Sex, Violence, and
Early Christian Texts

Sex, Violence, and Early Christian Texts

Edited by

Christy Cobb and Eric Vanden Eykel

LEXINGTON BOOKS
Lanham • Boulder • New York • London

Published by Lexington Books
An imprint of The Rowman & Littlefield Publishing Group, Inc.
4501 Forbes Boulevard, Suite 200, Lanham, Maryland 20706
www.rowman.com

86-90 Paul Street, London EC2A 4NE

Copyright © 2022 by The Rowman & Littlefield Publishing Group, Inc.

All rights reserved. No part of this book may be reproduced in any form or by any electronic or mechanical means, including information storage and retrieval systems, without written permission from the publisher, except by a reviewer who may quote passages in a review.

British Library Cataloguing in Publication Information Available

Library of Congress Cataloging-in-Publication Data

Names: Cobb, Christy, editor. | Vanden Eykel, Eric, editor.
Title: Sex, violence, and early Christian texts / edited by Christy Cobb and Eric Vanden Eykel.
Description: Lanham : Lexington Books, [2022] | Includes bibliographical references and index. | Summary: "Sex, Violence, and Early Christian Texts examines instances of sexual violence within a diversity of early Christian texts carefully, ethically, and with an eye toward shining a light on the scourge of sexual violence that is so often manifest in both ancient and contemporary Christian communities"— Provided by publisher.
Identifiers: LCCN 2022029742 (print) | LCCN 2022029743 (ebook) | ISBN 9781793637840 (cloth) | ISBN 9781793637864 (paper) | ISBN 9781793637857 (ebook)
Subjects: LCSH: Sex crimes—Religious aspects—Christianity. | Christian literature, Early. | Sex crimes in literature.
Classification: LCC BT708 .S4745 2022 (print) | LCC BT708 (ebook) | DDC 241/.66—dc23/eng/20220815
LC record available at https://lccn.loc.gov/2022029742
LC ebook record available at https://lccn.loc.gov/2022029743

Contents

Introduction   vii
   Christy Cobb and Eric Vanden Eykel

Chapter 1: Sexual Slander and Moral Supremacy in the *Elenchos*   1
   Tara Baldrick-Morrone

Chapter 2: Danaids and Dirces in Roman Corinth: Sexualized Violence and Imperial Spectacle in *1 Clement*   17
   Chance E. Bonar

Chapter 3: Euclia's Story: Coordinated Sexual Assault, Violence, and Willfulness in the *Acts of Andrew*   37
   Christy Cobb

Chapter 4: "Guardians of Chastity and Companions in Suffering": The Didactic and Rhetorical Function of Rape Threats in Ambrose of Milan   53
   Jennifer Collins-Elliott

Chapter 5: Corinthian Concerns and Textual Assault   71
   Arminta Fox

Chapter 6: Sexual Violence, Martyrdom, and Enslavement in Augustine's *Letter* 111   85
   Midori Hartman

Chapter 7: Virginity, Bestiality, and Virtue in Sozomen's Account of the Attack of the Consecrated Virgins of Heliopolis   107
   LaToya M. Leary Francis

Chapter 8: Tertullian of Carthage, Sexualized Violence, and the "Abjection" of the Female Flesh   123
   Travis W. Proctor

Chapter 9: Paul Trading Barbs: Sexual Invective as Gendered
    Violence   143
    Joshua M. Reno

Chapter 10: Ambivalent Wedding Imagery in Matthew's Jerusalem
    Narrative   169
    Laura Robinson

Chapter 11: Virgin Acts: Blinding, Castration, and the Violence of
    Male Chastity   185
    Jeannie Sellick

Chapter 12: Assaulting the Virgin: How the *Protevangelium of
    James* Hides Sexual Violence   201
    Eric Vanden Eykel

Chapter 13: Five Husbands: Slut-Shaming the Samaritan Woman   217
    Meredith J. C. Warren

Chapter 14: Revelation Naturalizes Sexual Violence and Readers
    Erase It: Unveiling the Son of God's Rape of Jezebel   239
    Stephen Young

Index of Ancient Sources   261

Index   273

About the Contributors   281

Introduction

Christy Cobb and Eric Vanden Eykel

Votives are common features in churches and other religious spaces around the world. Resting in neat, uniform rows, their flames dance in ways that mesmerize, comfort, and intoxicate. People light these tiny candles for different reasons. Many votives burn in memory of deceased loved ones. Others are lit as an indication of worry over a seemingly impossible decision or, perhaps, as an expression of peace with a decision recently made. Some votives shine as symbols of joy. Others still are lit in remembrance of survivors of sexual violence.[1] Together, these discrete flames blend to cast light into dark places and, for many, they stand as a reminder of the hopeful possibility that we are not alone.

But votives can also be dangerous. After all, fire can only exist because it destroys. As we marvel at the beauty of these candles, we behold their slow and inevitable self-destruction. The real danger of these twinkling flames, however, is not their ability to consume, but to conceal. Votives can be symbols of joy, thankfulness, hope, and even relief, but they can just as easily mask tragedy, victimization, sorrow, and violence. When a person lights a votive in a church, the beauty and sincerity of the moment is often obvious. What is often invisible is the pain, hurt, and trauma behind this action.

The ancient texts analyzed in this book are not unlike the votives on its cover. Many of them are undeniably beautiful in so many ways, and for centuries they have been sources of light, encouragement, and comfort for readers. But they are also dangerous things, for behind all of their light and beauty lurks a dark ugliness that is easily ignored or not easily seen. Like votives, these texts are dangerous precisely for what they are able to hide. Buried within the texts of early Christianity are numerous examples of sexual violence. For centuries these stories have been overlooked, their flames extinguished, and the violence within them has often gone unaddressed. This volume attempts to relight these candles, and to let their flames burn, dangerously. But also, we seek to address the violence found within these texts directly, ethically, and in meaningful ways.

The essays in this collection are part of an ongoing conversation about the language of abuse, assault, and rape in Christian texts, and how this language has functioned and continues to function to promote, normalize, and obscure the rhetoric and reality of sexual violence in various religious settings. We want to acknowledge at the outset that a project like this is only possible because of the pioneering work of other scholars and activists who have paved the way. In many respects, Phyllis Trible began the work of critical engagement with texts of sexual violence in her groundbreaking book, *Texts of Terror*.[2] This book focused on four stories found in the Hebrew Bible that are notably difficult to interpret or even read. First, Trible addresses the rape of Hagar in a chapter titled "Hagar: The Desolation of Rejection." For the second chapter, entitled "Tamar: The Royal Rape of Wisdom," Trible rereads the rape of Tamar. The horrific story of the concubine of the Levite is told in the third chapter, "An Unnamed Woman: The Extravagance of Violence." Finally, Trible tells the story of the sacrifice of Jephthah's daughter in a chapter titled "The Daughter of Jephthah: An Inhuman Sacrifice." Trible's approach is specifically feminist and also personal as she engages in the telling of these "sad stories."[3] While Trible's book tells the stories of these four women, it also attempts to redeem them. She writes of her approach: "It interprets stories of outrage on behalf of their female victims in order to recover a neglected history, to remember a past that the present embodies, and to pray that these terrors shall not come to pass again. In telling sad stories, a feminist hermeneutic seeks to redeem the time."[4]

Rhiannon Graybill's more recent book, *Texts After Terror*, continues the work begun by Trible. As is clear by the numerous citations in the present volume, Graybill's method and approach to addressing biblical rape stories has been profoundly influential for those of us who are working on sexual violence. In her work, Graybill addresses the complex and ambiguous nature of these religious texts that include and describe sexual violence. Through the lens of affect theory, Graybill suggests three terms that could help to identify and address sexual violence in the texts of the Bible: fuzzy, messy, and icky.[5] These terms are useful because the religious texts do not specifically designate rape or ask for consent, thus it is often difficult to identify texts of sexual violence using the terms found within the texts themselves. Instead, Graybill suggests that rape within the Bible is often fuzzy and messy, and that they might feel "icky" to contemporary readers. She writes: "Sexual violence in the Hebrew Bible is fuzzy, messy, and icky, and a feminist response to the Bible's 'texts of terror' demands that we take this seriously."[6] Our aim in this book has been to assume Graybill's charge as it relates to sexual violence in early Christian literature, and to take the often "fuzzy, messy, and icky" rhetoric of these texts seriously.

There is also work being done on sexual violence outside of the field of biblical studies. For example, Amy Kalmanofsky's edited volume, *Sexual Violence and Sacred Texts*, includes chapters written by scholars of the three Abrahamic religions: Judaism, Christianity, and Islam. As Kalmanofsky observes, "No religion has a monopoly on sacred texts that depict, justify, or even incite sexual violence."[7] In addition to its interreligious focus, this volume also offers a step toward healing survivors of sexual violence. In the first chapter in the volume, Kalmanofsky suggests that feminist scholarship can provide healing in two possible ways. The first possible way that scholarship can incite healing is through the identification of "factors that trigger, sustain, and condone the violence."[8] Additionally, Kalmanofsky notes that scholarship provides strategies of interpretation that can assist survivors of sexual violence "to engage with the ugliest biblical texts in ways that help them heal."[9] Echoing Kalmanofsky, our hope is that the chapters in the present volume might in some cases provide meaningful steps toward healing through their identification, interpretation, and rejection of the rhetoric of sexual violence in early Christian texts.

There is no shortage of conversation among scholars of antiquity on the importance of labels, particularly as they relate to the first-century Jesus movement that is more commonly called "Christianity." Terminology matters, and so we would like to be clear on some of the decisions we have made in the framing of this volume. For our purposes, "early Christianity" refers roughly to the first five hundred years of the Common Era. The individual chapters that follow draw from a broad range of texts during that span of time; the earliest are the Pauline Epistles, and the latest is Sozomen's *Ecclesiastical History*. When we speak here and in the pages that follow about "early Christianity," this should not be taken as a suggestion that "Christianity" is or ever has been a monolith. Similarly, when discussing sex and violence we have broadened our understanding to include both rhetorical and physical violence. While many of the texts analyzed in this volume may not be read strictly as history, we treat them as instances of violence regardless of whether they occurred. Ultimately, the violence in these texts represents violence that occurred in antiquity and continues to occur today. Moreover, texts such as these are often overlooked or justified, and our volume seeks to uncover and condemn sexual violence in all of its forms.

The chapters in this volume address a variety of early Christian texts. Some focus on writings from the New Testament, some from Christian apocrypha, and others from patristic authors. Contributors to the project were not given any specific methodological frameworks to follow, and as a result, the approaches and outcomes of their chapters differ from one another. Yet similarities can also be found throughout these chapters, through attention to ethical reading strategies, a focus on marginalized characters and voices, as well as a combined effort to take these passages seriously by considering the ramifications of stories such as these about sexual violence within religious texts.

Several authors wrote with the aim of unmasking the rhetoric of sexual violence that for any number of reasons has proven largely invisible to contemporary readers. Chance E. Bonar's chapter on *1 Clement* examines the role of two groups of women—Danaids and Dirces—whom the author mentions as having suffered immensely. Noting that their presence in the letter has long mystified interpreters, Bonar argues that these are best understood in the context of the Roman arena, and that the author uses this threat of sexualized violence as a warning to readers about the importance of obedience to Roman ecclesiastical structures. Christy Cobb's chapter on the apocryphal *Acts of Andrew* highlights Euclia, an enslaved woman whose enslaver—a woman named Maximilla—forces her to have sex with her husband so that she (Maximilla) can remain chaste. Reading Euclia's story alongside Sara Ahmed's *Willful Subjects*, Cobb suggests that Euclia persists within the *Acts of Andrew* as an example of Ahmed's willful characters. Although Euclia's story is tragic, Cobb's theoretical analysis illuminates her agency while it also brings to light Maximilla's culpability in this scene of horrendous sexual violence.

Arminta Fox focuses in her chapter on Paul's instructions to the unmarried in 1 Corinthians 7. The women in this passage are instructed by Paul to marry, Fox notes, and to thereby serve as passive and possibly unwilling "vessels" for the sexual impulses of the men in their community. Fox therefore frames these women as victims of "textual assault." Joshua M. Reno examines related rhetoric elsewhere in the Pauline corpus. Reno argues that at key points in 2 Corinthians and Galatians, Paul draws from a lexicon of sexual invective that, while foreign to most readers today, would have been commonplace in his first-century context. And in this context, Paul's statements against his opponents serve not to portray them not only as *wrong*, but also as sexual deviants.

Laura Robinson analyzes two "wedding parables" in Matthew's Gospel—the Parable of the Banquet (Matt 22:1–14) and the Parable of the Ten Virgins (Matt 25:1–13)—and she demonstrates that wedding imagery in these parables looks different when it is understood in light of ancient sources that speak of weddings as affairs that involve both a competition for property—in this case, the bride—and the severing of family connections. These dynamics are lost, Robinson argues, when these parables are read in light of so many modern assumptions about what weddings entail. Eric Vanden Eykel's chapter examines an overlooked instance of sexual violence in the *Protevangelium of James*, where a woman named Salome "examines" the body of Mary directly after she has given birth to Jesus. Vanden Eykel argues that this episode is best read as an instance of sexual assault, but that this reading might not register for most readers because it resists the categories generally used to define such things.

Meredith Warren's chapter addresses the scene from the Gospel of John that involves Jesus's conversation with a Samaritan woman at a well. Warren frames Jesus's interactions with this woman—in which he highlights that she has had five husbands and is currently living with someone who is not her husband—as an example of "slut-shaming." Warren points out not only the "invisible" nature of this problem, but also the ways that it continues to manifest in contemporary scholarship. Stephen Young's chapter examines a scene near the start of Revelation, where a woman called Jezebel is punished for unrepentantly promoting false teachings. While this "punishment" has generally been understood by readers as Jezebel being stricken by some type of plague or illness, Young argues that it is more accurately understood as an instance of martial rape. Such an interpretation is not considered by many readers because of their lack of familiarity with the concept of martial rape in the ancient world, but also because many readers of Revelation would rather not imagine one of the text's protagonists—in this case, the Son of God—as a rapist.

Other contributors in this collection address instances of sexual violence that are more explicit and, therefore, perhaps more obvious to contemporary readers. Tara Baldrick-Morrone explores Hippolytus of Rome's use of abortion language to criticize one of his opponents. His strategy, Baldrick-Morrone points out, treats the bodies of pregnant and enslaved women as mere rhetorical tools in service of maintaining power and a sense of moral superiority. Jennifer Collins-Elliott examines Ambrose of Milan's use of rape threats in his public and private discussion of virgins. In his (public) treatise on virgins, Ambrose notes several virgins who were threatened with sexual violence but who emerged unscathed and victorious. For Ambrose, threats of sexual violence in this text are pedagogical. But Collins-Elliott notes that his attitude toward such things shifts drastically in his (private) correspondence with the Bishop of Verona. When informed about the physical virginity test of an actual virgin in his own community, Ambrose recoils and argues that this test is reprehensible and amounts to rape.

In her chapter, Midori Hartman analyzes Augustine's rhetoric of sexualized violence in *Letter* 111. Hartman notes this in this letter—written in the year prior to the Visigoth sacking of Rome in 410 CE—Augustine frames the increasingly violent nature of the world as akin to an enslaved person who is being punished for willful disobedience to their enslaver, which Augustine understands as an analogy for humanity's rejection of the gospel. Hartman argues that Augustine realized the problematic trajectory of such a claim, however, particularly as it relates to sexualized violence toward enslaved persons, and that he adjusts his position accordingly in subsequent writings. LaToya M. Leary Francis examines Sozomen's account of a violent attack on the consecrated virgins of Heliopolis, in which their bodies are ripped open, shaved, stuffed with food, and fed to swine. Leary Francis argues that Sozomen imagines the perpetrators of this grizzly, horrifying scene as "pagans," and that he uses this scene to highlight what he sees as the profound differences between Christians and non-Christians. On her read, the virgins are meant to symbolize Christians during the reign of the Emperor Julian, and that the sexualized nature of the violence is meant to clarify and heighten a sense of vulnerability and danger.

Travis W. Proctor's chapter examines Tertullian's *On the Shows* through the theoretical lens of the "abject." In this text, Tertullian conceives of Roman "spectacles" as sexualized, demonic phenomena that should be avoided by Christians. Proctor argues that through Tertullian's rhetoric against the Romans, he abjectifies certain bodies (Roman and female, in particular) and presents them as more prone to sexualized, demonic violence. Tertullian therefore creates his own "spectacle" for his readers to behold. Finally, Jeannie Sellick analyzes episodes in the apocryphal *Acts of John* that involve acts of sexual violence not found in other chapters. In one, a young man castrates himself as a mark of conversion and an expression of his guilt for having committed adultery. In another, a man attempts to rape the corpse of a deceased Christian woman. Sellick argues that these episodes exist to emphasize the dangerous nature of male sexuality, and to reinforce a preference for chastity over against marriage. Sellick argues that the *Acts of John* more broadly, by intertwining sexuality with violence, "queers normativity and normalizes queerness; making the 'normative' illicit and the queer laudable."

While working on this volume, we had an opportunity to attend and present our work at a 2022 conference sponsored by the *Religion and Sexual Abuse Project*.[10] This conference gave us the opportunity to dialogue with scholars who are engaging this important topic outside of our own field of biblical studies. The experience affected both of us in a number of ways, and it helped us to articulate and clarify what we hoped to accomplish in this project. The conference organizers were intentional in providing space for reflection in the midst of presentations that emphasized the personal, emotional, and spiritual facets of this important work. Dr. Monica Coleman was one of the keynote speakers. Her work addresses the ways in which a church might respond to sexual violence against a member of the congregation, as well as strategies for resisting sexual violence before it occurs.[11] In the wake of this experience, we as the editors began to recognize more of the possible outcomes and applications of this project. We are immensely grateful for our experiences at this conference and for the many colleagues and friends that we met while there.

Like votives, the chapters in this volume are designed to stand alone, but they are also gathered in this binding so that they can work together to cast light into dark places. We hope that readers will approach this book with this in mind. Some will undoubtedly be drawn to specific chapters, while others will read the book cover to cover, noting the consistencies and contrasts throughout. Above all, we hope that this book inspires others to continue addressing the problem of sexual violence in early Christianity and our own contemporary contexts. We hope that these chapters can light a way for future research that will illuminate previously hidden texts and interrogate readings that obscure, defend, or normalize the sexual violence that is tragically common within the corpus of early Christian literature.

As we leave these candles burning, we dedicate this book to the myriad survivors of sexual violence in the church, in the academy, and beyond. Our sincere hope is that this book will serve not only as an acknowledgment of your experiences, but as part of the ongoing conversation to create a kinder and more just world.

NOTES

1. https://dailytrojan.com/2021/10/24/students-hold-vigil-honoring-sexual-assault-survivors/ For more information about Take Back the Night Foundation, an organization whose goal is to end sexual assault through awareness initiatives, see: https://takebackthenight.org/.

2. Phyllis Trible, *Texts of Terror: Literary-Feminist Readings of Biblical Narratives*, Overtures to Biblical Theology (Philadelphia: Fortress Press, 1984).

3. Trible, 1.

4. Trible, 3.

5. Rhiannon Graybill, *Texts After Terror: Rape, Sexual Violence, and the Hebrew Bible* (Oxford: Oxford University Press, 2021), 11; Other publications that address sexual violence in the Bible include: Rhiannon Graybill, "Fuzzy, Messy, Icky: The Edges of Consent in Hebrew Bible Rape Narratives and Rape Culture," *The Bible and Critical Theory* 15, no. 2 (2019): 1–28; Rhiannon Graybill, "Critiquing the Discourse of Consent," *Journal of Feminist Studies in Religion* 33 (2017): 175.

6. Graybill, *Texts After Terror*, 31.

7. Amy Kalmanofsky, *Sexual Violence and Sacred Texts* (Indianapolis: Feminist Studies in Religion Books, 2017), 1.

8. Amy Kalmanofsky, "How Feminist Biblical Scholarship Can Heal Victims of Sexual Violation," in *Sexual Violence and Sacred Texts*, ed. Amy Kalmanofsky (Indianapolis: Feminist Studies in Religion Books, 2017), 15.

9. Kalmanofsky, 15.
10. https://www.religionandsexualabuseproject.org/.
11. Monica A. Coleman, *The Dinah Project: A Handbook for Congregational Response to Sexual Violence* (Eugene, OR: Wipf and Stock Publishers, 2010).

WORKS CITED

Coleman, Monica A. *The Dinah Project: A Handbook for Congregational Response to Sexual Violence*. Eugene, OR: Wipf and Stock Publishers, 2010.

Graybill, Rhiannon. *Texts After Terror: Rape, Sexual Violence, and the Hebrew Bible*. Oxford: Oxford University Press, 2021.

Kalmanofsky, Amy, ed. *Sexual Violence and Sacred Texts*. Indianapolis: Feminist Studies in Religion Books, 2017.

Trible, Phyllis. *Texts of Terror: Literary-Feminist Readings of Biblical Narratives*. Overtures to Biblical Theology. Philadelphia: Fortress Press, 1984.

Chapter 1

Sexual Slander and Moral Supremacy in the *Elenchos*

Tara Baldrick-Morrone

In the introduction to the 1970 edited volume *The Morality of Abortion: Legal and Historical Perspectives*, Catholic professor of law John T. Noonan, Jr. begins by criticizing the burgeoning movement to decriminalize abortion. He states, "Abortion, once regarded as a secret and loathsome crime, a medical disaster, or a tragic manifestation of human weakness, has been justified by the draftsmen of the American Law Institute, defended by the American Medical Association, applauded by the American Public Health Association, championed by Planned Parenthood-World Population, and publicized by the *New York Times*."[1] Noonan's reproach here is not aimed at those who have abortions but, instead, at people in positions of power and influence who are supposedly allowing and perhaps even encouraging people to have them. While concern over the apparent moral laxity of those in power is a familiar refrain in most of Noonan's work, he is far from the first Christian author to express such a sentiment, particularly when it comes to the "permissibility" of abortion.

In this essay I aim to elucidate one of the first written examples of Christian moral panic over abortion as found in the *Elenchos* (or *Refutation of All Heresies*), the Greek text purportedly written by the third-century Roman bishop Hippolytus.[2] But more than simply demonstrating how the *Elenchos* mirrors later conflicts over Christian identity and positions on abortion, I explicate the larger themes at play concerning slander, claims of moral supremacy, and the use of enslaved and pregnant bodies as sites of contestations over authority. These bodies, which were more vulnerable to harm and sexual violence in the ancient Mediterranean world, became useful models through which early Christian authors asserted their moral superiority and dominance over their communal rivals. In the case of pregnant bodies, they operate in the *Elenchos* as a means for Hippolytus not only to enforce his own ideas of what kind of sex is deemed correct or "Christian," but also to use them as tools in his rhetorical attack on his enemies. Such is also the case with enslaved bodies in the *Elenchos*. Hippolytus's struggle over authority with Callistus (an apparent rival) is predicated on exploiting Callistus's embodiment as a former enslaved person, whose presumed sexual vulnerability and propensity for wickedness poses potential risks and ruin for the Christian community at large. That Hippolytus uses these bodies to meet his own ends points to the harm perpetuated by the text's rhetorical project. Said differently, the particular construction of these bodies is centered on harmful and violent assumptions about enslaved people, sexual behavior, and reproduction in the ancient Mediterranean world.

EARLY CHRISTIAN DISCUSSIONS OF ABORTION

To best explain how the *Elenchos* uses abortion as well as the bodies of enslaved and pregnant people as sites of contestation, it is necessary to address how (and why) early Christian texts talk about abortion. For an issue that seems to occupy the minds of many Christians in the twentieth and twenty-first centuries, it may come as a surprise that few early Christian texts mention abortion at all. And while discussions of abortion appear in a range of different genres, from texts like the second-century "manual" known as the *Didache* to the sixth-century sermons of Caesarius of Arles, none of these texts devotes a great deal of time to the issue. Yet this has not prevented some scholars interested in the development of Christian views on abortion from narrativizing these texts so as to create a linear and uniform story about Christian opposition to abortion.[3]

My previous work on this material has pushed back against this approach. More specifically, I have argued that we can develop a clearer and more comprehensive picture of how early Christians used abortion to develop contours of "true" Christianity by attending to the rhetorical strategies present in the texts.[4] Analyzing the texts through this lens reveals that early Christian authors found the topic of abortion to be useful for their own efforts to delimit communal boundaries, whether it be to determine which behaviors are deemed as authentically "Christian" or to slander a perceived opponent by calling their moral authority into question. We find such slander in the *Elenchos*, where the accusation is twofold: the ecclesial leader Callistus is accused of allowing illicit sexual behavior between women and enslaved and freedpersons *and* of permitting those who become pregnant to destroy "that which was conceived [*sullambanomena*]" (IX.12.25).[5]

Beyond how these Christian texts use abortion as a rhetorical device, we can also consider how the bodies of pregnant people themselves are used. In some instances, the pregnant person is nowhere to be found. For example, when abortion is proscribed in the *Didache* (2.2) and the *Epistle of Barnabas* (19.5), neither mention the body from which the *teknon* ("child") would be expelled. When the pregnant person does appear in a text's discussion of abortion, such as canon 63 from the Council of Elvira, it is often to associate them with the *scelus* (Latin, "crime") of *adulterium* (Latin, "adultery"). Compared to other early Christian texts that discuss abortion, the *Elenchos* makes use of the bodies of pregnant people in a distinct way: the pregnant body becomes evidence of not only *moicheia* ("adultery") and *phonos* ("murder"), but also *asebeia* ("impiety"). Yet it is not just those who are pregnant who are supposedly impious, but also Callistus, the supposed rival of the author. Thus, while the people who have abortions are criticized for their actions, they only appear as props in a lengthy attempt by the author to both prove Callistus's moral inferiority and undermine his legitimacy as leader of the community in Rome.

SEXUAL SLANDER

Though the *Elenchos* stands out for its discussion of abortion, it fits in alongside many other instances of ancient sexual slander used as a weapon against Christians and non-Christians alike. Though sexual slander was used often in the ancient Mediterranean world at large, scholars like Susanna Drake and Jennifer Wright Knust have demonstrated that early Christians were no strangers to this rhetoric.[6] Whether accusing (other) Jews of sexual immorality to legitimize violence against them or criticizing rival teachers for lax morals in order to authorize one's own teachings, early Christians frequently used sexual slander as a powerful tool in contests over authority and legitimacy. By linking their enemies to immoral behavior, early Christians delegitimized their opponents and cast them as outside the boundary of "true" Christianity. As we see with the *Elenchos*, Hippolytus accuses Callistus of permitting illicit sex and abortion to explicitly defame him, all in an effort to assert his own moral supremacy. At the same time that sexual slander is about establishing dominance, also at play is how Hippolytus defines what it means to be "Christian," particularly by establishing and defining the "right" kind of sexual behavior. In this sense, to accuse someone of allowing pregnant people to have abortions was to undermine their legitimacy as an arbiter of what it meant to be a "true" Christian.

Undergirding these more explicit examples of sexual slander is Callistus's own embodied social status as a former enslaved person, which Hippolytus drew to the fore by prefacing Callistus's "heresy" with a brief description of his life. I will talk about this at length below, but I find it important to mention here because of its implications. Since enslaved people (who were defined by their bodies) were considered to be equally as weak as they were deviant, Hippolytus's slander against Callistus draws on stereotypes of the enslaved as being morally inferior and subject to sexual violation all at the same time. Hippolytus's sexual slander is thus similar to other examples in early Christian texts, particularly in that it focuses on sexualized, enslaved bodies because of the presumed dangers they pose to the Christian community.

A SHORT HISTORY OF THE *ELENCHOS'S* MANUSCRIPT AND AUTHORSHIP ISSUES

Before discussing the contents of the *Elenchos*, it is important to note some of the authorship and textual issues present in the manuscript history.[7] Having a cursory understanding of these problems will make sense of some of my translation decisions, as well as suggestions related to the rhetorical nature of this passage and any possible historical realities behind it.

Though Book I of the *Elenchos* circulated on its own (and thus has its own transmission history), the rest of the work appears in a single manuscript that Constantinus Minoides Mynas acquired from a monastery in Greece in the 1840s.[8] In addition to physical damage to the parchment and the absence of Books II, III, and the beginning of IV, the text as found in the manuscript is replete with gaps, omissions, and numerous errors.[9] Included in these issues is also the fact that no name is attached to the work, which has left open the question of authorship. The attribution of Book I to Origen (based on its own manuscript tradition) influenced the first published edition of Books IV-X in 1851, which was similarly ascribed to him. Yet even at that time not all scholars were in agreement concerning authorship. In the same year, another edition attributed it to Hippolytus of Rome. There are several arguments in favor of Hippolytan authorship, including the fact that the author refers to themselves as a bishop in *Proem* 6 (which rules out Origen, as he was not a bishop). Moreover, early Christian authors like Eusebius and Jerome link a work such as this to Hippolytus, whom they refer to as a bishop during the reign of Alexander Severus (222–235 CE).[10] Additionally, the author's purported involvement in the ecclesial disputes in Rome as described in Book IX further point to Hippolytus as the author. Yet while the case for Hippolytus seems clear for some, there are still several questions and difficulties that prevent many scholars from making any declarative statements. For example, a statue outside the Vatican Library, which is purportedly of Hippolytus, includes an engraved list of his works that does not include the *Elenchos*. A few other scholars have also proposed theories that, though not entirely convincing, leave enough room for doubt.[11]

For the sake of ease and consistency with many of the contemporary scholars I study, I have chosen to refer to the person responsible for the text as Hippolytus (I sometimes also use "the author"). I find it important to acknowledge the problems with this highly corrupt and disputed text precisely in order to move beyond discussions of authorship. I acknowledge the importance of this work, especially as to how questions of authenticity and provenance shape the ways in which we make sense of the text. Yet my analysis of the *Elenchos* is independent of these issues. Instead, I am more interested in the text as we have it and, primarily, how it has been used by modern authors in their own efforts to claim moral supremacy.[12] The *Elenchos* often appears in historical narratives which attempt to authorize claims about Christian opposition to abortion in the ancient Mediterranean world. In these narratives, the *Elenchos* acts as simply one data point that, when connected to other data points, creates a portrait of the ancient world that speaks more to the particular scholar's own interests than any ancient reality. In the case of the *Elenchos*, I want to consider how its rhetorical use of enslaved and pregnant bodies and abortion has shaped its inclusion in these "grand narratives" about the history of abortion. Though one cannot necessarily determine the specific effect that one third-century text could have on discussions of reproduction in the twenty-first century, considering the "afterlife" of the *Elenchos* might help us to theorize about the ways that certain kinds of bodies are more likely to be used to generate moral authority, both in the ancient Mediterranean world and in our world today.

THE GENRE OF THE *ELENCHOS*

To make sense of how the author uses abortion to slander Callistus, we must begin with what leads him to do so in the first place. In form, the *Elenchos* is a heresiography, as the author catalogs so-called heresiarchs in order to reveal and dispel their "secret mysteries" (*aporrēta mustēria*; Proem 2). From Greek philosophers (Book I) to astrology (Book IV) and numerous heresies throughout (Books V-IX), Hippolytus sets out to detail the doctrines and practices of all who pose a threat to "the Church." But rather than reading the *Elenchos* as reporting factual information, we would do well to understand that the genre of heresiography uses ancient polemical strategies meant to discredit the author's opponents.[13] As such, this defamation was often based on misattribution and sometimes even wholesale fabrication.

At the same time that the author delegitimizes his rivals, he also bolsters his own position and standing. In particular, he accomplishes this by weaving various sources into his own narrative as a means to demonstrate his knowledge and skill as a defender of "true" Christianity against a litany of heresies. The author's descriptions of Callistus's life, along with his accusations, function to paint Callistus as not only heir to these heresies but also the creator of his own (IX.7.2–3). Given the threat that Callistus poses, it is no wonder that Hippolytus's work amounts to a "vitriolic 'character assassination,' written with a pen dipped in gall."[14]

CONTENTS OF THE *ELENCHOS*, BOOK IX

The central focus of the *Elenchos* begins in Book IX, as Hippolytus sets his sights on Callistus. Beyond simply giving readers an indication that this is indeed the author's own context, much of this book presents a possible view into the intracommunal strife in the Roman church during the third century. To begin with, the author foregrounds the main heretical school he aims to address: a type of monarchianism, which stresses the unity of God, Jesus, and the holy spirit.[15] According to the author, this particular "heresy" originated with the philosophy of Heraclitus. This "blasphemous folly" (*blasphēmos aphrosunē*; IX.2) is propagated among Christians by Noetus and further spread by Cleomenes and his *sunagōnistai* ("accomplices"; IX.7.2), Zephyrinus and Callistus, leaders of the community at Rome (IX.7.1–2). After presenting an overview of this *kakodidaskalia* ("evil teaching"; IX.8.1) and how it made its way into the hierarchy of the church (IX.8–11), the author launches into a lengthy description of Callistus's life and the allegedly underhanded ways in which he went from being an *oiketēs* ("a household slave"; IX.12.1) to succeeding Zephyrinus as the pope (IX.12.15). This emphasis on Callistus's former status as an enslaved person, as I will discuss below, is one of the central elements of Hippolytus's claim of moral superiority.

THE EVENTS LEADING UP TO CALLISTUS'S ALLEGED *ASEBEIA* ("IMPIETY") (IX.11.1–3; 12.1–15)

As described in the *Elenchos*, Callistus had been a domestic enslaved person whose owner, Carpophorus, was a Christian and a member of the imperial household (12.1). As a person of "faith" (*pistis*; 12.1) himself, Callistus was selected to handle Carpophorus's finances.[16] Others, such as widows and *adelphoi* ("brothers," here meaning Christians; 12.1), also began entrusting him with their own wealth. Yet Callistus took their money, quickly lost it all, and was left without anything (12.1). By the time Carpophorus was made aware of what happened and sent for Callistus to explain, he had already fled

(12.2). After a series of events, including a suicide attempt and subsequent arrest, Callistus was then sent to a Sardinian mine as punishment (12.9).

This short episode lays the foundation for Hippolytus's claim to moral supremacy. The first step for the author is calling attention to Callistus's status as an *oiketēs*, which signals that his morals should already be considered questionable.[17] The association of both enslaved people and freedpersons as inherently inferior beings who were predisposed to be deceitful and sexually immoral reflects a common idea found in numerous texts and genres in the ancient Mediterranean world.[18] Scholars like Sheila Briggs, Jennifer Glancy, Katherine Shaner, Chris L. de Wet, and J. Albert Harrill have demonstrated that far from challenging these ideas, early Christian authors had decidedly ambivalent attitudes toward enslavement.[19]

Enslavement and the enslaved permeate early Christian texts, from theological arguments for why an enslaved person should obey their enslaver in the deutero-Pauline letter to the Ephesians to the image of enslavement as a metaphor for marriage in the work of Augustine.[20] That Callistus's status would be used as part of Hippolytus's attack on his character makes all the more sense when considering that "Christian elites also shared a wider Roman perception that slaves, who laboured and lived side by side with slaveholders, were potential enemies lodged within the home. . . . "[21] Moreover, enslaved persons, whether they worked in agriculture or in a household, were expected to be both submissive and obedient.[22] In this description of his life, Callistus is characterized as willful and disobedient: all the attributes of an especially "bad" enslaved person. Added to Callistus's disobedience of Carpophorus is the fraud committed against widows and other Christians. While Callistus threatened stability in his enslaver's household, the harm done to others is further evidence for Hippolytus that Callistus poses a dangerous threat to the stability of the entire Christian community.

After the governor in Sardinia released Callistus from the mines under false pretenses and against the wishes of authorities in the church (12.10–13), Callistus ingratiated himself with Zephyrinus, the head of the church in Rome. Yet because Zephyrinus allegedly was an illiterate person who was ignorant of ecclesial matters (11.1), he was susceptible to Callistus's schemes, which included seeking the bishop's seat for himself and spreading a teaching that the Father and Christ were one (as opposed to later trinitarian concepts) (11.1, 3). Yet at the same time both Zephyrinus *and* Callistus advocated *against* this teaching (11.3). This "hypocrisy" (*hupokrisis*; 11.3) was all Callistus's doing, which not only sowed discord among the community but also aided in his ascension to bishop. After Zephyrinus's death, Callistus expelled those who espoused this so-called heresy from the community, so as "to get rid of" (*apotripsasthai*; 12.15) accusations against him.

As important as these doctrinal disputes are for determining the boundaries of Christian identity, what undergirds them is the image of Callistus as a former enslaved person. Hippolytus's description of Callistus plays directly into the stereotypical characterization of an enslaved person as inherently deviant. Thus, I suggest that it is Callistus's very status as a former enslaved person that makes him not only more susceptible to this "evil teaching" (*kakodidaskalia*), but also prone to spreading his own. Moreover, Callistus's former social status is an embodied one, inextricably linked to vulnerability and violation. This made Callistus both a walking liability and an immediate threat to his rivals.[23] As Hippolytus saw it, Callistus's status as a former enslaved person "exposed the body of Christ to the somatic vulnerabilities of enslaved members."[24] Callistus's position as a freedperson further heightened this concern, as it made explicit the anxieties that the boundaries between social categories were more fluid than fixed.[25] In this case, Hippolytus's allegations and defamation suggest that Callistus's leadership of the *ekklēsia* posed the greatest risk to the entire church body.

CALLISTUS'S TEACHINGS "AGAINST THE CHURCH" (*KATA TĒS EKKLĒSIAS*; 12.16–23)

Though this section largely includes repeated material from earlier in Book IX, it concludes with what I liken to "pearl-clutching": Hippolytus alleges that Callistus, whom at this point has "organized a school" (*sunestēsato didaskaleion*; 12.20), was amenable to any number of scandalous things, including: allowing men to have "pleasures" (*tas hēdonas*) and then forgiving them their sins (12.20); preventing any "bishop" (*episkopos*) from being deposed no matter the sin (12.21); and permitting members of the church hierarchy to be married more than once without fear of losing their position among the clergy (12.22).

This list suggests that issues concerning the "body" (of the individual and of the church) are the central focus of the *Elenchos*'s condemnation of Callistus. As mentioned above, Hippolytus's main contention is not Callistus's "pleasures" or that he himself remarries: the greater concern is that he *allows* these things to happen (and without repercussion). Having opposed Callistus's "heresy" while Zephyrinus was still alive (11.3), the author has already warned his community about Callistus, whom he repeatedly calls *panourgos* ("wicked"; 11.1, 12.16) and a *goēs* (an "impostor" or a "cheater"; 12.16, 20). To accuse him of being an impostor not only highlights the characteristics that former enslaved people were associated with (deceit, immorality, etc.); more importantly, it deems Callistus to be out of place. Callistus, as described by Hippolytus, is the epitome of the negative consequences that arise when the boundary between enslaved and freeborn people is breached. Yet Hippolytus is not solely concerned because of the shifting societal boundaries that led to Callistus, a former enslaved person, becoming the bishop of Rome. Rather, Hippolytus's concern is with the moral laxity and continued blurring of social boundaries that Callistus purportedly *permits*, particularly between freeborn women and both enslaved and freedpersons.

ACCUSATIONS OF PERMITTING "ADULTERY AND MURDER" (*MOICHEIAN KAI PHONON*; 12.23–26)

Callistus's following allegedly continued to grow, as those whom "delighted in his teaching" (*hēsthentes tois dogmasi*; 12.23) continued to visit his "school," particularly for "pleasures which Christ did not allow" (*tas hēdonas, has ou sunechōrēsen ho Christos*; 12.24). More shocking than the approved behavior in the previous section, Callistus

> even permitted freeborn women (if they burned with passion, were unmarried, [and] were unwilling to degrade their own dignity in order to marry a lawful spouse) to have whomever they might choose as a sexual partner, whether an enslaved person or a freedperson (*eite oiketēn eite eleutheron*). He permitted these women to deem that person in place of a spouse, though they had not been legally married. From that point, the so-called believers began to try contraceptive drugs or to bind themselves to expel what was conceived (*atokiois pharmakois kai tō peridesmeisthai pros to ta sullambanomena kataballein*), for the sake of not wanting to have a child by an enslaved person, nor by a lowborn person, for the sake of their nobility and excessive wealth. (12.24–25)[26]

"Look," Hippolytus exclaims, "the lawless one proceeded into such great impiety, teaching adultery and murder together" (*horate eis hosēn asebeian echōrēsen ho anomos, moicheian kai phonon en tō autō didaskōn*; 12.25). Given what he has just described, Hippolytus remarks that these people led by Callistus even dare to call themselves a "catholic church" (*katholikēn ekklēsian*; 12.25).[27]

Though there is some difficulty translating this passage into English, the overall situations described are relatively clear: first, Callistus allegedly allowed freeborn women not only to have sex with people of lower social status (enslaved people and freedpersons) but also to treat them as if they were legitimate spouses. In her brief discussion of this passage, Glancy notes that what Hippolytus "found outrageous was equally outrageous to other freeborn denizens of the Empire. They imagined a slave body penetrating, possessing, and mastering a free body."[28] The anxiety over blurred boundaries was such a concern that even imperial legislation policed and in some cases forbade such unions between free people and the enslaved.[29] Hippolytus does not use the term, but scholars referring to this passage usually consider these relationships as concubinage (*contubernium* in Latin). *Contubernium*, as defined in Judith Evans Grubbs's sourcebook on marriages in the Roman Empire, is "a quasi-marital union, entered into by those who were unable to make a legal marriage, particularly slaves."[30] Yet *contubernium* usually referred to freeborn men's relationships with enslaved women, as freeborn women's relationships with enslaved men upended expectations of social and sexual gender roles. Though this reflects a later period, a law from the early fourth century indicates as much, threatening a woman who has entered into a *contubernium* with losing her own liberty and enslaving her children to her partner's enslaver.[31] As shocking as the author makes it seem, the idea that Callistus supposedly legitimized the sexual behavior and marital unions of enslaved people and freeborn women was only one half of his *asebeia* ("impiety").

Of greater concern is that these women, "so-called believers" (*pistai legomenai*; 12.25) were then attempting to prevent pregnancy or have abortions to avoid having children by those same low-status people. Even though it does not explicitly say he permitted this, that Hippolytus includes adultery *and* murder as part of Callistus's apparent teaching is more than enough to imply it. At the same time, this accusation cannot be separated from that which engendered it: the illicit sexual behavior described above. With all of Hippolytus's accusations under consideration, we must take stock of how they function together in the *Elenchos*. Specifically, the purpose of these charges of *allowing* illicit sexual behavior and the attempts to cover it up by way of contraceptive drugs and abortion is to distinguish between those associated with the author and those whom he says follow Callistus. Accusing those associated with Callistus of sexual impropriety further distinguishes them from Hippolytus and his apparent supporters. As we have seen, the anxiety over fluid boundaries has been at the forefront of this text. At the same time that the concern largely focuses on the fluidity between free and enslaved bodies, it is also about the distinction between the "true" catholic church (*katholikēn ekklēsian*) and those whom Hippolytus calls *Kallistianoi* ("Callistians"; 12.26). In this sense, these accusations were not just rhetoric: as with other instances of sexual slander, vilifying his opponents was in service of Hippolytus's attempts to claim legitimacy and authority within the community.

Yet Hippolytus's use of abortion as slander could not have been successful had it not been for one crucial element: pregnant bodies. Whereas later Christian authors like Jerome and Ambrose made use of childbirth and pregnancy metaphors to discuss any number of topics, in those texts the pregnant body is often relegated to the background, sometimes disappearing completely.[32] But in a text like the *Elenchos*, the very presence of pregnant bodies is necessary to undermine Callistus's papal authority.[33] The pregnant body operates as part of Hippolytus's rhetorical toolbox, as an implicit example of his moral supremacy. Without it, his critique would not be as biting. For Hippolytus's claims about Callistus's moral inferiority to stick, these bodies must vacillate between being both pregnant and not-pregnant. The usefulness of their appearance extends only as far as they serve the author's purposes in compounding Callistus's (tolerance of) wickedness. Their bodies, implicated in both transgressing social boundaries and committing murders, become props for the author's rhetorical violence against Callistus. That is, linking Callistus to permissive sexual behavior (that leads to pregnancy) is one thing, but to also connect him to murder (by ending that pregnancy) is vital for challenging Callistus's authority. Though considering pregnant bodies as useful rhetorical models was not invented by Hippolytus (as other ancient Mediterranean authors also used them to their own ends),[34] what we see in the *Elenchos* is one of the first examples in early Christian texts of using abortion as sexual slander and, further, a rhetorical device that acts as "evidence" of moral decay.

SOME CLOSING CONSIDERATIONS

In my analysis of Hippolytus's attempts to undermine Callistus, I have demonstrated how sexual slander in this third-century Christian text relied on the "imaginative economy" of the world in which Christians lived.[35] That is, enslaved bodies represented the concern that many had about the potentiality of violation and the lack of fixed social boundaries. The pregnant bodies present in the *Elenchos* carried the same anxiety about boundaries while they similarly proved to be useful tools for representing the depths of an enemy's supposed moral failings (exacerbated by whether or not the fetus was present). In the struggle over ecclesial authority, Hippolytus used these bodies for his own rhetorical interests and to shape the contours of "true" Christianity as he saw them. A close reading of the *Elenchos* reveals that enslaved and pregnant bodies, as well as abortion, were useful tools that early Christian authors exploited in particular struggles over power and legitimacy. In this sense, the text's use of abortion is to achieve particular rhetorical ends, not to elucidate an explicit teaching on abortion. As I discussed earlier, modern histories of Christian opposition to abortion often excise the *Elenchos* from its ancient Mediterranean moorings of sexual slander and invective in an effort to claim Christian moral authority, particularly in the present. And though the author of the *Elenchos* and John Noonan share similar views about the permissibility of abortion as a sign of moral decline, paying attention to what makes each of their projects distinct allows us to understand how claims to moral authority are predicated on the presence (and absence) of certain kinds of bodies in particular historical contexts.

NOTES

1. John T. Noonan, Jr., "Introduction," in *The Morality of Abortion: Legal and Historical Perspectives*, ed. John T. Noonan, Jr. (Cambridge, MA: Harvard University Press, 1970), ix.

2. I discuss the issue of authorship in more detail below.

3. Beverly Wildung Harrison's work on the problems with masculinist (and often unethical) interpretations of ancient Christian texts on abortion is a formative influence on my thinking here (see Beverly Wildung Harrison, *Our Right to Choose: Toward a New Ethic of Abortion* [Boston: Beacon Press, 1983], 119–153]). For a reading of these texts which understands them as evidence of an ancient Christian concern for fetal life, see John T. Noonan, Jr., "An Almost Absolute Value in History," in *The Morality of Abortion: Legal and Historical Perspectives*, ed. John T. Noonan, Jr. (Cambridge, MA: Harvard University Press, 1970), 1–59. For a reading of these texts which understands them as evidence of an overarching pro-life ethic against violence and forsaking bloodshed in early Christian communities, see Michael J. Gorman, *Abortion and the Early Church: Christian, Jewish, and Pagan Attitudes in the Greco-Roman World* (Eugene, OR: Wipf & Stock Publishers, 1982).

4. Tara Baldrick-Morrone, "'Let's Not Retell This Myth about the History of the Thing': The Impact of John T. Noonan, Jr.'s Grand Narrative on the American Abortion Debate" (PhD diss., Florida State University, 2020), 23.

5. All the transliterated terms in this essay are Greek unless otherwise noted.

6. For more on sexual slander in early Christian texts, see the following work: Jennifer Wright Knust, *Abandoned to Lust: Sexual Slander and Ancient Christianity* (New York: Columbia University Press, 2005); Susanna Drake, *Slandering the Jew: Sexuality and Difference in Early Christian Texts* (Philadelphia: University of Pennsylvania Press, 2013).

7. For other scholarship that addresses these issues, see Miroslav Marcovich, *Hippolytus: Refutation omnium haeresium*, PTS 25 (Berlin: de Gruyter, 1986), 1–17; Jaap Mansfeld, *Heresiography in Context: Hippolytus' Elenchos as a Source for Greek Philosophy*, PhA 56 (Leiden: Brill, 1992), 317–325; Allen Brent, *Hippolytus and the Roman Church in the Third Century: Communities in Tension before the Emergence of a Monarch-Bishop*, VCSup 31 (Leiden: Brill, 1995), 204–367; Ronald Heine, "Hippolytus, Ps.-Hippolytus and the Early Canons," in *The Cambridge History of Early Christian Literature*, eds. Frances Young, Lewis Ayres, and Andrew Louth (Cambridge: Cambridge University Press, 2004), 142–151; M. David Litwa (trans. and ed.), *Refutation of All Heresies*, WGRW 40 (Atlanta: SBL Press, 2016), xxvii-liii.

8. Constantinus Minoides Mynas acquired the manuscript for the Bibliotheque de nationale France on one of his trips sponsored by the French Ministry of Public Instruction. Though much of the correspondence between Mynas and various ministers has been reproduced in a 1916 article by Henri Omont, the specific circumstances of the acquisition of this manuscript (as well as over fifty others) are unclear. For more on this, see Henri Omont, "Minoïde Mynas et ses missions en Orient (1840–1855)," *Mémoires de l'Académie des Inscriptions et Belles-Lettres* 40 (1916): 337–419.

9. Marcovich, *Hippolytus*, 6–7.

10. Marcovich, *Hippolytus*, 10–11; Eusebius, *Hist. Eccl.*, 6.20.2–6.22; Jerome, *Vir. ill*, 61.

11. In the most recent English translation of the text, M. David Litwa does a commendable job of summarizing the different theories on the text's authorship. Ultimately, Litwa comes down on the side of an unknown author (whom he refers to as "our author" throughout his notes).

12. Many thanks to Jennifer Collins-Elliott for helping me work through this argument.

13. For more on the *Elenchos* as heresiography and examples of the author's use of various sources, see Mansfeld, *Heresiography*, 44–316.

14. Marcovich, *Hippolytus*, 40.

15. The Latin term *monarchiani* is used by Tertullian to comment on a similar school of thought in *Against Praxeas*. Though the limited space here precludes me from engaging in an extended discussion of "modalistic monarchianism" as well as the problem of reifying rhetorical categories, the conflict centers on whether to emphasize the unity of the Father, Son, and Holy Spirit ("monarchianism") or to emphasize the distinction between the three ("trinitarianism"). For more on this, as well as the possible connections between Tertullian and Hippolytus, see Brent, *Hippolytus*, 501–535.

16. For other examples of the enslaved working as "financial agents" for their enslavers, see Jennifer A. Glancy, *Slavery in Early Christianity* (New York: Oxford University Press, 2002), 43.

17. Though the author does not state their own status in society (other than to mention that they are an *archierateia* ["bishop"; *Proem* 6]), there is no indication that they were formally enslaved.

18. Cf. Jennifer Glancy, "Slavery and the Rise of Christianity," in *The Cambridge World History of Slavery: Volume 1, The Ancient Mediterranean World*, eds. Keith Bradley and Paul Cartledge (Cambridge: Cambridge University Press, 2011), 469. To name a few examples, see Ulpian's discussion of enslaved people as prone to corrupt influence (*Digest* 11.3.1.5); the depiction of Trimalchio, a lewd and ostentatious freedperson in Petronius's first-century novel *Satyricon*; and Tacitus's description of the freedperson Antonius Felix, who "exercised the authority of a king with the spirit of a slave, plunging into all manner of cruelty and lust" (*Histories* 5.9; trans. Kenneth Wellesley).

19. These authors have written other works on the topic, but these are good places to start: Glancy, *Slavery*; J. Albert Harrill, *Slaves in the New Testament: Literary, Social, and Moral Dimensions* (Minneapolis: Fortress Press, 2006); Sheila Briggs,

"Gender, Slavery, and Technology: The Shaping of the Early Christian Moral Imagination," in *Beyond Slavery: Overcoming Its Religious and Sexual Legacies*, ed. Bernadette J. Brooten (New York: Palgrave Macmillan, 2010), 159–176; Katherine A. Shaner, *Enslaved Leadership in Early Christianity* (New York: Oxford University Press, 2018); Chris L. de Wet, *The Unbound God: Slavery and the Formation of Early Christian Thought* (London: Routledge, 2018).

20. For discussion of Ephesians, see Glancy, *Slavery*, 140–145; Harrill, *Slaves*, 85–117. For discussions about Augustine's use of slavery as metaphor, see Briggs "Gender, Slavery, and Technology," 170; de Wet, *The Unbound God*, 104–145.

21. Glancy, "Slavery and the Rise of Christianity," 469.

22. Glancy, *Slavery*, 138.

23. Glancy, *Slavery*, 70.

24. Glancy, *Slavery*, 70.

25. Glancy, *Slavery*, 93.

26. This translation is mostly my own, with some help from Litwa, *Refutation*, 657. As discussed earlier in this essay, there are many issues with this manuscript, which several editors have attempted to correct over the years (including this passage). Much of the disagreement over this passage hinges on the phrase *en axia*, which I have translated as "dignity." See, for example, A. Cleveland Coxe's note in the translation of the *Elenchos* in volume 5 of the Ante-Nicene Fathers series: "This passage, of which there are different readings, has been variously interpreted . . . The variety of meaning generally turns on the word *enaxia* in Miller's [1851] text. Bunsen alters it into *en axia . . . hēlikia*, i.e., were inflamed at a proper age. Dr. Wordsworth reads *hēlikiōtē . . . anaxiō*, i.e., an unworthy comrade. Roeper reads *hēlikia . . . anaxiou*, i.e., in the bloom of youth were enamoured with one undeserving of their choice" (*ANF* 5:131n7).

27. Before ending this section, Hippolytus also mentions that Callistus began to permit second baptisms (though for whom is not clear).

28. Glancy, *Slavery*, 96.

29. Glancy, *Slavery*, 27.

30. Judith Evans Grubbs, *Women and the Law in the Roman Empire: A Sourcebook on Marriage, Divorce and Widowhood* (London: Routledge, 2002), xvii.

31. Theodosian Code 4.12.1, 1 April, 314. The first part of the law concerns the same parties (free women and enslaved men), yet these free women "have suffered violence either at the hands of slaves or anyone else and have been joined against their will to men of servile status" (Grubbs, *Women and the Law in the Roman Empire*, 176).

32. Harold L. Short, "'On the Outskirts of Babylon': Representations of Motherhood in Fourth-Century Latin Christian Literature" (PhD diss., Florida State University, 2017), 229–275.

33. Cf. Denise Kimber Buell, *Making Christians: Clement of Alexandria and the Rhetoric of Legitimacy* (Princeton: Princeton University Press, 1999), 161. Buell makes a similar argument about Clement of Alexandria's use of "pregnant, birthing, and lactating bodies" to support his arguments in the *Paedagogus*.

34. For some ancient non-Christian and Christian examples, see Helen King, *Hippocrates' Woman: Reading the Female Body in Ancient Greece* (London: Routledge, 1998); Rebecca Flemming, *Medicine and the Making of Roman Women: Gender, Nature, and Authority from Celsus to Galen* (Oxford: Oxford University Press, 2000); David D. Leitao, *The Pregnant Male as Myth and Metaphor in Classical Greek Literature* (Cambridge: Cambridge University Press, 2012); Alicia D. Myers, *Blessed among Women?: Mothers and Motherhood in the New Testament* (Oxford: Oxford University Press, 2017); Meghan R. Henning, *Hell Hath No Fury: Gender, Disability, and the Invention of Damned Bodies in Early Christian Literature* (New Haven: Yale University Press, 2021).

35. Peter Brown, *The Body and Society: Men, Women, and Sexual Renunciation in Early Christianity* (New York: Columbia University Press, 2008), 153.

WORKS CITED

Baldrick-Morrone, Tara. "'Let's Not Retell This Myth about the History of the Thing': The Impact of John T. Noonan, Jr.'s Grand Narrative on the American Abortion Debate." PhD diss., Florida State University, 2020.

Brent, Allen. *Hippolytus and the Roman Church in the Third Century: Communities in Tension before the Emergence of a Monarch-Bishop*. Supplements to *Vigiliae Christianae* 31. Leiden: Brill, 1995.

Briggs, Sheila. "Gender, Slavery, and Technology: The Shaping of the Early Christian Moral Imagination." Pages 159–176 in *Beyond Slavery: Overcoming Its Religious and Sexual Legacies*. Edited by Bernadette J. Brooten. New York: Palgrave Macmillan, 2010.

Brown, Peter. *The Body and Society: Men, Women, and Sexual Renunciation in Early Christianity*. New York: Columbia University Press, 2008.

Buell, Denise Kimber. *Making Christians: Clement of Alexandria and the Rhetoric of Legitimacy*. Princeton: Princeton University Press, 1999.

De Wet, Chris L. *The Unbound God: Slavery and the Formation of Early Christian Thought*. London: Routledge, 2018.

Drake, Susanna. *Slandering the Jew: Sexuality and Difference in Early Christian Texts*. Philadelphia: University of Pennsylvania Press, 2013.

Flemming, Rebecca. *Medicine and the Making of Roman Women: Gender, Nature, and Authority from Celsus to Galen*. Oxford: Oxford University Press, 2000.

Glancy, Jennifer A. *Slavery in Early Christianity*. New York: Oxford University Press, 2002.

———. "Slavery and the Rise of Christianity." Pages 456–481 in *The Cambridge World History of Slavery: Volume 1, The Ancient Mediterranean World*. Edited by Keith Bradley and Paul Cartledge. Cambridge: Cambridge University Press, 2011.

Gorman, Michael J. *Abortion and the Early Church: Christian, Jewish, and Pagan Attitudes in the Greco-Roman World*. Eugene, OR: Wipf & Stock Publishers, 1982.

Grubbs, Judith Evans. *Women and the Law in the Roman Empire: A Sourcebook on Marriage, Divorce and Widowhood*. London: Routledge, 2002.

Harrill, J. Albert. *Slaves in the New Testament: Literary, Social, and Moral Dimensions*. Minneapolis: Fortress Press, 2006.

Harrison, Beverly Wildung. *Our Right to Choose: Toward a New Ethic of Abortion*. Boston: Beacon Press, 1983.

Heine, Ronald. "Hippolytus, Ps.-Hippolytus and the Early Canons." Pages 142–151 in *The Cambridge History of Early Christian Literature*. Edited by Frances Young, Lewis Ayres, and Andrew Louth. Cambridge: Cambridge University Press, 2004.

Henning, Meghan R. *Hell Hath No Fury: Gender, Disability, and the Invention of Damned Bodies in Early Christian Literature*. New Haven: Yale University Press, 2021.

Hippolytus. *The Refutation of All Heresies*. Pages 9–153 in vol. 5 of *The Ante-Nicene Fathers*. Edited by Alexander Roberts and James Donaldson. Translated by J. H. MacMahon. New York: Christian Literature Publishing Co., 1886.

King, Helen. *Hippocrates' Woman: Reading the Female Body in Ancient Greece*. London: Routledge, 1998.

Knust, Jennifer Wright. *Abandoned to Lust: Sexual Slander and Ancient Christianity*. New York: Columbia University Press, 2005.

Leitao, David D. *The Pregnant Male as Myth and Metaphor in Classical Greek Literature*. Cambridge: Cambridge University Press, 2012.

Litwa, M. David, trans. and ed. *Refutation of All Heresies*. Writings from the Greco-Roman World 40. Atlanta: SBL Press, 2016.

Mansfeld, Jaap. *Heresiography in Context: Hippolytus'* Elenchos *as a Source for Greek Philosophy*. Philosophia Antiqua 56. Leiden: Brill, 1992.

Marcovich, Miroslav. *Hippolytus: Refutation omnium haeresium*. Patristische Texte und Studien 25. Berlin: de Gruyter, 1986.

Myers, Alicia D. *Blessed among Women?: Mothers and Motherhood in the New Testament*. Oxford: Oxford University Press, 2017.

Noonan, John T., Jr. "An Almost Absolute Value in History." Pages 1–59 in *The Morality of Abortion: Legal and Historical Perspectives*. Edited by John T. Noonan, Jr. Cambridge, MA: Harvard University Press, 1970

———. "Introduction." Pages ix-xviii in *The Morality of Abortion: Legal and Historical Perspectives*. Edited by John T. Noonan, Jr. Cambridge, MA: Harvard University Press, 1970.

Omont, Henri. "Minoïde Mynas et ses missions en Orient (1840–1855)." *Mémoires de l'Académie des Inscriptions et Belles-Lettres* 40 (1916): 337–419.

Shaner, Katharine A. *Enslaved Leadership in Early Christianity*. New York, Oxford University Press, 2018.

Short, Harold L. "'On the Outskirts of Babylon': Representations of Motherhood in Fourth-Century Latin Christian Literature." PhD diss., Florida State University, 2017.

Tacitus. *The Histories*. Translated by Kenneth Wellesley. Revised with a New Introduction by Rhiannon Ash. London: Penguin Books, 2009.

Chapter 2

Danaids and Dirces in Roman Corinth

Sexualized Violence and Imperial Spectacle in 1 Clement

Chance E. Bonar

In the late first or early second century, a letter was sent from Rome to Corinth. Known to scholars as *1 Clement,* this letter is significant because of how it calls the Corinthian Christ-following assembly to conform to the will of its Roman counterpart by restoring previous church leadership. Near the beginning, the writer[1] explores ancient and contemporary examples of jealousy (*zēlos*) that have destroyed relationships and caused suffering for God's people. One specific example of this has caused commentators significant trouble:

> Being persecuted through jealousy, women—Danaids and Dirces—suffering in this way terrible and unholy mutilations, arrived at the secure race of faith and received a noble reward, being weak in the body. (*1 Clem* 6.2)[2]

The Corinthian assembly, residing at one of the seats of Roman colonial culture and power, were no strangers to the type of sexualized violence and mythological Greek women described in this passage. They likely congregated a kilometer away from the local amphitheater, within which spectators gathered to watch condemned individuals be dressed up and mutilated for entertainment. How, then, might the Corinthian recipients of *1 Clement* interpret this passage in light of local expressions of Roman colonial violence and sexualized spectacle?

The Danaids and Dirces in *1 Clement* have often troubled (male) scholars who struggle to make sense of their presence in the writer's argument. Despite the lack of manuscript evidence for corruption, scholars throughout the nineteenth and twentieth centuries offered various emendations to the phrase "Danaids and Dirces" in order to "fix" the passage and conform it to their vision of early Christian orthodoxy in Rome. To begin this chapter, I suggest that such emendations to hypothetical corruptions demonstrate not an ancient textual misunderstanding, but modern scholarly anxiety over how pagans and women might "corrupt" the letter often attributed to a Roman bishop.

In lieu of hypothesizing about the origins of the Danaids and Dirces, I offer an examination of the passage's function in *1 Clement* and potential reception among the Corinthians. The latter part of this chapter imagines how the Corinthian recipients of *1 Clement* may have understood its brief scene of violence against women and their purported overcoming of "being weak in the body." Building upon scholarship on the mythological staging of Roman executions as well as archaeological data at Corinth, I suggest that the unexcavated Corinthian amphitheater and Roman spectacle culture serve as essential for a correct understanding of *1 Clem* 6.2. The amphitheater, one of the first in mainland Greece built soon after the establishment of the Corinthian colony (*colonia*), was one of many features that typified Corinth's deep ties to Rome. Corinthian Christ-followers may have understood *1 Clement*'s exemplary women and the sexualized violence they experienced through their own participation in or viewing of Roman spectacles. Such spectacular images, I argue, highlight the dependency of Corinth on Rome for its prominent colonial status, and strengthens the case of the writer of *1 Clement* that Rome's ecclesiastical advice should be taken by their imperial and ecclesiastical *colonia*. The sexually violated women of *1 Clem* 6.2 are thus used by the Roman assembly as an example, as a veiled threat that violence might come upon those who cause enough internal dissent to be noticed and notable in the eyes of the (imperial and ecclesiastical) Romans.

1 CLEMENT 6.2 AND THE "PROBLEM" OF PAGAN WOMEN

1 Clement, a letter sent by "the assembly of God that sojourns in Rome to the assembly of God that sojourns in Corinth" (pref.), was likely written between 70–140 CE in order to quell strife (*stasis*) and rivalry (*eris*) caused by the deposition of local presbyters.[3] Borrowing from Paul's strategy when writing to the Corinthians, *1 Clement* uses deliberative rhetoric to convince Corinthian Christ-followers to achieve "peace and concord" (*1 Clem* 65.1; *eirēnēn kai homonoian*) and to send those who caused internal quarrels into self-exile. After praising the Corinthians' former concord and lamenting its recent decline (*1 Clem* 1–3), the writer turns to the problem of jealousy (*zēlos*) and envy (*phthonos*) as an explanation for the internal divisions in Corinth (*1 Clem* 4–6). After examining various examples of jealousy from the Jewish scriptures—including Cain and Abel, Joseph and his brothers, and Moses and the Egyptian—the writer turns to recent examples of those who have suffered, been persecuted, and been divided because of jealousy: Peter, Paul, the multitude of the elect, estranged wives, and persecuted women characterized as Danaids and Dirces.[4]

This final example of jealousy has caused numerous interpretive headaches for commentators who did not expect female martyrs to be compared to pagan women. Most commentators read this passage as referring to a Roman practice of mythological reenactment in the amphitheater or arena, in which criminalized people wear costumes during their condemnation.[5] Some, especially in recent years, have read it as symbolic or metaphorical for how these Christian women suffered.[6] This perplexity stems in part from the fact that comparison of martyred Christian women to both Dirce and the daughters of Danaus is difficult to square with the stories we have of them. Pseudo-Apollodorus's *Library* tells us that Dirce was murdered when Amphion and Zethus tied her to a bull for attempting to kill their mother Antiope.[7] The Danaids, on the other hand, are remembered as fifty daughters of Danaus who killed their soon-to-be cousin-husbands and were condemned to continually fill a perforated vessel with buckets of water in Hades.[8] While the former myth makes sense in the context of persecution and torture, the latter hardly seems like a fitting comparison. Some have tried to solve this conundrum by arguing that the Christian women were set up as prizes for a race, just as some of the Danaids were by their father.[9]

As a solution to this conundrum, from the seventeenth century onward some scholars have suggested that the text must be corrupt and have emended "Danaids and Dirces" accordingly, as the chart below demonstrates. These emendations, however, are often justified not only as attempts to clarify the language of *1 Clem* 6.2 or to remove references to myths that do not match the context of *1 Clement*, but to expunge the comparison of Christian women to pagan mythological figures altogether. Even as early as his 1633 edition of *1 Clement*, Patricius Iunius marked off "Danaids and Dirces" with square brackets and argued that "no one would, at first glance, not realize that these [words] are foreign to this passage, and clearly contrary to the mind of the author."[10] Christopher Wordsworth's emendation ("women, enslaved girls") was quickly followed by a defense of Clement's Christian integrity:

> It is very unlikely that S. Clement, a Christian Father, writing to a Christian Church, should have accepted the language of heathen insult and cruelty, and

have identified Christian saints with a jealous and savage adulteress like Dirce, and with heathen wives such as the daughters of Danaus, infamous for their treachery and cruelty for their husbands.[11]

Not long after, Christian Bunsen thanked Wordsworth for this emendation, expressing his "gratitude for being relived from two monsters which disfigured a beautiful passage in the Epistle of the Roman Clement."[12] Alphonse Dain likewise argued that Wordsworth's emendation was correct, and that "this intrusion of mythological terms" caused "a beautiful movement of thought to disappear"—in large part because "Clement, nourished by holy Scripture, attained to ignore pagan culture and even the pagan world."[13] Most recently, Otto Zwierlein suggested that the phrase was a marginal gloss that was incorporated into the body of *1 Clement,* arguing that its content did not match the broader text "because Pseudo-Clement keeps his letter to the Christian community free from any pagan mythology" and boldly claiming that the phrase was "repulsive."[14] For such scholars, the use of the Danaids and Dirces as exemplary in one of our earliest Christian texts led to the desire to purify *1 Clement* from women deemed monstrous, cruel, and terrifyingly pagan. Instead, these men suggested emendations that portrayed some of these persecuted women as enslaved, as girlish and weak, as unjustly and irreverently martyred, or like little lambs.

Recent scholarship on *1 Clement* has overwhelmingly demonstrated that the imagined division between "Christian" and "pagan" references that produced most of these conjectures does not hold up under scrutiny, since *1 Clement* is written largely in the style of Greek *homonoia* literature with the goal of unity among the Corinthians and occasionally uses so-called "pagan" motifs.[15] In response to these scholars' emendations and disdain for pagan women, the next two sections of this chapter will explore why it is possible or even likely that that *1 Clement* describes these Christian women as Danaids and Dirces, as well as how the Corinthian recipients of this letter might have interpreted this comparison in light of their colonial relationship to Rome.

IMPERIAL SPECTACLE AND SEXUALIZED VIOLENCE IN THE AMPHITHEATER

As Kathleen Coleman has convincingly demonstrated through her work on mythological staging of executions in the early Roman imperial period, *1 Clem* 6.2 is most likely referring to Christian women who were condemned and forced to wear costumes as part of a dramatic reenactment of famous stories.[16] In the late Roman Republic and early Empire—especially after the birth of the amphitheater and further technologies of spectacle and

Danaids and Dirces in Roman Corinth 21

Table 2.1

Manuscript	Text	Translation
Codex Alexandrinus (5th ct.)[i]	danaides kai dirkai	Danaids and Dirces
Codex Hierosolymitanus (1056 CE)[ii]	danaides kai deirkai	Danaids and Dirces
Latin (11th ct.)[iii]	Danaides et Dircae	Danaids and Dirces
Syriac (1169/70 CE)[iv]	d'n'yds wdirq'	Danaids and Dirces
Coptic (4th ct.)[v]	ndanais m^en ^endirkē	Danaids and Dirces

Scholar	Emendation	Translation
Jean Leclerc[vi]	aneu aidous kai dikēs	without reverence and justice
Wordsworth[vii]	neanides paidiskai	women, enslaved girls
Donaldson[viii]	gennaiai te kai doulai	brave and enslaved women
Lagarde[ix]	analkides kai kopikai	feeble and girlish
Haupt[x]	amnides dikaiai	just ewes

[i.] F. G. Kenyon, *The Codex Alexandrinus* (Royal ms 1 D v-viii) in Reduced Photographic Facsimile. New Testament and Clementine Epistles (London: British Museum, 1909).

[ii.] Joseph Barber Lightfoot, *The Apostolic Fathers, Part I,1: S. Clement of Rome* (Hildesheim/New York: Georg Olms, 1973 [1890]), 429; idem, *The Apostolic Fathers, Part I,2: S. Clement of Rome* (Hildesheim/New York: Georg Olms, 1973 [1890]), 33.

[iii.] G. Morin, *Sancti Clementis Romani ad Corinthos epistulae versio Latina antiquissima*. Anecdota Maredsolana 2 (Maredsous, Belgium, 1894), 7.

[iv.] R. L. Bensly and R. H. Kennet, *The Epistles of S. Clement to the Corinthians in Syriac* (Cambridge: Cambridge University Press, 1899), 7.

[v.] Carl Schmidt, *Der erste Clemensbrief in altkoptischer Übersetzung*, TU 32.1 (Leipzig: J. C. Hinrichs'sche Buchhandlung, 1908), 39. Unfortunately, our Akhmimic Coptic manuscript is fragmentary and only has text for this passage up to the word before "Danaids and Dirce." See Friedrich Rösch, *Bruchstücke des ersten Clemensbriefes, nach dem achmimischen Papyrus der Strassburger Universitäts- und Landesbibliothek* (Strasbourg: Schlesier and Schweikhardt, 1910), 19–22.

[vi.] PG 1:221. Migne (PG 1:220–222) notes alternate readings as danaides kai dirkē and danaē te kai dirkē, as well as that P. Young here suggests that the verse is a post-Clement of Alexandria addition, since Clement mentions the Danaids in Strom. 4.120.4.

[vii.] Christopher Wordsworth, *Theocritus: Codicum Manuscriptorum Ope* (Cambridge: Joannes G. Parker, 1844), 213; idem, Conjectural Emendations, 18–20.

[viii.] James Donaldson, "The New MS. of Clement of Rome," *The Theological Review* 14 (Jan. 1877): 45. Here, Donaldson argues that "the sedate letter of one church to another is not a document in which nicknames would be introduced under any circumstances," insisting that names from the amphitheater meant to mock martyrs would not be repeated by Christ-followers.

[ix.] Paul de Lagarde, *Armenische Studien* (Osnabrück: Otto Zeller, 1970 [1877]), 73.

[x.] M. Haupt, "Analecta," *Hermes* 3.1 (1869): 145–6. Haupt briefly considers the possibility of hagnai te kai dikaiai ("pure and just [women]"), but rejects this. Cf. Clement of Alexandria, Protrepticus 12, in which daughters of God are described as "fair lambs."

torture—we find that displays of imperial power and theatrical aesthetics go hand-in-hand. Martial's *On the Spectacles*, published around 80 CE at the inauguration of the Colosseum under Titus, contains a series of epigrams relaying mythological enactments within the arena: a woman enamored with a bull just like Pasiphae (the mother of the Minotaur), and Laureolus,

Daedalus, and Orpheus mauled by bears as condemned participants thrown to the beasts (*damnatio ad bestias*; see *Spect.* 6, 9, 10, 24).[17] Martial makes clear that the enactment of myth brings these stories to life: "whatever legend sings, the amphitheater offers you" (*Spect.* 6).[18] Likewise, at the turn of the third century, Tertullian mocked Roman deities and took aim at how they participated in blood sport in the arena by "executing their themes and stories through the condemned" (*Apol.* 15.4).[19] Tertullian notes contemporary cases of mythological enactment in the arena, such as the castration of Attis, a man burned alive while dressed as Hercules, and Mercury and Pluto examining and dragging corpses out of the arena (*Apol.* 15.5).

Roman blood spectacles became a prominent event for the convergence of administering justice, exhibiting (often sexualized) violence of Rome's imperial power (*imperium*) over criminalized bodies, and curating an aesthetically pleasing theatrical event for the masses. As James Harley has argued, such blood sport became popular in the Flavian period in large part through the incorporation of theatrical features to the juridical system.[20] Throughout the day, one would encounter animal hunters (*venatores/bestiarii*) in the morning, condemned criminals (*noxii*) allotted to be killed in the arena around lunchtime, and gladiators participating in obligations (*munera*) by fighting in the afternoon.[21] While we know of some instances of women participating in the arena as *venatores* or gladiators,[22] most female participants would either be *noxii* who had been sentenced to death as part of an entertaining show of force, or would be relegated to the nosebleed seats in accordance with Augustus's laws concerning dress and seating arrangements at the amphitheater.

Alongside *1 Clem* 6.2, other early Christian texts underscore how the theatricality of the arena often involved sexual and sexualized violence against women, particularly through animals.[23] In the *Acts of Paul and Thecla,* for example, Thecla is condemned to the beasts for defending herself against Alexander's attempted sexual assault, and is thereafter stripped and thrown into the arena with lions, bears, and a lioness. After miraculously surviving their attacks and baptizing herself, Alexander has Thecla's feet bound between two bulls and has their genitalia burned so as to provoke the bulls—yet this torture failed to kill Thecla.[24] Likewise, in the *Martyrdom of Perpetua and Felicitas,* Perpetua and her fellow *noxii* are coerced to wear robes of the priests of Saturn and priestesses of Ceres when they enter the amphitheater, and Perpetua justifies her refusal to do so (*Mart. Perp.* 18). When they enter the amphitheater, the women are confronted by a heifer that was chosen as their opponent so that "their sex might be matched with that of the beast." They are stripped naked and brought out in nets, and then given tunics once more in response to the spectators' horror (*Mart. Perp.* 20).[25] In both of these martyrological narratives, Thecla and Perpetua are sexually degraded, exposed, and compared to animals. In the case of Perpetua, we also have a glimpse of the theatrical clothing that she refuses to don.[26] Both women are stripped naked before being offered clothing once more—a tactic of humiliation that Sheila Briggs argues "took on sexual connotations that the amphitheater turned into sadistic spectacle."[27] In line with such treatment of condemned women, *1 Clement* portrays some Christian women in the arena as being forcibly animalized and coerced into dressing like a woman killed by a bull. Women's sexuality in such cases was both criminalized and put on display through dress (or lack thereof), bestiality, and sexual violence in the amphitheater.

In contrast to the long history of considering *1 Clem* 6.2 a noxious aberration in the text that wrongly compares Christian women to abhorrent "pagans," it is meant to bring to mind "those weak in the body"[28] suffering as Danaids and Dirces, being sexually violated and degraded as *noxii* in the arena, but in the end receiving their reward from God. We know well that early Christians attended events in the amphitheater and often imagined themselves on the giving end, rather than the receiving end, of imperial spectacular violence.[29] As I will argue in the final section, the Corinthian Christians were no different. Here, *1 Clem* 6.2 would not only evoke these specific persecuted and sexually degraded Christian women, but would elicit their own context as a Roman *colonia* and their participation in Roman spectacular culture.

READING *1 CLEM* 6.2 FROM CORINTH THE ROMAN *COLONIA*

How might the Corinthian *ekklēsia* that received *1 Clement* understand this treatment of persecuted women as Danaids and Dirces? I suggest that Corinth's position as a Roman *colonia* and its association with Roman spectacle frames both this passage and the end goal of *1 Clement*. That is, the writer uses amphitheatrical imagery to invoke Corinth's relationship with and dependence upon Rome as part of *1 Clement*'s broader persuasive and reconciliatory strategy.

Roman Corinth was highly prized and characterized as a wealthy trading center and producer of expensive goods,[30] and three writings from the early Roman Empire highlight Corinthian civic identity and Romanness: the Roman orator Favorinus's defense of his statue in Corinth (Ps.-Dio Chrysostom, *Orat.* 37), a letter from Argos regarding tributes to Corinth (Ps.-Julian, *Letter* 198), and Aelius Aristides's *Isthmian Oration* (*Orat.* 46).[31] Just as each of these writers highlight Corinth's ties to Rome, *1 Clement*'s reference to mythological (amphi)theatrical spectacles underscores how the Corinthian congregation ought to maintain unity and peace, lest jealousy (*zēlos*) cause them to suffer further sexualized violence at the hands of the Roman state. These first- and second-century writers each suggest that Corinth was a city breaking with other possible forms of Hellenism, and that was viewed at least by some as being too Roman. No doubt, the relationship between Hellenism and Romanness is complex and by no means mutually exclusive, but some ancient writers made normative judgments about Corinth's deep ties to Rome. Favorinus's early second-century speech against the Corinthians, for example, written in response to their pulling down of his statue in the city, compares their actions to those of other Greek cities. In defense of his own Hellenization as a Roman orator who acquired Greek dress, habits, and language, Favorinus subtly showers the Corinthians with mocking praise for not being Greek enough:

> Ought he [i.e. Favorinus] not to have a bronze statue in Corinth? Yes, and in every city—in yours because, though Roman (*Rhōmaios*), he has become thoroughly Hellenized (*apēllēnisthē*), even as your own city has. (Ps.-Dio Chrysostom, *Orat.* 37.26)[32]

Corinth, like Favorinus, is depicted as a Roman in Hellenic clothing and is urged to recognize their similarities and to re-erect his statue.

A few decades before Favorinus, a letter was sent from Argos that argued that the Argives should not be forced to offer tribute to Corinth in order to host games at the capital of the Roman province of Achaea.[33] Especially since Argos hosted so many festivals and other cities like Delphi were immune from this tribute, payment for Corinth's festival seemed unjust to the Argives. Of particular interest for *1 Clement* is the reason for which Argos protested payment:

> For it is not to furnish gymnastic or musical contests (*agōnōn gumnikōn ē mousikōn*) that the Corinthians need so much money, but they buy bears and panthers for the hunting shows (*kunēgesia*) which they often exhibit in their theaters (*theatrois*; Ps.-Julian, *Letter* 198, 408D-409A).

Rather than using finances of neighboring cities to host familiar events, the Argives accuse Corinth of wasting it all on extravagant events that are hardly representative of Hellenic culture. The letter soon after argues that the Argives are "enslaved to a foreign spectacle (*ksenikē thea;* 409B)" through this payment, and that the Corinthians must choose between "abiding by the laws and customs of ancient Greece (*tēs palaias Hellados*), or rather by those which it seems they recently took over from the sovereign city (*tēs basileuousēs poleōs*; 409C)." Two things are of note here. First is that the Argive letter depicts Corinthian participation in *venationes* (animal hunts) as part of their spectacular production as foreign—a Roman practice rather than a Greek one. The second is that the Argives go so far as to question whether the Corinthians have abandoned Greek customs more generally in favor of their colonizer's customs.[34]

Finally, Aelius Aristides produced a speech in 156 CE (*Orat.* 46) in honor of Poseidon for a Corinthian festival and heaped praised upon the city of Corinth. Aristides celebrates that Poseidon is a fitting deity to oversee Corinth and that Corinth, likewise, is a fitting city to represent the region of Achaea. However, such praise of Corinth as the crown jewel of the Hellenic world also highlights its role as the colonial capital of Achaea:

> The city is the starting-point for good order (*eunomias*), and even now distributes justice (*ta dikaia*) to the Greeks. (*Orat.* 46.27)[35]

Here, Corinth simultaneously represents the heart of Panhellenic identity and functions as an arm of Roman imperial rule and jurisdiction in Greece.

Alongside these three writers, Corinth's entanglement with Roman institutions, cultic practices, and public monumental display all underscore the close relationship between the imperial center and its colonial capital.[36] Whether or not other Greek city-states and their inhabitants were content with it, Corinth's civic identity—and likely its ecclesiastical identity—was shaped by its status as a Roman *colonia* and capital of the Achaean province.

One particular feature of the Roman Corinthian colonial landscape of interest for reading *1 Clem* 6.2 is the unexcavated amphitheater. The site sits roughly one kilometer east of the Temple of Apollo and Corinth's forum and was likely among the first architectural projects of the first-century BCE Roman colonial settlers (See Fig. 2.1). In her investigation of the emergence of the Roman amphitheater, Katherine Welch demonstrated that Corinth was likely the first location in Greece to construct a Romanesque stone

Figure 2.1. Amphitheater at Corinth. *Source:* Petros Dellatolas, American School of Classical Studies at Athens, Corinth Excavations. Used with permission.

amphitheater as a permanent structure, unlike the more common practice of a temporary wooden structure.[37] The Corinthian amphitheater and Corinthian love of gladiatorial games was well-known and criticized in the first and second centuries CE by the likes of Apollonius of Tyana, Demonax, and Dio Chrysostom, all of whom mocked Athens for mimicking Corinth by converting the Theater of Dionysius near the Acropolis to host gladiatorial shows:[38]

> The Athenians used to assemble in their theater (*theatron*) below the acropolis and watch human slaughter, so that it was more popular there than it now is in Corinth (*en Corinthō nun*). (Philostratus, *Vit. Apoll.* 4.22.1)[39]

> When the Athenians, out of rivalry with the Corinthians (*kata zēlon ton pros Korinthous*), were thinking of holding a gladiatorial show (*thean monomachōn*), he came before them. (Lucian, *Demon.* 57)[40]

> For instance, in regard to the gladiatorial shows (*monomachous*) the Athenians have so zealously emulated the Corinthians (*ezēlōkasi Korinthous*), or rather have so surpassed both them and all others in their mad infatuation. (Dio Chrysostom, *Orat.* 31.121)[41]

Just as *1 Clement* opens by lamenting the internal division caused by jealousy (*zēlos*) at Corinth, Lucian and Dio Chrysostom see the rivalrous and zealous emulation of Corinthian spectacle as an instance of *zēlos* that is harmful to the Athenian (and broader Hellenic) lifestyle. To be like Corinth is to be too Roman, to enjoy blood sport too much, and to wrongly amplify *zēlos*.

It is not an accident that the writer of *1 Clement* alludes to the mythological reenactment and torture of women in the amphitheater when writing from Rome to Corinth. The reference in *1 Clem* 6.2 is meant to underscore and remind its readers of their cultural ties to Rome and their obligation to listen to the Roman assembly. As David Horrell has suggested, *1 Clement* builds upon Paul's Corinthian correspondence in order to support "the interests of the socially dominant, and which ideologically legitimates the established social, domestic and ecclesiastical order."[42] The impetus for sending *1 Clement* to Corinth may not be fraternal obligation or papal authority, but rather an expectation of colonial submission to the desire of the imperial center. Unlike our aforementioned writers who mocked Corinth for its Romanness, *1 Clement* leans into this trope to add legitimacy to its argument that the Corinthians ought to reinstate its deposed presbyters and harmoniously return to the status quo.[43] As we see by the end of *1 Clement*, the Roman assembly sent envoys to Corinth that were expected to report back to Rome when "peace and concord"—phrased as "adopting the attitude of obedience (*hupakoēs*)" slightly earlier in the letter—was achieved (*1 Clem* 63.1; 65.1).[44]

Upon hearing *1 Clem* 6.2, we might imagine the Corinthian assembly thinking of their own experiences as spectators at the amphitheater and their fear of becoming a victim of Roman imperial sexualized violence. Corinth had been stripped and violated once before by the Romans, as had these Christian women; what could prevent this from happening again? Rome's message, then, was to put an end to internal strife and jealousy that would prompt further violence from the imperial juridical and spectacular complex. We see such a message one chapter earlier, as David Eastman has demonstrated in his reassessment of *1 Clement*'s account of the deaths of Peter and Paul. *1 Clem* 5, he argues, posits that internal dissent and jealousy between factions of Christ-followers is what gained imperial attention and caused the apostles' deaths in Rome, and that *1 Clement* urges Corinth to avoid further instigation that would catch the eye of Rome.[45]

1 Clem 6.2 can be read in a similar light. Just as Peter and Paul died in an untimely way because "unjust jealousy" (*zēlon adikon*) among Christ-followers caught the attention of the Roman state, so too did a vast multitude of the elect and these persecuted women suffer because of internal strife. The overturning of ecclesiastical leaders at Corinth caused enough of an uproar that the Roman assembly felt compelled to intervene and advocate for the status quo, for ecclesiastical and political quietism, lest more Christ-followers unjustly die. Just as the gladiator was an ambiguous figure—both conqueror and conquered, loved and loathed, as Maia Kotrosits has explored[46]—so too are Peter, Paul, and the women of *1 Clem* 6.2. While these women are tortured and sexually degraded as Danaids and Dirces in a Roman spectacular display, they are also upheld at reaching "the goal in the race of faith." As Laurence Welborn notes, "Clement raises here the spectre of action by the Roman authorities"[47]—a veiled threat against the Corinthians who fail to act in the interest of the Roman assembly and state. *1 Clement* does not necessarily advocate for their deaths to be emulated or celebrated. Rather, they are presented as case studies of jealousy (*zēlos*) and as examples of what violence need not happen if the Corinthian assembly submits to the will of Rome.

CONCLUSION

This chapter responds to a longstanding misunderstanding of persecuted women being described as "Danaids and Dirces" in *1 Clem* 6.2. Rather than treating the phrase as an anomaly or interpolation, I suggest that women dressed as Danaids and Dirces fits well with attested practices of mythological staging in the Roman imperial arena. While we do not know the details of the "terrible and unholy tortures" that the women of *1 Clem* 6.2 faced, we can compare their circumstances to those of other martyrs and *noxii*. In light of Corinth's intimate relationship with Rome as the colonial capital of Achaea and its emulation of Roman amphitheatrical architecture, the writer of *1 Clement* stresses that ecclesiastical conservativism is the ideal way to avoid further imperial violence. *1 Clement* itself explains the function of these examples:

> We write these things, dear friends, not only to admonish (*nouthetountes*) you but also to remind (*hupomimnēskontes*) ourselves. For we are in the same arena (*skammati*), and the same contest (*agōn*) awaits us. (*1 Clem* 7.1)

The Roman assembly seemingly fears that rocking the boat will put both communities in further danger, and trusts that colonial ties between Rome and Corinth will be efficacious for their call to quietism. Just as Roman imperial structures made an example out of the women persecuted as Danaids and Dirces by sexually degrading and torturing them as *noxii,* Roman ecclesiastical structures make an example out of them as unnecessary consequences of jealousy and strife among Christ-followers.

NOTES

1. I do not believe that Clement of Rome penned *1 Clem,* but rather that *1 Clem* was quickly associated with Clement as a prominent presbyter in Rome. By the late second century, Dionysius of Corinth knows of "the letter sent to us before by Clement" that is read by the Corinthian congregation (Eusebius, *His. eccl.* 4.23.11), so the tradition of associating this letter with Clement likely emerged by the mid-second century. Cf. Irenaeus, *Haer.* 3.3.3; Clement of Alexandria, *Strom.* 4.105.1–113.3.

2. I am using the Greek text of *1 Clement* from Michael W. Holmes, *The Apostolic Fathers: Greek Texts and English Translations,* 3rd ed. (Grand Rapids, MI: Baker Academic, 2007), 52. The English translation is my own.

3. See esp. *1 Clem* 1.1, 3.1–4, 54.2, 63.1–65.2. On the dating of *1 Clement* beyond the traditional date of 96 CE, see Andrew Gregory, "Disturbing Trajectories: *1 Clement,* the *Shepherd of Hermas,* and the Development of Early Roman Christianity," in *Rome in the Bible and the Early Church,* ed. Peter Oakers (Carlislee: Paternoster, 2002), 144–49. On the strife at Corinth, see Laurence L. Welborn, "Jealousy, Envy, Strife and Discord in First Clement," *JBV* 38.2 (2017): 173–79; idem, *The Young Against the Old: Generational Conflict in First Clement* (Lanham: Lexington; Minneapolis, MN: Fortress Press, 2018)*;* Clare Rothschild, *New Essays on the Apostolic Fathers,* WUNT 375 (Tübingen: Mohr Siebeck, 2018), 69–80; Harry O. Maier, *The Social Setting of the Ministry as Reflected in the Writings of Hermas, Clement and Ignatius* (Waterloo: Wilfrid Laurier, 2002), 87–134.

4. On these *exempla,* see James Petitfils, *Mos Christianorum: The Roman Discourse of Exemplarity and the Jewish and Christian Language of Leadership,* STAC 99 (Tübingen: Mohr Siebeck, 2016), 150–81.

5. Kathleen M. Coleman, "Fatal Charades: Roman Executions Staged as Mythological Enactments," *JRS* 80 (1990): 44–73.

6. Hocario E. Lona, *Der erste Clemensbrief,* KAV 2 (Göttingen: Vandenhoeck & Ruprecht, 1998), 169–70. Jan M. Kozlowski ("'Danaïdes et Dircés': Sur 1 Cl 6.2," *ETL* 82.4 [2006]: 467–78) suggests that this passage is an allegory for women who refused their husbands' sexual advances (i.e., Danaids) and who were sexually violated for doing so (i.e., Dirces).

7. Ps.-Apollodorus, *Libr.* 3.5.5; Hyginus, *Fab.* 7–8; Pausanias, *Descr.* 9.25.3; Euripides, *Antiope* frag. 179–227. The two most famous Roman-era depictions of this scene are a painting in the House of the Vettii at Pompeii and the Farnese Bull from the Baths of Caracalla. See Lillian B. Joyce, "Dirce Disrobed," *ClAnt* 20.2 (2001): 221–38.

8. Ps.-Apollodorus, *Libr.* 2.1.5; Hyginus, *Fab.* 168–70; cf. Tatian, *Orat.* 26. Sian Lewis ("Women and Myth," in *A Companion to Greek Mythology,* ed. Ken Dowden and Niall Livingstone [Malden, MA: Blackwell, 2011], 447) helpfully notes that Greek myths are plastic and only occasionally crystallized; thus, it would be difficult to pin down what version of the Danaids myth *1 Clem* works with.

9. A. Plummer, "Contributions and Comments: 'Danaids and Dirces' in the Epistle of Clement to Corinth," *ExpTim* 26.12 (1915): 560–62; Hanns Christof Brennecke, "Danaiden und Dirken: zu 1 Cl 6,2," *ZKG* 88.2–3 (1977): 306–8. Tassilo Schmitt ("Des Kaisers Inszenierung Mythologie und neronische Christenverfolgung," *ZAC* 16.3 [2012]: 491) suggests that the Danaids may be a symbol for the senselessness of the Christian women's deaths.

10. Patricius Iunius, *Clementis ad Corinthos Epistola Prior* (Oxford, 1633), 9, O2: *Nemo est qui primo intuit, non videat haec aliena esse ab hoc logo, et plane contra authoris mentem.*

11. Christopher Wordsworth, *Conjectural Emendations of Passages in Ancient Authors with other Papers* (London: Rivingtons, 1883), 19.

12. Christian Charles Josias Bunsen, *Hippolytus und IIis Age; or, The Beginnings and Prospects of Christianity.* Vol. 1: Hippolytus and the Teachers of the Apostolical Age, 2nd edition (London: Longman, Brown, Green, and Longmans, 1854), xviii.

13. Alphonse Dain, "Notes sur le texte grec de l'Épître de saint Clément de Rome," *RSR* 39 (1951): 356: "cette intrusion de terms mythologique [. . .] disparaissait un beau movement de pensée [. . .] Clément, nourri d'Écriture sainte, affecte d'ignorer la culture païenne et même le monde païen." Dain contradictorily argues that "women, enslaved girls" was an example of classical asyndeton, but that "Danaids and Dirces" was an error that would have required a conjunctive *kai.*

14. Otto Zwierlein, "Danaïden und Dirken (1Clem 6,2)," in *Petrus und Paulus in Jerusalem und Rom: Von Neuen Testament zu den apokryphen Aposteakten* (Berlin: De Gruyter, 2013), 153: "weil Ps.Clemens sein Schreiben an die Christengemeinde zu Korinth frei von jeglicher heidnischen Mythologie halt"; 154: "anstößig."

15. Odd Magne Bakke, *"Concord and Peace": A Rhetorical Analysis of the First Letter of Clement with an Emphasis on the Language of Unity and Sedition*, WUNT 2.141 (Tübingen: Mohr Siebeck, 2001); W.C. van Unnik, "Studies on the So-Called First Epistle of Clement: The Literary Genre," in *Encounters with Hellenism: Studies on the First Letter of Clement*, ed. Cilliers Breytenbach and Laurence L. Welborn (Leiden: Brill, 2003), esp. 128–163; Cilliers Breytenbach, "Civic Concord and Cosmic Harmony: Sources of Metaphoric Mapping in 1 Clement 20.3," in *Encounters with Hellenism*, 182–96.

16. Coleman, "Fatal Charades." Cf. Tacitus, *Ann.* 15.44 in which Nero inflicts "the most exquisite tortures" (*quaesitissimis poenis*) upon Christians; Suetonius, *Nero* 11 on spectacles more broadly.

17. On related performances of Pasiphae and the bull, see Suetonius, *Nero* 12.2. James Harley ("The Aesthetics of Death: The Theatrical Elaboration of Ancient Roman Blood Spectacles," *THS* 18 [1998]: 92) notes that the victim may have not been dressed as Laureolus, but simply framed or identified as such before the execution.

18. *quidquid Fama canit, praestat harena tibi.* Latin text and English translation from Kathleen M. Coleman, *Valerii Martialis Liber spectaculorum* (Oxford: Oxford University Press, 2006), 62.

19. *argumenta et historias noxiis ministrantes.* Latin from Paulus Frassinetti, ed. *Q. Septimi Flornetis Tertulliani Apologeticum* (Paravia, Torino: Proprietà Letteraria, 1965), 41.

20. Harley, "The Aesthetics of Death," 89–97. Schmitt ("Des Kaisers Inszenierung," 495–96) and Coleman ("Fatal Charades," 53) note that we do have at least one example of a pre-Neronian mythological execution held in the Forum (Strabo, *Geogr.* 6.273), but this practice emerged more prominently during and after Nero's reign.

21. Coleman, "Fatal Charades," 55–56; Alison Futrell, *Blood in the Arena: The Spectacle of Roman Power* (Austin, TX: University of Texas, 1997), 10–33.

22. Stephen Brunet, "Women with Swords: Female Gladiators in the Roman World," in *A Companion to Sport and Spectacle in Greek and Roman Antiquity*, ed. Paul Christensen and Donald G. Kyle (Malden, MA: Wiley Blackwell, 2014), 478–491.

23. Many of these examples stem from Johannes N. Vorster, "The Blood of the Female Martyrs as the Sperm of the Early Church," *R&T* 10.1 (2003): 66–99.

24. *Acts of Paul and Thecla* 9: "And he bound her from the feed to the midst of the two bulls and he stirred up a flaming hot iron under their genitals." English translation from Barrier, *The Acts of Paul and Thecla,* 165. Importantly, Maia Kotrosits ("Penetration and Its Discontents: Greco-Roman Sexuality, the *Acts of Paul and Thecla,* and Theorizing Eros without the Wound," *JHS* 27.3 [2018]: 363) notes that, unlike the death of the female martyrs in *1 Clem* 6.2, Thecla "thwarts *both* the traumatic conclusion of execution and the happy resolution of marriage."

25. *sexui earum etiam de bestia aemulatus.* Latin text and English translation from Herbert Musurillo, *The Acts of the Christian Martyrs* (Oxford: Clarendon Press, 1972), 128–89.

26. We find a similar connection between the sexualization of condemned women and animals in Apuleius (*Met.* 10.19–35). Lucius, the human-turned-ass, is taken by his enslaver to Corinth to participate in the spectacles. Lucius is forced to have sex with a wealthy Corinthian matron, as well as is almost forced to rape a woman condemned to the beasts in the arena. See H. J. Mason, "Lucius at Corinth," *Phoenix* 25.2 (1971): 160–165.

27. Sheila Briggs, "Gender, Slavery, and Technology: The Shaping of the Early Christian Moral Imagination," in *Beyond Slavery: Overcoming Its Religious and Sexual Legacies,* ed. Bernadette J. Brooten and Jacqueline L. Hazelton. Black Religion / Womanist Thought / Social Justice (New York, NY: Palgrave Macmillan, 2010), 164.

28. *hai astheneis tō sōmati.* Compare with Blandina, an enslaved woman in the *Martyrs of Lyons and Vienna* whose enslaver worried that she would fail to confess her faith under torture "due to the weakness of her body" (*Mart. Lyons* 1.18; *dia to asthenes tou sōmatos*). While Blandina famously does not experience the pain of her torture, her martyrdom, like the women of *1 Clem* 6.2, contains athletic metaphors concerning her putting on the athlete Christ and winning the crown of immortality through her contest (*Mart. Lyons* 1.42). See Stephanie L. Cobb, *Divine Deliverance: Pain and Painlessness in Early Christian Martyr Texts* (Berkeley, CA: University of California Press, 2016), 66, 74–77; Ronald Charles, *The Silencing of Slaves in Early Jewish and Christian Texts* (London/New York: Routledge, 2019), 178–83.

29. Revelation and Tertullian's *On the Spectacles* are prime examples of this phenomenon. See Christopher A. Frilingos, *Spectacles of Empire: Monsters, Martyrs, and the Book of Revelation* (Philadelphia: University of Pennsylvania Press, 2004); Maia Kotrosits, "Seeing is Feeling: Revelation's Enthroned Lamb and Ancient Visual Affects," *BibInt* 22 (2014): 473–504; Kimberly B. Stratton, "The Eschatological Arena: Reinscribing Roman Violence in Fantasies of the End Times," *BibInt* 17 (2009): 45–76; Elizabeth A. Castelli, *Visions and Voyeurism: Holy Women and the Politics of Sight in Early Christianity,* ed. Christopher Ocker (Berkeley, CA: Center for Hermeneutical Studies, 1995); David Frankfurter, "Martyrology and the Prurient Gaze," *JECS* 17.2 (2009): 215–45.

30. Strabo, *Geography* 8.6.20–23; Juvenal, *Satires* 6.295 and 8.114; Martial, *Epigrams* 9.59, 10.65, 10.68.

31. For an overview of these four texts, see Jason König, "Favorinus' 'Corinthian Oration,' in its Corinthian Context," *Proceedings of the Cambridge Philological Society* 47 (2001): 152–65.

32. Greek text and English translation from Dio Chrysostom. *Discourses 37–60,* trans. H. Lamar Crosby. Vol. 4, LCL 376 (Cambridge, MA: Harvard University Press, 1946), 24–27.

33. Greek text and English translation from Julian, *The Works of the Emperor Julian,* trans. Wilmer Cave Wright, Vol. 3, LCL 157 (London: William Heinemann, 1923), 84–97. For a detailed examination of this letter, see Antony J.S. Spawforth, "Corinth, Argos, and the Imperial Cult: Pseudo-Julian, Letters 198," *Hesperia* 63.2 (1994): 211–32. Spawforth tentatively dates the letter between 80–120 CE, and provides compelling evidence that its description of Argive festivals fits the time period (211–14).

34. See Pausanias, *Descr.* 2.1.2, regarding how Corinth is not settled by "the ancient Corinthians" (*Korinthiōn* [. . .] *tōn archaiōn*), but by "colonists" (*epoikoi*)—freedpeople sent by Rome. König ("Favorinus' 'Corinthian Oration,'" 156–58) argues that Pausanias subtly foregrounds Corinth's Romanness and denies their Greek status—along with various Greek institutions (*Descr.* 3.2.7). Also see Cavan W. Concannon, *Assembling Early Christianity: Trade, Networks, and the Letters of Dionysios of Corinth* (Cambridge: Cambridge University, 2017), 128–31.

35. Greek text from Aelius Aristides, *Aelii Aristidis Smyrnaei quae supersunt omnia,* ed. Bruno Keil, Vol. 2 (Berlin: apud Weidnammos, 1893), 370. English translation my own.

36. See esp. Margaret L. Laird ("The Emperor in a Roman Town: The Base of the *Augustales* in the Forum of Corinth," in *Corinth in Context: Comparative Studies on Religion and Society,* ed. Steven J. Friesen, Daniel N. Schowalter, and James C. Walters (Leiden: Brill, 2010), 67–116) regarding how the imperial cult in Corinth was maintained by the *augustales,* a group of freedpeople municipal organizers who purposefully built monuments that blended Hellenic and Roman features.

37. H. N. Fowler and R. Stillwell, *Corinth: Results of Excavations conducted by The American School of Classical Studies at Athens. Vol. I: Introduction: Topography, Architecture (= Corinth I)* (Cambridge, MA: Harvard University Press, 1932), 89–91 and figs. 54–56; Katherine E. Welch, *The Roman Amphitheatre: From its Origins to the Colosseum* (Cambridge: Cambridge University Press, 2007), 255–59; idem, "Negotiating Roman Spectacle Architecture in the Greek World: Athens and Corinth," in *The Art of Ancient Spectacle,* ed. Bettina Bergmann and Christine Kondoleon (Washington, DC: National Gallery of Art; New Haven: Yale University Press, 1999), 133–40.

38. Welch, *The Roman Amphitheatre;* 165–78; idem, "Negotiating Roman Spectacle," 125–33. Coleman ("Fatal Charades," 52n68) notes that Julius Caesar built the first wooden amphitheater in 46 BCE It is worth noting that along with the stone amphitheater, Corinth converted both its theater and odeon for gladiatorial shows in the second or third centuries CE. See Richard Stillwell, *Corinth: Results of Excavations conducted by The American School of Classical Studies at Athens. Vol. II: The Theatre. (= Corinth II)* (Princeton, NJ: The American School, 1952), 84–98 on the theater and its frescoes of *venationes*; O. Broneer, *Corinth: Results of Excavations conducted by The American School of Classical Studies at Athens. Vol. X: The Odeum. (= Corinth X)* (Cambridge, MA: Harvard University Press, 1932), 142–148, 225 on the odeon and its potential traces of animal cages.

39. Philostratus, *The Life of Apollonius of Tyana,* trans. Christopher P. Jones, LCL 16 (Cambridge, MA: Harvard University Press, 2005), 366–67.

40. Lucian, *Lucian, Vol. 1,* trans. A. M. Harmon, LCL 14 (London: William Heinemann, 1913), 168–69.

41. Dio Chrysostom, *Discourses* 31–36, trans. J. W. Cohoon and H. Lamar Crosby, LCL 358 (Cambridge, MA: Harvard University Press, 1995 [1940]), 124–27.

42. David G. Horrell, *The Social Ethos of the Corinthian Correspondence: Interests and Ideology from 1 Corinthians to 1 Clement* (Edinburgh: T&T Clark, 1996), 263–65, 287 (quote from 287). Cf. Maier, *The Social Setting,* 118–25. van Unnik

("Studies," 124–27) notes how previous scholars have explained the impetus for *1 Clement* as a utilization of papal power, an extension of *imperium Romanum* into an ecclesiastical sphere, or fraternal responsibility from one congregation to another.

43. On harmony on a political and cosmic level in *1 Clem*, see Breytenbach, "Civic Concord."
44. See Welborn, *The Young Against the Old*, 224–46.
45. David L. Eastman, "Jealousy, Internal Strife, and the Deaths of Peter and Paul: A Reassessment of *1 Clement*," ZAC 18.1 (2013): 34–53. Cf. Suetonius, *Claudius* 25.4; Dio Cassius, *Hist. rom.* 60.6.6 on expulsion of Jews from Rome because of instigation.
46. Kotrosits, "Seeing is Feeling," 493–94.
47. Welborn, "Jealousy," 178.

WORKS CITED

Aelius Aristides. *Aelii Aristidis Smyrnaei quae supersunt omnia*. Edited by Bruno Keil. Vol. 2. Berlin: apud Weidnammos, 1893.

Bakke, Odd Magne. *"Concord and Peace": A Rhetorical Analysis of the First Letter of Clement with an Emphasis on the Language of Unity and Sedition*. WUNT 2.141. Tübingen: Mohr Siebeck, 2001.

Bensly, R. L. and R. H. Kennet. *The Epistles of S. Clement to the Corinthians in Syriac*. Cambridge: Cambridge University, 1899.

Brennecke, Hanns Christof. "Danaiden und Dirken: zu 1 Cl 6, 2." *Zeitschrift für Kirchengeschichte* 88.2–3 (1977): 302–308.

Breytenbach, Cilliers. "Civic Concord and Cosmic Harmony: Sources of Metaphoric Mapping in 1 Clement 20.3." Pages 182–196 in *Encounters with Hellenism: Studies on the First Letter of Clement*. Edited by Cilliers Breytenbach and Laurence L. Welborn. Leiden: Brill, 2003.

Breytenbach, Cilliers, and Laurence L. Welborn, eds. *Encounters with Hellenism: Studies on the First Letter of Clement*. Leiden: Brill, 2003.

Briggs, Sheila. "Gender, Slavery, and Technology: The Shaping of the Early Christian Moral Imagination." Pages 159–176 in *Beyond Slavery: Overcoming Its Religious and Sexual Legacies*. Edited by Bernadette J. Brooten and Jacqueline L. Hazelton. Black Religion/Womanist Thought/Social Justice. New York, NY: Palgrave Macmillan, 2010.

Broneer, O. *Corinth: Results of Excavations conducted by The American School of Classical Studies at Athens. Vol. X: The Odeum. (= Corinth X)*. Cambridge, MA: Harvard University, 1932.

Brunet, Stephen. "Women with Swords: Female Gladiators in the Roman World." Pages 478–491 in *A Companion to Sport and Spectacle in Greek and Roman Antiquity*. Edited by Paul Christensen and Donald G. Kyle. Malden, MA: Wiley Blackwell, 2014.

Bunsen, Christian Charles Josias. *Hippolytus and His Age; or, The Beginnings and Prospects of Christianity.* Vol. 1: Hippolytus and the Teachers of the Apostolical Age. 2nd edition. London: Longman, Brown, Green, and Longmans, 1854.

Castelli, Elizabeth A. *Visions and Voyeurism: Holy Women and the Politics of Sight in Early Christianity.* Edited by Christopher Ocker. Berkeley, CA: Center for Hermeneutical Studies, 1995.

Charles, Ronald. *The Silencing of Slaves in Early Jewish and Christian Texts.* London: Routledge, 2019.

Cobb, L. Stephanie. *Divine Deliverance: Pain and Painlessness in Early Christian Martyr Texts.* Berkeley, CA: University of California, 2016.

Coleman, Kathleen. "Fatal Charades: Roman Executions Staged as Mythological Enactments." *Journal of Roman Studies* 80 (1990): 44–73.

———. *M. Valerii Martialis Liber Spectaculorum.* Oxford: Oxford University, 2006.

Concannon, Cavan W. *Assembling Early Christianity: Trade, Networks, and the Letters of Dionysios of Corinth.* Cambridge: Cambridge University, 2017.

Dain, Alphonse. "Notes sur le texte grec de l'Épître de saint Clément de Rome." *Recherches de science religieuse* 39 (1951): 353–361.

Dio Chrysostom. *Discourses 37–60.* Translated by H. Lamar Crosby. Vol. 4. LCL 376. Cambridge, MA: Harvard University Press, 1946.

———. *Discourses 31–36.* Translated by J. W. Cohoon and H. Lamar Crosby. LCL 358. Cambridge, MA: Harvard University Press, 1995 [1940]).

Donaldson, James. "The New MS. of Clement of Rome." *The Theological Review* 14 (Jan. 1877): 35–49.

Eastman, David L. "Jealousy, Internal Strife, and the Deaths of Peter and Paul: A Reassessment of *1 Clement.*" *Zeitschrift für antikes Christentum* 18.1 (2013): 34–53.

Fowler, H. N. and R. Stillwell. *Corinth: Results of Excavations conducted by The American School of Classical Studies at Athens.* Vol. I: Introduction: Topography, Architecture (= Corinth I). Cambridge, MA: Harvard University, 1932.

Frankfurter, David. "Martyrology and the Prurient Gaze." *Journal of Early Christian Studies* 17.2 (2009): 215–245.

Friesen, Steven J., Sarah A. James and Daniel N. Schowalter, eds. *Corinth in Contrast: Studies in Inequality.* Leiden: Brill, 2014.

Friesen, Steven J., Daniel N. Schowalter, and James C. Walters, eds. *Corinth in Context: Comparative Studies on Religion and Society.* Leiden: Brill, 2010.

Frassinetti, Paulus, ed. *Q. Septimi Flornetis Tertulliani Apologeticum.* Paravia, Torino: Proprietà Letteraria, 1965.

Frilingos, Christopher A. *Spectacles of Empire: Monsters, Martyrs, and the Book of Revelation.* Philadelphia: University of Pennsylvania, 2004.

Futrell, Alison. *Blood in the Arena: The Spectacle of Roman Power.* Austin, TX: University of Texas, 1997.

Gregory, Andrew. "Disturbing Trajectories: *1 Clement*, the *Shepherd of Hermas*, and the Development of Early Roman Christianity." Pages 142–166 in *Rome in the Bible and the Early Church.* Edited by Peter Oakes. Carlislee: Paternoster, 2002.

Harley, James. "The Aesthetics of Death: The Theatrical Elaboration of Ancient Roman Blood Spectacles." *Theatre History Studies* 18 (1998): 88–97.
Haupt, M. "Analecta." *Hermes* 3.1 (1869): 140–155.
Horrell, David G. *The Social Ethos of the Corinthian Correspondence: Interests and Ideology from 1 Corinthians to 1 Clement.* Edinburgh: T&T Clark, 1996.
Iunius, Patricius. *Clementis ad Corinthos Epistola Prior.* Oxford, 1633.
Joyce, Lillian B. "Dirce Disrobed." *Classical Antiquity* 20.2 (2001): 221–238.
Julian. *The Works of the Emperor Julian.* Translated by Wilmer Cave Wright. Vol. 3. LCL. London: William Heinemann, 1923.
Kenyon, F. G. *The Codex Alexandrinus (Royal ms 1 D v-viii) in Reduced Photographic Facsimile. New Testament and Clementine Epistles.* London: British Museum, 1909.
König, Jason. "Favorinus' 'Corinthian Oration,' in Its Corinthian Context." *Proceedings of the Cambridge Philological Society* 47 (2001): 141–171.
Kotrosits, Maia. "Penetration and Its Discontents: Greco-Roman Sexuality, the *Acts of Paul and Thecla,* and Theorizing Eros without the Wound." *Journal of the History of Sexuality* 27.3 (2018): 343–366.
———. "Seeing is Feeling: Revelation's Enthroned Lamb and Ancient Visual Affects." *Biblical Interpretation* 22 (2014): 473–504.
Kozlowski, Jan M. "'Danaïdes et Dircés': Sur 1 Cl 6.2." *Ephemerides Theologicae Lovanienses* 82.4 (2006): 467–478.
Lagarde, Paul de. *Armenische Studien.* Osnabrück: Otto Zeller, 1970 [1877].
Laird, Margaret L. "The Emperor in a Roman Town: The Base of the *Augustales* in the Forum of Corinth." Pages 67–116 in *Corinth in Context: Comparative Studies on Religion and Society.* Edited by Steven J. Friesen, Daniel N. Schowalter, and James C. Walters. Leiden: Brill, 2010.
Lewis, Sian. "Women and Myth." Pages 443–458 in *A Companion to Greek Mythology.* Edited by Ken Dowden and Niall Livingstone. Malden, MA: Wiley Blackwell, 2011.
Lightfoot, Joseph Barber. *The Apostolic Fathers, Part I,1: S. Clement of Rome.* Hildesheim/New York: Georg Olms, 1973 (1890).
———. *The Apostolic Fathers, Part I,2: S. Clement of Rome.* Hildesheim/New York: Georg Olms, 1973 (1890).
Lona, Horacio E. *Der erste Clemensbrief.* Kommentar zu den Apostolischen Vätern 2. Göttingen: Vandenhoeck & Ruprecht, 1998.
Lucian, *Lucian, Vol. 1.* Translated by A. M. Harmon. LCL 14. London: William Heinemann, 1913.
Maier, Harry O. *The Social Setting of the Ministry as Reflected in the Writings of Hermas, Clement, and Ignatius.* Waterloo: Wilfrid Laurier University, 2002.
Mason, H. J. "Lucius at Corinth." *Phoenix* 25.2 (1971): 160–165.
Morin, G. *Sancti Clementis Romani ad Corinthos epistulae versio Latina antiquissima.* Anecdota Maredsolana 2. Maredsous, Belgium, 1894.
Musurillo, Herbert. *The Acts of the Christian Martyrs.* Oxford: Clarendon, 1972.
Petitfils, James. *Mos Christianorum: The Roman Discourse of Exemplarity and the Jewish and Christian Language of Leadership.* Tübingen: Mohr Siebeck, 2016.

Philostratus. *The Life of Apollonius of Tyana*. Translated by Christopher P. Jones. LCL 16. Cambridge, MA: Harvard University Press, 2005.

Plummer, A. "Contributions and Comments: 'Danaids and Dirces' in the Epistle of Clement to Corinth." *The Expository Times* 26.12 (1915): 560–562.

Rösch, Friedrich. *Bruchstücke des ersten Clemensbriefes, nach dem achmimischen Papyrus der Strassburger Universitäts-und Landesbibliothek*. Strasbourg: Schlesier and Schweikhardt, 1910.

Schmidt, Carl. *Der erste Clemensbrief in altkoptischer Übersetzung*. Texte und Untersuchungen 32.1. Leipzig: J. C. Hinrichs'sche Buchhandlung, 1908.

Schmitt, Tassilo. "Des Kaisers Inszenierung Mythologie und neronische Christenverfolgung." *Zeitschrift für Antikes Christentum* 16.3 (2012): 487–515.

Spawforth, Antony J. S. "Corinth, Argos, and the Imperial Cult: Pseudo-Julian, Letters 198." *Hesperia* 63.2 (1994): 211–232.

Stillwell, Richard. *Corinth: Results of Excavations Conducted by The American School of Classical Studies at Athens. Vol. II: The Theatre. (= Corinth II)*. Princeton, NJ: The American School, 1952.

Stratton, Kimberly B. "The Eschatological Arena: Reinscribing Roman Violence in Fantasies of the End Times." *Biblical Interpretation* 17 (2009): 45–76.

van Unnik, W. C. "Studies on the So-Called First Epistle of Clement: The Literary Genre." Pages 115–181 in *Encounters with Hellenism: Studies on the First Letter of Clement*. Edited by Cilliers Breytenbach and Laurence L. Welborn. Leiden: Brill, 2003.

Welborn, Laurence L. "Jealousy, Envy, Strife and Discord in First Clement." *Journal of Beliefs & Values* 38.2 (2017): 173–179.

———. *The Young Against the Old: Generational Conflict in First Clement*. Minneapolis, MN: Fortress, 2018.

Welch, Katherine E. "Negotiating Roman Spectacle Architecture in the Greek World: Athens and Corinth." Pages 125–145 in *The Art of Ancient Spectacle*. Edited by Bettina Bergmann and Christine Kondoleon. Washington, DC: National Gallery of Art; New Haven: Yale University, 1999.

———. *The Roman Amphitheatre: From its Origins to the Colosseum*. Cambridge: Cambridge University, 2007.

Wordsworth, Christopher. *Conjectural Emendations of Passages in Ancient Authors with other Papers*. London: Rivingtons, 1883.

———. *Theocritus: Codicum Manuscriptorum Ope*. Cambridge: Joannes G. Parker, 1844.

Vorster, Johannes N. "The Blood of the Female Martyrs as the Sperm of the Early Church." *Religion & Theology* 10.1 (2003): 66–99.

Zwierlein, Otto. "Danaïden und Dirken (1Clem 6,2)." Pages 151–158 in *Petrus und Paulus in Jerusalem und Rom: vom Neuen Testament zu den apokryphen Apostelakten*. Untersuchungen zur antiken Literatur und Geschichte 109. Berlin: De Gruyter, 2012.

Chapter 3

Euclia's Story

Coordinated Sexual Assault, Violence, and Willfulness in the Acts of Andrew

Christy Cobb

In the *Acts of Andrew*, an enslaved woman named Euclia is sexually exploited, harassed, raped, mutilated, and then left to die. The sexual violence enacted upon Euclia is planned, coordinated, and implemented by Maximilla, an elite Christian female enslaver who functions as the text's protagonist. Euclia's story is horrific. In this volume filled with numerous examples from early Christian literature of sexual violence, rape, and abuse, Euclia's narrative is quite possibly the worst, especially as one considers the way in which the text attempts to blame Euclia for her own abuse while uplifting Maximilla as the heroine of the narrative. After Euclia's gruesome death, which lingers in the reader's imagination, the text simply erases her from the narrative and she is not mentioned again.

In this essay, I read Euclia's story as an example of premeditated sexual assault, rape, and murder. I argue that Maximilla, as Euclia's enslaver, intentionally coordinated the sexual harassment that led to Euclia's murder. Then, using Sara Ahmed's theory of willful subjects, I offer a reading of Euclia's story as an example of Ahmed's willfulness.[1] While the narrative intentionally depicts Euclia in negative ways (rebellious, greedy, sensual, etc.), it is this aspect of Euclia's character that reveals her willfulness, her refusal to submit to authority. Euclia's will is a tension in the narrative that Maximilla must overcome in order to attain her own sexual purity. Yet, Euclia's willfulness is also subtle resistance to power. As Ahmed puts it, willfulness is an "inheritance" and is affective in its effect upon us.[2]

This rereading of the *Acts of Andrew* is not an attempt to erase the violence done to Euclia. Instead, this feminist theoretical reading condemns the violence done to Euclia while at the same time shifting the focus to her as the most oppressed and abject character, yet also the one who is the most willful. This reading of Euclia enhances Ahmed's theory of willfulness by providing a literary example of an enslaved female character who is defiant, willful, and punished severely for it. As Ahmed notes: "The punishment for willfulness is a passive willing of death, an allowing of death."[3] Euclia is indeed punished through death yet her willfulness remains persistent within the narrative, even after death.

One important factor fosters the victim-blaming, coordinated harassment, rape, violence, and murder of Euclia: Euclia is enslaved. This fact is primary; Euclia is an enslaved woman working in the house of free, elite Maximilla. The author of this early Christian narrative dehumanizes Euclia's character and provides rationalization for the unjustified treatment of her within the text. As the rhetoric of the narrative supposes, Maximilla's desires matter more than Euclia's because she is free, elite, and Christian. As an enslaved character, Euclia's desires are unimportant and irrelevant. Ronald Charles analyzes this dynamic and concludes: "Euclia is set up in contrast to Maximilla, to enrich Maximilla's function as a major character in the text. To put it simply, Maximilla needed Euclia to make herself look good."[4] As is clear, the narrative is written through the lens of a free elite enslaver and Euclia is continually portrayed negatively. This is not uncommon for texts from a culture entrenched in slavery such as the Greco-Roman world.[5] In these texts, enslaved characters are usually portrayed as stereotypically "good" or "bad," which illustrates the expectations of enslaved persons in antiquity. The *Acts of Andrew*, although an early Christian text, is no different. Euclia is portrayed negatively and thus the reader is led to believe that Euclia deserves her fate, no matter how gruesome or inhumane.

Euclia's story is found in part III of the fragmented *Acts of Andrew* which is usually titled the "Passion of Andrew" as it ends with a description of the apostle's death.[6] Maximilla is the female protagonist in this section of the *Acts of Andrew*. She is an elite woman who is married to the proconsul named Aegeates, who is a clear antagonist of the narrative as he is not a follower of Andrew's message. When Maximilla meets the apostle Andrew she becomes convinced of his message and converts to Christianity, to the dismay of her husband. Andrew's message is not only one about Christ, however; as many of the apostles in the Apocryphal Acts, Andrew preaches a message of abstinence and a rejection of sex, even for a newly married believer such as Maximilla. For example, Andrew prays over Maximilla: "Lord, may her soul remain forever pure, sanctified by your name—protect her especially, Master, from this disgusting pollution. As for him, our savage and perpetually boorish enemy: enable her to sleep apart from her visible husband and be wed to her inner husband" (16.3–4). Maximilla, who is portrayed as a strong follower of Andrew and of his message, then strategizes ways that she can escape sexual intercourse with her husband, Aegeates. Ultimately, she decides to use her enslaved attendant, Euclia, to accomplish this plan. She approaches Euclia and offers to be her "benefactor" if Euclia will do what she is told. The text indicates that Euclia "gave her word agreeing to it" (17.3). Then Maximilla dressed Euclia in her own clothes and sent her in to sleep with Aegeates in her place. Apparently, this subterfuge worked for eight months, at which time Euclia "demanded that her lady obtain her freedom for her" (18.1). Even though the text indicates that Maximilla "granted her what she asks," it seems that Euclia was still enslaved within the household as later Euclia asked for money and jewelry. At this point, the plot is unveiled and other enslaved workers in the house tell Aegeates the whole story. Aegeates then goes directly to Euclia and tortures her. In his fury, and with a desire to keep the whole matter a secret, Aegeates mutilates Euclia, cuts out her tongue, and then throws her body outside. Euclia's story ends with this morbid sentence: "There she stayed, without food for several days, before she herself became food for the dogs" (22.5).

I want to be clear that this text is not sympathetic toward Euclia. Rather, it rhetorically and purposefully portrays her in negative ways. Her body is on display and described in sexual terms. She appears greedy, wanting more than just freedom through her requests for money and jewelry from Maximilla. The narrative subtly suggests that Euclia is enjoying her time with Aegeates and that she desires attention from the other enslaved workers in the house. By contrast, the text attempts to show that Maximilla is virtuous and pure. She is described as going out of her way to appease Euclia, who is the stereotypical "bad slave," even though it is through Euclia's body that Maximilla is able to resist sex with her husband and therefore spend more time with the apostle Andrew. The text wants the reader to view Maximilla as the fair and generous enslaver and as a new convert who is completely devoted to her asceticism.[7]

In order to resist this rhetoric, I read the text through a feminist lens which enables me to uncover Euclia's story even as it is hidden within the narrative which is focused on Maximilla. I am also contemplating Euclia's "will" within this story. My reading is informed by the theory of willfulness outlined by Ahmed in *Willful Subjects*. Ahmed considers the idea of the will which is grounded in her rereading of the Grimm brother's story "The Willful Child," which she reads alongside several George Eliot novels, continental philosophy, as well as feminist and queer theory. The heroine of Eliot's *The Mill on the Floss*, Maggie Tulliver, sparked Ahmed's interest in the will. She writes: "We might share affection for Maggie as feminist readers, as we might share affection for the many willful girls that haunt literature."[8] Spurred by these questions about "female trouble-making fiction," Ahmed interrogates the idea of willfulness by asking what types of people are described as willful and when does this identification surface.[9] She writes: "No wonder that the figure of the willful subject—often but not always a child, often but not always female, often but not always an individual—has become so familiar."[10]

These familiar willful characters are problematic and troubling. They are faulty characters who resist the demands placed upon them by society and by the narrative. Ahmed contends that willfulness is more often placed on children and women: "I would argue that feminist history involves a history of becoming conscious of how troubling attributions such as willfulness fall, unevenly, on subjects."[11] Historically, this spirit of rebellion was often extinguished. Yet, when the willfulness is unable to be eliminated and the character's will succeeds, we might feel admiration at some level for the character's persistence. As Ahmed observes: "If the attribution of willfulness sticks, something becomes a willful thing, what prevents a will from being completed. There is agency in this becoming; *there is life*."[12] It is this willfulness, this agency, this *life*, that I want to bring into Euclia's story, indeed even into her death, as found in the *Acts of Andrew*.

Ahmed opens *Willful Subjects* with the story of the willful child by the Brothers Grimm. In this gruesome story, a young girl is described as "willful" as she disobeys her mother constantly, which displeases God.[13] Because of her strong will, God allows her to fall ill and ultimately the child dies. When her body is buried, the girl's arm refuses to stay under the earth and continually and repeatedly pokes out of the grave. Finally, the mother goes to the grave and hits the arm with a rod and only then does the girl's body remain buried. This story, with its violence and affirmation of corporal punishment, leads Ahmed to consider how many subjects are willful even as being willful is viewed as problematic.[14] The Grimm's story of the willful child is a thread that runs throughout Ahmed's book. The young girl's persistent arm becomes a symbol for Ahmed of the will, a feminist and queer illustration for the ways that certain groups of people are targeted and silenced, yet rise again and again.

Ahmed concludes *Willful Subjects* with a discussion of the connection between enslavement and the willfulness. She writes: "A history of willfulness would thus include a history of objects that are not empty enough to be filled by human will, objects that refuse to provide containers."[15] Ahmed then offers a rereading (as she notes "some would say a willful misreading") of Hegel's master/slave dialectic alongside Grimm's willful child fable. While many read Hegel's well-known dialectic as representative of the universal consciousness, Ahmed views it as a "master's fable."[16] In Hegel's dialectic, the master needs the slave in order to recognize the "other" and the slave needs the master for similar reasons.[17] Yet, Ahmed rereads Hegel and suggests that the master can receive validation from other masters; thus, the dialectic is only providing the view of the master, not the view of the slave. From there, Ahmed addresses the inconsistencies of even discussing the will of a slave. In the ideology of a slavery context, an enslaved person is viewed as property and thus does not have a will of her own, but instead is viewed as a container for the enslaver's will. Yet, a slave *is* a person. As Ahmed writes, "The slave is both person a property; *a property of will that has will.*"[18] When an enslaved person exercises their will, then they are being willful even if they are submitting to the will of their enslaver. Further, when an enslaved person resists the will of their enslaver, they become the arm of the willful child that repeatedly rises out of the ground in which their body is buried.

Ahmed revises Hegel's fable through the lens of colonial slavery as well as the Grimm fable of the willful child. Because an enslaved person was "both person and property" then an enslaved person has a will of their own and they must submit to the will of their enslaver. This is especially true when considering female enslaved persons. Here Ahmed turns to the work of Saidiya Hartman, bell hooks, and Hortense Spillers and brings in the historical context of Black enslaved persons in the American context. Enslaved Black women were used as sexual objects for the enjoyment of male enslavers and often as breeders; they were forced to produce (birth) more enslaved workers for the enslavers' will. Thus, as Ahmed writes, Black female slaves "became the arms, the hands, the genitals, and the womb: parts cut off from a body . . . "[19] When an enslaved person exercises their will, they are already resisting their own status as enslaved, as so-called property. This view rejects Hegel's view that the slave is working for the enslaver.[20] Thus, Ahmed revises Hegel's fable along with Grimm's in this way: "The slave recognizes that she has a will of her own, a will that belongs to herself and not to the master. She recognizes will through her laboring body. The master in treating the slaves as arms ceases to use his own arms. They become flaccid organs. This is the scandal of the colonial relation."[21]

Using Ahmed's theory of willfulness, I argue that Euclia is willful. In order to develop this reading, I focus on the brief passages from the *Passion of Andrew,* beginning at section 17 through section 22 where Euclia is raped, tortured, and killed. I place the blame upon Maximilla (as well as Aegeates) for the sexual abuse and rape of Euclia. Using a feminist lens, my reading highlights the willfulness of Euclia, who exercises her will in various ways throughout the story. The *Acts of Andrew* depicts Euclia as willfully submitting to the will of Maximilla when she agrees with her plan. For months, Euclia masquerades as Maximilla, burying her own will in favor of Maximilla's desires. Then, she exercises her will through asking Maximilla for her freedom (Hegel's dialectic is at work here, perhaps). Then, her will surfaces again as she requests money, jewelry, and gifts. In the end, like the child in the Grimm fable, Euclia's arm (body) is broken when Aegeates mutilates her and leaves her to die. Yet even after her death, Euclia's story remains. As Ahmed writes: "The arms can smash the Hegelian dialectic."[22] Reading with Ahmed, I view Euclia's willfulness as a "hopeful sentiment" which does not (and should not) eliminate the unethical and inhumane treatment that she receives.[23]

First, I argue that Maximilla intentionally coordinates the sexual violence done to Euclia.[24] Within the context of the narrative, Maximilla is a devoted follower of Andrew and spends as much time as possible with the apostle listening to his message. Maximilla is convinced that she must remain pure and chaste in order to be completely devoted to God. In this way, the text justifies Maximilla's actions and treatment of Euclia. My own reading resists this tendency and highlights the places in the text that illustrate Maximilla's culpability. For example, section 17 of the Passion of Andrew begins: "Maximilla then planned (*skeptomai*) the following (17.1)." My focus here is on the verb from *skeptomai*, which has a number of meanings including "to think beforehand, premeditate."[25] The typical translation is "planned," as used by MacDonald, but I suggest this secondary meaning, to premediate, is necessary here in order to show the way in which Maximilla planned and coordinated the continual rape of Euclia which led to her torture and death at the hands of Aegeates. As Kate Cooper notes, "Maximilla's liberation from the conjugal debt, however, is portrayed as the result not of divine intervention but of her very earthly cunning."[26]

In order to ensure Euclia's cooperation and silence, Maximilla offers herself as a benefactor to Euclia: "You will have me as a benefactor of all that you require, provided that you go along with my scheme and carry out what I tell you to do" (17.2). The word *euergetēs,* meaning "benefactor," is not always used in cases of manumission. In fact, benefactors in the Greco-Roman world could function in a variety of ways not directly involved with slavery.[27] Yet, the subsequent narrative in the *Acts of Andrew* makes it clear that Euclia and Maximilla understood this promise to lead to Euclia's manumission. This is exemplified in 18.1 when Euclia asks that Maximilla grant her freedom (*eleutheria*) and Maximilla agrees, at least according to the text (Euclia does not seem to actually be free as later in the narrative she remains in the house and is tortured by Aegeates).

This promise of Maximilla's was likely very tempting to Euclia. As Jennifer Glancy notes, "Slaves dreamed of a day when they would be free, the most precious of hopes."[28] Maximilla then preys upon Euclia's status as a *paidiskē* and offers manumission if Euclia goes along with Maximilla's plan. Yet, Euclia does not have a *real* choice here. As Ahmed astutely notes: "A feminist account of gender as a social relation might need to include analysis of how women willingly agree to situations in which their safety and well-being are compromised."[29] While the rhetoric of the *Acts of Andrew* makes it appear that Euclia agrees to Maximilla's plan, readers knowledgeable of slavery practices in the Greco-Roman world would recognize the impossible situation that Euclia is in. Euclia appears to "willingly agree," to use Ahmed's language. Yet, what would happen to Euclia if she were to refuse?[30] Likely, this would lead to corporal punishment or even death. Ahmed suggests: "we also need to hear the cases in which yes involves force but is not experienced as force, when for instance a woman says yes to something as the consequences of saying no would be too much (loss of access to children, to resources or benefits, to residence, etc.)."[31] This applies to Euclia as she does agree to help Maximilla, in that she is not forced necessarily, yet the consequences of her saying no could entail not only corporal punishment but other forms of extreme violence which were commonly imposed upon enslaved persons. Maximilla recognized this and capitalized on it when offering to be Euclia's benefactor if she carries out the plan. Even though Maximilla asks Euclia for her help with this plan, there is an assumption within the text that Euclia must agree. Euclia's will must align with Maximilla's will. Ahmed describes this facet of enslavement when she writes, "bodies become objects, become arms, what is assumed to carry and to carry out the master's will, becoming *where* the will of the master *resides*."[32]

Second, the text rhetorically blames Euclia which results in victim-blaming within the text. The text describes Euclia as "a shapely, notoriously wanton servant-girl" (17.1b, MacDonald's translation). I want to focus on this description of Euclia which is in the Greek: "*paidisken panu eumorphon kai phusin atakton.*" The words used here are full of connotations and insinuations. The first word, *paidiskē*, indicates that Euclia is enslaved. *Paidiskē* is also used to mean a young female child, but in many contexts, it indicates an enslaved female worker who often worked in domestic contexts.[33] The phrase "*panu eumorphon*" indicates that she was very attractive especially in terms of her body shape. MacDonald translates this "shapely," which I think is accurate here. The phrase "*phusei*" means by nature and "*atakton*" has a number of meanings such as "disorderly" but another option denotes "sensually of excess." My translation of this phrase is: "a very shapely and especially sensual by nature enslaved woman named Euclia."[34] This sentence describing Euclia is, in essence, blaming Euclia for her own rape for her body image and sexuality, a practice which is not unfamiliar to our modern contexts as well.

Euclia's body is described in such a way that the reader is led to believe she is sexually available; yet also Euclia is identified as a *paidiskē*, an enslaved female worker and a word that was often connected to a female child, or a young enslaved girl. As I noted, the use of *paidiskē* does not necessarily indicate that the enslaved person must have been young (the implicit use of this word could have also been used for enslaved persons to dehumanize and infantilize them, even if they are not technically young). Yet, the word choice is significant when applying Ahmed's theory to it. As Ahmed notes, persons described as willful were often children and often female. Here, Euclia is described as both, which furthers my reading of Euclia as a willful subject.

Even while describing Euclia's body in sensual terms, the text suggests that Euclia looks like Maximilla, or rather, Euclia is able to be disguised to look like Maximilla so to trick Aegeates into believing that Euclia is his wife. This is described in 17.4: "Just as a woman customarily dresses herself up to look like her rival, so Maximilla groomed Euclia in her own finery and dispatched her to sleep with Aegeates in her stead." While it might have been Euclia's beauty and sensuality that is to blame for Euclia being chosen for this role, yet also Maximilla must be imagined in similar ways. On the other hand, as Charles observes, the focus of the text is not Maximilla's beauty, but her chastity, or the "beauty of her soul" that is the most important.[35] Ultimately, though, this deception is done in order to secure Maximilla's purity, and Euclia's body is (ab)used in order to procure this purity. As Glancy concludes: "Maximilla, a slaveholder drawn to the ascetic renunciation of sexual relations with her husband, thinks nothing of relying on her slave Euclia as an erotic body double: her humiliation purchases Maximilla's sexual purity. Maximilla relies on an enslaved body to secure the freedom of her own body."[36]

By forcing Euclia to have sex with Aegeates, Maximilla coordinates Euclia's rape. As an enslaved woman, Euclia had no ability to consent to these sexual acts, and as mentioned above, even though Maximilla asked her to go along with this plan, Euclia was not in a position to decline the request of her enslaver. As the work of Rhiannon Graybill has shown, discussing rape and consent in the ancient and biblical world is complicated. Graybill employs the term "fuzzy" to refer to the "ambivalence that surrounds many situations of sexual violence."[37] When considering the experiences of an enslaved person in antiquity, sexual violence and rape is extremely "fuzzy." An enslaved person in antiquity was viewed as property and as such would be unable to provide consent.[38] Likewise, enslavers used their enslaved workers sexually, both male and female.[39] In antiquity, this was not viewed as "rape" and, as we will see in the early Christian narrative of the *Acts of Andrew*, it was not even viewed as immoral.

There are two wills at play in this part of the narrative: Maximilla's and Euclia's. Maximilla wills to not have sex with her husband. As an enslaved woman, Euclia's will is irrelevant to Maximilla. Her will must be the will of her enslaver. In this way, Maximilla's willfulness is applauded by the text. She is following the words of Andrew reflected in his will and the will of Christ, as she views it. In this way, Andrew's will and God's will are aligned, both of which Maximilla embraces as her own will. Dressing Euclia to pretend to be herself, Maximilla's deception is not nefarious. Above all, Maximilla's will to remain pure must triumph.[40] Because she is Maximilla's enslaved attendant, Euclia's will is not considered beyond its submission to the will of her enslaver. As Ahmed writes, "A willful submission is one in which the slaves are willing to extend to the will of the master."[41]

Euclia dressed as Maximilla and slept with Aegeates for eight months, according to the text (18.1), after which time Euclia asked Maximilla for her freedom. There is much to unpack in this brief note within the text. The inclusion of eight months suggests to me and to several other scholars that Euclia might have become pregnant and Maximilla's plan would soon be exposed if she continued this masquerade.[42] When rereading this narrative through the lens of Euclia and her persistent willfulness, a different story comes to light. For instance, if one reads and considers that Euclia is indeed pregnant and believes she will be manumitted, then her requests for "a large sum of money" (18.2) as well as some of Maximilla's jewelry could be used in order to support her life outside Maximilla's house as well as her future child. In this way Euclia's will is at first submissive to Maximilla; as Ahmed reminds us: "The slaves exercise the will they are not supposed to have in submitting to the will of the master: a willing submission is thus a willful submission."[43] But then when there is more at stake, Euclia's will resists for her own life and (perhaps) the life growing within her.

Moreover, Ahmed theorizes about the reproductive will and notes that the willful person might refuse or not be willing to reproduce. Here, of course Euclia has no choice as an enslaved character. Yet, if one reads this as Euclia having been impregnated by Aegeates then Euclia does have some leverage with which to assert her will. As Ahmed writes, "If women exist as wombs, as child makers, then they inherit the reproductive will, as that which if thwarted or blocked, causes illness and damage."[44] It is in this scenario that Maximilla's plan begins to unravel. If the reader is supposed to assume that Euclia is pregnant, then the fear is that Maximilla's scheme will be discovered. In this moment, Euclia's will surfaces again as she has a small amount of leverage in this situation. The two wills are still at war, yet Euclia's will appears clearer in juxtaposition to Maximilla's.

The narrative, however, portrays Euclia as greedy and boastful. The text indicates that "Euclia regularly took clothing, fine linen, and headbands from Maximilla" (18.3). In addition to this, the narrative describes Euclia bragging to other enslaved workers in the house (18.3) and then mocking them when they did not respond to her (18.5). Similarly, the text portrays Maximilla as completely ethical, fair, and loyal to Euclia. She is in every way the virtuous enslaver. In fact, the narrative notes: "Maximilla no doubt supposed that Euclia was true to her word and to be trusted because of the gifts given her . . ." (19.1). Yet this contrast can also be overturned. If Euclia was supposed to regularly dress up and pass as Maximilla to her own husband, she would certainly be wearing Maximilla's clothing and headbands. Additionally, it is well documented that in antiquity free persons did not assume that an enslaved person would be "true to their word," as the text says here. In fact, the opposite was often assumed about enslaved persons: their words were not assumed to be truthful unless under torture.[45] The ancient reader of this story would likely recognize that and understand here that the rhetoric of the narrative assumed Euclia could not be trusted.[46]

Ultimately, Maximilla's plan fully collapses because the enslaved workers in her house discover Maximilla's scandalous betrayal of her husband Aegeates, who is also their enslaver. Some of these enslaved workers wanted to immediately tell Aegeates but others had "ambivalent" feelings toward Maximilla (20.5) and "feigned fondness for her and silenced the others" (20.5). Maximilla uses bribery once again and pays a large sum (1,000 denarii) to each of the enslaved workers who had "hypocritically simulated affection for her" and then "commanded them to stay silent about the ruse (21.3). Even still, as Andrew predicted, the enslaved workers took the money they received, went to Aegeates, and told him about Maximilla's plan to refuse sex and about her use of Euclia. Yet, Aegeates placed the blame squarely on Euclia and not Maximilla, for as the narrative notes, he was "still affectionate for his spouse." After torturing Euclia, she confessed to the promises and rewards that Maximilla gave to her for dressing up as his wife and having sex with Aegeates (22.2). Even after the torture, Aegeates wanted to be certain that no one else found out about the scandal, so he commits further violence to Euclia. Even though Maximilla was the mastermind behind this deceitful plan, Aegeates is the instigator of the extreme violence enacted upon Euclia.

The violence done to Euclia in this one sentence is horrendous. First, he cut out her tongue (*glōssotomaō*). Then he mutilates (*akrōtēriazō*) Euclia. The Greek word used here refers to the amputation of hands and/or feet, but can also refer to the mutilation of genitals.[47] After this extreme violence, Aegeates orders her to be thrown outside (22.4). Euclia remained outside yet alive, it seems, for many days until dogs ate her body. The biblical connection to Jezebel's body, who was also eaten by dogs (2 Kings 9:30–37), seems obvious.[48] The author here wants to imply that Euclia, like Jezebel, deserved her fate, and also likely to capitalize on the sexualized views of Jezebel. As Charles argues, Euclia is silenced once and for all.[49]

The ending to Euclia's story is even worse than the beginning. Euclia was promised her freedom by Maximilla. Then, Euclia is forced to have sex with her enslaver, Aegeates. This continual rape and sexual violence continued for eight months. Then, even after receiving her freedom (or the promise of freedom), Euclia does not escape her enslavement. She is tortured. Her body is mutilated. In the end, Euclia dies a horrific and inhumane death. The violence done to Euclia is undeniable. Yet the *Acts of Andrew* quickly moves the plot back to Maximilla and her devotion to Andrew and her newfound love for Christ. Euclia is not mentioned again.

Euclia's will disrupts the narrative which is so clearly aligned with Maximilla's plight and focus on sexual purity. In this way, Euclia's will interrupts the aims of the narrative especially when she requests her own freedom as well as more money and gifts. Maximilla is also willful in her own refusal to sleep with her own husband, Aegeates. Yet, Maximilla's willfulness is affirmed by the narrative. Maximilla's willfulness is not Ahmed's willfulness because she aligns with the focus of the author and the narrative itself is on her side. She is not the child with her arm coming out of the grave; Maximilla is the mother returning to hit the arm of the child (in this case, Euclia).

Aegeates's own will is similarly rejected in this text. He wills to sleep regularly with his own wife, Maximilla (as the canonical Paul might argue he should be able to do; see 1 Cor 7); yet, the will of Aegeates is subverted by his wife. Aegeates believes that his will is honored. It is not. Instead, he is sleeping with Euclia dressed as Maximilla. Maximilla's will succeeds here. When Aegeates discovers the ruse, his resolute will is to destroy Euclia. In this part of the narrative, then, Aegeates's will succeeds through his torturing, mutilation, and murder of Euclia. As such, he is transformed into the mother from the Grimm fable who makes the final blow to force her daughter's arm back into the grave.

What are we to do with a text such as this one, which affirms sexual violence and murder for the sake of one elite woman's purity? In addition to reading for entertainment, early Christian readers might have read texts such as the *Acts of Andrew* for edification, that is, to impart knowledge, ethics, or information on how to live as a Christian.[50] When considering this possible pedagogical purpose, in a slave society, readers could also learn from this text how enslaved persons should be treated and how they should act. When one considers this from the perspective of an enslaver, perhaps the story functioned this way. We know, for example, numerous enslavers who identified as Christian yet mistreated their enslaved workers.[51] When reading from the perspective of the enslaved, Euclia's story could be a part of what Ahmed calls "stone pedagogy." As she writes: "Stones might be willing, or not. At one level, stones appear as willful, insofar as willfulness is often related to being obstinate and unyielding. . . . Perhaps stones are willing inasmuch as what they do not let us do; in how they resist our intentions. They can be checking powers, reminders that the world is not waiting to receive our shape."[52] Here Ahmed connects her theory to religion and the ways in which people are often assigned places in society based on a divine plan, or rather, God's will. Yet Ahmed's theory resists, as does Euclia's story. The traditional view is that "we as humans must be satisfied with the place we have been given within the divine order."[53] Ahmed offers that willfulness and dissatisfaction can be a gift, and perhaps even a lesson. Like Euclia, we can "inhabit the room of willfulness."[54] When we embrace the inheritance of willfulness, then we join in kinship with others who are willful. Ahmed calls this a "stony kinship, a kinship of strangers."[55] To push this further, we could consider the possibility that enslaved persons who encountered Euclia's story could be challenged and even inspired by Euclia's willfulness.

Yet, Euclia's story ends in her death. Euclia's will is pushed back into the grave like the arm of the young girl in the Grimm fable. We cannot find value in her death as narrated in the *Acts of Andrew*. To illustrate this, I turn to the poignant work of Saidiya Hartman who writes of the horrors of the Atlantic slave trade alongside her own journey traveling a similar route in search of her past. After describing the numerous tortures inflicted upon the memory of St. George, the martyr, Hartman notes that when saints are tortured, faith and the promise of eternal life can be a comfort. Yet, death for an enslaved person does not provide that comfort. Hartman writes: "But no solace can be found in the death of a slave, no higher ground can be located, no perspective can be found from which death serves a greater good or becomes anything other than what it is."[56] I think this quote applies well to Euclia's story in the *Acts of Andrew*. Her death is not redeemable, nor are Maximilla's actions. The rereading of Euclia's story offered here as an example of Ahmed's willfulness cannot and should not validate the sexual violence and torture done to Euclia. However, my reading of Euclia as willful can perhaps provide another ending to her story, just as Ahmed provides a retelling of Hegel's dialectic as well as the Grimm fable.

Euclia is willful. She submits to the will of her enslaver, Maximilla, out of necessity, yet this in and of itself is an act of will, as her identity as *paidiskē* suggests that she does not have a will of her own. Later, after the eight months of aligning her will with Maximilla's will, Euclia requests the freedom she was promised. Ahmed describes Euclia's search for freedom: "Even if the slave in laboring is on the way to freedom (more so than the master) that freedom is described as limited. And (we are ready for this, we expected this) *willfulness then becomes the slave's assignment.* . . . "[57] Euclia's willfulness persists (her arm surfaces) as she tells the other enslaved workers in the house about what she has been doing for Maximilla. She is told to be silent, yet she is not. Euclia's will does not diminish in this narrative but instead grows stronger with each passing month. Yet, Euclia does not tell Aegeates about Maximilla's plan until she is forced to speak under torture. This, too, is an act of will. Euclia's willfulness is present through the story, just as the child in the Grimm story, until Aegeates, just as the Grimm child's parent, has to cut off her limbs in order to impede her will from surfacing. In the end, Euclia is an arm, a leg, a tongue, a body. She is the willful child in the Grimm story, rising out of her own grave again and again. Euclia's will persists through the narrative, refusing to let the reader forget her gruesome story. I conclude with Ahmed's words: "we can and do wander away from the subject of will, and by wandering away, *we take her with us*."[58]

NOTES

I am grateful to my friends and colleagues Bailey Freeburn, Jennifer Glancy, Maia Kotrosits, and Katherine Shaner for their thoughtful comments and dialogue about this essay.

1. Sara Ahmed, *Willful Subjects* (Durham and London: Duke University Press, 2014).
2. Ahmed, *Willful Subjects*, 18.
3. Ahmed, *Willful Subjects*, 1.
4. Ronald Charles, *The Silencing of Slaves in Early Jewish and Christian Texts*, Routledge Studies in the Early Christian World (London & New York: Routledge, 2020), 200.
5. Resources on slavery in antiquity and early Christianity: Keith Bradley, *Slavery and Society at Rome* (Cambridge; New York, NY: Cambridge University Press, 1994); Jennifer A. Glancy, *Slavery in Early Christianity* (New York: Oxford University Press, 2002); Page DuBois, *Slavery: Antiquity and Its Legacy* (Ancients and Moderns; London: I. B. Tauris, 2010); Sandra R. Joshel, *Slavery in the Roman World* (Cambridge Introduction to Roman Civilization; New York, NY: Cambridge University Press, 2010).
6. The *Acts of Andrew* now survives in three parts which includes the *Acts of Andrew and Matthias in the city of the Cannibals* (Part I), *Gregory's Latin Epitome* (Part II), and the *Passion of Andrew*, which is where Euclia's story is found. Dennis Ronald MacDonald, *The Acts of Andrew* (Santa Rosa, CA: Polebridge Press, 2005), 12–13. English translations in this essay will be from MacDonald's translation, unless otherwise noted. When the Greek text is referenced it is from: Jean-Marc Prieur, trans., *Acta Andreae* (Corpus Christianorum Series Apocryphorum 5–6; Turnhout: Brepols, 1989).
7. For more on Maximilla, see: Kate Cooper, *The Virgin and the Bride: Idealized Womanhood in Late Antiquity* (Cambridge: Harvard University Press, 1996); Caroline T. Schroeder, "Embracing the Erotic in the Passion of Andrew. The Apocryphal Acts of Andrew, the Greek Novel, and Platonic Philosophy," in *The Apocryphal Acts of Andrew*, ed. Jan N. Bremmer (Leuven: Uitgeveriji Peters, 2000), 110–26; Saundra Schwartz, "From Bedroom to Courtroom: The Adultery Type-Scene and the Acts of Andrew," in *Mapping Gender in Ancient Religious Discourses*, ed. Todd C. Penner and Caroline Vander Stichele (Leiden: Brill, 2007), 267–311.
8. Ahmed, *Willful Subjects*, 3.

9. The ideas Ahmed outlines in *Willful Subjects* are based upon her previous work. See Sara Ahmed, *The Promise of Happiness* (Durham: Duke University Press, 2010).
10. Ahmed, *Willful Subjects*, 17.
11. Ahmed, *Willful Subjects*, 90.
12. Ahmed, *Willful Subjects*, 47.
13. As Ahmed notes, in the original story written in German, the child is not gendered. In various subsequent translations of this story, the child is a girl and sometimes a boy. Ahmed intentionally genders the child female because she "argue[s that] willfulness *tends* to be registered as a feminine attribute." Ahmed, *Willful Subjects*, 205 fn1.
14. The problem of the will connects directly to Ahmed's previous work on happiness, as willfulness and unhappiness both are viewed as an error or a fault. Ahmed, *Willful Subjects*, 4.
15. Ahmed, *Willful Subjects*, 200.
16. Ahmed, *Willful Subjects*, 201.
17. Ahmed's analysis of Hegel focuses on the section titled "Independence and Dependence of Self-Consciousness: Lordship and Bondage" in Georg Wilhelm Friedrich Hegel, *Phenomenology of Spirit*, trans. Arnold V. Miller (Oxford: Oxford University Press, 1977), 111–19.
18. Ahmed, *Willful Subjects*, 201 (author's emphasis).
19. Ahmed, *Willful Subjects*, 201.
20. Hegel famously uses the terms bondsman/lord here, but Ahmed uses "slave and master" instead in order to note the "political histories" of these words (*Willful Subjects*, 252, fn 30).
21. Ahmed, *Willful Subjects*, 202.
22. Ahmed, *Willful Subjects*, 203.
23. Ahmed, *Willful Subjects*, 173.
24. Because Maximilla is the protagonist of the narrative, my reading of her resists the rhetoric of the narrative.
25. LSJ, s.v. "skeptomai."
26. Cooper, *The Virgin and the Bride*, 48.
27. For a thoughtful analysis of patron/client relationships in the Greco-Roman world as they relate to slavery, see: Glancy, *Slavery in Early Christianity*, 124–26.
28. Glancy, *Slavery in Early Christianity*, 93.
29. Ahmed, *Willful Subjects*, 55.
30. As Charles notes, "The text does not say anything about what might happen to Euclia if she refuses the powerful woman" (*The Silencing of Slaves in Early Jewish and Christian Texts*, 197).
31. Ahmed, *Willful Subjects*, 55.
32. Ahmed, 200.
33. Mark Golden, "Pais, 'Child' and 'Slave,'" *L'Antiquite Classique* 54 (1985): 91–104; Christy Cobb, *Slavery, Gender, Truth, and Power in Luke-Acts and Other Ancient Narratives* (London: Palgrave Macmillan, 2019), 1–2.
34. Here I am intentionally translating *paidiskē* as "enslaved woman" instead of "girl," as the Greek implies, in order to describe more accurately Euclia's identity and

place within the household. I view *paidiskē* as used within this narrative as a tool to dehumanize and infantilize Euclia, not as a reference to her age.

35. Charles, *The Silencing of Slaves in Early Jewish and Christian Texts*, 197.
36. Glancy, *Slavery in Early Christianity*, 156.
37. Rhiannon Graybill, "Fuzzy, Messy, Icky: The Edges of Consent in Hebrew Bible Rape Narratives and Rape Culture," *The Bible and Critical Theory* 15, no. 2 (2019): 2.
38. For more on the complexity of consent, see: Rhiannon Graybill, "Critiquing the Discourse of Consent," *Journal of Feminist Studies in Religion* 33 (2017): 175.
39. Glancy, *Slavery in Early Christianity*, 23.
40. For other instances where sexual purity is used as a justification for violence, see Jeannie Sellick's chapter in this volume.
41. Ahmed, *Willful Subjects*, 201.
42. Christy Cobb, "Hidden Truth in the Body of Euclia: Page DuBois' Torture and Truth and Acts of Andrew," *Biblical Interpretation* 25, no. 1 (2017): 28–29; Schwartz, "From Bedroom to Courtroom," 305; Anna Rebecca Solevåg, *Birthing Salvation: Gender and Class in Early Christian Childbearing Discourse* (Leiden; Boston: Brill Academic Publications, 2013), 191.
43. Ahmed, *Willful Subjects*, 201.
44. Ahmed, *Willful Subjects*, 118–19.
45. Page duBois, *Torture and Truth* (New York; London: Routledge, 1991), 35.
46. Cobb, *Slavery, Gender, Truth, and Power in Luke-Acts and Other Ancient Narratives*, 161.
47. LSG, s.v. "akroteriazo."
48. Solevåg, *Birthing Salvation*, 194; Cobb, "Hidden Truth in the Body of Euclia," 35.
49. Charles, *The Silencing of Slaves in Early Jewish and Christian Texts*, 201.
50. For an overview of this argument about the purpose and genre of the Apocryphal Acts, see David Edward Aune, *The New Testament in Its Literary Environment* (Philadelphia: Westminster Press, 1987), 149–52.
51. Glancy, *Slavery in Early Christianity*, 13.
52. Ahmed, *Willful Subjects*, 189.
53. Ahmed, *Willful Subjects*, 191.
54. Ahmed, *Willful Subjects*, 192.
55. Ahmed, *Willful Subjects*, 192.
56. Saidiya Hartman, *Lose Your Mother: A Journey Along the Atlantic Slave Route* (New York: Farrar, Straus, and Giroux, 2007), 67.
57. Ahmed, *Willful Subjects*, 202.
58. Ahmed, *Willful Subjects*, 173 (author's emphasis).

WORKS CITED

Ahmed, Sara. *The Promise of Happiness*. Durham: Duke University Press, 2010.
———. *Willful Subjects*. Durham and London: Duke University Press, 2014.

Aune, David Edward. *The New Testament in Its Literary Environment*. Philadelphia: Westminster Press, 1987.

Bradley, Keith. *Slavery and Society at Rome*. Cambridge; New York, NY: Cambridge University Press, 1994.

Charles, Ronald. *The Silencing of Slaves in Early Jewish and Christian Texts*. Routledge Studies in the Early Christian World. London & New York: Routledge, 2020.

Cobb, Christy. "Hidden Truth in the Body of Euclia: Page DuBois' *Torture and Truth* and *Acts of Andrew*." *Biblical Interpretation* 25, no. 1 (2017): 19–38.

———. *Slavery, Gender, Truth, and Power in Luke-Acts and Other Ancient Narratives*. London: Palgrave Macmillan, 2019.

Cooper, Kate. *The Virgin and the Bride: Idealized Womanhood in Late Antiquity*. Cambridge: Harvard University Press, 1996.

DuBois, Page. *Slavery: Antiquity and Its Legacy*. Ancients and Moderns; London: I. B. Tauris, 2010.

———. *Torture and Truth*. New York; London: Routledge, 1991.

Glancy, Jennifer A. *Slavery in Early Christianity*. New York: Oxford University Press, 2002.

Golden, Mark. "Pais, 'Child' and 'Slave.'" *L'Antiquite Classique* 54 (1985): 91–104.

Graybill, Rhiannon. "Critiquing the Discourse of Consent." *Journal of Feminist Studies in Religion* 33 (2017): 175.

———. "Fuzzy, Messy, Icky: The Edges of Consent in Hebrew Bible Rape Narratives and Rape Culture." *The Bible and Critical Theory* 15, no. 2 (2019): 1–28.

Hartman, Saidiya. *Lose Your Mother: A Journey Along the Atlantic Slave Route*. New York: Farrar, Straus, and Giroux, 2007.

Hegel, Georg Wilhelm Friedrich. *Phenomenology of Spirit*. Translated by Arnold V. Miller. Oxford: Oxford University Press, 1977.

Joshel, Sandra R. *Slavery in the Roman World*. Cambridge Introduction to Roman Civilization. New York, NY: Cambridge University Press, 2010.

MacDonald, Dennis Ronald. *The Acts of Andrew*. Santa Rosa, CA: Polebridge Press, 2005.

Prieur, Jean-Marc, trans. *Acta Andreae*. Corpus Christianorum. Series Apocryphorum 5–6. Turnhout: Brepols, 1989.

Schroeder, Caroline T. "Embracing the Erotic in the Passion of Andrew. The Apocryphal Acts of Andrew, the Greek Novel, and Platonic Philosophy." In *The Apocryphal Acts of Andrew*, edited by Jan N. Bremmer, 110–26. Leuven: Uitgeveriji Peters, 2000.

Schwartz, Saundra. "From Bedroom to Courtroom: The Adultery Type-Scene and the Acts of Andrew." In *Mapping Gender in Ancient Religious Discourses*, edited by Todd C. Penner and Caroline Vander Stichele, 267–311. Leiden: Brill, 2007.

Solevåg, Anna Rebecca. *Birthing Salvation: Gender and Class in Early Christian Childbearing Discourse*. Leiden; Boston: Brill Academic Publications, 2013.

Chapter 4

"Guardians of Chastity and Companions in Suffering"

The Didactic and Rhetorical Function of Rape Threats in Ambrose of Milan

Jennifer Collins-Elliott

Ambrose, a fourth-century Bishop of Milan, frames his longest treatise on virginity with apologies for his lack of expertise with and knowledge of virginity, and by bolstering his admitted inexperience with a preemptive self-defense and a divine mandate: "And indeed distrusting my ability, but being encouraged by examples of divine mercy, I dare to devise a speech, for, God willing it, even an ass spoke" (*Virg.* 1.1.2). In this treatise, Ambrose is caught between a desire to both learn from and teach virgins, and a realization that he does not actually have sufficient experience for this task (*Virg.* 2.1.2). Misgivings aside, he engages in this didactic project using examples that are mediated through his own retelling.

In each of the examples considered here, both from *De virginibus* and his correspondence with Bishop Syagrius of Verona, virgins are confronted with the threat of sexual violence, which Ambrose highlights as a defining moment in their constitution as virgins. Rape threats serve as a key element in Ambrose's didactic and rhetorical strategy, and I argue that he uses the threat of sexual violence to teach his audience about expectations for virgins, crafting the "specifically (and socially recognizable) feminine body" through sensationalized, sexualized, and voyeuristic stories of virgin martyrs.[1] It is also notable that when Ambrose encounters a threat of sexual violence within his own community, such violence becomes an affront, unimaginable, and offensive. Rape threats can then be both tantalizing in the imaginary and inexcusable in reality.

This chapter highlights four of the virgins featured by Ambrose in *De virginibus* who are threatened with but avoid sexual violence, either through death or divine deliverance. Ambrose introduces each of these examples—Agnes, Thecla, the unnamed Antiochene virgin, and Pelagia—to teach virgins, and Christians more broadly, what proper virginity looks like. I then consider an epistolary exchange with Bishop Syagrius of Verona, in which Ambrose's tone changes dramatically when faced with the potential real-life threat to the chastity of a virgin named Indicia. Through *De virginibus,* Ambrose publicly celebrates the triumphs of Christian virgins over their Roman persecutors who threaten sexual violence. Privately, however, Ambrose fights an intra-Christian battle over the appropriateness of physical virginity tests as he tries to defend the modesty of a virgin who has been accused of sexual impropriety.

AMBROSE AND *DE VIRGINIBUS*

Ambrose's *De virginibus* was composed in 377 CE, just three years after he became bishop. Little is known about Ambrose's life prior to his consecration.[2] He was born around 339 CE in Trier,[3] and, according to *De virginibus*, had a sister (Marcellina) who was a consecrated virgin, and a relative (Soteris) who was allegedly martyred during the Diocletianic persecution.[4] Ambrose also had a brother (Satyrus), and his father died when he was young. His family relocated to Rome, where Marcellina dedicated herself to virginity (*Virg.* 3.1.1), and where Ambrose completed his education in liberal arts (Paulinus, *Vita* 2.5). He then left the city to work for the praetorian prefect Probus, under whom he achieved the rank of *consularis* and was made the governor of the provinces of Liguria and Aemilia, which is what brought Ambrose to Milan (Paulinus, *Vita* 2.5). He was famously selected as bishop by a child who called out Ambrose's name in the wake of the death of the Arian bishop Auxentius. He was then baptized and eight days later consecrated as the bishop of Milan (Paulinus, *Vita* 3.9).

Almost three years later Ambrose published *De virginibus*. The text is a composite, based primarily on two sermons, one given by Ambrose on the feast day of Saint Agnes and the other given by Pope Liberius for Ambrose's sister Marcellina (*Virg.* 1.2.5, 3.1.1).[5] Although he begins *De virginibus* with skepticism about his own ability to write on the subject, he was familiar with the virginal life. He even attributes some inspiration to Marcellina, as it was allegedly at her suggestion that he address virgin self-killing in the third book of *De virginibus*.⁶ Beyond his familial connections to the subject matter, Ambrose demonstrates his knowledge with a multitude of biblical references. Neil McLynn describes Ambrose as creating "a public voice of his own, learned and weighty" through *De virginibus*.⁷ McLynn also attributes Ambrose's defensiveness and reticence to his need to establish himself as an authority with acceptable theological credentials among the Milanese.⁸ And while he may have been struggling to reach his Milanese audience, Ambrose boasts of women coming from Piacenza, Bologna, and even Mauretania to take the veil from him (*Virg.* 1.10.57).

In his treatise, Ambrose writes and speaks for the benefit of virgins, but he also indicates that he desires to reach a broader audience with their example: "These are not precepts for virgins but examples by virgins. Our speech has painted a portrait of your virtue, and you all perceive an image of your dignity reflected as if in the mirror of this talk ... And since there are as many people as there are opinions, if there is anything refined in our talk, let everyone read it" (*Virg.* 2.6.39). As Peter Brown has argued, Ambrose composed *De virginibus* and his several other treatises on virginity⁹ not only for those already dedicated to a life of virginal asceticism like his sister Marcellina, but also for powerful, elite Romans:

> [The treatises on virginity] were written so as to change upper-class opinion—to persuade emperors, prefects, and provincial governors to allow wealthy widows and virgins to remain dedicated to the Church and to tolerate the redirection of parts of the wealth of great families, through such women, to pious causes.¹⁰

Thus, his work was meant to be consumed by a broader Christian audience. Ambrose's senatorial background, his knowledge of Greek and Greek philosophy, and his vision for the Catholic Church as an uncompromised body standing in opposition to its enemies helped him bring sheltered, ascetic sensibilities into a Roman, public domain, particularly through the bodies and lives of Christian women. In this context, I first want to call attention to the role played by one of the narrative devices used by Ambrose to shape expectations for Christian women, namely, the threat of sexual violence via the stories of virgins and virgin-martyrs such as Agnes, Thecla, the unnamed Antiochene virgin, and Pelagia in *De virginibus*.

AGNES

The first virgin-martyr discussed in *De virginibus* is Agnes, who Ambrose says is twelve years old at the time of her death. Notwithstanding her youth, Ambrose highlights her mature demeanor at the prospect of her impending martyrdom. For example, he describes Agnes as going more joyfully to the place of her punishment than any bride going to her wedding (*Virg.* 1.2.8). The executioner initially attempts to scare Agnes and flatter her while others express their desire to marry her, but she rejects them by publicly declaring her fidelity to Christ. She goads on the executioner, asking why he is delaying to kill her. While his hand trembles, she has no fear as she achieves her double martyrdom of modesty and religion (*Virg.* 1.2.9).

The interchange between Agnes and her executioner exemplifies what Stephanie Cobb describes as a dual social significance placed on female martyrs: "while Christian women were expected to display masculinity in the face of external opposition, they were to maintain traditional women's virtues within the Christian community."[11] Ambrose feminizes Agnes in ways that would be recognizable to his Christian audiences, but he also emphasizes masculine characteristics to be contrasted against her non-Christian persecutor. Ambrose has the audience weep at the sight of Agnes going to her death, but she is dry-eyed (*Virg.* 1.2.8). The executioner is described first as arrogant, but he loses this bravado when it comes time to actually kill the young girl (*Virg.* 1.2.9). Agnes takes charge of the situation, bowing her head to accept the blow, but the executioner is shaking and pale (*Virg.* 1.2.9). Agnes displays the masculine virtue of self-mastery while her non-Christian executioner exhibits fear and distress, effectively masculinizing her and feminizing him by contrast.[12]

But Ambrose is not engaged in a wholesale subversion of gendered characteristics in describing Agnes's martyrdom. Even as her masculinity is apparent during the scene of her execution, she remains feminized in particularly Christian and virginal ways. Ambrose after all describes her as a child coming of age through sexualized taunting, death, and her spiritual marriage to Christ. He paints her as a joyful and virtuous bride.[13] He also highlights her physical description as small, young, and vulnerable, saying that her body is so small that there is no room for the executioner's blow, amplifying her readiness to "offer her whole body to the raving soldier's sword" (*Virg.* 1.2.7). This dual significance that is so apparent in Agnes's death is not Ambrose's innovation. Such elements recall Perpetua's death in *Martyrdom of Perpetua and Felicitas* 21, for example, and how she guided the executioner's sword to her throat. Sexualized elements of Agnes's and Perpetua's deaths, wherein both women welcome the sword of their male executioners, has likewise been noted by David Frankfurter and Virginia Burrus.[14]

THECLA

The same pattern is carried over to the example of Thecla. While Thecla is not a martyr in the traditional sense, Ambrose describes her as such and uses her story as an explicit lesson "in how to be sacrificed" (*Virg.* 2.3.19).[15] This overt didactic emphasis is further borne out by the specific episode that Ambrose chooses to focus on, that of Thecla's impending execution in the arena. Like Agnes, Thecla is brought into a public space to be sexually shamed, but she instead reverses nature itself to maintain her modesty and to teach the audience, inside and outside the text, how to treat a virgin.

Thecla's story is from the second-century apocryphal *Acts of Paul and Thecla* and was well-known by the fourth century CE. Ambrose gives little detail on the apocryphal tale in *De virginibus* itself. In the *Acts of Paul and Thecla*, the titular heroine breaks off her engagement after hearing Paul's preaching, and is intent on following Paul and living a life of chastity. In her pursuit of Paul, Thecla is threatened with sexual violence and humiliation on several occasions. In one such episode, a socially influential man named Alexander sees Thecla and lusts after her (*Acts Paul Thec.* 26). After trying and failing to tempt Paul with money and gifts in exchange for Thecla, Alexander embraces Thecla, who resists and strips him of his cloak and crown, publicly making him a laughingstock. In retaliation, Alexander takes Thecla to the governor where she confesses and is sentenced to death by wild animals. Thecla however expresses her concern that her virginity would be imperiled if she were imprisoned, and so the governor arranges for her to stay with a wealthy woman (*Acts Paul Thec.* 27, 31). Once thrown to the animals, Thecla not only survives, but she baptizes herself in the arena and changes the minds of the audience who have witnessed her miraculous feats (*Acts Paul Thec.* 28–39). She is said to have lived the rest of her days proselytizing, having faced but never succumbing to sexual violence (*Acts Paul Thec.* 41–43).

Focusing in his account on Thecla's experience in the arena, Ambrose portrays her with the same masculine steadfastness that he employed with Agnes. Ambrose cast the sexual threats which Thecla faces as a force of nature. Thecla combats the male gaze of her audience by her bold confrontation with the lion, which could not "violate the sacred body of a virgin" (*Virg.* 2.3.20). Watching the lion lick Thecla's feet, the crowd changes its view of her and learns from the lion's example. The beasts teach men how to adore a martyr and how to chastely engage with a virgin, who demonstrates a self-mastery that Thamyris, her abandoned betrothed, and the men in the audience do not. Like Agnes, Thecla defies a public display of sexual violence within the story, but is nevertheless publicly sexualized by Ambrose via his writing. Listeners and readers are reminded of her nakedness in the arena, and they are reminded of the lecherous eyes of the internal audience, objectifying Thecla via her modesty to the point of voyeurism.

THE UNNAMED ANTIOCHENE VIRGIN

Following Agnes and Thecla, Ambrose further explores the importance of public displays of virginity by examining a case where a woman attempts to keep herself secluded and declares publicly her celibacy, only to still fall victim to the same threat of violence. The story of the unnamed Antiochene virgin is perhaps the most suggestive virgin-martyr tale in *De virginibus*. In it, an especially chaste woman keeps herself hidden from public view but is desired by men all the more because she avoids their gaze. In the hopes of quelling their lust for her, the Antiochene virgin declares "chaste celibacy [*integritatem pudoris professa*]," but this only turns the men to hatred and persecution.[16] The Antiochene virgin is unable to escape, and even though she did not fear death, she did fear the men who sexually desired her. Her persecutors realize that they need to attack her chastity if they want to harm her religious devotion, and so they take her to a brothel. After the Antiochene virgin prays for the protection of her chastity, a soldier comes to the brothel to rescue her. The Antiochene virgin puts on the soldier's cloak and escapes the brothel still a virgin.[17] After having discovered the soldier in disguise, the persecutors sentence him to death in place of the virgin. The soldier accepts his fate, but the Antiochene virgin protests. After explaining to the soldier her need to die, the Antiochene virgin's story ends with both her and the soldier achieving martyrdom.

Ambrose combines his didactic aims with an apostrophe to virgins, building a sense of sensationalism in instructing them how to receive this story appropriately, just before the incidents in the brothel:

> Now for a long time my speech has been modest, as if fearing to approach and to explain the shameful series of events. Close your ears, virgins. A girl of God is being led to a brothel. But open your ears, virgins. A virgin of Christ can be made to prostitute herself, but she cannot be made to commit adultery ... Learn the miracles of the martyrs, holy virgins, but unlearn the vocabulary of these places. (*Virg.* 2.4.26–27)

This warning, however, creates the opposite of Ambrose's stated goal. In prefacing the brothel scenes with such a statement, the audience's attention has been piqued, preparing readers and listeners for potentially lurid and erotic imagery and events to follow. But Ambrose does not turn the general or virginal audience away. The warning is an invitation to consume something that could defile, but the lessons yielded from the corrupting scenes is greater than the damage they could do. It is, in other words, worth the brush with sin to witness the virgin martyr's miracles. As David Frankfurter has argued, "early Christian martyrologies allowed their audiences to contemplate in safe form scenes that were so fascinating, even titillating, that they could not legitimately be enjoyed otherwise."[18] The potential rape of the Antiochene virgin is a thrilling and even erotic plot point. And the closer she comes to sexual defilement, the more exciting and triumphant her maintained virginity becomes. Packaging all of this in a martyrology makes the otherwise erotic and violent story morally acceptable, even laudable.

The convergence of didacticism and voyeurism is again apparent for both audiences. That is, the audience inside the narrative—the libidinous men and the curious onlookers—and the audience outside the narrative—those hearing or reading *De virginibus*. As with the spectacle of Thecla in the arena, Ambrose's audience is confronted with the prospect that they are likewise observers whose unchaste eyes and intentions pose a threat to the virgin. But, in contrast to Agnes and Thecla, the unnamed Antiochene virgin is determined to avoid this prurient gaze. When the Antiochene virgin hid herself from men, the result was not that their passions were subdued, but the opposite, as they were inflamed all the more. Her dedication to celibacy is meant to put a stop to those desiring her, but instead it prompts the men to become bitter and hostile. The line between desire and destruction is impossibly small in this scenario. When denied the object of their desire, the men turn to persecution and sexual punishment. This dynamic of being hidden, increasing desire, and being faced with rape or death is further explored and taken to an even greater extreme in the last account of a virgin martyr, Pelagia.

PELAGIA

The last virgin martyr in *De virginibus* is Pelagia, a young woman about fifteen years old. She has sisters (who are also virgins) and a mother, but Pelagia is home alone when she is assailed by a group of men. Shut up in her house, she prays to God about the appropriateness of killing oneself in the face of persecution. She resolves to die at her own hand, dresses like a bride, and kills herself in an unspecified way. Pelagia's persecutors find her dead and thus decide to track down her mother and sisters, trapping the women between themselves and a river. Like Pelagia, the mother and virginal sisters are faced with the choice of sexual violence or killing themselves. At the mother's prompting, the women drown themselves, and together they become martyrs.

Ambrose's writing suggests that it was his sister Marcellina who brought to his attention the question of the appropriateness of killing oneself to avoid being caught by your persecutors and subjected to sexual violence. Using Pelagia as an example, Ambrose makes a distinction between martyrdom and "using violence against oneself," which he says the Scripture forbids (though he does not reference any particular passage). He describes Pelagia's position as a "situation of constraint," and thus he determines her decision is martyrdom (*Virg.* 3.7.32). Ambrose uses Pelagia's martyrdom as his prime example of acceptable self-harm in the face of persecution and the threat of sexual violence. Virginity and choosing to die to protect one's virginity are defining features of a pious female martyr in *De virginibus*. Rape threats not only come with the territory; they define the landscape.

Pelagia's story contains clear parallels to some previous virgin martyrs in *De virginibus*. Like Agnes, Pelagia is a young teen when she faces sexual violence and death. Pelagia, like the unnamed Antiochene virgin, shuts herself up in her house, alone, to protect herself from the men who have come to rape and kill her. And while Pelagia is alone in killing herself, Agnes and the Antiochene virgin are active participants in their own deaths. Each of these virgin martyrs seek out and embrace death not only to achieve the crown of martyrdom but also to avoid sexual violence and thus achieve the crown of virginity. Pelagia furthermore makes her impending self-inflicted death righteous, describing it as toppling a sacrilegious altar with her blood extinguishing its flames (*Virg.* 3.7.33). In a more explicitly matrimonial move than Agnes, Pelagia dresses herself as a bride to meet her bridegroom in death.

Unlike the previously discussed virgins, the erotic gaze of Pelagia's story is focused less on her, and more on her mother and sisters. After Pelagia's persecutors "saw the plunder of purity that they had seized for themselves," they turned their attention to Pelagia's mother and sisters (*Virg.* 3.7.34). Now caught between the roving band of men and a river, the mother guided her daughters to the water, declaring it their baptistry and watery tomb. The women had to move quickly, but even so, Ambrose highlights their dedication to modesty, saying that they hitched up their dresses only enough for them to move freely into the river (*Virg.* 3.7.35). Though drowning themselves in a rushing river, Ambrose reports that their corpses remained miraculously clothed. Again, Ambrose invites readers and listeners to imagine hitched up dresses and exposed bodies by underscoring the covered virginal body. When telling the story of a group of vulnerable women trapped and trying to escape sexual violence, modesty itself becomes erotically charged, as it reminds the audience of what they are not seeing.

A PEDAGOGY OF SEXUALIZED VIOLENCE

In the stories of Agnes, Thecla, the unnamed Antiochene virgin, and Pelagia, the threat of sexual violence serves a key narrative purpose: it titillates the audience, intensifies the virgins' purity, and feminizes them. The virgins' chastity, in soul and body, is tested. Both inside and outside the text they are subjected to leering and lecherous eyes, which do not cause physical harm but are nevertheless sexually threatening and can cause psychic harm. The ultimate test of the virgins' purity is the act of publicly sexually shaming and threatening them. This network of power—the "sado-erotic"[19] interplay between martyr, persecutor, and audience—produces virgins through threats of sexual violence. Moreover, these moments produce virgins who demonstrate masculine self-mastery while simultaneously reinforcing their particularly Christian femininity. As Ann Cahill argues, "the specifics of the feminine body, particularly feminine bodily comportment, reflect the power relations that have produced them and the myriad ways this production is accomplished."[20] In moments of sexual peril, virgins are born, as are the mechanisms that shape the minds and bodies of Christian women.

Just as martyrologies are didactic, so too are rape threats.[21] The threats serve not only as warnings about proper and improper behavior, but they also excite the audience. As Frankfurter says of the violence of martyrologies: "spectacles we should not gaze at, that should not excite on their own terms, are sanctioned as legitimate, even pious, through their framing as the monstrous acts of Romans or heathens or savages and as the heroic resistance of comely Christian martyrs."[22] This is one of the lessons of sexual violence; because it is declared taboo and scandalous, this makes it exciting and alluring. Additionally, there is a safety and acceptability because it is threatened by persecutors who will surely be bested by the end of the tale. In each of the virgin martyr stories shared by Ambrose, rape lives in the imaginary. No one is sexually harmed, physically or mentally. Sexual violence remains a thrilling plot point in a miraculous tale. Moving out of the legendary and into real, contemporary life, however, sexual violation becomes substantially more complicated, as we will see in Ambrose's handling of the virgin Indicia's case.

THE VIRGIN INDICIA: AMBROSE'S CORRESPONDENCE WITH BISHOP SYAGRIUS

In *De virginibus*, Ambrose uses stories of virgins threatened with sexual violence to teach moral lessons about chastity, modesty, and acceptable behavior for virgins. There is a certain safety in these stories, wherein the audience already knows the outcome and thus can be assured that any fascination with the tale is harmless. They can enjoy the tension and excitement of leering eyes, scenes in brothels, and young vulnerable bodies because no virgins were defiled in the making of these stories.

As a contrast, I turn now to a case from Ambrose's *Letters* involving a virgin named Indicia, who is accused of sexual impropriety and is facing a physical virginity test. As I will show, the pragmatic need of Ambrose's response illustrates a remarkable shift in tone. There is no titillation, but only anger when Ambrose confronts Syagrius, the Bishop of Verona, about the proposed examination. What was praiseworthy in *De virginibus* is suddenly a material threat to the body and reputation of a contemporary person. Ambrose, who deployed rape threats as a narrative and didactic device in *De virginibus*, has crafted a set of expectations for the behavior and bodies of virgins through Agnes, Thecla, the unnamed Antiochene virgin, and Pelagia. But, when those expectations are visited upon a living person like Indicia, Ambrose's moral abstractions suddenly have consequences that he struggles with. Rather, the precepts offered in *De virginibus* lead to manifestly damaging expectations for virginity, which in turn must be protested in Indicia's defense.

The incident is discussed in two letters (*Ep.* 5, 6 [56, 32; 57, 33]) that Ambrose wrote to Syagrius, the Bishop of Verona, sometime between 380 and 396 CE.[23] Unlike *De virginibus,* which was crafted as a didactic treatise on virginity and intended for a broad Roman Christian audience, Ambrose's correspondence with Syagrius was intended to address specific accusations against Indicia and to argue against the use of physical virginity tests. In the first letter (*Ep.* 5), Ambrose expresses his displeasure with the way in which Syagrius dealt with accusations of unchastity lodged by Indicia's brother-in-law, Maximus.[24] Ambrose claimed that Syagrius had endangered the virgin by holding her without knowledge of her accuser nor alleged witnesses. He raises objections not just to the physical examination, but also to what he claims is a lack of due process. Referencing Susanna in Daniel 13, Ambrose demands that Indicia's accuser, Maximus, be investigated. Because Ambrose believes Maximus's accusations are baseless—Maximus had even retracted them—he is concerned that this will make any virgin vulnerable to the same kind of mockery and likewise be forced to undergo inspections of their genitalia. The sensitivity of the matter is evident, Ambrose says, in the modest way in which Syagrius wrote his letter. And yet Syagrius expects that a virgin could be subjected to such an inspection without shame, a notion that Ambrose roundly rejects.

The shame and danger of such an inspection is compounded by the prospect of a "cheap slave" conducting the virginity test. Ambrose's response can be characterized as not only alarmed but insulted, and he further is keen to keep issues related to individual virginity out of the public eye. As Ambrose says, people who hear about this case will lose their sense of shame, and the virgin will suffer the exposure of her modesty, since nothing is holier in a virgin than her sense of shame (*Ep.* 5.6). Furthermore, this public display is not only damaging, but also unnecessary, as Ambrose says that God requires no proof aside from the virgin's modesty, which is evident to everyone via her conduct. These two points—that hearing such a story will cause moral damage and that a public display of virginity is unnecessary and damaging—are in stark contrast with the stories Ambrose tells in *De virginibus*, which highlight overt acts of virginal chastity that are mediated through suspenseful and salacious accounts about virgins in sexual peril. After all, a crucial part of solidifying a virgin's modesty was a public challenge to her virginity via threats of sexual violence. But Ambrose's *De virginibus*, produced years earlier than these letters, helped to establish the very expectations that he is now raging against.

Ambrose repeats a familiar sentiment, that the only true sign of virginity is in the behavior of a virgin. Outward signs—such as an obviously pregnant belly, the awkward walk of a heavily pregnant woman, a child who has been given up or killed—make the loss of chastity publicly known, and this knowledge is then disseminated through gossip. Indicia, Ambrose contends, showed nothing in her behavior that would betray a secret loss of chastity, and no one who knew her had heard anything that would suggest this either. This public evaluation and character judgment are more persuasive to Ambrose than the results of a physical virginity test. Instead, the desire to conduct a physical examination, the bishop contends, is born not out of respect for modesty or chastity, but out of fear of reprisal. In Ambrose's estimation, Bishop Syagrius fears a potential punishment or the loss of respect if he does not conduct the test. Ambrose's position is succinctly stated when he says that, "The case is going badly when the body is more preferable than the claim of the mind. I prefer that virginity be manifested by the seal of behavior [*morum signaculo*] than the door bolt of the physical body [*corporis claustro*]" (*Ep.* 5.14). The rest of the letter supports this belief that virginity is witnessed through a virgin's behavior, as Ambrose systematically undermines the character of Indicia's accusers, while including the voices of those who testify to Indicia's holy and modest behavior.

Letter 6 continues in the same vein as Letter 5 in its rebuke of Syagrius, but further engages in a lengthy narrative example of fighting against sexual violators and the importance of guarding chastity. As Julia Kelto Lillis notes, Letter 6 to Syagrius could suggest that Indicia's physical exam has already happened.[25] Ambrose's strong language indicates that he regards such an inspection as a form of sexual violence, and as such he rebukes Syagrius, saying that their ancestors held chastity in reverence and would wage war on "violators of modesty" (*Ep.* 6.2).

In support of this assertion, a large part of Letter 6 is dedicated to Ambrose's version of the story of the Levite and his concubine from Judges 19–20.[26] One difference in Ambrose's account is the demand that the mob makes when they arrive at the old man's home where the Levite and his concubine are staying. In Judges 19:22, the mob demands the male guest be given over to them for sex. Instead, Ambrose says that the lustful young men wanted the female guest, as they were seduced by her beauty.[27] And when the old man offered up his virgin daughter, Ambrose says that the lustful crowd rejected her in favor of the Levite's concubine because the more the strange woman was denied to them, the more they desired her (*Ep.* 6.8).

This detail, unique to Ambrose's retelling, conforms to a theme explored previously in *De virginibus*. When, for example, the Antiochene virgin publicly declared her dedication to chastity in the hopes that this would abate suitors, it only inflamed their lusts. The threat of sexual violence in both cases is driven by rejection. When told that a particular woman was not sexually available to them, the perpetrators of violence became more aggressive. Desire is linked with what a person cannot have, and, in some cases, what is hidden from them. Seclusion, though thought to be a safeguard, could actually further endanger women by heightening their desirability. Ambrose closes Letter 6 with a reminder that the violation of consecrated virginity is truly a heavenly matter, with no mention of Indicia's earthly trial at the end (*Ep.* 6.19).

When compared to Indicia's story, the choice of the Levite and his concubine (Judges 19–20) as the illustrative example of the treatment of sexual violators is a curious one. It is an exceptionally violent story in which there is no question of the sexual violation of a woman's body. If readers are meant to see Indicia's treatment in the treatment of the concubine (wife), Ambrose is not at all ambiguous in how he regards virginity testing of consecrated virgins: it is an assault tantamount to rape.

CONCLUSION

Rape and the threat of sexual violence are specifically gendered forms of violence. Here, I have sought to examine how Ambrose engages with the gendered violence of rape threats on two levels: first, within the internal narratives that Ambrose gives in *De virginibus* and his correspondence, and second, within the religious community in which Ambrose was himself a leader. Rape threats are used to fashion a feminine body by serving as a reminder of vulnerability and potential subjection.[28] It is not just the case that this threat of sexual violence shapes those who are immediately targeted, but the effects of the threat also extend to those who could potentially be targets: "the threat of rape is a formative moment in the construction of the distinctly feminine body, such that even bodies of women who have not been raped are likely to carry themselves in such a way as to express the truths and values of a rape culture."[29]

Ambrose uses the voyeuristic elements of rape threats to draw his audience into his didactic aims of defining virginity. Thus, Agnes, Thecla, the unnamed Antiochene virgin, and Pelagia in *De virginibus* can be masculine in their self-mastery while still being made appropriately feminine via the threats to their bodies and virginity. Simultaneously, the men threatening sexual violence in Ambrose's stories express their loss of masculine self-control by lashing out sexually at the virgins, who remain steadfast. Nevertheless, the specter of potential sexual violence lingers, reminding Ambrose's audience of the vulnerability of feminized bodies.

While this works well for Ambrose as a rhetorical device in the stories of legendary virgins and virgin-martyrs, the practical consequences of such rhetoric are unsettling, even abhorrent, when confronted with their application to a member of his own community. Yet, Ambrose's *De virginibus* helped create an atmosphere in which the purity of Christian virgins had to be unassailable. By raising the standards of virginity to that of the miraculous, Ambrose left vulnerable flesh-and-blood women like Indicia, who now faced sexual violation not by stereotypical non-Christian bogeymen, but by members of her own community.

NOTES

1. Ann Cahill, *Rethinking Rape* (Ithaca, NY: Cornell University Press, 2001), 147.

2. In addition to Ambrose's own writings, two ancient historians and biographers wrote about Ambrose's life and work: Rufinus of Aquileia and Paulinus of Milan. Rufinus translated Eusebius's *Historia Ecclesiastica* and extended it to the death of Theodosius in 395 CE, and it was published in 402/403. The fuller account of Ambrose's life comes later, however, from Paulinus, a friend and secretary to the bishop, who wrote *Vita Sancti Ambrosii* in 422. See, Rufinus of Aquileia, *The Church History of Rufinus of Aquileia: Books 10 and 11*, trans. Philip R. Amidon (New York: Oxford University Press, 1997), and Boniface Ramsey, *Ambrose* (London: Routledge, 1997).

3. Ramsey, *Ambrose*, 16; F. Homes Dudden, *The Life and Times of St. Ambrose*, 2 vols. (Oxford: The Clarendon Press, 1935) 1:2; John Moorhead, *Ambrose: Church and Society in the Late Roman World* (London: Longman, 1999), 1.

4. Ramsey, *Ambrose*, 224 n. 52; Moorhead, *Ambrose*, 21 n. 17.

5. Ramsey, *Ambrose*, 71. Ramsey suggests that Ambrose perhaps also used a third sermon, but he does not elaborate on this. Neil B. McLynn, citing Duval and Rosso, argues that Ambrose's text is "derivative" as it draws from an Athanasian text and

from the work of Cyprian. See, Neil B. McLynn, *Ambrose of Milan: Church and Court in a Christian Capital* (Berkeley: University of California Press, 1994), 56; Y.-M. Duval, "L'originalité du 'De virginibus's dans le movement ascetique occidental: Ambroise, Cyprien, Athanase," in *Ambroise de Milan: dix études*, ed. Y.-M. Duval (Paris: Études augustiniennes, 1974), 9–66; and Giuseppe Rosso, "La 'lettera alle vergini': Atanasio e Ambrogio," *Augustinianum* 23 (1983): 421–452.

6. Ramsey, *Ambrose*, 72.

7. McLynn, *Ambrose of Milan*, 56.

8. McLynn, *Ambrose of Milan*, 57.

9. Namely, *De virginitate* (ca. 378 CE), *De institutione virginis* (ca. 391/2 CE), and *Exhortatio virginitatis* (ca. 393–395 CE).

10. Peter Brown, *The Body and Society: Men, Women and Sexual Renunciation in Early Christianity* (New York: Columbia University Press, 1988), 345.

11. L. Stephanie Cobb, *Dying to Be Men* (New York: Columbia University Press, 2008), 15. See also Virginia Burrus, "Reading Agnes: The Rhetoric of Gender in Ambrose and Prudentius," *JECS* 3.1 (1995): 25–26: "The immediate objective is to trace the literary transformation of would-be 'manly' women—*viragines*—into feminine docile *virgins*, exploring how female audacity was both entertained and firmly restrained through two fourth-century tellings of the of the tale of the virgin martyr Agnes."

12. For more on self-mastery as a masculine virtue and its presence in martyr stories, see Stephen Moore and Janice Capel Anderson, "Taking It Like A Man: Masculinity In 4 Maccabees," *JBL* 117.2 (1998): 249–273, and Cobb, *Dying to Be Men*.

13. Agnes's youth and her sudden transition from child to bride is emphasized across in other late antique versions of her story as told by Damasus in his *elogium* and Prudentius is the *Peristephanon*. Damasus describes Agnes as suddenly leaving her nurse's lap to being persecuted by a tyrant. Prudentius describes her as just a child, barely sexually mature, when she took a stand for Christ, refusing to sacrifice to Minerva. For Damasus's *elgoium*, see, Dennis Trout, "From the *Elogia* of Damasus to the *Acta* of the *Gesta Martyrum*," in *Attitudes towards the Past in Antiquity. Creating Identities: Proceedings of an International Conference held at Stockholm University, 15–17 May 2009*, ed. Brita Alroth and Charlotte Scheffer (Stockholm: Stockholm University, 2014), 311–320, and Dennis Trout, *Damasus of Rome: The Epigraphic Poetry* (Oxford: Oxford University Press, 2015). For Prudentius's *Peristephanon*, see, Anne-Marie Palmer, *Prudentius on the Martyrs* (Oxford: Clarendon Press, 1989), and Prudentius, *Prudentius's Crown of Martyrs:* Liber Peristephanon, trans. Len Krisak (Abingdon, Oxon: Routledge, 2020).

14. David Frankfurter, "Martyrology and the Prurient Gaze," *JECS* 17.2 (2009): 224. Virginia Burrus, *"Begotten, Not Made": Conceiving Manhood in Late Antiquity* (Stanford: Stanford University Press, 2000), 142–143. Virginia Burrus, "Reading Agnes: The Rhetoric of Gender in Ambrose and Prudentius," *JECS* 3.1 (Spring 1995): 31. Virginia Burrus, *The Sex Lives of the Saints: An Erotics of Ancient Hagiography* (Philadelphia: University of Pennsylvania Press, 2004), 53. Prudentius's "The Passion of Agnes" is more grotesque, lurid, and sexually suggestive than Ambrose and

Damasus's versions of Agnes's story. The phallic imagery of the executioner's sword is especially pronounced in "Hymn to Agnes" ln. 63–90.

15. On Thecla as a living martyr, see Elizabeth A. Castelli, *Martyrdom and Memory: Early Christian Culture Making* (New York: Columbia University Press, 2004), 134–171. On living martyrs more generally, see Diane Shane Fruchtman, "Living in a Martyrial World: Living Martyrs and the Creation of Martyrial Consciousness in the Late Antique Latin West" (PhD diss., Indiana University, 2014).

16. As translated by Ramsey, *Ambrose*, 97. Ramsey's translation of *integritatem pudoris* as "chaste celibacy" captures the narrative sense that the Antiochene virgin is declaring her intention to maintain the integrity of her chastity in the hopes that this will stop the unwanted attention from men. Instead, this declaration only inflames them further and angers them.

17. The unnamed Antiochene virgin's story shares narrative tropes with a number of other late antique Christian stories. There are parallels with Prudentius's "The Passion of Agnes" in the *Peristephanon*, as Agnes was said to have been taken to a brothel and to have left it purer than before she entered. The imagery of the virgin in the brothel as a dove being preyed upon is very similar to imagery invoked in the story of Mary, the Niece of Abraham from the *Life of Abraham of Qidun*. Mary, like the Antiochene virgin, is also rescued from the brothel by a solider who disguises her to escape the brothel before she can be raped. The soldier in Mary's story, however, is actually her uncle in disguise and not a true soldier as in the Antiochene virgin's story. As Ramsey also notes, this virgin's story is similar to that of Theodora of Alexandria, who was also rescued from a brothel by a soldier, and then the two were put to death. See, Ramsey, *Ambrose*, 222 n. 20; Prudentius, "The Passion of Agnes," *Prudentius's Crown of Martyrs*, 170–173; Sebastian P. Brock and Susan Ashbrook Harvey, "Mary, the Niece of Abraham of Qidun," *Holy Women of the Syrian Orient* (Berkeley: University of California Press, 1998), 27–37.

18. Frankfurter, "Martyrology and the Prurient Gaze," 217.

19. Frankfurter, "Martyrology and the Prurient Gaze," 217.

20. Cahill, *Rethinking Rape*, 151–152.

21. Frankfurter, "Martyrology and the Prurient Gaze," 233.

22. Frankfurter, "Martyrology and the Prurient Gaze," 230.

23. There is no consensus on the date of letters 5 and 6 (CSEL 56 and 57, FOTC 32 and 33). Mary Beyenka notes that the traditional date for letter 5 (56, 32) is 380, which is the date she uses for letter 6 (57, 33). But several scholars have argued for a significantly later date. Jean-Rémy Palanque dates letters 5 and 6 (56, 32; 57, 33) to 395–396. More recently, Kevin Uhalde dates letter 5 (56, 32) to 394, and Dyan Elliott dates the letter to 383. See, Ambrose, *Letters*, Fathers of the Church 26, trans. Mary Melchior Beyenka (Washington, D.C.: Catholic University of America Press, 1954), 152 n. 1, 163; Jean-Rémy Palanque, *Saint Ambroise et l'Empire romain: Contribution à l'histoire des rapports de l'église et de l'état à la fin du quatrième siècle* (Paris: E. de Boccard, 1933), 554; Kevin Uhalde, *Expectations of Justice in the Age of Augustine* (Philadelphia: University of Pennsylvania Press, 2013); Dyan Elliott, *The Bride of Christ Goes to Hell: Metaphor and Embodiment in the Lives of Pious Women, 200–1500* (Philadelphia: University of Pennsylvania Press, 2012).

24. Ambrose of Milan, *Letters*, trans. Beyenka, 152 n. 1.

25. Lillis (299) suggests that perhaps letter 32 (5; 56) could be Ambrose trying to stop the exam while letter 33 (6; 57) is his admonishment following the exam. Alternatively, she argues that the exam could have happened before the first letter, 32 (5; 56). There is no consensus as to whether or not the physical exam has already happened when Ambrose wrote to Syagrius. Kathleen Coyne Kelly (32), Joy Schroeder (106), and Kevin Uhalde (68) also assume that the exam has taken place. Michael Rosenberg describes the exam as if it had not yet taken place (186), while Dyan Elliott explicitly rejects the claim that the inspection had taken place before letter 32 (5; 56) (309 n.122). See, Julia Kelto Lillis, "Virgin Territory: Configuring Female Virginity in Early Christianity" (PhD diss., Duke University, 2017), 299; Kathleen Coyne Kelly, *Performing Virginity and Testing Chastity in the Middle Ages* (London: Routledge, 2000); Joy Shcroeder, *Dinah's Lament: The Biblical legacy of Sexual Violence in Christian Interpretation* (Minneapolis: Fortress Press, 2007); Michael Rosenberg, *Signs of Virginity: Testing Virgins and Making Men in Late Antiquity* (Oxford: Oxford University Press, 2018); Uhalde, *Expectations of Justice in the Age of Augustine*; Elliott, *The Bride of Christ Goes to Hell*.

26. As Joy Schroeder notes, his rendition draws heavily from Josephus's account in *Jewish Antiquities* 5.2.8–12. Ambrose and Josephus's accounts of this story depart in significant ways from the biblical account. See, Schroeder, *Dinah's Lament*, 106.

27. Ambrose, *Ep.* 6.7; Josephus, *Jewish Antiquities* 5.2.8. Josephus adds that they had seen her earlier in the marketplace and had noticed her beauty. This detail of the marketplace is not in Ambrose's letter nor in Judges 19.

28. See, Renée J. Heberle, "Rethinking the Social Contract: Masochism and Masculinist Violence," in *Theorizing Sexual Violence* (New York: Routledge, 2009), 125–146, and Louise du Toit, *A Philosophical Investigation of Rape: The Making and Unmaking of the Feminine Self* (New York: Routledge, 2009).

29. Cahill, *Rethinking Rape*, 143

WORKS CITED

Primary Sources

Acta Pauli et Theclae: Maximilien Bonnet and Richard A. Lipsius, ed.s, *Acta Apostolorum Apocrypha*. Leipzig: H. Mendelssohn, 1891.

Ambrose. *De virginibus*: PL 16:187a-232c; Boniface Ramsey, *Ambrose*. The Early Church Fathers. London: Routledge, 1997.

———. *Epistolarum Classis I*: PL 16:875b-1219a; Mary Melchior Beyenka, trans., *Letters*. Fathers of the Church 26. Washington, D.C.: Catholic University of America Press, 1954.

Passio Sanctarum Perpetuae et Felicitatis: Thomas J. Heffernan, ed. & trans., *The Passion of Perpetua and Felicity,* New York: Oxford University Press, 2012.

Paulinus of Milan. *Vita Sancti Ambrosii*: PL 14:27a-46c; Boniface Ramsey, *Ambrose*. The Early Church Fathers. London: Routledge, 1997.

Prudentius. *Peristephanon*: LCL 398 vol. II; Len Krisak, trans., *Prudentius' Crown of Martyrs: Liber Peristephanon*. Routledge Later Latin Poetry. Introduction and notes by Joseph Pucci. Abingdon, Oxon: Routledge, 2020.

Secondary Sources

Amidon, Philip R. *The Church History of Rufinus of Aquileia: Books 10 and 11*. Translated by Philip R. Amidon. New York: Oxford University Press, 1997.
Brock, Sebastian, and Susan Ashbrook Harvey. *Holy Women of the Syrian Orient*. Updated Edition. The Transformation of the Classical Heritage 13. Berkeley, CA: University of California Press, 1998.
Brown, Peter. *The Body and Society: Men, Women and Sexual Renunciation in Early Christianity*. New York: Columbia University Press, 1988.
Burrus, Virginia. "Reading Agnes: The Rhetoric of Gender in Ambrose and Prudentius." *Journal of Early Christian Studies* 3:25–46, 1995.
———. *"Begotten, Not Made": Conceiving Manhood in Late Antiquity*. Stanford, CA: Stanford University Press, 2000.
———. *The Sex Lives of Saints: An Erotics of Ancient Hagiography*. Divinations: Rereading Late Ancient Religion. Edited by Daniel Boyarin and Virginia Burrus. Philadelphia: University of Pennsylvania Press, 2004.
Cahill, Ann. *Rethinking Rape*. Ithaca, NY: Cornell University Press, 2001.
Castelli, Elizabeth A. *Martyrdom and Memory: Early Christian Culture Making*. Gender, Theory, and Religion. New York: Columbia University Press, 2004.
Cobb, L. Stephanie. *Dying to Be Men: Gender and Language in Early Christian Martyr Texts*. Gender, Theory, and Religion. New York: Columbia University Press, 2008.
Dudden, F. Homes. *The Life and Times of St. Ambrose*. Vol. 1. Oxford: The Clarendon Press, 1935.
Duval, Y.-M. "L'originalité Du De Uirginibus Dans Le Movement Ascétique Occidental: Ambroise, Cyprien, Athanase." Pages 9–66 in *Ambroise de Milan: XVIe Centenaire de Son Élection Épiscopale*. Edited by Y.-M. Duval. Paris: Études Augustiniennes, 1974.
Elliott, Dyan. *The Bride of Christ Goes to Hell: Metaphor and Embodiment in the Lives of Pious Women, 200–1500*. Philadelphia: University of Pennsylvania Press, 2012.
Frankfurter, David. "Martyrology and the Prurient Gaze." *Journal of Early Christian Studies* 17:215–45, 2009.
Fruchtman, Diane Shane. "Living in a Martyrial World: Living Martyrs and the Creation of Martyrial Consciousness in the Late Antique Latin West." PhD diss., Indiana University, 2014.
Heberle, Renée. "Rethinking the Social Contract: Masochism and Masculinist Violence." Pages 125–46 in *Theorizing Sexual Violence*. Edited by Renée Heberle and Victoria Grace. Routledge Research in Gender and Society 21. New York: Routledge, 2009.

Kelly, Kathleen Coyne. *Performing Virginity and Testing Chastity in the Middle Ages.* London: Routledge, 2000.

Lillis, Julia Kelto. "Virgin Territory: Configuring Female Virginity in Early Christianity." PhD diss., Duke University, 2017.

Mclynn, Neil B. *Ambrose of Milan: Church and Court in a Christian Capital.* Berkeley, CA: University of California Press, 1994.

Moore, Stephen, and Janice Capel Anderson. "Taking It Like a Man: Masculinity In 4 Maccabees." *Journal of Biblical Literature* 117:249–73, 1998.

Moorhead, John. *Ambrose: Church and Society in the Late Roman World.* The Medieval World. London: Longman, 1999.

Palanque, Jean-Rémy. *Saint Ambroise et l'Empire Romain: Contribution à l'histoire Des Rapports de l'église et de l'état à La Fin Du Quatrième Siècle.* Paris: E. de Boccard, 1933.

Palmer, Anne-Marie. *Prudentius on the Martyrs.* Oxford: Clarendon Press, 1989.

Ramsey, Boniface. *Ambrose.* The Early Church Fathers. London: Routledge, 1997.

Rosenberg, Michael. *Signs of Virginity: Testing Virgins and Making Men in Late Antiquity.* Oxford: Oxford University Press, 2018.

Rosso, Giuseppe. "La 'Lettera Alle Vergini' Atanasio e Ambrogio." *Augustinianum* 23:421–52, 1983.

Schroeder, Joy. *Dinah's Lament: The Biblical Legacy of Sexual Violence in Christian Interpretation.* Minneapolis: Fortress Press, 2007.

du Toit, Louise. *A Philosophical Investigation of Rape: The Making and Unmaking of the Feminine Self.* Routledge Research in Gender and Society 19. New York: Routledge, 2009.

Trout, Dennis. "From the Elogia of Damasus to the Acta of the Gesta Martyrum." Pages 311–20 in *Attitudes towards the Past in Antiquity. Creating Identities: Proceedings of an International Conference Held at Stockholm University, 15–17 May 2009.* Edited by Brita Alroth and Charlotte Scheffer. Acta Universitatis Stockholmiensis: Stockholm Studies in Classical Archaeology 14. Edited by Arja Karivieri. Stockholm: Stockholm University, 2014.

———. *Damasus of Rome: The Epigraphic Poetry Introduction, Texts, Translations, and Commentary.* Oxford Early Christian Texts. Oxford: Oxford University Press, 2015.

Uhalde, Kevin. *Expectations of Justice in the Age of Augustine.* Philadelphia: University of Pennsylvania Press, 2013.

Chapter 5

Corinthian Concerns and Textual Assault

Arminta Fox

From the walls of the Sebasteion in Aphrodisias, Turkey, scenes of the mortal conquest of various people groups reach out with affective power through over 2,000 years and thousands of miles. Each nation is portrayed synecdochally. In several, such as the ones from Bretagne and Armenia, the nation is a woman whose clothes have been ripped and torn, just as her life will be torn from her when the emperor takes mercy on her with his sword. The gendered, sexualized, and racialized violence of the Empire makes my soul ache with pain, shame, and fear.[1] Yet even as this image terrorizes, it is also immanently familiar: women made to bear the fear and shame of sexualized violence from men, in an effort to save their communities. At the Sebasteion, these images make up part of the Aphrodisian temple complex, forming simultaneous sacred and secular space. The gods, it seems, are complicit in the sexual violence suffered by these women and the peoples they represent.

In this essay, I argue that a similar affective theme resonates through the rhetoric of 1 Corinthians 7. Women are told to get married and have sex against their will for the sake of the community's harmony, cleanliness, and salvation on account of the sexual immorality of men. This "textual assault" creates an affective culture of fear and communal shame of *porneia*, as judged by a divine agent, that will resonate within Christian culture for centuries. The same cultural affects appear in the later New Testament texts of 2 Corinthians 11 and 1 Timothy 2. After introducing this textual challenge in its socio-historical context, I will identify several helpful strands of affect theory which I will use to analyze 1 Corinthians 7. Then I will describe similar resonances in other New Testament texts before gesturing toward implications for today.

CONTEXT

In the first century, the Corinthian Christ communities were trying to figure out what it meant to follow Christ and to be a "Christian." The formula often stated at baptism from before Paul's time asserts that "There is no longer Jew or Greek, there is no longer slave or free, there is no longer male and female; for all of you are one in Christ Jesus" (Gal 3:28). But what does it mean to live that way? To what extent do differences of gender, for example, matter in the Christ community among the baptized? How does that radical egalitarian ethic work within the extremely patriarchal context of the Roman Empire?

The Corinthian correspondence with Paul, or at least what is preserved in the canonical 1–2 Corinthians, shows an ongoing relationship, maintained through a letter exchange, oral reports, and visits. The correspondence shows that there are many things, many feelings at stake in this relationship; the letters range from loving, heartfelt praise to tears and anguish, to anger and frustration. Both 1–2 Corinthians are longer in comparison to other Pauline letters, shorter than Romans alone. This lengthy correspondence suggests that Paul is invested in the community's success. 1 Corinthians reveals that Paul has visited the community in Corinth (also mentioned in Acts 18), written to them previously (5:9), read letters from them (7:1), and heard oral reports from them (1:11; 16:17). The topics in 1 Corinthians range from how to get along, to how to deal with wrongdoing, to ritual and worship practices and beliefs regarding baptism, communion, and even resurrection.

In 1 Corinthians 7, Paul responds to matters about which they wrote, particularly regarding celibacy and marriage: "Now concerning the matters about which you wrote:. . . . " (1 Cor 7:1). Their perspective, as recorded by Paul, is that it is good for a man not to touch a woman. The term for touching used in this verse is from *hapto*, which Liddell and Scott define as a touch that grasps or binds, in which someone takes hold of someone or something else.[2] This touch alters, changes, or influences the object or person, in such a way as to make an impact.[3] It is a touch that ignites or kindles fire. This is the same word used in the synoptic tale of the hemorrhaging woman in Mark 5:27–31, where healing power goes out of Jesus by the woman's touch. This word is also used in John 20:17 when Jesus tells Mary not to touch him, for he has not yet ascended to God.[4] 1 Corinthians 5–7 deals with matters of sex, celibacy, and marriage. Given this context, and the direction of Paul's succeeding argument, it seems appropriate to translate this term as referring to sexual touch in this passage. So, the Corinthian perspective is that it is good for a man to not sexually touch a woman in a way that makes an impact, changing or affecting the touched person. This can be interpreted in a number of ways. Are the Corinthians saying that it is good for men not to engage in sex with women? Or that it is good for women to not be touched sexually (by men)?[5] Regardless of the person, it seems clear that the Corinthians, in writing to Paul, argue against this kind of touch.

While some leaders in Corinth argue that celibacy is best, Paul wants most people to get married. He fleshes out his reasons for wanting people to get married: to account for cases of *porneia,* often translated as "sexual immorality," and that it is better for them to marry than to burn with passion. Are they concerned about *porneia*?[6] As Antoinette Wire points out: "The success of his argument depends on their being ready to understand immorality as a present threat and a severe danger. Without the premise that the existing state of immorality is intolerable, it would not make sense to argue that marriage is necessary in order to prevent it."[7] If they are not concerned about *porneia* before receiving his letter, 1 Corinthians 5–6 would encourage their sense of danger and concern for their communal and individual bodies.

Indeed, the larger context of chapters 5–7 displays Paul's arguments against male sexual immorality, particularly the kind committed against women. In chapters 5–6, Paul presents three major cases in which immorality is a danger, and all of them deal with male immorality that disadvantages women in some way.[8] In the first case, in 1 Corinthians 5:1–20, a man "has" his father's wife. Paul places guilt on the community and on the man in his description: there is *porneia* among you (5:1). Paul includes the description of the behavior almost reluctantly, as if it is not the main focus: a man has sexually possessed his father's wife (5:1). This dangerous behavior is presented as worthy of a harsh judgment that takes communal and divine power to subdue. The lack of detail only seems to add to the danger. Which man? He did what, exactly? Without additional details, one can only imagine that it must be terrible! There is a dangerous, unidentified man hiding in your midst, suggests the text. With the community assembled and Paul joining them in spirit with the power of the Lord Jesus, the community is to hand the man over to Satan for the destruction of the flesh (5:4–5).[9] Paul argues that the community must deal with their problem. There are already questions about the reputation of the Corinthian community (5:1). Their communal cleanliness is at stake, with a little yeast threatening the whole batch (5:6–8). The father's wife, a relation dangerously close to the man's mother, is presented with no agency of her own as she is preyed upon in her vulnerability, grasped by the man. Paul's instructions that follow are for the community to guard who they associate with, even within the community (5:9–13). There is a dangerous man among you, in your very community, and the women, the wives and mothers, are the most vulnerable.

In 1 Corinthians 6:1–11, Paul responds to a reported concern about brother taking brother to court. Wire suggests that brother may take brother to court particularly when there were disagreements about dowries and the trade and possession of women. Yet, women were not allowed to speak in the Corinthian courts except through male representatives. This second example of immorality is focused on a primarily male space and likely between male offenders.

The third major example in 1 Corinthians 6:12–20 involves the visiting of prostitutes. Here, it is not the prostitutes themselves who are condemned, but rather those who visit them who were almost exclusively men. As Wire argues, "By challenging the practice of going to prostitutes Paul indicates the existence of a double standard that commonly applied in Corinthian marriages. The husband might have many sexual partners with impunity, but the wife did not."[10] By focusing on male space and male actions, each of these cases highlights male immoral actions.

However, Paul's condemnation is not directed toward these particular male offenders. He brings up these cases in the letter in order to elicit a sense of communal responsibility. In Wire's words: "Paul's charges against offenders are embedded in a sustained challenge to all his readers to put an end to immoral conduct. The blame does not fall on the individuals who have strayed, but on the community that has not reacted appropriately."[11] This sense of communal responsibility extends throughout the letter as he argues for unity and order in the face of difference and debate. As we approach 1 Corinthians 7, then, Paul has already cultivated in his audience both the sense of danger from immoral/bad men faced by women and the sense of communal shame and responsibility to respond appropriately. It is to these affects that this essay now turns.

AFFECT THEORIES AND COMMUNAL FEELINGS

Affect theories help to explain how feelings penetrate communities and spaces. In their essay introducing ways to read with feeling, Fiona Black and Jennifer Koosed offer a description of affect theory as "a critically informed analysis of emotions and bodily sensations, one that resists any neatly bifurcated analysis of emotions as either interior states or as social-political conditions."[12] They also suggest that biblical scholars tend toward a Deleuzian approach to affect theories in which "affects are what preexist all perception, cognition, and language; they preexist even the bodily sensations we experience as emotions."[13]

Affect theories can inspire readings that go beyond a notion of static, individual identity. I see affect theory as allowing interpretations that speak to the shifting multiplicity of identity, where individual identities bump up against and seep into those around them. These identity processes are shaped by power and politics which seek and often fail to dictate limits and boundaries on identities. In her affective work on early Christian texts, Maia Kotrosits describes similar appeals in affect theory as she uses a cultural studies approach to rethink early Christian identity:

> Affect takes the concept of the constructedness of the subject and identity performance seriously, but reimagines it with a new degree of rigor. It strips the term *identity performance* of its implications of individuality, ontology, and coherence (identity), and of its appeal to an act and an actor (performance), implications that are inimical to the very impulse for such theories in the first place. [. . .] Affect theory . . . re-orients one towards process, queer or surprising affiliations, and futurity.[14]

This sentiment is echoed in Felicity Colman's summary of Deleuze in which "affect is the change, or variation, that occurs when bodies collide, or come into contact."[15]

So, if the Corinthians are concerned about a type of sexual touch (*haptomai*) that changes the touched, attention to the *affect* of this moment is an attention to the details of these changes: what, exactly, is altered, and how?[16] In this approach the focus shifts from individuals—such as Paul the author or a particular toucher/touched person—to the ways in which, the processes by which, many people are altered by the potential of sexual touch, wanted or unwanted.

FEELINGS IN 1 CORINTHIANS 7

In 1 Corinthians 7, several patterns in the language of the text indicate affects of fear/danger and (communal) shame that may correspond to a communal feeling of assault.[17] These affects are produced through a discussion of the rules and limits for community and the high stakes of deviating from the rules or authorities. This section of the letter involves Paul's responses to various matters about which they wrote, as he indicates in 1 Cor 7:1. The format assumes that Paul offers his opinions on various things, commending them in some ways and critiquing them in others. The imperative form and the use of "should" language are abundant, as Paul imposes his preferred practices on the community. The prescribed behaviors are also connected to goals of Pauline imitation (v. 7) and divine commands (v. 10). Relatedly, there is language of control, authority, and ownership. Each person is to have their own spouse (v. 3). Paul inscribes rules around who has authority over the body in 7:4. There is the threat that individuals are not in control of their own bodies.

The text produces affects of fear and shame within the readers when it lays out consequences for following or failing to follow the rules or obey authority. The actions and their consequences endanger both the individual and the community. Yet, communal shame is produced when the community is adjoined to the individual who commits *porneia*. Eve Kosofsky Sedgwick notes that shame is contagious: "someone else's embarrassment, stigma, debility, bad smell, or strange behavior, seemingly having nothing to do with me, can so readily flood me—assuming I'm a shame-prone person—with this sensation whose very suffusiveness seems to delineate my precise, individual outlines in the most isolating way imaginable."[18] While 1 Cor 5–6 presented particular cases of *porneia*, there are no details about the cases of *porneia* in 1 Cor 7:2, which reads: "Because of *porneia*, each man should have his own wife and each wife her own husband." This lack of details generalizes the *porneia*, making it an omnipresent and limitless threat, endangering and infecting the community. Indeed, in 1 Cor 7:5, the threat of *porneia* from *others* seeps into the self as the text's concern becomes *one's own* lack of self-control (*dia tēn akrasian humōn*). In this way it is seemingly aimed at anyone in the community with its second person plural form. Anyone, any relationship, might be subsumed by or succumb to *porneia*. The temptations of *porneia* and their related affects are also personified in the figure of Satan (1 Cor 7:5), (*hina mē peirazē humas ho Satanas dia tēn akrasian humōn*). The reader is assumed to fear Satan as a powerful external agent who can lead someone, particularly when weak, from the right path.[19] While *porneia* can be one's own, it is also external, inherently relational.

In 1 Cor 7:9, Paul speaks to the unmarried and the widows, arguing that they should remain unmarried, unless they cannot control themselves. If one doesn't live under the controls of either marriage or self-regulation, the danger is that one will be consumed by fire, presumably with passion (*gar estin gamēsai ē pyrousthai*). This fire harkens back to the fire of sexual touch from *haptomai* in verse 1. Sexual touch alters someone—whether the person touching or the person touched—so that they are out of control, on fire with passion. Such a progression to being on fire would produce an affect of fear in the reader. While Paul states that it is best for the unmarried to remain unmarried, the presentation of the risks of doing so and the easy association with fire make it unlikely that the unmarried would feel safe or confident to stay unmarried. The fear and shame are contagious.

For the married who may wish to separate, Paul has additional instructions (7:10–11). That he singles out this group indicates their size and prevalence, suggesting that separating from spouses upon baptism may have been a regular practice in Corinth.[20] The text argues that the unbelieving spouse is made holy through the believing spouse, which also makes the children clean (7:12–14). The dangers in this passage center on holiness and cleanliness rather than Satan or fire. If a believing spouse separates from an unbelieving spouse the unbelieving spouse is not made holy and their children are not clean. This is a major risk for women in the Christ community who may want to leave a spouse but who are concerned about the status of their children. The contagion of shame and fear are highlighted in these verses, as a lack of cleanliness is said to spread to others in the family. The danger and related fear for the reader escalates in 7:15–17 as the text highlights the lack of peace (7:15), threat of death (7:16), and social or divine alienation (7:15–19) that results from unregulated touch and *porneia*.

Each reader or member of the audience would not be affected in the same way, however. Paul's arguments against *porneia* would particularly touch women in the community. Wire explains Paul's efforts to persuade women:

> First, throughout the argument against immorality it is not the offending Paul has addressed, but the community, including its women, which must make structural changes in its life. Second, the way Paul has appealed to the community with images of yeast pollution and violation of the union with Christ suggests that he may be addressing those who have set aside sexual relations for the gospel. Third, men who renounce sexual relations are the least important for Paul to persuade, since their choices already ward off immorality. It is the women rejecting sexual contact who must be persuaded if he is to succeed in stemming immorality by Christian marriage or remarriage of those men not willing to forgo sexual relations. Apparently, Paul sets out to persuade women to give up what they have gained through sexual abstinence in order that the community and Christ himself may be saved from immorality.[21]

Wire's interpretation of these chapters points to a concerted effort by the apostle to convince Corinthian women to go against their own convictions in order to engage in marriage and sex with sexually immoral men.

Expanding on Wire's reading by highlighting the affects of fear and shame within this passage, my reading demonstrates that the way this text is felt touches and attacks women in a way that is akin to a sort of textual assault. In particular, women who have rejected sexual relations are coerced into fear of male sexual immorality and made to feel a related shame and even responsibility for that immorality.

CONTAGION

Leaning into the affective resonances of fear/danger of male sexuality and communal shame within this text of 1 Corinthians 7 compels identification with other similar stories and other times when communities of people have been made to feel afraid, ashamed, and responsible for (male) sexual immorality. The same affective coupling notably returns within 2 Corinthians and in the post-Pauline Pastoral literature, further contributing to an affective culture of shame and fear within early Christianity.

In 2 Corinthians 11, concerns of fear and shame regarding *porneia* return as devices to inspire communal responsibility. Indeed, Paul says that *he* is afraid that the community will stray, a confession meant to inspire fear in the audience (2 Cor 11:3, 12:20–21). He presents alternative leaders as rival male suitors, battling over the chastity of the effeminized community.[22] The concern over leadership in the community is presented by Paul as a concern over women's bodies in marriage and sex.[23] By listening and submitting to these alternative leaders, Paul suggests that the Corinthians are being taken advantage of, and that he, by contrast, is shamed by *not* taking advantage of them (2 Cor 11:20–21). While this is ostensibly a discussion of authority in the community, the underlying fear is that male sexuality and authority is immoral and dangerous to this effeminized communal body.[24] The idealized response assumes the community, like Paul, feels shame regarding this danger and correspondingly changes its/her behavior to better correspond with Paul's authority that guards their/her chastity and purity, (regarding the gospel, of course). The affective message is consistent: a woman must sacrifice her own desires in order to be married (to Christ, in this case) because it will protect the community from danger and impurity.

While the community is to repent and make themselves a bride of Christ in 2 Corinthians 11, salvation comes to one's Christ community through women's childbearing in 1 Tim 2:15. In her work on Christian discourses of childbearing, Anna Rebecca Solevåg argues that "to be within the realm of possible salvation, a woman has to submit to marriage and potential childbearing."[25] In the Pastoral Letters, the key metaphor for the community shifts from body to household, where "each believer has a place and a responsibility as a member of his or her household, and that place in turn requires a particular kind of behavior or certain duties in the *ekklesia.*"[26] The fears of the devil resurface in this letter, as he stokes the young widow's sensual desires and leads women astray from their duties of marrying, bearing children, and managing the household (1 Tim 5:11, 14–16).[27] Yet, it is not only a fear about particular women who may be led astray, but rather that they would not be able to perform their mothering duties in the household of God, thus threatening the salvation of all. In spite of some who would wish for a life in the Christ community where gendered distinctions no longer limit one's choices, an affective reading of 1 Timothy suggests that fears of sexual immorality stemming from a male adversary (the devil) asserted that women should not only get married but be involved in childbearing and rearing in order to secure salvation for themselves and others around them.

Indeed, imperial logic points to women bearing children, regardless of their own wills, in order to populate the empire with new heirs, citizens, and slaves.[28] Returning to the walls of the Sebasteion, Davina Lopez has argued that the visual rhetoric of these walls conveys the idea that "the emperor continues to manufacture children—heirs to Roman world order—through the defeat of and acquisition of nations, thereby ensuring peace and the maintenance of the Roman family and race inaugurated by the first father, Augustus."[29] In the Pastoral Letters, similarly, women are the vessels by which these new heirs are born and taught to properly participate in the household of God.

CHRISTIAN AFFECTIVE DETRITUS

Feelings of fear, communal shame, and responsibility are uncomfortably common rhetorical features of early Christian biblical texts, as this affective reading highlights. Previous affective readings of early Christian texts also point to the reconfiguring of identity that is produced when texts are read in this way. This affective reading of 1 Cor. 7 disrupts a notion of Christian identity as it reiterates the point that early Christians and Christian leaders are not wholly distinct from the larger Roman world, including in regards to how gendered dynamics are configured. We might ask of early Christ communities the same questions we might ask about how ancient peoples felt and perceived the reliefs from the Sebasteion: What does it do to a community when the women are viewed as vulnerable and the men are viewed as possible sexual deviants? What would the effects be on the lived theologies in the Corinthian community? How does someone relate to and/or resist the empire of God and its power? If women thought of themselves as being at risk, I imagine that they would be more likely than their male counterparts to seek out rescue through salvation or to seek out safe communities. Men, on the other hand, might avoid the Christ community for fear of appearing weak, as if they cannot control or defend themselves and their wives/women. Or, perhaps resistance to Paul's words allowed some in Corinth to reaffirm the idea that, in Christ Jesus, there is no male and female for all are one. Some of these possible scenarios are evident in other early Christian texts. Indeed, within this very volume it is possible to see some of the ways legacies of "textual assault" continued to ripple throughout Christian communities.

This reading is disruptive of identity in ways that break through the historical divide. This is the Living Word, after all. Even today, people continue to feel its power. The assumption certainly haunts our communities today that women, in particular, should forfeit their own lives and bodies in the most intimate ways for the sake of badly behaving men. As in antiquity, twenty-first-century Christian communities are not immune. Indeed, it would seem that they are integral to the perpetuation of this idea. Yet, if "textual assault" continues to affect people in this moment, then this connection through time can also help elicit faith, that just as Christian women are surviving and resisting today, in part by the sharing of their stories, so too must they have done in the first century.

NOTES

1. See Davina C. Lopez's excellent analysis of this monument in Lopez, *Apostle to the Conquered: Reimagining Paul's Mission, Paul in Critical Contexts* (Minneapolis: Fortress Press, 2008), 42–48.
2. Henry George Liddell et al., *A Greek-English Lexicon* (Oxford: Oxford University Press, 1996), 231.
3. "Touch." *Oxford English Dictionary,* 3rd edition. (New York: Oxford University Press, 2022).
4. 2 Corinthians 6:17 extends the meaning to ethnic groups, as Paul says that Christ followers should not touch, have contact with, Gentiles. Colossians 2:21 considers certain foods as untouchable.
5. What about sexual touching between women? It seems that if the Corinthians had continued their argument to Paul in that direction, that Paul may have had more to say on the topic. For more on this topic, see Bernadette Brooten, *Love Between Women: Early Christian Responses to Female Homoeroticism* (Chicago: University of Chicago Press, 1996).
6. There is scholarly debate on how to translate *porneia*. Luise Schottroff argues that the term refers to "unlawful sexual relationships" where the "law" refers to the Torah and *halakha*. Luise Schottroff, "1 Corinthians," in *Feminist Biblical Interpretation: A Compendium of Critical Commentary on the Books of the Bible and Related Literature*, ed. Luise Schottroff (Grand Rapids: William B. Eerdmans, 2012), 723. Whether there are elements of moral judgment in addition to legal judgment is also a concern, as noted in Brooten, *Love Between Women*, 291. Throughout this essay, I often leave it untranslated in order to allow for multiple possible translations.
7. Antoinette Clark Wire, *The Corinthian Women Prophets: A Reconstruction Through Paul's Rhetoric* (Minneapolis: Fortress Press, 1990), 73.
8. Wire, *The Corinthian Women Prophets*, 73–79.
9. "In the name of our Lord Jesus, when you have gathered together and my spirit is present with the power of our Lord Jesus, hand this one over to Satan for the destruction of the flesh so that his spirit may be saved in the day of the Lord." (1 Cor. 5:4–5)
10. Wire, *The Corinthian Women Prophets*, 76.
11. Wire, *The Corinthian Women Prophets*, 76.
12. Fiona C. Black and Jennifer L. Koosed, *Reading with Feeling: Affect Theory and the Bible* (Atlanta: SBL Press, 2019), 1.
13. Black and Koosed, *Reading with Feeling*, 4.
14. Maia Kotrosits, *Rethinking Early Christian Identity: Affect, Violence, and Belonging* (Minneapolis: Fortress Press, 2015), 10.

15. Black and Koosed, *Reading with Feeling*, 4. Ann Cvetkovich touches on this thought as she describes the history of the "Public Feelings" group in developing her own discussion of depression as a public feeling. Cvetkovich suggests that the community shares not only in one's identity formation but also in the lived experiences of feeling. In her work *Depression: A Public Feeling*, she uses personal memoir as something that indicates not only an individual's own experience, but of the communities within which one lives. Approaching depression from the perspective of cultural studies rather than biology, her story is rooted in places, and the peoples of those places. For example, she returns to her grandparents' house and feels a homecoming that helps her identify her own feelings, her own self, not only in the interactions with her grandmother, but also in the spaces of the house, the spaces of the land, and even the native peoples of that land. She connects her feelings to the forced migrations and social displacement of the native peoples of that land, as well as to those of her own ancestors. At other times, she roots her feelings and experiences in the cultural moments of 1990s queer culture and awakenings, which she experiences most directly in certain places in NYC, but also in yoga classes in Austin, etc. The feel of the cultural histories of various places are reflected in her own ways of feeling. Affectively reading 1 Corinthians 7 may similarly encourage the creative envisioning of the collective feelings that haunt the community from prior experience of trauma in Corinth.

16. This type of cultural and collective affect that rethinks and resists individual identity has resonances with previous affective work focused on the Corinthian correspondence. Joseph Marchal has investigated the simultaneous push and pull of disgust within the letters, in which the audience is attracted and repulsed as the letters rhetorically construct disgusting others (and reveal Paul as both disgusted and disgusting as well). (See Joseph Marchal, "The Disgusting Apostle and a Queer Affect between Epistles and Audiences" in *Reading with Feeling*, edited by Black and Koosed) Also, Joseph Marchal, *Appalling Bodies: Queer Figures Before and After Paul's Letters*. (New York: Oxford University Press, 2019.) Laura Nasrallah lays out a topography of grief in Corinth that acts as a sort public feeling. Her approach allows for a weightier understanding of Paul's discussion of death and resurrection in 1 Corinthians 15. See Laura Nasrallah. "On Grief: Roman Corinth and 1 Corinthians." *Archaeology and the Letters of Paul*. (New York: Oxford University Press, 2019). Jaime Gunderson's 2020 dissertation focuses on grief and other feelings in 2 Corinthians. Gunderson argues that attention to affect reveals new ways of thinking about authority and relationships in the community. Affects such as grief and disgust often work together in 2 Corinthians to both rebuke and evaluate in ways that prompt the reorganization of the communal body. (Gunderson, Jaime. *Affecting Corinth: Grief and Other Feelings in 2 Corinthians*. Ph.D. Dissertation, The University of Texas at Austin, 2020.) These previous studies provide excellent grounding for this chapter. Yet, my focus is more particularly tied to affects of fear/danger and (communal) shame which I see as present in 1 Corinthians 5–7 and some of the primary affects associated with sexual violence.

17. While there are many possible affective responses to the trauma of sexual violence, those of fear and shame are perhaps most obvious from the standpoint of

the victim. It is worth noting that perpetrators of sexual violence may experience additional affects such as power, control, and pleasure.

18. Eve Kosofsky Sedgwick, *Touching Feeling: Affect, Pedagogy, Performativity* (Durham: Duke University Press, 2003), 36.

19. See Fiona C. Black, "Public Suffering? Affect and the Lament Psalms as Forms of Private-Political Depression," in *Reading with Feeling: Affect Theory and the Bible*, ed. Jennifer L. Koosed and Black, Fiona C. (Atlanta: SBL Press, 2019), 77–80. (Black cites Ahmed, Cvetkovich, and Brennan).

20. Wire argues that 1 Cor 7:1 "shows Paul's ambiguous response to a pattern of withdrawing from long-term sexual relationships in the Corinthian church. Some people have remained formally married, others have left believing spouses, still others have left non-believing spouses. This suggests that married people who come to believe do not automatically, perhaps do not normally, continue in previous sexual relationships," (*Corinthian Women Prophets*, 72).

21. Wire, *Corinthian Women Prophets*, 78–79.

22. Arminta M. Fox, *Paul Decentered: Reading 2 Corinthians with the Corinthian Women* (Lanham: Fortress Academic, 2019).

23. Shelly Matthews, "2 Corinthians," in *Searching the Scriptures*, ed. Elisabeth Schüssler Fiorenza, vol. 2 (London: SCM Press, 1995), 196–217; Caroline Vander Stichele, "2 Corinthians: Sacrificing Difference to Unity," in *Feminist Biblical Interpretation: A Compendium of Critical Commentary on the Books of the Bible and Related Literature*, ed. Luise Schottroff (Grand Rapids: William B. Eerdmans Pub., 2012). Arminta Fox, *Paul Decentered: Reading 2 Corinthians with the Corinthian Women.* (Lanham: Lexington Books, 2019).

24. The fears regarding purity (*akatharsia*), sexual immorality (*porneia*), and licentiousness (*aselgeia*) and the shame associated with them are stated directly in 2 Cor 12:21.

25. Anna Rebecca Solevåg, *Birthing Salvation: Gender and Class in Early Christian Childbearing Discourse* (Leiden: Brill, 2013), 133.

26. Solevåg, *Birthing Salvation*, 97. Solevåg continues this point: "The idea seems to be that younger women should focus on their responsibilities in their own households, serving husbands and raising children, whereas older women/widows can take on a 'mothering' role in the household of God, the *ekklesia*, by training younger women in their household duties and serving as widows." (103)

27. Solevåg roots the ideas of the devil in readings of Adam and Eve, where Eve's temptation and sin are seen as sexual deviancy and adultery. For her thorough analysis of this history of interpretation, see Solevåg, *Birthing Salvation*, 123–28.

28. For her discussion on the importance of procreation for Aristotelian logic, see Solevåg, *Birthing Salvation*, 96–100.

29. Lopez, *Apostle to the Conquered*, 45.

WORKS CITED

Black, Fiona C. "Public Suffering? Affect and the Lament Psalms as Forms of Private-Political Depression." In *Reading with Feeling: Affect Theory and the Bible*, edited by Jennifer L. Koosed and Black, Fiona C., 71–94. Atlanta: SBL Press, 2019.

Black, Fiona C., and Jennifer L. Koosed. *Reading with Feeling: Affect Theory and the Bible*. Atlanta: SBL Press, 2019.

Brooten, Bernadette. *Love Between Women: Early Christian Responses to Female Homoeroticism*. Chicago: University of Chicago Press, 1996.

Cvetkovich, Ann. *An Archive of Feelings: Trauma, Sexuality, and Lesbian Public Cultures*. Durham, NC: Duke University Press, 2003.

———. *Depression: A Public Feeling*. Durham, N.C.: Duke University Press, 2012.

Fox, Arminta M. *Paul Decentered: Reading 2 Corinthians with the Corinthian Women*. Lanham: Fortress Academic, 2019.

Gunderson, Jaime. "Affecting Corinth: Grief and Other Feelings in 2 Corinthians." PhD diss, University of Texas at Austin, 2020.

Kotrosits, Maia. *Rethinking Early Christian Identity: Affect, Violence, and Belonging*. Minneapolis: Fortress Press, 2015.

Liddell, Henry George, Robert Scott, Henry Stuart Jones, and Roderick McKenzie. *A Greek-English Lexicon*. New York: Oxford University Press, 1996.

Lopez, Davina C. *Apostle to the Conquered: Reimagining Paul's Mission*. Paul in Critical Contexts. Minneapolis: Fortress Press, 2008.

Marchal, Joseph. "The Disgusting Apostle and a Queer Affect between Epistles and Audiences." In *Reading with Feeling: Affect Theory and the Bible*, edited by Fiona C. Black and Jennifer L. Koosed. Atlanta: SBL Press, 2019.

Marchal, Joseph A. *Appalling Bodies: Queer Figures before and after Paul's Letters*, 2020.

Matthews, Shelly. "2 Corinthians." In *Searching the Scriptures*, edited by Elisabeth Schüssler Fiorenza, 2:196–217. London: SCM Press, 1995.

Nasrallah, Laura Salah. "On Grief: Roman Corinth and 1 Corinthians." In *Archaeology and the Letters of Paul*. New York: Oxford University Press, 2021.

Schottroff, Luise. "1 Corinthians." In *Feminist Biblical Interpretation: A Compendium of Critical Commentary on the Books of the Bible and Related Literature*, edited by Luise Schottroff, 718–42. Grand Rapids: William B. Eerdmans, 2012.

Sedgwick, Eve Kosofsky. *Touching Feeling: Affect, Pedagogy, Performativity*. Durham: Duke University Press, 2003.

Solevåg, Anna Rebecca. *Birthing Salvation: Gender and Class in Early Christian Childbearing Discourse*. Leiden: Brill, 2013.

"Touch." In *Oxford English Dictionary*. New York: Oxford University Press, 2022.

Vander Stichele, Caroline. "2 Corinthians: Sacrificing Difference to Unity." In *Feminist Biblical Interpretation: A Compendium of Critical Commentary on the*

Books of the Bible and Related Literature, edited by Luise Schottroff. Grand Rapids: William B. Eerdmans Pub., 2012.

Wire, Antoinette Clark. *The Corinthian Women Prophets: A Reconstruction Through Paul's Rhetoric*. Minneapolis: Fortress Press, 1990.

Chapter 6

Sexual Violence, Martyrdom, and Enslavement in Augustine's *Letter* 111

Midori Hartman

In 409 CE, Augustine of Hippo responded to a letter from Victorian, a priest who was concerned about recent barbarian invasions across the Roman Empire. This letter (*Letter* 111) represents his theological struggle with the question of violence and sin, which would become a central issue in his major treatise, *City of God* (413–426 CE).[1] Writing this letter a year prior to the devastating 410 CE sacking of Rome, Augustine frames regional violence in terms of equating humanity with a willfully disobedient enslaved person who must be punished.[2] He uses Luke 12:47–48 as scriptural support, and argues that God allows such violence to happen to the world because the world rejects the gospel. However, even Augustine recognizes the challenge of certain real-life experiences to this broad claim, namely, when the violence happens to God's most faithful followers in the form of death or sexual violence.

This paper explores how Augustine utilizes enslavement in *Letter* 111 in order to frame the general increase of violence found within and at the borders of the imperial realm as a just punishment for a gospel-rejecting world that he saw in the early fifth century. I argue that his use of slavery to explain violence proves problematic when considering individual victims—most especially the sexually violated servants of God—whom he claims have obtained the wounds of martyrdom as a result. Augustine's intention is to distance God from blame in response to questions of theodicy by focusing on human agency in sin: perpetrators of violence are the sinners, not the victims. However, as I will argue, Augustine's use of enslavement metaphors and the language of martyrdom to explain and justify the violence apart from God fails to address adequately the inherent sex-based abuse behind his rhetorical use of enslavement and captivity in this letter.

A main consideration here is that Augustine's rhetoric in *Letter* 111 contextualizes his return to this same topic in *City of God*.[3] Here we may observe an erasure of his willingness in *Letter* 111 to elevate victims of sexual violence to martyrdom, as well as a de-emphasis of the connection between enslavement and God's suffering servants. Thus, although we may see continuity in his thinking that mental chastity protects the body from the sin of violation, we also see marked difference. His inclusive charity for victims of violence in *Letter* 111 has become replaced in his larger project by pessimism over humanity to defend Christianity. Overall, this analysis will help us consider how Augustine changes his approach and tact with respect to difficult topics like sexual violence depending upon his audience and purpose.

VIOLENCE: HUMANITY'S PUNISHMENT FOR ORIGINAL SIN

In order to contextualize Augustine's argument that violence itself is a natural compensatory force for humanity's sin in the world, we must address his conceptualization of sin itself. First introduced into his theology in 396 CE, original sin (*peccatum originale*) was Augustine's theory that humanity has inherited the sin of Adam and Eve's first disobedience in the garden of Eden, which has been passed along to subsequent generations through the act of procreation.[4] This first sin of disobedience was not simply breaking a rule: it was the sin of turning away from God, a form of idolatry.

While it was a common enough idea in late antiquity that there must be some great sin that explained evil in the world, it was Augustine who located it within a reproductive inheritance: in Genesis, the first humans covered their genitals with fig leaves out of shame, which is the source from where the sin is passed on.[5] Given this tie to human reproduction, Augustine conceived of original sin as inevitable and not simply something one can overcome with free will.[6] In other words, it was a kind of stain that could not be washed away from human actions, therefore establishing human responsibility for evil in the world. This is directly counter to his opponents who saw evil as an aspect of fatalism (e.g., Manichaeanism) or who imagined human ability to overcome sin through free will (e.g., Pelagianism).[7] For Augustine, only God's grace could save humanity from sin even though it was not God's fault that humans used their free will in incorrect ways. Moreover, the punishment for the sin is the sin itself,[8] namely, that it is proof of humanity's continued willful turning away from God.

One problem with the theory of original sin is that it is a reductive way of approaching theodicy: misfortune is the result of individual tendency to abuse free will, namely, to do actions that induce suffering. The gift of free will removes God from being critiqued for lack of response to events, and it can lead to victim blaming, in that it is conceived that victims must deserve violence enacted upon them if God chooses not to intervene directly. As we shall see with the case of *Letter* 111, Augustine imagines that because humanity itself has rejected the gospel, it is unsurprising that such a sin would result in a collective increase in violence. Augustine's answer to why God "allows" this punishment to fall upon those undeserving such as his own followers—that God has some intention for their suffering to be teachable models—does not give a fully satisfying answer. This is especially true when it comes to rape and its implicit relationship with enslavement.

AUGUSTINE'S USE OF LUKAN ENSLAVEMENT METAPHORS

Fundamentally, enslavement is the domination and exploitation of another person for gain without the other's ability to consent and/or be compensated. This exploitation is more than simple extraction of labor and economic value; it is ideological and social, and it is also inherently connected to sexual abuse. Being a free citizen was associated with masculine rationality and self-control, while enslaved people were associated with feminized subjugation. Gender played a role, but the logic was more top-bottom in nature, a pyramid of the one and few over the many. It mirrored the basic Roman patron-client system, in which the patron is the one with power over the many layers of his *familia* (household) and clients. This made enslavement a particularly fruitful metaphor to explain many kinds of asymmetrical relationships, even the relationship between the divine and humanity.

Augustine is not unique in using slavery as a metaphor for humanity's relationship to the ultimate *dominus*, God, in what we would define as highly ambivalent ways. The Bible itself is a source for this contradictory "both/and" approach to the system of enslavement as a useful tool to get certain ideas across even if it was understood as a problematic human institution. Christy Cobb, for example, illustrates how the author of the Gospel of Luke uses the metaphor of enslavement ambivalently, especially in the "sayings of Jesus" sections, which "often appear to overturn typical hierarchies of domination."[9] The power of enslavement metaphors to argue for the overturning of hierarchies paradoxically stems from the fact that it also depends upon the re-inscription of those same hierarches for the metaphor to have meaning for the audience.[10] We can see this re-inscription of power hierarchies in Augustine's citation of Luke to support his view that humanity should understand itself to be enslaved, and therefore must submit to God with full obedience.

Augustine cites just two lines from a larger "sayings passage" in Luke, the parable of the faithful or the unfaithful slave (12:41–48),[11] using this as evidence for his argument that humanity deserves violence in the present age. In the larger parable, Jesus speaks of the faithful and prudent steward (*fidelis dispensator et prudens*) that the master (*dominus*) sets over his household (*familia*) to ensure that everyone gets their share of wheat (12:42). This is set up as the ideal model in contrast to the undiligent slave (*servus*) who is lazy because the Lord is delayed in his return, and who beats the slave-boys and girls (*pueros et ancillas*) under his care and takes food and drink in excess (12:45).[12] This trope of the good slave, who executes the will of his master as though an extension of his own limb, versus the bad slave, who is immoderately greedy and lazy, was a common trope in the Roman literary mindset.[13] However, it is telling that Luke's parable of the faithful versus the lazy slave stems from a question by Peter, which was based upon a previous parable concerning watchful slaves (12:35–40), to which Augustine does not choose to refer to make his point. As with other slavery parables attributed to Jesus, the enslaved person's "condition of utter subjection to another's will" ultimately symbolizes the relationship between humanity and God.[14] This is the logic that Augustine uses to explain why humanity is the reason for so much suffering in the world: people collectively fail to be good slaves of their master, God.

It is evident here that time, therefore also eschatology, is an important aspect both of Luke's parable of the faithful and unfaithful slave and Augustine's own approach to violence in his time: one day God will come back and judge humanity for what it has done during this waiting period. As Robert Markus has asserted, Augustine and other late ancient intellectual leaders were wrestling with the paradox of being inheritors of a perpetually delayed apocalyptic tradition: the end is both here but also not yet here.[15] In concert with the issue of delay, supporters of orthodoxy felt they had to contend with competing ideologies deemed "heresies" that signaled division over the kind of idealized unity of those awaiting the return of the Son of Man.[16] As has been established in scholarship, whoever could control the memory and worship of the martyrs could claim authority and establish a narrative of unity and orthodoxy.[17] As such, *Letter* 111 participates in this ongoing cultural production of martyrdom and orthodoxy in its embrace of the sexually violated as martyrs.[18]

Another aspect for consideration within both biblical and late antique perspectives on waiting for judgment day is the role of space in the intersection between enslavement and violence. On the one hand, both interreligious and intrareligious conflicts were tied to visions of larger systemic violence of competition for imperial dominance.[19] Augustine's defense of Christianity in *City of God* is an example of interreligious competition between Christianity and non-Christians, while his ongoing work of attacking opponents like the Donatists is an example of intrareligious competition within the Christian community.[20] However, violence was also implicit in the small-scale and daily system when it came to slaves, for which space and place were connected to obedience, as well as discipline and punishment.

In the Roman mindset, slaves were associated with space, as both material property and in light of what functions they performed on the property. This point that can be lost to us today because their placement and engagement in that same space is not easily recognizable in the archaeological record.[21] For example, in Petronius's *Satyricon*, a notice on the doorpost of the wealthy freedman Trimalchio's house is inscribed with a warning that any slaves leaving the house without permission will receive one hundred lashes (28). This frankly over-the-top threat nevertheless signals information: Roman enslavers were hyper-concerned with the embodied and ideological placement of the enslaved, whether they themselves were present or absent.[22] This same ideology of expectant enslavers finding their enslaved people at intended work—properly oriented in their duties, and therefore properly placed with respect to that work—is part of the Lukan parable itself (12:43). To do otherwise will incur punishment in increasing severity with respect to intentionality (12:45–47).[23] This extended metaphor uses real and quotidian expectations of the enslaver-enslaved relationship to contextualize how followers of Jesus should approach the wait (time) on earth (place). In this way, Luke's Jesus advocates that the disciples must be completely prepared and ready "to be open to the Master at any moment"[24] (12:35–40), and that those who are pastoral leaders must be faithful and uphold the teachings because of their responsibility in positions of power (12:42–48).[25]

Augustine works with this normative assumption that Christians who have not lived up to their obligations while awaiting the Day of Judgment must be punished. He narrows his focus on the punishment of bad slaves by directly citing only two lines from this parable in Luke, namely 12:47–48. The severity of their punishments depends upon whether slaves know the will of their master or not. The slave who knows the master's will (*voluntatem domini*) and purposefully does wrong deserves a harsher punishment than the slave who did not know the master's will and still did wrong. A master will flog the former many [times] (*vapulabit multas*) (12:47), while the latter he will flog fewer [times] (12:48). In the Lukan perspective, these beaten "slaves" are to be understood as the "bad" followers of Christ, namely those who do not fulfill divine commission as leaders of the community with greater responsibilities to those under their care as stand-ins for Christ in his absence.

Augustine, however, sees the punishments of "bad slaves" as a more expansive picture to represent general humanity's lack of response to God's message. For him, humanity has had plenty of forewarning about this violence through prophets and the gospel, so at this point unbelievers are willfully rejecting God, which equates them with slaves who intentionally resist doing what the master wants and deserve the harshest of punishments (2). This interpretation of Lukan leadership as representative of all humanity allows Augustine to begin his explanation of theodicy, namely how evil can be in the world and how it is not God's fault that it is so. Rather, it is humanity's collective fault for not paying attention to God's message over the long arc of time.

Here it is worth observing the line order of Luke 12:47 and 12:48 as they are represented in Augustine's letter, starting first with the lesser beating (12:48) and ending with the greater beating (12:47). Although this arrangement may be a result of manuscript differences, this is may also be intentional as a means to set up his argument with respect to both time and space. If those who sin accidentally receive less punishment than those who willfully disregard God's will, then of course overall humanity should be suffering the punishment to a greater degree, which explains widespread violence in the world. However, Augustine also concedes that those who do not commit sins—such as saints who follow God's will—become the receptacles of double the suffering:

> Why, therefore, is it a surprise if in the age of Christianity [*christianis temporibus*] this world receives many blows just as the slave who already knows the will of his Master, and doing things worthy of beatings? Those [in the world] are aware of how quickly the Gospel is proclaimed, but they are not aware of how perversely it is condemned. However, the humble and holy slaves of God, who suffer doubly in evil times because they suffer them both from the impious and with the pious have their consolation and hope of the world about to be. (2)

In other words, because the world has had enough time to learn God's will through the gospel, Augustine believes that humanity broadly deserves whatever punishment comes to it, even if that means that good people will suffer now in the world. Just like bad "slaves," humanity overall deserves violence as punishment because it cannot claim ignorance. Rather, it has committed actions out of willful disobedience. And just like good "slaves," holy people represent the will of God, but they come to suffer because they are caught up in the material world punishment but are rewarded for being justified in God's Kingdom. In this framework, everyone ends up suffering to a degree in awaiting the Second Coming as a result of improper use of free will because of original sin.[26]

Augustine ends this crucial paragraph by quoting Romans 8:18 to justify a future-focused mindset on the suffering of the present moment (2). However, in the following paragraph he responds to critiques of those who would raise theodicy-related questions against those who are in tune with God's will and still are made to suffer. It is here that Augustine is able to set up his embracement of the logic of suffering servants and reclaiming violence against certain Christians in his day as social capital by equating them with martyr's wounds.

THE SUFFERING SERVANTS OF GOD

For Augustine, the suffering servants in Israel's history are evidence against any who question how the violence against servants of God can be justified if violence is supposed to be punishment against sinners (3). This is ultimately a question about theodicy. Augustine's interest is not to address God's role in either activating or permitting violence; rather, it is the character that these righteous people display when violence is imposed upon them. However, upon closer examination, we can see that they are imperfect legendary models to equate with the present and real violence of Augustine's day.

Augustine supports his view of suffering servants with a long quotation from Daniel 3 concerning the three Hebrews in the fiery furnace. This allows him to focus on their holiness and courage, as well as their important confession of sins. However, even Augustine concedes that God spared them the actual pain and suffering of the fire, taking what is a humorous scene in the text and trying to equate it with contemporary murder and human trafficking.[27] He then turns to the figure of Daniel as another suffering servant, whose trials and confession of the righteousness of God proves that God even scourges his own holy ones according to their sins. Augustine acknowledges that these righteous people do not suffer the fires and lions because of their outstanding holiness in order to compare non-holy people as unequal to their measure (4). Again, this answer does not satisfyingly answer why the present righteous people *do* actually suffer, but he may be implying that holy people of the present age are but pale imitations of historic holy people.

In order to address any critics wondering why present holy people cannot simply thwart the violence brought upon them like these previous suffering servants, Augustine must address God's role in this process (5). For him, God produces these "miracles" (*miracula*) in order to have kings, like Antiochus IV Epiphanes (cf. 2 Maccabees 7), come to believe that holy people worship the true God. In other words, God had a legitimate and explicit purpose in allowing the torture of select righteous people. This logic will continue to be the framework for explaining the limits of human understanding of God's will concerning the captivity of holy people by barbarians: just as humanity cannot know why God chooses some to suffer, it cannot know exactly what "miracles" they are serving in a "barbarian land" (*terra barbarica*) (7). It is important to note here that Augustine tries to infuse suffering with meaning in order to sidestep why God chooses not to intervene, regardless of intention. As we shall see, Augustine must both minimize the impact of death at the same time as he elevates victimization within the longer history of Christian memorialization of violence, namely the martyrdom tradition.

To trivialize death itself as inconsequential, Augustine questions whether there is any difference between dying from a fever and being killed by the sword with the exception of length of suffering. Both forms of death result in release from the body, and a long illness is greater suffering than a quick death (6). By comparing dying of a fever or by the sword, he seeks to minimize being killed by violence by making it the "better" death with respect to degree of suffering. However, Augustine has greater difficultly addressing the captivity of the chaste and holy women that Victorian mentioned to him, which is seen in part by the greater length of address that he gives this subject in comparison with death by barbarian sword. The concern is no longer sudden and unexpected death by sword, but extended suffering in the form of sexual violence against women.

The capture and subjugation of women in ancient warfare was common, a reality that has been obscured by the avoidance of the issue in our literary sources and our own still-developing understanding of the history of rape as a tool of warfare.[28] For the Romans, the issue of sexual violence was tied to anxiety over its impact on those of freeborn status (*ingenuus*).[29] As Jonathan Walters notes:

> The status of being a respectable, freeborn Roman citizen was thus marked, at least in theory, on the corporeal level by bodily inviolability. Roman citizens, however low their social status, were not to be beaten, raped, or otherwise assaulted. Sexual penetration and beating, those two forms of corporeal assault, are in Roman terms structurally equivalent.[30]

Bodily inviolability was important for both Roman men and women, and its reliance on free status brings us back to the issue of enslavement: there is presumption of the sexual violability of the enslaved that is counterbalanced by the "ideal of physical inviolability of the free Roman citizen."[31] And sexual inviolability, particularly for free Roman women, required modesty (*pudicitia*). Conflict between Rome and its enemies ("barbarians") introduced its citizens to this potential of being sexually violated and unable to protect their modesty, as seen in the events of *Letter* 111. How does Augustine respond?

His first line of defense is assurance of God's own status and support of his people who have been captured:

That captivity of those chaste and holy women is indeed a most serious thing to be suffered, but God is not a captive of them, nor does he desert his captives, if he knows his own. For those holy ones of whose sufferings and confessions I recalled in the holy Scriptures, when they had been led away by enemies and placed into captivity, said those compositions which were being read by us in order that we might discover that captive servants of God are not to be deserted by their Master. (*Letter* 111, 7)

The biblical accounts of holy people being led off into captivity are proof for Augustine that the "Master" (*Dominus*) does not abandon "captive servants of God" (*captivos Dei servos*). As we noted earlier, human trafficking becomes for him a means of providing "miracles" in barbarian territories, just as figures like the three Hebrews and Daniel represented in the past. Augustine encourages further investigation of what has happened to such present-day captives in order to focus on providing such people consolation. He raises the example of the trafficking of the niece of Bishop Severus in Sitifis (modern-day Algeria). Apparently, she was returned in great honor to her parents, having prayed for the healing of the severely ill sons in the house of her captors in return for her release. According to Augustine, God intended this all to happen for the purpose of teaching God's power to the barbarians.

There are several issues with Augustine's choice of example to support his argument that the suffering of these holy women might have educational purposes. On the one hand, it is difficult to distinguish cases of temporary captivity such as ransom and cases of more permanent enslavement in antiquity.[32] The niece represents the former as an idealized, best-case scenario, because she obtained her freedom with her honor intact and magnified by her effectively paying her own ransom; this would not have been the normative reality for most captives in war. Moreover, it is unclear what actually has happened to these women except they have become captives of the enemy. While the church or loved ones could try to ransom the women back, it would have been a serious financial endeavor for the community, with the probable outcome of reinforcing the system of human trafficking in the provincial parts of the empire if ransom was paid.[33] If ransom was not part of the arrangement, then by Roman legal standards, these holy women were facing a more permanent reality of enslavement. Capture was political and economic strategy against enemies, as well as an understood benefit in which people would engage in conflicts to obtain human capital.[34] Within the Roman legal framework of *ius gentium* (the law of nations), it was considered a universal right for nations to enslave their enemies in war as a part of human culture.[35]

Having established a connection between the contemporary example of the niece and how God uses holy people to teach lessons, Augustine then invites comparison between the situation of the holy women and his earlier contemplation of suffering servants. The connection point in his mind is forced exile, not enslavement or sexual violence. He compares the captive women to the diasporic Jews in Daniel not being able to sacrifice in the traditional way at the Temple in Jerusalem (8). The response to both situations of "exile" is to be the same: prayers and confession of sins. He quotes Daniel 3:38–45 to reinforce the connection. This is not a true equivalency because it does not address the gendered violence inherent in the act of captivity as "exile," namely the serious potential of enslavement and sexual violence. However, Augustine turns to address this issue in his last paragraph of the letter:

> And they say these things [prayers], those ones groaning to God, who is accustomed to being present to His people, and either will permit nothing to be perpetuated against the most chaste members by the lust of enemies, or if it is permitted, then He will not accuse them. For when the mind is [not] stained by a shame-worthy consent, then it also defends the flesh from reproach. And whatever she endures that she neither committed nor permitted in desire, it will be the blame solely of the one who did to her; and so all that violence suffered will not be considered a shameful corruption, but to be a wound of the passion [martyrdom]. For the integrity of chastity has such an influence in the mind that, as long as it is not violated, then modesty is unable to be violated in the body, of whose members are able to be conquered. (*Letter* 111, 9)

While these women are not outright named as Virgins of God by Augustine,[36] his emphasis on their chasteness earlier in the letter and his argument for the women's continued state of modesty as a result of mental chastity at the close of his letter suggests the connection. Whether or not these women were technically Virgins of God, at minimum Augustine's compulsion to address these compromised women arises his need to distance God from such acts of violence even as he must also address Victorian's concerns with empathy. As such, he is unable to equate actual rape with teachable lessons for humanity as he could with biblical suffering servants or with positive tales like Bishop Severus's niece. His answer in *Letter* 111 about humanity's general punishment through the violence it creates, while emphasizing that the sin of rape falls upon the rapist and not the victim, fits within his larger theory of original sin. Augustine can argue that sexual violence against these women does not compromise their modesty and that it elevates them to the level of martyrdom because he believed violence to be inevitable due to original sin; therefore, he shifts the question from why God allows the violence to how humanity is to respond to the violence it enacts. For Augustine the shame of rape is offset by its gain: a wound of martyrdom.

ATTRIBUTING AND DENYING "WOUNDS OF PASSION"

Augustine's rationale for equating rape with a wound of martyrdom in *Letter 111* is that if the one does not mentally consent to the act, then the sin is wholly upon the rapist. At first glance, this logic displaces any blame on the victim for the physical violation at the same time as it distances God from criticism over lack of intervention in preventing the act. The perpetrator misuses God's gift of free will to commit evil in the world, proving that the inheritance of original sin continues into the present. This seems, at face value, to be a surprisingly positive take on the side of the victim. As we noted earlier, Roman free status was tied to control and protection of the free body from physical violation; in the case of Roman women, their moral value and status depended upon protection of their own modesty. To argue mental chastity over physical unchastity in rape appears to disconnect these women from the negative stigma associated with presumed sexual violence in the process of enslavement through captivity. Moreover, what is a terrible tragedy for God's most virtuous is reframed as an empathetic concession: these women have achieved elite martyr status. Yet as we shall see in what follows, Augustine's willingness to elevate Christian victims of rape to the level of martyrs in *Letter 111* is not extended to his conversation on the same topic in *City of God*. Ultimately, this reveals his desire to distance God from the cause of violence (i.e., original sin) and it reinforces his pessimistic view of the inevitable sinfulness of humanity, especially those living in his present age.

The desire to distance the physical act of rape from consent in virtuous women was not a uniquely Christian perspective, as seen in the infamous tale of the rape of Lucretia by the Roman historian Livy (64 BCE—12 CE). Livy attributes Roman nobility to Lucretia in response to her rape, namely her own tenacious resistance to the act and her immediate suicide by sword.[37] Important here is Lucretia's own words: "What can be well with a woman who has lost her chastity? . . . *My body only is violated; my mind is guiltless*; death will be my witness. Swear that the adulterer will be punished."[38] As we shall see, Augustine uses Lucretia in *City of God* to address the rape of Christian women in the 410 CE sacking of Rome in far less sympathetic terms than in *Letter 111*.

Early in *City of God*, Augustine meditates on Christian forms of suffering as a charge by non-Christians as proof of Christianity's ineffectiveness in the face of recent violence. In Book 1, he makes the assertion that virtue governs the body and that having a holy will protects against whatever happens unwillingly to the body (1.16). He does this in order to address criticisms of Christian victims' responses to the rape, namely suicide or the refusal of suicide (1.17). He cites the story of Lucretia in order to challenge Romans to recognize that they, too, have their own lauded example of the nobility of a woman violated and that the male perpetrators are the ones who commit the sin against those who are chaste of mind (1.19). Ultimately, this becomes a set-up for Augustine to assert that there are no divine precepts that permit a Christian to commit suicide under the commandment against killing (1.20). In other words, a conversation about the rape of women is ultimately a conversation about the condemnation of suicide, not consolation of the victims.

Scholars have focused heavily upon Augustine's use of Lucretia and his address of the sexually violated in *City of God*. For example, Dennis Trout argues that Augustine's denial of Lucretia as a moral model for committing the crime of murder in suicide allows him to both address the recent violence in a way that moves the issue of sexual purity from human arbitration to God's judgment.[39] While Augustine's use of Lucretia appears to be support for mental chastity over bodily violation, Trout suggests that Augustine doubts her true inner chastity and questions the sexually violated women in 410 CE in similar terms: perhaps they were being judged by God for the sin of pride over their chastity.[40] In exploration of the way in which ancient Christian texts embraced shame as means of challenging the limitations of the honor-shame system, Virginia Burrus argues that Augustine reinscribes Lucretia's shame so as to rewrite Roman history in order to revise salvation history itself and its relationship to the eschatological body.[41]

Building upon Trout and Burrus, Jennifer Barry highlights the recently sexually violated women in order to show their erasure from "collective Christian memory" by Augustine in *City of God*.[42] By observing that Augustine's word choice of *stuprum* (violation) without a corresponding idea of force (e.g. *per vim*), Barry argues that this ultimately results in the dismissal of all claims of female chastity because they are inherently suspect in God's judgment of pride, offering minimal consolation but not the condemnation of rape.[43] In general, recent scholarship has been attentive to how Augustine uses Lucretia and the violence against Christian women in ways that suit his theological interests when it is to claim Christian superiority over interpreting recent events, past history, and the moral behavior of victims.

What is necessary to consider, then, is how Augustine's address of the violated women in *City of God* uses ideas he has already developed in *Letter* 111 in drastically different ways. In *City of God*, he begins his discussion of forms of Christian suffering by speaking about how many were led into captivity during the sacking of Rome (1.14). What constitutes the bulk of *Letter* 111—an explanation of why God's servants suffer for the purpose of teaching—becomes a simple reference line for captivity in the *City of God*:

There are in the Holy Scriptures also great consolations of this calamity: There were the three boys in captivity, there was Daniel, there were other prophets; God, the consoling one, did not desert them. Therefore, if he did not desert his faithful ones under the domination of nations, even if barbarians, nevertheless they are human, and he is the one who did not desert the prophet in the innards of a monster. (*City of God* 1.14)

Having swapped out the Job reference in *Letter* 111 with Jonah, Augustine then turns to critique those non-Christians who do not believe in such miracles by referencing Arion's mythical salvation on the back of a dolphin and the story of the Roman general Marcus Regulus who was a captive of the Carthaginians (1.15). As such, we can see that there is a dramatic difference in space dedicated to explaining the purpose of suffering servants between *Letter* 111 and *City of God*. With the letter, we have seen that Augustine uses it as a chance to teach about the purposes of miracles, while in the treatise the purpose of suffering in miracles is not so important as the sign of a lack of desertion by God.

Most important for the focus of this paper is that Augustine's equation of Christian victims of rape with obtaining the wounds of martyrdom in *Letter* 111 is not highlighted in this section of *City of God* concerning violated women. Rather, its denial is intensified. Burrus has observed that Augustine in *City of God* "distract[s] attention from actual deaths that might have been narrated as martyrdoms."[44] Working off this point, Barry charges that Augustine "subsumes the memory of the potential female martyr in [*City of God*] 1.16 and . . . the memory of the violated women."[45] It is here we can see that Augustine's larger intention in this section of *City of God* is to condemn Christian suicide, in order to deny its potential identification with martyrdom. Even when he acknowledges martyrs who committed suicide to avoid violation, he feigns ignorance of divine intention and posits that the veneration of those particular saints does not justify contemporary people committing suicide. For Augustine in *City of God*, it seems that historic martyrs are not to be models of emulation, and temporal problems like sexual violation should not invoke a response like the eternal sin of suicide as a self-murder (1.26).

When comparing the two texts, it appears that Augustine has subsumed his previous openness to the category of martyrdom for women who have been sexually violated.[46] His use of Lucretia's tale perhaps explains the origin of *Letter* 111's logic concerning the validity of mental chastity of sexually violated women, but this logic no longer represents a sympathetic response from one bishop to another on a troubling report of violence. Rather, it becomes a defensive way to critique Christian suicide and non-Christian criticisms that God does not help his own people. This section of *City of God* is striking in its intentional rejection of equating rape with martyrdom for the sexual violence of women in 410 CE in comparison with his earlier willingness to apply it to the events of 409 CE Similarly, it is important to note the comparative absence of *Letter* 111's language of enslavement and submission with this section of *City of God*, even if it itself is a repetitive theme in the work overall.[47]

If our analysis of sexual violation in *City of God* demonstrates how Augustine used it in order to dissuade any from seeking to gain martyrdom through suicide, then what are we to make of the role of sexual violence in his earlier work, *Letter* 111? By focusing on imagining good Christians as suffering servants and martyrs for Victorian, Augustine is ultimately trying to extract God from culpability. An enslaved humanity is being punished for sins through violence because it rejects the gospel and acceptance of the Second Coming. Holy people are caught up in this wave of violence, but even they have their own sins to confess and their roles to play to teach lessons to others through miracles. Even when the violence is the least justifiable—in the case of the rape of God's servants—he offers what appears to be a valuable consolation prize: martyrdom.

Here I suggest that in the years prior to the *City of God*, at least, Augustine was willing to remember these women named by Victorian as martyrs. His reaction is ultimately more pastoral than explanatory, seeking to comfort a fellow bishop who could not comprehend the violence, turning suffering into a teachable moment concerning God's commitment to explain that adversity is not an abandonment. Ultimately, he seeks to extract God from intentionality in this violence, beginning the process of addressing why God does not intervene when he has historically been understood as a God who liberates his people from their suffering. While this puts a critical light on his approach to the victims of sexual violence in *Letter* 111, it is still far better than the pessimistic rejection of similar victims in *City of God*.

CONCLUSIONS

Augustine appears to negate victim blaming in *Letter* 111. He is attentive to a legitimate problem in which chaste and holy women are sexually violated as a result of a larger issue of regional violence. By elevating these "compromised" women to the status of martyrs, Augustine expands the definition of what a "martyr" was—at least until he begins to write *City of God*. However, as this paper has sought to illuminate, Augustine's ultimate purpose is to disassociate immoral actions in the world such as rape from God's intention and/or lack of intervention. For him, this is solely a human-made problem, even if there is delayed God-provided solution: Judgment Day. Augustine's turn to the language of suffering servants and enslavement reinforces the issue of violence as an expectation for Christians in his age: even while he defends the mediocrity of his present age,[48] he will use scriptural exemplars of suffering to shamefully remind people to "do better." By framing contemporary violence in terms of humanity's failure to submit to God by means of acceptance of the gospel, Augustine uses the language of enslavement to contextualize humanity's disobedience in ways that reinscribe violence, as seen in his choice of scriptural references (e.g. Luke 12:47–48). This interpretive turn does not attend with care to the actual victims of the violence, especially given the fact that sexual violence was an inherent aspect of ancient enslavement. In trying so hard to save God from critique, Augustine attempts to provide comfort in ways that fall short of their initial aim in *Letter* 111.

NOTES

All translations are mine unless otherwise noted. The Latin text is from the digitized version of *S. Aurelii Augustini, Opera Omnia, Tutte le opere*, 45 vols (ed. Franco Monteverde; Rome: Nouva Biblioteca Agostiniana & Città Nouva, 1967). Any infelicities are mine and mine alone. My gratitude to volume editors, Christy Cobb and Eric Vanden Eykel, for their invitation and guidance.

1. Augustine wrote *City of God* as a defense of Christianity against non-Christian claims that it was the cause of the 410 CE sacking of Rome. His major argument was that the Roman Empire was always subject to such violence because humanity itself is subject to sin; therefore it is illogical to blame Christians for something that is part of the human condition.

2. A note on terminology: In this paper, I use the term "enslaved" as a replacement for the term "slave," as well as use the term "enslaver" to replace the words "master" and "owner" in my own discussion and analysis. This is an active choice to separate the condition of being enslaved from the status of "being" a slave, since the latter is dehumanizing. However, when referencing Augustine's own words and views and ancient tropes (e.g., "the lazy slave" versus the "good slave"), I retain the original slave/master language. I continue to use the term "slavery" to denote the system in which people were forced to become enslaved interchangeably with the term "enslavement." For more information, see P. Gabrielle Foreman, et al. "Writing about Slavery/Teaching about Slavery: This Might Help," https://naacpculpeper.org/resources/writing-about-slavery-this-might-help/.

3. Scholarship that directly addresses Augustine's approach to sexual violence in *Letter* 111 with *City of God* is limited. Jennifer Collins-Elliot makes this connection in her forthcoming PhD dissertation, "'Bespattered with the Mud of Another's Lust: Rape and Physical Embodiment in Christian Literature of the 4th–6th centuries CE" (Florida State University), which builds upon an unpublished 2014 NAPS paper, "Blameless Wounds: Augustine on Bodies in Orthodoxy." See Jennifer Barry, "So Easy to Forget: Augustine's Treatment of the Sexually Violated in the City of God," *JAAR* 88.1 (2020): 235–253, 238n9 for more information about this connection. My

argument in this present paper, in attending to the aspect of enslavement involved in Augustine's rhetoric, nuances my own very brief take and use of *Letter* 111 in my dissertation, "Enslaveable: Citizenship & Slavery in Late Antiquity (Augustine's Letter 10*)," Drew University, 2019.

4. Laura Holt, "Original Sin," in *Augustine Through the Ages*, ed. Allan D. Fitzgerald (Grand Rapids: Eerdmans, 1999/2009), 607–615, 608.

5. See *Sermon* 151.7 (c. 419 CE); Peter Brown, *Augustine of Hippo* (Berkeley: University of California Press, 1967), 388–9.

6. Jaroslav Jan Pelikan, *The Christian Tradition: A History of the Development of Doctrine, Volume 1: The Emergence of the Catholic Tradition (100–600)*, (Chicago: University of Chicago Press, 1971), 280.

7. Holt, "Original Sin," 607.

8. See *City of God* 14.15.

9. Christy Cobb, *Slavery, Gender, Truth, and Power in Luke-Acts and Other Ancient Narratives* (New York: Palgrave Macmillan, 2019), 30.

10. In other words, the use of metaphors of enslavement to signpost the upheaval of hierarchy and power structures depends on the same hierarchy and power structures embedded in the metaphor for it to *make sense*, perhaps even requiring their continuation beyond the author's need of the metaphor. Here Cobb's use of the Bakhtinian carnivalesque to read Luke-Acts can help us think about how hierarchical structures persist in such "reversals," but that the moment of reversal still retains some power in the memory of that event as signposting the possibility of there being another option or way to the world as it is. See Cobb, *Slavery, Gender, Truth, and Power*, 69.

11. "The slave not knowing the will of his master, and doing actions worthy of being struck, will be flogged a few times; however, the slave knowing the will of his master, and doing actions worthy of being struck, will be flogged many times" (*Letter* 111, 2; citing Luke 12:47–48).

12. Note here that I am using Augustine's Latin translations of Luke instead of the original Greek text. This figure of the lazy enslaved person who has authority over others, but abuses said power (as a warning for those who are unprepared for the Parousia), is an interesting metaphor to contrast with the character of the "dishonest manager" found in the parable of Luke 16:1–8. Both enslaved people have managerial power but do something either unjustifiable in response to lack of pressure or abnormal in response to pressure. In Luke 12, the "lazy slave" abuses others and his "master's" interests because he feels he is unwatched/unmanaged (there is no pressure), while in Luke 16, the soon-to-be demoted "dishonest manager" to find ways to "cook the books" of his master's debtors in order to show he is not as poor a manager as previously assessed (a great deal of pressure). Note that Harrill connects this "dishonest manager" with the stock character of the parasite (*parasitus*) and clever slave (*servus callidus*), a trickster figure in ancient classical drama that is intended to invoke further insights by the audience that "play to ancient slave-holding tastes and sensibilities" (3–4). See J. Albert Harrill, *Slaves in the New Testament: Literary, Social, and Moral Dimensions* (Minneapolis: Fortress, 2006).

13. For an overview of this trope, see Joseph Vogt, *Ancient Slavery and the Ideal of Man* (trans. Thomas Wiedemann; Cambridge: Harvard University Press, 1975),

129–145. It is worth noting here that as Vogt explains it, prior to Christianity, the historical recognition of the loyalty of an enslaved person would have required him or her to show extreme loyalty to be mentioned in the literary record; for example, giving up opportunities to obtain freedom for providing evidence against their enslaver. After Christianity, the requirements to count as a faithful slave change in the literature, namely that she or he "does nothing particularly heroic, but merely performs his [or her] duties with devotion" (142–3).

14. Vogt, *Ancient Slavery and the Ideal of Man*, 143.

15. Robert Markus, *The End of Ancient Christianity* (Cambridge: Cambridge University Press, 1990), 88. Note also with Markus that there was a concerted effort to map Christian time onto existing forms of temporal structuring, namely seen through such actions as the appropriation of the Roman calendar festival time with replacement with Christian saints and holidays.

16. Markus, *The End of Ancient Christianity*, 90.

17. In particular, see Candida R. Moss, *Ancient Christian Martyrdom: Diverse Practices, Theologies, and Traditions* (New Haven: Yale University Press, 2012); Harold A. Drake, "Intolerance, Religious Violence and Political Legitimacy in Late Antiquity," *JAAR* 79.1 (2011): 193–235; Elizabeth A. Castelli, *Martyrdom and Memory: Early Christian Culture Making* (New York: Columbia University Press, 2004).

18. Note as Moss shows that the title of martyr was not fixed or unified but could be applied to those who have not technically died such as Thecla. Moss reminds us that ancient "usage," not contemporary presumptions about martyrs with respect to death or voluntary choice should be the guideline for understanding martyrdom (Moss, *Ancient Christian Martyrdom*, 4). This is important when considering the sexually violated in Letter 111, who are framed as not being killed and did not choose what happened to them.

19. For example, interreligious conflict in late antiquity can be seen in Christian appropriation of other religious spaces and places such as temples, as well as enacting violence upon material culture, such as defacing and adding crosses to statues.

20. In the beginning of *Letter* 111 (1), Augustine references the violence of the Donatists and Circumcellions with respect to attacks upon orthodox clerics, robbing, and forced rebaptisms in order to explain to Victorian that this is not simply barbarian violence to the empire, but a widespread reality of the age itself. Concerning Augustine's competition with the Donatists with respect to imperial acceptance, see Brent D. Shaw, *Sacred Violence: African Christians and Sectarian Hatred in the Age of Augustine* (Cambridge: Cambridge University Press, 2011).

21. For more on this phenomenon of the absence of the enslaved in the archaeological record and how to reframe our approaches to it in order to see their presence, see Sandra R. Joshel and Lauren Hackworth Petersen, *The Material Life of Roman Slaves* (New York: Cambridge University Press, 2014).

22. It also implies literacy of enslaved people within the household in order to heed the warning, as well as perhaps serving a performative function for elite visitors reading the sign, namely signposting the enslaver's ability to control his household by verbal command AND force, if the latter is necessary.

23. Charles H. Talbert, *Reading Luke: A Literary and Theological Commentary on the Third Gospel*, Reading the New Testament 3 (rev.; Macon: Smyth & Helwys, 2002), 160.

24. Talbert, *Reading Luke*, 159.

25. Talbert, *Reading Luke*, 160.

26. This fits in with De Bruyn's (1999) observation that Augustine used biblical passages about paternal discipline to argue that even the faithful must "accept misfortune and injustice as salutary correction intended to prepare them for the inheritance of eternal life." See Theodore S. De Bruyn, "Flogging a Son: The Emergence of the *pater flagellans* in Latin Christian Discourse," *JECS* 7.2 (1999): 249–290, 264 and 266n105's reference to *Letter* 111.

27. On reading the original scene from Daniel 3 satirically, see David M. Valeta, *Lions and Ovens and Visions: A Satirical Reading of Daniel 1–6* (Sheffield: Sheffield Phoenix, 2008).

28. Kathy L. Gaca, "Girls, Women, and the Significance of Sexual Violence in Ancient Warfare," in *Sexual Violence in Conflict Zones: From the Ancient World to the Era of Human Rights*, ed. Elizabeth D. Heineman (Philadelphia: University of Pennsylvania Press, 2011).

29. Craig A. Williams, *Roman Homosexuality: Ideologies of Masculinity in Classical Antiquity* (New York: Oxford University Press, 1999), 104.

30. Jonathan Walters, "Invading the Roman Body: Manliness and Impenetrability in Roman Thought," in *Roman Sexualities*, eds. Judith P. Hallet and Marilyn B. Skinner (Princeton: Princeton University Press, 1997), 38–9.

31. Williams, *Roman Homosexuality*, 99.

32. Noel Lenski, "Captivity and Romano-Barbarian Exchange," in *Romans, Barbarians, and the Transformation of the Roman World: Cultural Interaction and the Creation of Identity in Late Antiquity*, eds. Ralph W. Mathisen and Danuta Shanzer (London: Routledge, 2011), 186.

33. I explore how Augustine's frustration with the drain of the church paying ransoms in *Letter* 10* may be a potential sign of a larger human trafficking ring that may have incentivized "capture for ransom" in my dissertation (81–94, especially 82n136).

34. Lenski, "Captivity and Romano-Barbarian Exchange," 186–8.

35. William Warwick Buckland, *The Roman Law of Slavery: The Condition of the Slave in Private Law from Augustus to Justinian* (Cambridge: Cambridge University Press, 1908; repr. 2010), 1.

36. Virgins of God became an occupation for women in the late antique church, a counterbalance to exclusion from male-dominated positions such as bishop, elder, and deacon. As such, these women's dedication to chastity on behalf of the church gave them power and agency, offering an alternative to normative expectations for Roman women (i.e., producing legitimate heirs and helping families network through marriage). For the connection between agency and modesty for Christian women in late antiquity, see Kate Wilkinson, *Women and Modesty in Late Antiquity* (Cambridge: Cambridge University Press, 2015), 1–2.

37. Note that swords were considered a masculine form of suicide, compared with the noose or poison. See Nicole Loraux, *Tragic Ways of Killing a Woman* (trans. Anthony Forster; Cambridge: Harvard University Press, 1987), 17. Cf. Sandra R. Joshel's discussion of the sword as a metaphor for sexual penetration; "The Body Female and the Body Politics: Livy's Lucretia and Verginia," in *Pornography and Representation in Greece and Rome*, ed. Amy Richlin (New York: Oxford University Press, 1992), 120.

38. Joshel, "The Body Female and the Body Politics," 116. Italics mine.

39. Dennis Trout, "Re-Textualizing Lucretia: Cultural Subversion in the *City of God*," *JECS* 2.1 (1994): 53–70, especially 63–66.

40. Trout, "Re-Textualizing Lucretia," 64–65. See *City of God* 1.28.

41. Virginia Burrus, *Saving Shame: Martyrs, Saints, and Other Abject Subjects* (Philadelphia: University of Pennsylvania Press, 2008), 125–126, 129.

42. Barry, "So Easy to Forget," 238.

43. Barry, "So Easy to Forget," 238.

44. Virginia Burrus, "An Immoderate Feast: Augustine Reads John's Apocalypse," *AugStud* 30.2 (1999): 183–194, 192.

45. Barry, "So Easy to Forget," 245.

46. Note also the lack of the term *stuprum* (violation) in *Letter* 111, a word that Augustine disassociates with anticipated language of force.

47. Examples include historical accounts of Roman enslavement, biblical references, and use of metaphorical language related to slavery (e.g., being a slave to sin). It is only at the end of his magnum opus where Augustine connects general enslavement as a sign of humanity's sinfulness in the world that is "justly imposed" because the "first cause of slavery, therefore, is sin, with the result that man is made subject to man by the bondage of this condition, which can only happen by the judgement of God" (*City of God* 19.15).

48. Markus, *The End of Ancient Christianity*, 53.

WORKS CITED

Critical Edition

Monteverde, Franco, ed. *Aurelii Augustini, Opera Omnia, Tutte le opere*, 45 volumes. Rome: Nouva Biblioteca Agostiniana & Città Nouva, 1967).

Secondary Sources

Barry, Jennifer. "So Easy to Forget: Augustine's Treatment of the Sexually Violated in the City of God." *Journal of the American Academy of Religion* 88.1 (2020): 235–253.

Brown, Peter. *Augustine of Hippo*. Berkeley: University of California Press, 1967.

Buckland, William Warwick. *The Roman Law of Slavery: The Condition of the Slave in Private Law from Augustus to Justinian*. Cambridge: Cambridge University Press, 1908. Repr., 2010.

Burrus, Virginia. "An Immoderate Feast: Augustine Reads John's Apocalypse." *Augustinian Studies* 30.2 (1999): 183–194.

———. *Saving Shame: Martyrs, Saints, and Other Abject Subjects*. Philadelphia: University of Pennsylvania Press, 2008.

Castelli, Elizabeth A. *Martyrdom and Memory: Early Christian Culture Making*. New York: Columbia University Press, 2004.

Cobb, Christy. *Slavery, Gender, Truth, and Power in Luke-Acts and Other Ancient Narratives*. New York: Palgrave Macmillan, 2019.

De Bruyn, Theodore S. "Flogging a Son: The Emergence of the *pater flagellans* in Latin Christian Discourse," *Journal of Early Christian Studies* 7.2 (1999): 249–290.

Drake, Harold A. "Intolerance, Religious Violence and Political Legitimacy in Late Antiquity." *Journal of the American Academy of Religion* 79.1 (2011): 193–235.

Gaca, Kathy L. "Girls, Women, and the Significance of Sexual Violence in Ancient Warfare." Pages 73–88 in *Sexual Violence in Conflict Zones: From the Ancient World to the Era of Human Rights*. Edited by Elizabeth D. Heineman. Philadelphia: University of Pennsylvania Press, 2011.

Harrill, J. Albert. *Slaves in the New Testament: Literary, Social, and Moral Dimensions*. Minneapolis: Fortress, 2006.

Hartman, Midori E. "Enslaveable: Citizenship & Slavery in Late Antiquity (Augustine's Letter 10*)," Ph.D. diss., Drew Theological School, 2019.

Holt, Laura. "Original Sin." Pages 607–615 in *Augustine Through the Ages*. Edited by Allan D. Fitzgerald. Grand Rapids: Eerdmans, 1999/2009.

Joshel, Sandra R. "The Body Female and the Body Politics: Livy's Lucretia and Verginia." Pages 112–130 in *Pornography and Representation in Greece and Rome*. Edited by Amy Richlin. New York: Oxford University Press, 1992.

Joshel, Sandra R., and Lauren Hackworth Petersen, *The Material Life of Roman Slaves*. Cambridge: Cambridge University Press, 2014.

Lenski, Noel. "Captivity and Romano-Barbarian Exchange." Pages 185–198 in *Romans, Barbarians, and the Transformation of the Roman World: Cultural Interaction and the Creation of Identity in Late Antiquity*. Edited by Ralph W. Mathisen and Danuta Shanzer. London: Routledge, 2011.

Levine, Amy-Jill. "The Gospel According to Luke," In *The Jewish Annotated New Testament*. 2nd edition. Edited by Amy-Jill Levine and Marc Zvi Brettler. New York: Oxford University Press, 2017.

Loraux, Nicole. *Tragic Ways of Killing a Woman*. Translated by Anthony Forster. Cambridge: Harvard University Press, 1987.

Markus, Robert. *The End of Ancient Christianity*. Cambridge: Cambridge University Press, 1990.

Moss, Candida R. *Ancient Christian Martyrdom: Diverse Practices, Theologies, and Traditions*. New Haven: Yale University Press, 2012.

Pelikan, Jaroslav Jan. *The Christian Tradition: A History of the Development of Doctrine, Volume 1: The Emergence of the Catholic Tradition (100–600)*. Chicago: University of Chicago Press, 1971.

Shaw, Brent D. *Sacred Violence: African Christians and Sectarian Hatred in the Age of Augustine*. Cambridge: Cambridge University Press, 2011.

Talbert, Charles H. *Reading Luke: A Literary and Theological Commentary on the Third Gospel*. Reading the New Testament 3. Rev. Macon: Smyth & Helwys, 2002.

Trout, Dennis. "Re-Textualizing Lucretia: Cultural Subversion in the *City of God*." *Journal of Early Christian Studies* 2.1 (1994): 53–70.

Valeta, David M. *Lions and Ovens and Visions: A Satirical Reading of Daniel 1–6*. Sheffield: Sheffield Phoenix, 2008.

Vogt, Joseph. *Ancient Slavery and the Ideal of Man*. Translated by Thomas Wiedemann. Cambridge: Harvard University Press, 1975.

Walters, Jonathan. "Invading the Roman Body: Manliness and Impenetrability in Roman Thought." Pages 29–43 in *Roman Sexualities*. Edited by Judith P. Hallet and Marilyn B. Skinner. Princeton: Princeton University Press, 1997.

Wilkinson, Kate. *Women and Modesty in Late Antiquity*. Cambridge: Cambridge University Press, 2015.

Williams, Craig A. *Roman Homosexuality: Ideologies of Masculinity in Classical Antiquity*. New York: Oxford University Press, 1999.

Chapter 7

Virginity, Bestiality, and Virtue in Sozomen's Account of the Attack of the Consecrated Virgins of Heliopolis

LaToya M. Leary Francis

In his *Ecclesiastical History*, Sozomen recounts a cruel "act of barbarity" that led to the tortuous death of Christian consecrated virgins. In the text, the inhabitants of Heliopolis assault "sacred virgins" by stripping the women naked and subjecting them to public exposure, hurling insults at them, shaving and ripping them open, and implanting them with food and allowing them to be eaten alive by swine. This account prompts a number of questions. Was it an attack that was perpetrated by Jews, Pagans, and/or Christians who were not deemed "Christian" on account of Jewish or non-Catholic practices? How is this act of violence supposed to function? Are the victims of Sozomen's account sexually violated by pigs? Does this account have any historical roots or is it a fabrication? Why the use of pigs?

This chapter will examine this incident with these questions in mind. I contend that Sozomen's account of the violence perpetrated against the sacred virgins is a creative project wherein Sozomen employs rhetoric to further exacerbate the differences between Christians and Pagans. He does this by casting pagans as bestial and by presenting the barbarity of the pagans as threatening to a vulnerable church. I will support this argument in three stages. I commence with a detailed description of the incident as reported by Sozomen, along with a brief discussion on how this account differs from the reports of Gregory of Nazianzus, Theodoret's *Ecclesiastical History*, and the *Chronicon Paschale*. The discussion will then shift to considerations regarding the rhetorical use of text. More specifically, this section will compare the features of Sozomen's account with other accounts of this incident in order to think about how this account expresses Christian views of non-Christians and pagan views of Christians. I conclude by discussing potential tropes that Sozomen might have employed in this account, and formulate some suggested avenues for future research.

DESCRIPTION OF THE INCIDENT

Sozomen's account of this incident begins with a note concerning the heightened cruelty displayed by the Heliopolitans compared to the inhabitants of Gaza and Alexandria. He offers a trigger warning by stating that the incident is so barbarous that it would lack credibility had there not been the testimonies of witnesses. Sozomen then reports the incident by first identifying the victims as "holy virgins who had never been looked upon by the multitude" (*Hist. eccl.* 5.10.5–7).[1] The first act of barbarity that he mentions is the stripping and exposed nudity of the virgin women. After the virgins were stripped and exposed to the multitude, undisclosed violent acts were inflicted upon them. These acts were followed by the shaving and violent opening of their bodies. The bodies of the virgins were then implanted with food and fed to swine, who were unable to distinguish between their ordinary food and human entrails. Sozomen concludes his report of this incident with an explanation concerning his opinion of why this violent act was perpetrated. Sozomen sees it as revenge for Constantine's abolition of a tradition that required the prostitution of virgin women on the eve of their marriage.

Sozomen's account of the atrocity against the virgins at Heliopolis is in three other sources: Gregory of Nazianzus's *Oration* 4.86–87, Theodoret's *Ecclesiastical History* 3.7.1, and the *Chronicon Paschale* 362. All of these sources present accounts of the murder of virgins and the consumption of their bodies by swine. When compared to Sozomen's report, these accounts vary in terms of location, rationale, and the nature of the violence experienced by the consecrated virgins. These variances are essential for understanding what Sozomen might have attempted to communicate in his entry.

Like Sozomen, Gregory of Nazianzus locates the incident in Heliopolis. Theodoret and the *Chronicon Paschale* place it in Ascalon/Gaza. Hans Carol Teitler argues that both Theodoret and the *Chronicon Paschale* employed Gregory of Nazianzus as their source and "read their source less than carefully."[2] Teitler uses Sozomen's reference to his grandfather's rearing in Gaza (*Hist. eccl.* 5.15.14–17) to contend that "Sozomen knew the history of Gaza too well to confuse Heliopolis and Gaza."[3] This suggests that Sozomen also employed Gregory of Nazianzus as a source but did not misunderstand Gregory's writing due to his knowledge of the history and landscape of Gaza.[4]

WHO WERE THE PERPETRATORS?

Sozomen's vague identification of the perpetrators of this atrocity leaves room for speculation. One can ask: Who are "the inhabitants of Heliopolis?" Are they Jewish, "Pagan," or Christians? Is Sozomen's vagueness intentional? Is the phrase "the inhabitants of Heliopolis" some form of a blanket identification or filler purposed to represent the enemy of Christians who might employ this text for their own means? While Sozomen is unclear in his identification of the perpetrators at the onset of his account, he obliquely identifies the culprits as pagan, and he suggests that this act of barbarity was an act of retaliation against the prohibition of a pagan custom:

> I am convinced that the citizens perpetrated this barbarity against the holy virgins from motives of revenge, on account of the abolition of the ancient custom of yielding up virgins to prostitution, when on the eve of marriage to those to whom they had been betrothed. This custom was prohibited by a law enacted by Constantine, after he had destroyed the temple of Venus at Heliopolis, and erected a church upon its ruins. (*Hist. eccl.* 5.10.5–7)

Sozomen's rationale is interesting for a number of reasons. I focus here on two: first, the "ancient custom" that was abolished by Constantine, and second, the destruction of the temple of Venus in Heliopolis. Both of these references are essential, as they work to expunge the idea that "the inhabitants of Heliopolis" could be a filler for any enemy outside of the pagans. Sozomen's rationale divulges his exposure to a number of Greek and Roman historians, including, but not limited, to Herodotus, Strabo, and Eusebius of Caesarea. Sozomen is clearly using Eusebius's *Life of Constantine* to further identify the offenders of this incident as pagans. In the *Life of Constantine*, Eusebius mentions the destruction of the temple of Venus in Heliopolis and the erection of the first Christian church. As in Sozomen's account, the destruction of the temple of Venus follows the abolition of the custom that resulted in the "unlawful commerce of women and adulterous intercourse" (*Vit. Const.* 3.55–58). While Eusebius lacks specifics concerning what sounds like some form of sacred prostitution, Sozomen specifically identifies this custom as entailing the prostitution of virgin women before marriage. Could this be a reference to the ritual prostitution in which the Greeks participated in the worship of Aphrodite?[5] Sozomen's text might suggest that this was the case. Both Sozomen and Eusebius allude to this custom as aged: Sozomen specifically calls the custom "ancient," while Eusebius mentions the abolition of the custom as a means of purging the empire of "any hidden vestiges of error" that might have still existed (*Vit. Const.* 3.55). In an attempt to present their cultures as superior to the licentious cultures of neighboring territories,

Herodotus and Strabo repeatedly mention the ritual practices of the worshippers of Aphrodite. In his history, Herodotus records:

> The Babylonians have one custom in the highest degree abominable. Every woman who is a native of the country is obliged once in her life to attend at the temple of Venus, and prostitute herself to a stranger. (*Hist.* 1.199)

In worship to Aphrodite/Venus, the woman must tie a string around her head and wait for a stranger to throw a coin into her lap (the coin will later go into the temple's treasury) and lead her away from the temple to "enjoy her person" (*Hist.* 1.199). Herodotus emphasizes that this ritual act is performed once in every female worshipper's life, regardless of social status. He notes that the inhabitants of Cyprus participated in the same ritual act. Like Herodotus, Strabo provides an account of the one-time sacred prostitution of Babylonian women (*Geogr.* 16.1.20). Strabo's account is shortened, but nonetheless, comparable to Herodotus's.[6] Strabo and Herodotus mention additional reports of Babylonian, Armenian and Lydian prostitution. These accounts discuss what might be deemed sacred prostitution as a multiplicitous act for both dedicated male and female slaves, as well as daughters before marriage (Strabo, *Geogr.* 11.14.16), a commercially minded professional enterprise (*Geogr.* 12.3.36), and an economic act purposed to help financially destitute women collect a decent dowry before marriage (*Geogr.* 11.16; Herodotus, *Hist.* 1.93).

While both Strabo and Herodotus lack specificity concerning the nature of these later accounts, epigraphical evidence suggests that Lydian prostitution was indeed religious. Bonnie MacLachlan employs the work of William Ramsay to describe a surviving Lydian inscription that suggests that the custom of dedicating young girls to the temple as sacred prostitutes may have been in practice well into the Roman period. Both MacLachlan and Ramsay argue that this tradition might have been practiced as late as the third century CE.[7]

This might very well support both Constantine's supposed fear that "hidden vestiges of error might still exist" and Sozomen's contention that the violence perpetrated against the Christian virgins was in response to the abolition of a custom that called for the sacred prostitution of virgin women (so Eusebius, *Vit. Const.*, 3.55). The historical prevalence of customs that mandated sacred prostitution in the fourth century remains a conjecture, but Sozomen's allusion to these ancient customs solidifies the identity of "the inhabitants of Heliopolis": the perpetrators of the violence in Sozomen's account are indeed pagans. There is no question in the accounts of Gregory of Nazianzus, Theodoret and the *Chronicon Paschale*: the incident in all three accounts is located in chapters that discuss the acts that were perpetrated by pagans against the Christians.[8]

RHETORICAL USE OF THE INCIDENT

This incident is lacking the evidence necessary to speak absolutely of its historicity. One can, however, consider potential uses of this text: namely, one can ask questions regarding how specific elements within the text communicate how Christians might have communicated the threat of pagan violence and how components within the text disclose Christian views concerning pagans. The discussion below considers these things by comparing the features of Sozomen's report with the accounts of Gregory of Nazianzus, Theodoret, and the *Chronicon Paschale*.

As mentioned before, Sozomen begins his report of the violence that occurred in Heliopolis by emphasizing the barbarity of the account. Sozomen views this act as displaying "greater cruelty" compared to the violence of the inhabitants of Gaza and Alexandria. He alludes to the crime as being so cruel, that it is unbelievable and accentuates its credibility by claiming that the act was corroborated by witnesses. The report of the actual violence commences with the first violation: the stripping of "the holy virgins who had never been looked upon by the multitude" (*Hist. eccl.* 5.10.5–7). His account then reports two other bodily violations perpetrated against the sacred virgins: the shaving and mutilation of their bodies and the subjection of the virgins to sexual violation and consumption by swine. The identification of the victims as virgins and the report of the victims' involuntary loss of virginity or rape seems to work as Sozomen's support for his contention regarding the heightened cruelty of the Heliopolitans. Sozomen's trigger warning is essential to this text, as it sets the stage for a dichotomous characterization of Christians and Pagans.

Like Sozomen, Gregory of Nazianzus identifies the incident at Heliopolis as exceedingly cruel.[9] Gregory's account, nevertheless, not only mentions the shameful exposure of the virgin victims who were "superior to the world, and unpolluted almost by even the eyes of males," but it also indicates that the bodies of the virgins were feasted upon by both humans and swine. Gregory's account is rhetorically gruesome and extremely detailed in respect to the act of cannibalism. The details of his account prompt valid questions concerning the nature of the cannibalism divulged—questions regarding the literal nature of the text. Is Gregory attempting to present a report of literal or figurative cannibalism? Are the inhabitants of Heliopolis tasting the sacred virgins with their eyes? Is this a figurative representation of the exposure and derision of the sacred virgins? While Gregory's detailed account can be a rhetorical move to figuratively display the effects of the violence of the exposure and derision perpetrated against the Christian church, Gregory includes details that implicate the portrayal of a literal act of cannibalism. He reports that the pagans "gorged themselves with their raw livers" (*Orat.* 4.87). Furthermore, he suggests that these acts were abominable and strategic on the part of the pagans. The Pagans are not only mindless in their inhumanity, but they are strategic in their attacks on Christians. Like Sozomen's sexualized account, Gregory's report further accentuates the barbarous nature of the pagans in contrast to the saintliness of the Christians.

Gregory's account, however, is interesting for reasons beyond his detailed references to cannibalism: his account lacks allusions to some form of sexual violation by swine. He is also extremely vague about how or where the virgins are ripped and cut open. His references to the consumption of their raw livers suggests that they were disemboweled, an understanding found also in the accounts of Theodoret and the *Chronicon Paschale* further emphasize this understanding. Sozomen's account, however, omits any suggestion of cannibalism.[10] This omission is quite curious, and prompts questions concerning both its omission of allusions to cannibalism and Sozomen's additional accentuation of the virginity of the victims and their bestial sexual violation. Sozomen's insinuation that this incident was an act of vengeance for the abolition of the ancient custom of sacred prostitution might suggest that the extreme cruelty of the violence perpetrated against the virgins at Heliopolis is much bigger than their exposure and molestation: the exposure and molestation of the virgins might allude to the Christian virgin's forced participation in idolatry via ritual sacrifice. While this claim is speculative, Sozomen's knowledge of allusions to the custom of the worshipers of Aphrodite/Venus, along with his decision not to record the human cannibalism within Gregory's account could suggest that Sozomen is employing the ancient custom of ritual prostitution as a means of highlighting the bestial nature of pagans in contrast to Christians and emphasizing pagan practices as threatening to Christians. In this way, Sozomen chooses a group that is viewed as one of the most vulnerable, and employs pornographic language as a means of portraying the pagans as barbaric in their intentional violation of that group. The pagans calculatingly strip the virgins of their clothing to visually molest them, and later they subject them to further violation via forced sexual engagement with swine. The ritual prostitution that is presented in Sozomen's account differs significantly from the ancient custom that is reported by Herodotus and Strabo: in lieu of a stranger and later their betrothed, the Christian virgins are given over to swine and then to death. This variant emphasizes both the impiety of the pagans and Sozomen's rationale for the perpetration of the incident: the virgins' torturous death entailed some form of ritual prostitution and punishment for transgression against the gods.[11]

Sozomen drafts his report of this incident to produce a response from the reader. Upon reading the account, the reader is expected to identify with the horrid experience of the sacred virgins and to respond by anathematizing pagan practices as threatening, especially to the most vulnerable of Christians. David Frankfurter supports this contention in his acknowledgement that Sozomen's account of the violence perpetrated against the sacred virgins employs female nudity as a means of heightening the monstrous effects of the incident and thus allows for the punishment of the sexually excited:

> The nude female, source of excitement, must be framed clearly as monstrous or as suffering at monsters' claws in order to sanction the erotic gaze and even allow masochistic identification with her suffering. Titillation itself becomes confused with anxious repudiation, leading to those scenes of sado-eroticism that punish viciously those who sexually excite the reader for eliciting that excitement.[12]

Sozomen's use of pornographic scenery is interesting. The identification of the victims both of this incident and of the incidents that precede and follow the account of the murder of the sacred virgins, however, may point to additional uses of the text. These supplementary uses might be better captured by focusing on the consistencies within the accounts of Sozomen, Gregory, Theodoret, and the *Chronicon Paschale*, namely, emphasis on the virginal state of the victims, the use of swine to consume the bodies, and a context that features violence against church leadership.

THREATS AGAINST CHRISTIAN LEADERSHIP

Virginity was instrumental in shifting the status of women in antique Christianity; it was employed as a means of overcoming the perceived innate sexual nature of the female gender. Through the embrace of virginity, women shifted into a liminal position, whereby women were unavoidably female in body, but male in their display of virtue in their renunciation of "the world."

Karen Jo Torjesen contends that virginity was a means of gaining autonomy in response to the subordination of the status of women during the institutionalization of the church. She argues that women assumed leadership roles in the early Church and identifies the Christian scandal as the diminished status endured by Christian women after the institutionalization of Christianity. She employs the writings of Augustine and Jerome, that associate virginity with a "return to the original state of human life," and identifies virginity as a mode by which women "gained control over their own sexuality."[13]

Athanasius of Alexandria further emphasizes the relationship between virginity and original sin in his *Apologia ad Constantium*. For Athanasius, virginity is a state that was offered to all human beings by the sacrifice of Jesus. It is a choice that is admired and deemed virtuous by both Christians and pagans:

> The Son of God, our Lord and Savior Jesus Christ, having become man for our sakes . . . in addition to all His other benefits bestowed this also upon us, that we should possess upon the earth, in the state of virginity, a picture of the holiness of the angels. Accordingly, such as have attained this virtue, the Catholic Church has been accustomed to call these *the brides of Christ*. And the heathen who see them express their admiration of them as the temples of the Word. (*Apol. Const.* 33.49)[14]

Athanasius accentuates virginity as entailing a change in both form and ownership: the Church characterizes Christian virgins as "brides of Christ" and the pagans identify these virgins as "temples of the Word." Brown furthers this portrayal by employing the work of Eusebius of Emesa to highlight the virgin's reclassification "as a human *ex voto:* she was no longer a woman; she had become a 'sacred vessel dedicated to the Lord.'"[15]

Could this be Sozomen's rationale behind the decision to feature consecrated virgins as the victims of the heinous violence? Could the violation of the sacred virgins in Heliopolis be likened to the destruction of Christian property? If so, his use of sexual imagery in the victimization of the consecrated virgins intimates a regression in the state of both the virgins and the Church at large. The classification "holy virgins" in Sozomen's account thus acts as a placeholder for the Christian Church. The pagans of Sozomen's account victimize the Christian virgins as a means of signaling the defilement and reversion of the status of the Christian Church. The ritual offering of the virgins becomes an offering of the Church to the gods of paganism. Sozomen, Gregory Nazianzus, Theodoret, and the *Chronicon Paschale* emphasize this in the accounts that precede and follow the report of the violence perpetrated against the sacred virgins.

In all of these reports, the virgins are likened to sacred property. Carolyn Connor confirms this objectified view of virgins in her description of ascetic women in late antiquity. She compares the dedication of a virgin to the freezing of community assets and quotes Brown, who likens women to wealth that "were there to circulate."[16] Sacred virgins in this case are objectified in that they are "seen as part of the wealth controlled by the early church."[17] These accounts communicate the existence of a heightened fear concerning the desecration of Christian "property." In Sozomen's and Gregory of Nazianzus's accounts, this includes the bodies of the sacred virgins. As a much later text that was most likely influenced by the ecclesiastical history of Theodoret, the *Chronicon Paschale* extends concern of defilement by including references to the exhumation and scattering of the remains of John the Baptist and Saint Patropolis. The context of these references suggests that the remains of both John the Baptist and Saint Patropolis should be included in the list of Christian "property." In fact, the classification as icon can be extended even to the bodies of the bishops and priests within all of these accounts. The violent acts within each of these accounts can, therefore, be interpreted as tools that communicate a threat against the sanctity and distinguishing nature of the Christian Church. Sozomen's sexualization of the incident regarding the violence perpetrated against the virgins at Heliopolis strongly emphasizes this threat. The diminished status and deadly end experienced by the virgins at Heliopolis acts as an exhortation for Christians to stand their ground and boldly refuse to be common. Sozomen's presentation of Julian's impiety showcases a direct threat to the distinct identity of the Christian Church.

This becomes much clearer when considering the dichotomy that Sozomen presents in his account; namely, the saintliness of the Christians compared to the bestiality of the pagan multitude. Sozomen's rationale for the violent actions—vengeance for the abolition of a custom that legalized the prostitution of virgin girls—compares the sacred nature of the Christian virgins, "who had never been looked upon by the multitude," to the pagan virgins whose prostitution this ancient custom legalizes. Sozomen furthers this by employing the sensational nature of violence against virgins to casts the perpetrators as callous, heartless, and inhuman. The sexualization of his account further dehumanizes the pagan perpetrators; the pagans not only strip the virgins of their shame, but they violate their bodies and subject them to bestiality. Gregory of Nazianzus further accentuates this dichotomy in his identification of this violent acts as spectacle. After reporting on the human feasting of the livers of the Christian virgins, Gregory says that:

> others, sprinkling the yet panting entrails with swine's food, and letting in the fiercer sort of swine, exhibited a show—and what a show!—to behold the flesh eaten up, and chewed together with the barley—a food not to be approached, and then for the first time seen, or even heard of. (*Orat.* 4.87)

Gregory characterizes the violence experienced by the sacred virgins as an abominable spectacle that was not previous seen or heard of. He later suggests that this act of violence (and others) was perpetrated to feed Julian's demons. The violence reported in Gregory's *Oration* 4 is a treatise concerning the impiety of Julian. The mindless acts of the inhabitants of Heliopolis further emphasize the immorality of Julian. As a result, we can surmise that the title "sacred virgins" is not the only placeholder in Gregory or Sozomen's report of this incident. The pagan perpetrators are also placeholders, multitude standing in for Julian. In light of this, Gregory's account of the violence perpetrated against the virgins of Heliopolis not only highlights the dichotomous relationship between Christians and Pagans, but it also contrasts the mannerisms of Christian leadership and Pagan leadership. The same can be said of Theodoret's *Ecclesiastical History* and the *Chronicon Paschale*. All four of these accounts present details that accentuates the dichotomy between the sacred Christians and the inhuman Pagans. Sozomen's account stands out due to its strong pornographic elements. Whether through the use of a sensational topic or via allusions to Christian forced participation in pagan practices, Sozomen creatively uses violence against virgin bodies to "think with."

POTENTIAL TROPES

Thus far, this chapter has explored variances and consistencies in the accounts concerning the atrocious treatment of the virgins at Heliopolis. As shown, Sozomen (and the other chroniclers) employs a number of techniques as a means of communicating the threat that pagan violence poses against Christians. There are, however, a myriad of other potential tropes that could be at play in these texts. This section will include brief entries regarding these potential tropes. I introduce these tropes here as a means of offering suggestions for future work.

Disembowelment

Disembowelment is referenced in all of the accounts of this incident. It is also featured in Theodoret and the *Chronicon Paschale*'s record of Cyril's persecution. While the use of disembowelment might simply work to emphasize the inhuman nature of the pagans, the consistent use of disembowelment might allude to something more. It is common knowledge that the act of disembowelment was common in other ancient traditions, including, but not limited to the traditional method of ritual sacrifice and execution of the samurai of feudal Japan (seppuku),[18] punishment for treason in England (thirteenth century–nineteenth century),[19] the supposed punishment for removing the bark from a tree in fifteenth-century Germany,[20] and the self-inflicted punishment for adultery by two women in sixteenth-century Germany. While these accounts are much later than the disembowelment reported in the chronicles referenced in this chapter, validation of disembowelment as a common practice or punishment in Greco-Roman (or even Persian and/or Babylonian) accounts could lead to profitable investigations on the use of disembowelment as a rhetorical theme in Christian sources.

Human Sacrifice and Cannibalism

The disembowelment of both the sacred virgins and Cyril leads to the act of cannibalism in the accounts of Gregory of Nazianzus, Theodoret, and the *Chronicon Paschale*. Theodoret and the author of the *Chronicon Pascale* actually include a small anecdote regarding the consumption of Cyril's liver and the adverse effects faced by its consumer(s). Gregory specifically identifies the livers of the virgins as the object of consumption. This prompts questions concerning human sacrifice and the divinatory practice of haruspicy/extispicy. It is well-known that extispicy was practiced in the ancient world. The practice, however, entailed the examination of the livers/entrails of sacrificial animals. It would be interesting to examine writings that discuss ancient practices (particularly ancient Near Eastern and Greco-Roman practices) of extispicy for associations with human sacrifice, legal executions, and/or suicides. If such references can be located in the works of Herodotus or Strabo, it could be further argued that Gregory of Nazianzus or perhaps even Theodoret employed Herodotus or Strabo as a means of boundary making in their reports of both the violence perpetrated against Cyril and the virgins at Heliopolis.

Ritual Sacrifice, Sacred Prostitution, and the Economy

As noted, Sozomen's sexualization and references to the heightened brutality of the violence perpetrated against the virgins at Heliopolis suggests that the barbarity experienced by the sacred virgins resulted in a physical and spiritual change in status. Sozomen's account not only involves the exposure and disembowelment of the sacred virgins, but also suggests some form of sexual violation. His rationale for pagan violence—Constantine's abolition of the ancient custom that mandate the forced prostitution of virgins on the eve of their marriage—might suggests that the account is insinuating that the Christian virgins were subjected to forced participation in the ancient custom abolished by Constantine. This contention prompts questions concerning the use of animals in the sacrifice and the death that followed. It would be helpful to locate additional accounts where forced ritual prostitution occurs where the victim(s) (whether male or female are within or outside of the community in question) is/are subjected to sexual acts with beasts.

The accounts of Herodotus and Strabo (noted earlier) regarding the practices of the Babylonians, Armenians, and Lydians prompt questions about the relation between ritual prostitution and the economy. My question here specifically concerns the supposed effect of the abolition of ritual prostitution and its association with violence and the economy. In "Sacred Prostitution and Aphrodite," MacLachlan emphasizes adherence to the ancient custom of sacred prostitution to Aphrodite/Venus for the sake of fruitful management of the nation. She mentions the account of Pompeius Trogus, where he reports the effects of a lapsed vow to Venus.[21] While in a time of war, the Locrians vowed that if they won the war they would prostitute their virgin daughters on the annual feast-day dedicated to Venus. After winning the battle, however, the Locrians lapsed on their vow and experience economic and political hardship as a result. During the reign of Dionysius the Second, however, adherence to the sacred prostitution of virgins returned on account of Dionysius's deceptive employment of the custom to require the sacred prostitution of Locrian virgins for his own benefit. While manipulating the ritual practices of the cult of Aphrodite/Venus, Dionysius maintained control over Locri for six years. MacLachlan sees this turn of events as an example of what happens when the divine power of Aphrodite/Venus is obstructed. She says, "the women kept their virginity and lost the city. Dionysius took control of the city and held it for six years. Aphrodite had the last word."[22]

When considering the relationship between political and economic protection and the ritual prostitution of virgin women, one cannot help but to consider whether the violence perpetrated against the virgins of Heliopolis is a means of appeasing the presumed anger of the gods (in this case Aphrodite/Venus). Are the Christian virgins forced into some form of sacred prostitution as a means of restoring the power of the cult of Aphrodite/Venus? Is there support for economic hardship that might be useful in forging a relationship between poverty and ritual violence? Is the forced ritual prostitution of the Christian virgins in Sozomen's account an example of Aphrodite/Venus having the last word?

CONCLUSION

This chapter has engaged Sozomen's account concerning the torturous death of the consecrated virgins at Heliopolis. Using reports of this incident in the works of other chroniclers, I have attempted to fill the gaps of unclear allusions in Sozomen's account. This chapter argues that the perpetrators of this incident were pagans who were retaliating against the imperial decrees that prohibited participation in pagan rituals and justified the destruction of pagan temples. This chapter also contends that Sozomen's sexualization of this account employs rhetoric to amplify the dichotomous characterization of pagans and Christians and to exacerbate the threat that pagan violence poses against the identity and distinction of the Christian Church. The consecrated virgins of Sozomen's account acts as a representation of the Christian Church that finds itself in a vulnerable position during the reign of Julian. Sozomen sexualizes the violence perpetrated against the Christian virgins as a means of heightening the threat of vulnerability. I concluded with brief summaries of tropes that might have been employed by Sozomen, Gregory of Nazianzus, and Theodoret. The potential use of these tropes could provide additional implications concerning Christian perspectives of both pagan ritual practices, Christian identity, and Christian responses to pagan violence.

NOTES

1. The translation that is provided for this incident in Sozomen's history here and elsewhere comes from Sozomen. *The Ecclesiastical History of Sozomen: Comprising A History of the Church from A.D. 324 to A.D. 440.* (Henry G. Bohn, 1855): 217–219.

2. H.C. Teitler, *The Last Pagan Emperor: Julian the Apostate and the War Against Christianity* (New York: Oxford University Press, 2017): 95.

3. Teitler, *The Last Pagan Emperor*, 95.

4. Sozomen might have also employed another source. His account differs significantly from Gregory of Nazianzus, particularly in the extent to which the perpetrators violated the consecrated virgins: Sozomen's account is written in manner that suggest that the virgins were sexually violated by pigs, while Gregory's account suggest bodily violation via human consumption. Both Sozomen and Gregory's accounts introduce elements that are present in ritual sacrifice; this will be briefly discussed later in this chapter.

5. It is important to note that there is some doubt concerning the historicity of claims of sacred prostitution. Robert Olden contends that sacred prostitution did not exist in the ancient Near East. He argues that sacred prostitution was a common indictment against neighboring groups employed to forge clear boundaries between religious, social, and ethnic groups. He employs Sozomen's account of the violence perpetrated against the sacred virgins as support for his argument. Unlike Olden, Elsie Parsons explores human perspectives and ritual practices that center around interactions between the living and the dead. She employs a myriad of primary sources from a wide variety of places and time periods, including, but not limited to the Tonga, Africa, Cambodia, India, Rome, Sweden, Babylonia, and the Canary Islands. She includes Sozomen's account of the torture and death of the sacred virgins in a well-sourced appendix as a reference concerning the influence of Paganism on Christianity. Parson's reference to Sozomen's account is not related to any of the arguments in her work; she simply includes Sozomen's account as an example of a text that mentions a reactionary violence perpetrated against virgins due to religious and political societal changes. For further information, see Robert A. Oden, *The Bible without Theology: The Theological Tradition and Alternatives to It* (Cambridge: Harper & Row, 1987): 131–153 and Elsie W. Parsons, *Religious Chastity: An Ethnographic Study* (New York: AMS Press, 1975): 321–324.

6. There are minor variations when comparing both accounts. Bonnie MacLachlan contends that the minor variations suggest that Strabo is not using Herodotus's account as a source. Instead, she posits that Strabo is either using an independent source or an earlier source that might have been used by Herodotus. For further information, see Bonnie MacLachlan, "Sacred prostitution and Aphrodite," *SR* 21, no. 2 (1992): 149.

7. The inscription features Aurelia Aemilia's claim of following the both the command of an oracle and the custom of her family and serving in the temple as a *hetairai*. The text of the inscription can be found in W. M. Ramsay, "Unedited Inscriptions of Asia Minor," *Bulletin de Correspondance Hellenique* 7 (1983): 276, and Bonnie MacLachlan,. "Sacred Prostitution and Aphrodite," 151.

8. When read outside of its context, Sozomen's account of this incident lacks specificity in regard to time: the only time marker in Sozomen's account is the dating of the abolition of the ancient custom requiring ritual prostitution. As mentioned before, Sozomen employs Eusebius's *Life of Constantine* to date the prohibition to the rule of Constantine (early fourth century). If one can believe Eusebius's account that activities deemed "impure superstitions" were abolished by use of the military, it can be assumed that barbarous retaliation against Constantine's prohibition would most likely occur after Constantine's reign. Theodoret, Gregory of Nazianzus, and the *Chronicon Paschale* all locate this incident within the reign of Julian. This makes sense when considering Julian's Christian identification as "Julian, the Apostate." Julian's satirical oration, *The Misopogon*, confirms pagan violence when Julian, satirized through the philosopher's beard, describes the affection of the people for the worship of the gods by restoring pagan temples, destroying "the tombs of the atheists" and by punishing individuals who "transgressed against the gods." Petau, La Bleterie, and Gibbon include Sozomen's reference to the violation and murder of the sacred virgins as an example of the punishments endured by those who "transgressed against the gods." Sozomen's account confirms a date during the reign of Julian in the report of the murder of Mark of Arethusa that immediately follows the account of the sacred virgins. According to Sozomen, Mark of Arethusa was murdered by Pagans after refusing to hearken to an imperial edict by Julian to pay for the re-erection of a pagan temple. For an English translation of the *Misopogon*, see Julian, Emperor of Rome, *The works of the Emperor Julian, and Some Pieces of the Sophist Libanius, Volume 1* (London: T. Cadell, 1798).

9. Gregory of Nazianzus, however, identifies the actions of the inhabitants of Heliopolis, Gaza, and Arethusa as notorious, not only because it is "distinguished conduct that renders people famous, but also any wickedness that surpasses other people's reputation for evil" (*Oration* 4.86).

10. This omission is also present in Theodoret and the *Chronicon Paschale*.

11. Each of the accounts record consumption by swine as the demise of the virgin women. Given the discussion, thus far, concerning defilement and forced ritual prostitution, the use of swine is even the more curious. Is Gregory and/or Sozomen (or some other independent source) intentionally employing swine in this narrative? Is this a reference to some form of conflation of Jewish and Christian ritual practices? Might this be a reference to another pagan practice (Demeter festivals)? Scholarship

on this incident (at least scholarship in English) is lacking. While these questions may not fit the scope of this chapter, they are worth considering for future scholarship in this area.

12. Frankfurter, "Martyrology and the Prurient Gaze," *JECS* 17.2 (2009): 226.

13. Karen Jo Torjesen, *When Women Were Priests: Women's Leadership in the Early Church & the Scandal of Their Subordination in the Rise of Christianity* (New York: Harper One, 1993), 209–210.

14. Peter Robert Brown, *The Body and Society: Men, Women, and Sexual Renunciation in Early Christianity*. (New York: Columbia University Press, 1988): 259; cf. Athanasius, Saint, Patriarch of Alexandria, and Miles, Headmaster of St. Bees School Atkinson. *Historical tracts of S. Athanasius, Archbishop of Alexandria.: Translated [by Miles Atkinson] With notes and indices*. (Oxford, J. H. Parker, 1843): 185.

15. Brown, *Body*, 260; cf. Eusebius of Emesa, *Homily* 6.18.

16. Connor, Carolyn L. *Women of Byzantium*. (New Haven: Yale University Press, 2004):16–17 c.f. Brown, "Daughters of Jerusalem" in Brown, *Body*, 258–284.

17. Brown, *Body*, 17.

18. Seppuku is the Japanese term that references the cutting of the abdomen. It was practiced by the Japanese as a means of dying an honorable death. It was also used as a form of capital punishment for samurais.

19. The Treason Act of 1351 established the definition and punishment of high and petty acts of treason. The punishment for high treason was death by hanging, drawing, and quartering.

20. A fifteenth-century ordinance from Taunus dictates that individuals who strip bark off of a standing tree will be punished by disembowelment.

21. The account of Pompeius Trogus is accounted for in Justin's *Apologia* 21.3. For McLachlan's treatment of this text, see Bonnie MacLachlan, "Sacred prostitution and Aphrodite," 159–162.

22. Bonnie MacLachlan, "Sacred Prostitution," 162.

WORKS CITED

Brown, Peter Robert Lamont. *The Body and Society: Men, Women, and Sexual Renunciation in Early Christianity*. (New York: Columbia University Press, 1988).

Clark Liassis, Nora. *Aphrodite and Venus in Myth and Mimesis*. (Newcastle upon Tyne, UK: Cambridge Scholars Publishing, 2015).

Connor, Carolyn L. *Women of Byzantium*. (New Haven: Yale University Press, 2004).

Frankfurter, D. "Martyrology and the Prurient Gaze." *Journal of Early Christian Studies* 17.2, (2009): 215–245.

Gwatkin, Henry Melvill. *Studies of Arianism: Chiefly Referring to The Character and Chronology of The Reaction Which Followed The Council of Nicaea*. (New York: AMS Press, 1978).

Herodotus. *The History of Herodotus: Translated from the Greek. With notes by William Beloe. In four volumes*. (London: printed for Leigh and Sotheby, 1791).

Julian, Emperor of Rome, "The Works of the Emperor Julian, and Some Pieces of the Sophist Libanius." Volume 1 (London: T. Cadell, 1798).
MacLachlan, Bonnie. "Sacred Prostitution and Aphrodite." *Studies in Religion*/Sciences Religieuses 21 (1992): 145–162.
Nazianzen, Gregory. "Gregory Nazianzen, "Julian the Emperor" (1888). Oration 4: First Invective Against Julian." Gregory Nazianzen, "Julian the Emperor" (1888). Oration 4: First Invective Against Julian, http://www.tertullian.org/fathers/gregory_nazianzen_2_oration4.htm.
Oden, Robert A. *The Bible without Theology: The Theological Tradition and Alternatives to It.* (Cambridge: Harper & Row, 1987).
Parsons, Elsie W. *Religious Chastity: An Ethnographic Study* (New York: AMS Press, 1975).
Ramsay, W.M. "Unedited Inscriptions of Asia Minor," *Bulletin de Correspondeance Hellenique* 7 (1983): 258–278.
Raymond, Janice G. *A Passion for Friends: Toward a Philosophy of Female Affection.* (Boston: Beacon Press, 1986).
Schaff, Philip, and Henry Wace. *A Select Library of Nicene and Post-Nicene Fathers of the Christian Church: Second Series.* (New York, The Christian Literature Company; Oxford, Parker and Company, 1890).
Sozomen. *The Ecclesiastical History of Sozomen: Comprising A History of the Church from A.D. 324 to A.D. 440.* (Henry G. Bohn, 1855): 217–219.
Teitler, H.C. *The Last Pagan Emperor: Julian the Apostate and the War Against Christianity* (New York: Oxford University Press, 2017).
Torjesen, Karen J. *When Women Were Priests: Women's Leadership in the Early Church & the Scandal of Their Subordination in the Rise of Christianity* (New York: Harper One, 1993).
Whitby, Mary, et al. *Chronicon Paschale 284–628 AD.* (Liverpool: Liverpool University Press, 1989): 36–37.

Chapter 8

Tertullian of Carthage, Sexualized Violence, and the "Abjection" of the Female Flesh

Travis W. Proctor

What kind of body gets to count as "Christian"? And what are the consequences for those that do not? In this essay, I explore these questions through the lens of the "abject," a theoretical category popularized by the psychoanalytic work of Julia Kristeva and, later, by the gender theorist Judith Butler, which designates those elements of embodiment that are "expelled" and "othered" as part of the consolidation of individual and collective identity.[1] Recent studies have noted how early Christian writers positively valued elements of the body, such as the flesh, that were considered "abject" within Greco-Roman culture more broadly. I argue that such analyses have too often ignored how Christian writers created their *own* forms of abjectivity, which, in turn, made certain bodies more liable to sexualized violence.

My analysis comprises three parts. In part 1, I explore the theoretical background of the abject, with its contemporary roots in the work of Kristeva and Butler. I note that scholars have frequently used this category to explicate affirmations of the "flesh" in early Christian literature, with a particular focus on the writings of Tertullian of Carthage. I argue that such analyses employ a "thin" version of abjectivity, which looks only (or at least primarily) at how Christian writers co-opted previously-abject bodily attributes as *positive* elements in their constructions of Christian subjectivity. I argue instead for utilizing abjectivity in a "thicker" approach, which attends sufficiently to what bodies Christian writers *exclude* in their own constructions of ideal corporeality. A more capacious use of abjectivity, I argue, aids in exploring how Christian writers created classes of "debilitated" bodies, whose corporeal identity made them more liable to experience divinely and socially sanctioned acts of violence. Part 2 provides a case study on the writings of Tertullian of Carthage, whose positive valuations of the "flesh" have often featured in analyses of Christian abjectivity. I turn instead to Tertullian's construction of his own forms of abjection, including the bodies of wayward Christian women as well as non-Christian Romans. Tertullian abjectifies such bodies by narrating their repeated association with demonic entities. Notably, as part of his discussion of Christian baptism, Tertullian construes the demonic body as an entity that was abjected as part of the Christian initiatory rite; Tertullian's ascription of demonic corruption to certain bodies (e.g., unruly Christians, non-Christian Romans), therefore, functions as an abjectification-by-association. Part 3 notes the consequences of such abjectifications: Tertullian positions those bodies construed as non- or insufficiently-Christian as liable to (and even deserving of) violence, whether at the hands of demons or the Christian God. I conclude the study by noting how rethinking abjectivity within early Christian studies has consequences for reorienting our understanding of embodiment, identity, and violence in antiquity.

THE ABJECT IN THEORY AND PRACTICE

The abject has gained prominence in the scholarly lexicon primarily through the work of Julia Kristeva, a Bulgarian-French philosopher and psychoanalyst who uses abject to signal the excluded elements of human subjectivity.[2] Drawing upon Lacanian theories of psychosexual development, Kristeva argues that humans first perceive their own individual subjectivity as part of an exclusionary process, whereby they distinguish their "self" as distinct from other persons and objects. The abject, then, stems from the "immemorial violence" of "casting off" certain bodily drives and attachments (e.g., one's maternal attachments) in order to create the subject.[3]

In the wake of Kristeva's work, the abject has emerged as a prominent category in analyses of the body and identity, particularly in contemporary studies of sex, gender, and sexuality. Gender theorist Judith Butler, most notably, utilizes the abject to consider how regimes of knowledge "produce . . . a domain of unintelligible, abject, unlivable bodies,"[4] which in turn, "circumscribe the domain of the subject."[5] In this way, Butler utilizes the abject to catalogue how societies' idealized notions of subjectivity are subtended and bounded by excluded modes of embodiment.[6] Despite the establishment of such borders, Butler claims, the abject "haunts" the subject because it threatens "to expose [its] self-grounding presumptions" by reminding the subject of its excluded former "self."[7] According to Butler, therefore, constructive discourses must fortify bodily boundaries through the prescription of bodily performances that reinforce the exclusion of the abject.[8]

As outlined by Kristeva and adapted by Butler, the abject helps to explicate the simultaneous contingency and resiliency of cultural constructions of human corporeality. Abjectivity points to the "excluded" aspects of this constructive process, and thus aids in excavating the destructive "underside" of cultural systems of corporeality. The abject compels us to ask: what bodies are left out in our constructions of human corporeality? How do such bodies contest the coherency of the subject itself? Put another way, the abject "is a challenge, asking us who the hell we think we are."[9]

EARLY CHRISTIAN STUDIES AND THE ABJECT

Who the hell did Christians think *they* were? Due to the enduring influence of both Kristeva and Butler, the abject has recently occupied a prominent place in scholars' attempts to answer such questions. Virginia Burrus has argued, for example, that early Christians reveled in the "abjection of flesh," which, through Jesus's incarnation, they associated with the "exaltation of divinity."[10] Thus, early Christian literature includes extensive narrations of the "shameful" nature of Jesus's crucifixion, as well as Jesus's "humiliation" in taking on the human fleshly form.[11] More recently, Manuel Villallobos Mendoza has traced similar insights back into the Gospel of Mark, arguing that Jesus's suffering highlights his possession of an "abject body" which, contra prevailing Roman corporeal norms, promoted "a kingdom of abject bodies."[12]

Burrus's and Mendoza's studies reflect a broader trend in early Christian studies: scholars tend to use the category of the abject to highlight how Christians *valorized* bodily attributes (e.g., the "flesh") otherwise viewed as repugnant by mainstream cultures. Such studies draw upon Kristeva's claim that the subject often responds to the abject (e.g., bodily excretions such as feces or vomit) with disgust and repudiation; Kristeva posits that this occurs because such formerly internal substances blur the internal/external boundaries of the human subject.[13] Burrus and Villalobos Mendoza, among others, suggest that early Christians counterintuitively *embraced* the disgusting and abject elements of the human body and society more broadly.[14] Similar themes surface in other studies. Judith Perkins, for example, has argued that whereas Roman society regarded some bodies as "abject" and therefore "unworthy of . . . respect," early Christians "reinscribed" the positive value of the body by accepting its most abject elements.[15] One of the important figures in Perkins's exploration is Tertullian, who, according to Perkins, affirmed the value of abject fleshly experience as part of his defense of bodily resurrection.[16] Charlotte Radler likewise points to Tertullian for evidence of early Christian reorientation of the "abject squalor of the flesh" as "curative," which "destabilized long-standing hierarchical cultural notions of honor and shame."[17]

Such studies have called attention to the important ways in which some early Christian writers, including Tertullian, revalued and positively appropriated abject modes of embodiment. These readings have employed a "thin" notion of abjectivity, however, which, while attending to Christian *positive* valuations of otherwise abject bodies, nonetheless ignores the *negation* (i.e., the abject-ing) of other types of bodies. The deficiencies in such an approach are evident in the misleading attributions of corporeal egalitarianism to early Christian authors. Perkins, citing the example of Tertullian (among others), argues that "Christians destabilized the grounds for the hierarchical configurations" associated with the body; as a result, "[n]o group is allowed to deny its members' embodiment or to foist the body onto an 'other.'"[18] Radler similarly proposes that Tertullian "suggests the possibility of redrawing societal and communal structures," such that "marginalized embodied human beings" become "agents and victors."[19] According to Radler, therefore, Tertullian constructs "a more capacious, inclusive understanding of God's salvific work."[20]

Such analyses neglect the many ways that Christian writers carried out their own acts of marginalization that created abject bodies. Tertullian, one of the main early Christian authors cited for his affirmation of the abject, exhibits a highly hierarchized and inequitable corporeal system. Taylor Petrey notes that "Tertullian does not advocate a neutral flesh," but concentrates the shame of the flesh "on women, and especially on the womb."[21] Along similar lines, Carly Daniel-Hughes traces how, with regard to Tertullian's prescriptions regarding female adornment, "a qualitative difference pertains to male and female fleshly bodies . . . [that] supports a gender economy figured in a hierarchical mode."[22] As Maia Kotrosits and Daniel-Hughes have recently stressed, therefore, "Tertullian picks up precarity *only to locate it elsewhere* . . . [which he] assigns to damnable others, or off-loads onto female bodies."[23]

Studies of the abject in early Christianity have rarely called attention to these aspects of Tertullian's writings, instead suggesting that he held to "non-hierarchical" or "inclusive" views of the body.[24] How might we explain this dissonance between scholarly perspectives on early Christian corporeality, and Tertullian in particular? I would suggest here that such disagreements stem from broader scholarly inclinations in the use of the abject. Imogen Tyler has noted, for example, that feminist theoretical approaches to the abject have largely valued the "transgressive potential" of the term, seeking to read for abject bodies that might "destabilize and/or subvert misogynistic representations of women."[25] So also in early Christian studies, where scholars have largely identified the flesh (and the body writ large) as a transgressive abject affirmed by Christians. Tyler notes, however, that such readings have too often failed to consider how abjection, as classically formulated, is a "perpetual process that plays a central role within the project of subjectivity"; thus, in its fullest sense, the category of the abject assumes that "*all subjects* are fundamentally 'abjecting subjects.'"[26] Studies of the abject in early Christianity, therefore, have employed a "thin" version of the abject by too often neglecting how early Christians acted as "abjectors" themselves, creating forms of abjection as part of their own exclusionary modes of subjectivity.[27] Appreciation for the multivalent aspects of Christian subjectivity requires, then, a "thicker" form of abjectivity that acknowledges these processes.

CHRISTIAN ABJECTION IN TERTULLIAN'S *ON THE SHOWS*

To trace out this ampler version of the Christin abject, I return to the writings of Tertullian of Carthage. I shift attention away from Tertullian's *valorization* of the Roman abject, however, and instead ask how Tertullian himself abjects certain modes of corporeality. Put another way, what kinds of bodily performances or states does Tertullian construct as incompatible with Christian identity? Tertullian's exposition *On the Shows* provides an ideal case study for such questions.[28] Much to the chagrin of Tertullian, Carthaginian Christians had apparently been attending Roman entertainment events (e.g., gladiatorial battles, athletic events, and theatrical performances). To counter this practice, Tertullian's treatise *On the Shows* lays out a proper behavioral program for Christians, forbidding several "idolatrous" Roman "spectacles" such as athletic contests, the circus, cultic practices, civic ceremonies, and even leisurely activities like horseback riding (6–12).

According to Tertullian, Roman entertainment activities "are not in concord [*non competant*] with true sacred observance [*verae religioni*]" (1),[29] and rob Christians of their distinctive "mark": "From this . . . [non-Christians] understand that someone has become a Christian—i.e., that they scorn the shows. Accordingly, anyone who takes away that (mark) by which they are known openly denies (their faith)" (24). For Tertullian, therefore, the Christian body is defined by its avoidance of particular Roman cultural performances. To trace out this opposition further, Tertullian evocatively juxtaposes the habits of the Roman body at the shows with the dispositions he demands of his Christian readers:

> Can it be that a person, sitting in that place [i.e., the shows] . . . will . . . think of God? They will have peace in their soul, I suppose, as they shout for the

charioteer; they will come to know modesty as they are astonished by the mimes ... But while the tragedian cries, they will think of the sayings of some prophet! Amongst the rhythms of an effeminate pantomime actor, they will recite a psalm! While the athletes are toiling, they will say that returning punch for punch is not allowed! And then they will be aroused by compassion, as they are transfixed by the bears biting and the chain-mail of the net fighters! ... Those hands you have raised to God, afterwards to tire them out commending an actor? And from the mouth with which you have spoken "Amen" over the sacred thing, to render praise to a gladiator? (25)

Through this series of juxtapositions, Tertullian constructs a corporeal binary of Roman and Christian bodies, stressing their incongruity. The Christian body seeks peace, the Roman the fights of the gladiator. The Christian chants the psalms, the Roman enjoys the music of "effeminate" entertainers. The lips of the Christian body utter prayer, while the Romans cheer for athletes.

In this way, the cultural activities of Romans emerge as the excluded element of Christian subjectivity, a kind of bodily comportment from which the Christian subject must remain distanced. Elizabeth Grosz notes that the abject elucidates "the constitution of a proper social body, the processes of sorting, segregating, and demarcating the body so as to conform to but not exceed cultural expectations."[30] Tertullian here abjects Roman bodily performances so as to "sort" and "segregate" the body according to his own "cultural expectations," such that Roman spectacles constitute for Tertullian the defining and excluding limit of Christian subjectivity. Far from forwarding a "non-hierarchical" or "inclusive" scheme, therefore, Tertullian here interprets Christian subjectivity through a corporeal index that privileged certain bodies over "abject" others.

Tertullian deepens his abjectification of the Roman body by associating it with evil forces: "What is it like to go from the assembly of God to the assembly of the Devil [*diaboli ecclesiam*]?," he mockingly asks his audience (25). Tertullian argues that the Devil and his demonic minions have made the shows their "assembly" by pretending to be the Roman "gods" and thus infiltrating the cultural activities of Romans. He declares that horseback riding, for example, is part of the "service of demons" (*daemonorium officia*) due to its inclusion in Greco-Roman games, which honor the Greco-Roman gods (9). Tertullian extends this demonic corruption to other practices: he argues that horses in general are attached to Castor and Pollux, the theater to Venus and Bacchus, depictions of gods to demonic spirits, and athletic contests to dead humans (9–12). He also argues that the origins, names, equipment, location, and artistic accompaniments of Roman civic ceremonies are all dedicated to the Roman pantheon, which themselves are nothing more than the masks of demonic spirits (9–13).

Tertullian's demonization of the shows intensifies his abjectification of the Roman body, in so far as he construes freedom from demonic corruption as a foundational element of Christian corporeality. This is evident in Tertullian's belief that baptism, the Christian rite of initiation, entails the removal of demons from the soul: "[W]hen the soul embraces the faith, *it is regenerated by this new birth in water* . . . Then it is welcomed by the Holy Spirit as, *at its physical birth, it was met by the evil spirit [sicut in pristina nativitate a spiritu profano]*" (*On the Soul* 41, emphasis mine).[31] In Tertullian's thought, therefore, "baptism is the second birth, on which occasion the Holy Spirit pushes away the evil spirit that might have associated itself with one's soul."[32] The Christian soul's "pushing away" of evil spirits is encapsulated, Tertullian claims, by the "renouncing" of Satan and his minions at the time of baptism (*On the Shows* 4, 24). By definition, therefore, the baptized Christian body is distinguished from its former Roman corporeality primarily through the abandonment of the demonic entity that had pervaded its former flesh and soul.

In this way, Roman non-Christian bodies are abject not only because they are excluded from the Christian community, but because their bodies are corrupted by the demonic entities that are "cast off" as part of the creation and consolidation of the Christian "self." The abject calls attention, then, to the ways in which Tertullian positions the exclusion of the demonic (and its attendant Roman cultures) as a *foundational* element in the creation of the Christian; that is, the interconnections between demonic and Christian bodies stretch back even to the formative moments of Christian subjectivity (i.e., baptism), when the *disconnecting* of the demonic from the human body was a requisite step in abandoning the corrupted Roman body and creating a new Christian corporeality. The demonic, in this way, comes to constitute the "defining limit of the subject's domain" even as it is excluded from that subjectivity.[33]

Since Roman cultural activities are marred by the presence of "spirits of the Devil [*diaboli spīrītus*]" (8), Christians must avoid them lest they "renounce and annul [*eieramus et rescindimus*]" the "seal" of baptism by "rescinding its testimony" (24). According to Tertullian, therefore, the renouncement of Satan and his "angels" during the baptismal ceremony ultimately entails not only the cleansing of the Christian body, but also the anticipatory eschewal of all activities associated with the adversary's wicked company. If they do not, Tertullian claims, they risk becoming "liable to penetration by demons [*daemoniis penetrabiles*]" (26). In this way, as Grosz notes, "what is excluded (i.e., the abject) can never be fully obliterated but hovers at the borders of our existence, threatening the apparently unsettled unity of the subject with disruption and possible dissolution."[34]

Likewise for Tertullian, the demonic unsettles the Christian body with a reminder of its former (Roman, demon-possessed) self. In response,

Tertullian calls on his readers to take up an interrelated collection of ritualized actions designed to fortify the Christian against demonic reintegration. Christians must take up habits such as fasting, sexual abstinence, proper bodily adornment, and appropriate partaking of ritual meals, among other ethical instructions.[35] Such practices are designed to position the abject at a "safe distance" such that it does not threaten the solidity of the subject.[36] It is through this performance of normative codes of subjectivity, framed by their ritualized eschewing of the abject demonic, that the Christian body materializes.[37] The abject, therefore, not only defines the limits of Christian subjectivity, but informs the ritualization of a particular type of Christian body.

THE ROMAN ABJECT AND CHRISTIAN SEXUALIZED VIOLENCE

The preceding analysis has demonstrated that, contrary to previous proposals, Tertullian creates an exclusionary corporeal system, which classifies certain bodies as "abject." In this final section, I trace how Tertullian's corporeal hierarchy construed such abject bodies as "debilitated," or more liable to divinely-sanctioned violence. Imogen Tyler notes that "if a person and their bodily appearance is designated the abject thing . . . , they are subject to dehumanizing violence."[38] Indeed, Tertullian makes explicit connections between Roman cultural activities, demonic possession, and the receipt of violence. In *On the Shows*, Tertullian claims that two women of his own time had attended Roman theatrical shows and been infected by demons. Tertullian cites one example of a woman who experienced such an attack:

> For there is the case of that woman . . . , who went to the theater and thereafter came back with a demon [*cum daemonio*]. And so during the exorcism, when the unclean spirit was being overwhelmed because he had dared to attack [*aggredi*] a believer [*fidelem*], he answered firmly, "I was certainly most justified in doing so, since I came upon her in my own territory." (26)

Tertullian's claim that the demon "dared" (*ausus*) to attack a believer suggests that he imagines pious Christians normally to be less susceptible to demonic assault. Christians' participation in the shows, however, opens their body to the danger of demonic "attack" (*aggredi*). Tertullian provides another example to similar effect: "to another woman, a linen sheet was shown to her in a dream on the night of that day that she had listened to a tragedian . . . And not even five days later, that woman was not alive in the world" (26).[39] Tertullian asserts that both of these women faced violent attacks (and, in one case, even death) because they had experienced an "association with the devil at the shows [*cum diabolo apud spectacula communicando*]" (26).

It is noteworthy that the cases to which Tertullian draws his readers' attention implicate *women* specifically in the inducement of demonic attack. Tertullian here likely appeals to the common perception in antiquity that women were more prone to infiltration by external spiritual forces (whether divine or demonic) due to their having more "porous" bodies.[40] Tertullian also subtly draws upon the ancient stereotype that it was dangerous for women to traverse excessively in the public sphere, here signaled by their vulnerability to demonic attack. I would add, moreover, that a significant element in Tertullian's disproportionate narration of demon-possessed women is his attendant claim that women possess particularly shameful and inferior bodies. Daniel-Hughes has elsewhere noted how Tertullian positions women's bodies as "negatively charged," chiefly in their association "with procreation, which [for Tertullian] is linked to death, the very signifier of sin."[41] Most notably, in *On the Flesh of Christ*, Tertullian challenges his opponent Marcion, daring him to acknowledge Jesus's contact with the "sordid" elements of the flesh through the Savior's involvement in maternal processes:

> Beginning then with that nativity you so strongly object to, . . . attack now, the nastinesses of genital elements in the womb, the filthy curdling of moisture and blood, and of the flesh . . . nourished on that same mire . . . You shudder, of course, at the child passed out along with his afterbirth, and of course bedaubed with it. (4.1–3)[42]

Radler finds in this passage an affirmation of the "abject" fleshly body, arguing that Tertullian "creates a reordered soteriological structure that classifies flesh, filth, and dishonor as curative," which, in turn, "destabilized long-standing hierarchical cultural notions of honor and shame."[43] As Petrey has noted, however, Tertullian's affirmation functions only as far as it accentuates the flesh's inherent shame: "Tertullian himself ultimately holds to the same association of the body as inherently scatological."[44] Daniel-Hughes points out, moreover, that woman's "connection with the processes of birth . . . [come] to associate her fleshly body more closely with the looming threat of corruption and mortality."[45] In this way, Tertullian displaces "the filth associated with human birth . . . onto Mary, and, implicitly, onto woman as well."[46] In other words, "[w]ombs are dirty places, and womb-bearers are dirty people."[47] Through his narration of the shamefulness of birth, therefore, Tertullian reinscribes and perpetuates a hierarchical view of the human body where women possess uniquely-shameful and inferior flesh.[48]

In this regard, it is notable that Tertullian likewise associates the origins of demonic corruption of Roman culture with maternal and birthing processes.

Tertullian claims that demons begin their attack on humans as part of the invocation of Roman deities at birth:

> All men are born surrounded by the idolatry of the midwife: the wombs from which they are born are still wrapped in the ribbons which were hung on the idols, *and thus the child is consecrated to the demons* [*daemoniorum ... profitentur*]; in labor, they chant prayers to Lucina and Diana; for a whole week a table is set in honor of Juno; on the final day, the "Writing Fates" are invoked; and the child's first step is sacred to Statina. (*On the Soul* 39, emphasis mine)

Tertullian here references parturition rituals (*dies natalis*), cultic practices that traditionally accompanied Roman childbirths and early infancy. During and after labor, Roman mothers, midwives, and female relatives (men were not typically involved in childbirth procedures) dedicated special offerings to Greco-Roman goddesses of fertility (e.g., Artemis/Diana, Hera/Juno), chanted incantations to protect mother and child, and sometimes performed ritualistic gestures to protect the newborn from the evil eye.[49] Such rites were designed to invoke divine protection for children from early infancy's many dangers, including sickness and sinister forces. For Tertullian, however, such rites accomplish the reverse: they endanger the child by allowing evil spirits to "trap" the souls of newborn children "from the moment of their birth" (39). As a result, Tertullian declares, "there is hardly a single person that is unaffected by a demon" (*nullum paene hominem carere daemonio*) (57).[50] By associating humanity's initial "demonization" with parturition rites, Tertullian once again centralizes the origins of shame and corruption in the moments of birth, and, thus, in gynocentric practices. This serves Tertullian's purpose of universalizing demonic infiltration to the entirety of Roman culture, and yet also once again associates abject demonic entities with women.

As noted already, previous treatments of the abject in early Christian literature have too often neglected these aspects of Tertullian's writings. In doing so, they have risked replicating, rather than contesting, Tertullian's exclusionary corporeal paradigms.[51] In this regard, it is significant that Tertullian associates the abject flesh specifically with maternal processes. Imogen Tyler has argued that Kristeva's notion of the abject, which posits the rejection of the mother as the formative moment of human subjectivity, problematically construes maternal bodies as inherently "abject." According to Tyler, this construal has manifested in the over-representation of maternal bodies in contemporary narrations and artistic representations of abject bodies.[52] Such unreflective applications of the abject to the maternal, Tyler argues, unwittingly reinscribe gender dichotomies and "risk marginalizing *lived experiences* of being the thing deemed abject."[53] By affirming Tertullian's disproportionate shaming of the maternal body, scholars of early Christianity have similarly replicated the abjectification of modes of corporeality associated with the female body, while also ignoring the cultural consequences that could result for women (and other marginalized persons) as a result of their disproportionate association with abjection.

The abjectification of the female flesh carried dire consequences. While Tertullian does imply that all Christians are vulnerable to attacks by demons (*On the Shows* 26), he nonetheless disproportionately narrates such attacks as occurring against women (see discussion above). In such a way, Tertullian reinscribes the female body as being distinctively prone to the receipt of (demonic) violence. Tertullian's construction of the abject functions, then, as an act of "debilitation," or the "practice of rendering populations available for . . . likely injury."[54] Tertullian, by marking a strong connection between demonic and women's bodies, construes the female flesh as prone to abjection, and, thus, to being made "available" for violence and "maiming."

Tertullian's dual abjection and debilitation of the female flesh is evident likewise in his narration of divine violence against Roman bodies as part of the final judgment. At the time of Christ's second coming, Tertullian claims, "indeed other shows remain to be performed—that ultimate and perpetual day of judgment . . . What an immense show it will be, then!" (30). In Tertullian's recounting, the "show" of judgment day will primarily consist of divine acts of violence carried out as revenge against non-Christian bodies:

> What to admire, what to laugh at? In what thing will I take delight, while I watch so many and so great kings who were admitted into heaven, it was claimed, . . . moaning in the depths of darkness? Likewise the governors who persecuted the name of the Lord, melting in flames more ferocious than those they kindled as they raged against the Christians? And who else? Those wise philosophers red-faced in the presence of their pupils as they burn together, those (pupils) to whom they had suggested that nothing was of concern to God, those to whom they asserted either that souls did not exist or that they (or their souls) would not return in their previous bodies! (30)

Through this apocalyptic "tour de force of viewing," Tertullian "substitutes a violent Christian spectacle for the pagan shows,"[55] assigning to each Roman a punishment that is in accord with his mocking stereotypes. In doing so, Tertullian constructs a "juridical setting" where he can act out a "fantasy of power" through judgment and punishment of non-Christian bodies.[56]

Prominent Roman citizens who had opposed or enticed Christians will be punished in ways that invert their stereotypical activities:

> And then there will be the tragedians to be heard, certainly more vocal in their own misfortune; then the pantomime actors to be watched, a great deal more flexible in the fire; then the charioteer to observe, entirely red on their flaming

wheel; then also the athletes to look upon, not in their gymnasium but being cast into the fire. (*On the Shows* 30)

Note here the highlighting of the tragic actor's voice, the actor's flexibility, the charioteer's association with the wheel, and the athlete's physique, all of which are transmuted so that they contribute to the visualization of the Roman's body's torture. Through this evocative scene, Tertullian casts the Roman body from the seats of the coliseum into the arena itself, where they become the spectacle of punishment that they had enjoyed for earthly entertainment. The Christian body, through the eyes and imagination of Tertullian, takes the place of its Roman persecutors, watching with laughter and joy as the Roman body is tortured and the imperial gaze of punishment is reversed. Tertullian displays here "a Tarantino-esque desire for vengeance," carried out in lurid fashion against the Roman body.[57] Thus, despite his condemnations elsewhere of fellow Christian's zealous participation in the shows, Tertullian here "positively reveals in and savours the power of his role as spectator," to such an extent that he at times struggles to decide in which mode of torture he will take the most delight (30).[58]

Tertullian underwrites this desire by casting the Roman spectacles as sexualized and feminized spaces that transgress the proper boundaries of the sexed flesh. Tertullian claims, for example, that Christians "in the entire show . . . will encounter no greater temptation than the overwrought clothing of women and men," while their interaction with other crowd members "creates an exchange that kindles the sparks of desire" (25). Tertullian here constructs Roman entertainments as erotic visual and physical encounters between spectators, characterized by overwrought temptations and desires.[59] The presence of such desires, it seems, implicitly justifies Tertullian's own pleasure in viewing the divinely-sanctioned torture of the shows' participants.

Tertullian elsewhere emphasizes that Roman shows participated in gender-bending practices that violated sexual norms. He argues that the repugnance of the theater is signaled by its inclusion of male actors "effecting effeminate displays, dismissing (their) sense of sex and decency [*per muliebres res repraesentat, sensum sexus et pudoris exterminans*]" (17).[60] In a later discussion of the Roman entertainments, Tertullian similarly condemns any man who "dresses (himself) in effeminate clothing [*muliebribus vestietur*]," as well as the man who "feigns voice, sex, or age [*vocem, sexus, aetates mentientem*]," and finally the "pantomime actor [*pantomimo*]" who "is procured to play effeminate roles [*muliebribus curatur*]" (23).[61] Along similar lines, Tertullian elsewhere condemns Christian enjoyment of the "effeminate [pantomime] actor [*effeminati histrionis*]" while at the shows (25). Notable here are the examples cited by Tertullian to underscore the transgressive nature of the theater: each instance of gender-bending wickedness is performed by a man "play-acting" as a woman. In such a way, Tertullian constructs Roman entertainments as overtly queered and feminized spaces, where men improperly cross gender boundaries and disregard their "sense of sex and decency."

Tertullian's simultaneous sexualization and feminization of Roman spectacles serves as an implicit justification for his garish narration of violence against the Roman body. It is notable, for example, that as part of his detailing of the tortures of the Roman body, Tertullian cites (among other tortured Romans) the "tragic actors" (*tragoedi*) and "(pantomime) actors" (*histriones*) (30). In doing so, Tertullian reminds the reader of his previous detailing of the gender-bending practices of Roman spectacles, and thus provides an unspoken rationalization for God's violent punishment of Roman bodies. Tertullian's thoroughgoing sexualization and feminization of the Roman shows, therefore, constructs the Roman body (as well as Christian participants) as debilitated—i.e., available for divinely-sanctioned scorn and violence. In so far as Tertullian underwrites his debilitation of the Roman body through its association with abject women's flesh and an abject demonic pantheon, his writings emerge as an example of the ways that Christian constructions of abject bodies created modes of exclusion by which certain bodies were made more liable to sexualized judgment and violence.

CONCLUSION

This essay has traced how Tertullian's abjectification of women's flesh, primarily through his demonization of maternal processes, functions as a foundational maneuver in his articulation of Christian "collective existence." By abjecting women's and non-Christian Roman's bodies, Tertullian constructs a specific brand of Christian subjectivity built upon a gendered hierarchy of the body. This abjectification, in turn, fashioned a realm of "debilitated" bodies—populated most prominently by wayward Christian women and feminized Romans—who were made available for divinely-sanctioned violence.

Previous treatments of the abject in Tertullian have largely overlooked such aspects of his writings. I have argued that this stems at least in part from a "thin" utilization of abject, used largely for the purposes of noting Christian affirmation of otherwise-despised aspects of corporeality. As other commentators have noted, however, Tertullian's affirmation of "abject" bodies or bodily components is only one part of a more wide-ranging corporeal scheme, which itself creates (and makes available for harm) certain bodies classified as abject. Most notably, through association with demonic corruption, Tertullian implies that disobedient Christian women and non-Christians stand in danger of demonic infiltration, and thus to bodily dissolution or harm.

By attending to these aspects of abjectification in Tertullian's writings, my essay pushes scholars of early Christianity to utilize the abject in a more capacious fashion, to consider not only Christian affirmations of formerly-abject bodies, but also how Christians themselves created classes of abject bodies as part of their articulations of Christian subjectivity. In doing so, we might be better able to understand who got to count as "Christian" in the ancient Mediterranean, as well as the consequences for those that did not. In other words, we may yet develop a deeper understanding of who the hell Christians thought they were.

NOTES

1. This definition of the "abject" is adapted from Judith Butler, *Gender Trouble: Feminism and the Subversion of Identity* (New York: Routledge, 1999 [1990]), 169–170.

2. See especially Julia Kristeva, *Powers of Horror: An Essay on Abjection*, translated by Leon S. Roudiez. (New York: Columbia University Press, 1982). For a pre-Kristevan use of the abject, see Georges Bataille, "Abjection and Miserable Forms," in Sylvere Lotringer, ed., *More & Less* (Brooklyn, NY: Semiotext(e)/Autonomedia, 1999), 8–13; Rina Arya, *Abjection and Representation? An Exploration of Abjection in the Visual Arts, Film and Literature* (Basingstoke, UK: Palgrave Macmillan, 2014), 66–72.

3. Kristeva, *Powers of Horror*, 9–10.

4. Judith Butler, *Bodies That Matter: On the Discursive Limits of "Sex"* (New York: Routledge, 1993), x.

5. Butler, *Bodies That Matter*, xiii. See also Judith Butler, *Undoing Gender* (New York: Routledge, 2004), 12–13.

6. Imogen Tyler, *Revolting Subjects: Social Abjection and Resistance in Neoliberal Britain* (London: Zed Books, 2013), 28.

7. Butler, *Bodies That Matter*, x, xiii. On this element of the abject, see also Georges Bataille, *Œuvres Complètes* (Paris: Gallimard, 1970), II.217; Kristeva, *Powers of Horror*, 4, 9–10; Elizabeth Grosz, *Sexual Subversions: Three French Feminists* (Sydney: Allen & Unwin, 1989), 71; Arya, *Abjection and Representation*, 72.

8. Butler, *Bodies That Matter*, xix.

9. Maggie Hennefeld and Nicholas Sammond, "Introduction: Not It, or, the Abject Objection," in Hennefeld and Sammond, *Abjection Incorporated: Mediating the Politics of Pleasure & Violence* (Durham: Duke University Press, 2020), 1–31 [27].

10. Virginia Burrus, *Saving Shame: Martyrs, Saints, and Other Abject Subjects* (Philadelphia: University of Pennsylvania Press, 2008), 47.

11. Burrus, *Saving Shame*, 47.

12. Manuel Villalobos Mendoza, *Abject Bodies in the Gospel of Mark* (Sheffield: Sheffield Phoenix Press, 2012), 94.

13. Kristeva, *Powers of Horror*, 2–3.

14. Burrus, *Saving Shame*, 52–3.
15. Judith Perkins, *Roman Imperial Identities in the Early Christian Era* (New York: Routledge, 2009), 101–4.
16. Perkins, *Roman Imperial Identities*, 103–4. In Perkins's analysis, Tertullian takes this position against Christians, like Marcion, who devalued the salvific value of the human flesh.
17. Charlotte Radler, "The Dirty Physician: Necessary Dishonor and Fleshly Solidarity in Tertullian's Writings," *VC* 63 (2009): 345–368 [347, 365].
18. Perkins, *Roman Imperial Identities*, 102.
19. Radler, "The Dirty Physician," 368.
20. Radler, "The Dirty Physician," 354.
21. Taylor G. Petrey, *Resurrecting Parts: Early Christians on Desire, Reproduction, and Sexual Difference* (New York: Routledge, 2016), 99.
22. Carly Daniel-Hughes, *The Salvation of the Flesh in Tertullian of Carthage: Dressing for the Resurrection* (New York: Palgrave Macmillan, 2011), 67. On this point see also Carly Daniel-Hughes, "'Wear the Armor of Your Shame!': Debating Veiling and the Salvation of the Flesh in Tertullian of Carthage" *SR* 39.2 (2010), 179–201.
23. Maia Kotrosits and Carly Daniel-Hughes, "Tertullian of Carthage and the Materiality of Power," in Kotrosits, *The Lives of Objects: Material Culture, Experience, and the Real in the History of Early Christianity* (Chicago: University of Chicago Press, 2020), 85–106, 193–201 [200 n. 84], emphasis mine.
24. The exception to this general approach is the work of Burrus, who acknowledges that Tertullian "displaces the defensive affect of shame onto others" (Burrus, *Saving Shame*, 53; cf. Rivera, *Poetics of the Flesh*, 46).
25. Imogen Tyler, "Against Abjection," *FT* 10.1 (2003): 77–98 [77, 82–3].
26. Tyler, "Against Abjection," 80. Emphasis mine. For an important critique of the "universality" assumed in the concept of the abject, see Giyatri Spivak, "Extreme Eurocentrism," *Lusitania: A Journal of Reflection and Oceanography* (1992): 55–60 [56–59]. I should stress here that my proposal is not designed to enforce some kind 'canonical' use of abject, as if the concept can only be used in as part of particular theoretical maneuvers. But it is to push for recognizing the full theoretical potential of the category, and thus for the use of a more capacious concept for analyzing Christian corporeality and subjectivity.
27. I adapt the term "abjector" from Sabine Broeck, *Gender and the Abjection of Blackness* (Albany, NY: State University of New York, 2018), 71, 84.
28. I develop this analysis at greater length in *Demonic Bodies and the Dark Ecologies of Early Christian Culture* (Oxford: Oxford University Press, 2022).
29. Translations of *On the Shows* are my own, based on the Latin text of Marie Turcan, ed., *Tertullien: Les Spectacles*, Sources Chrétiennes 332 (Paris: Éditions du Cerf, 2012 [1986]), and in consultation with T.R. Glover, tr., *Tertullian: Apology, De Spectaculis*, Loeb Classical Library 250 (Cambridge, MA: Harvard University Press, 1931).
30. Elizabeth Grosz, *Volatile Bodies: Toward a Corporeal Feminism* (Bloomington, IN: University of Indiana Press, 1994), 193.

31. Translations of *On the Soul* are from Edwin A. Quain, tr., "Tertullian On the Soul," in Rudolph Arbesmann, Sister Emily Joseph Daly, and Edwin A. Quain, trans., *Tertullian Apologetical Works and Minucius Felix Octavius* (New York: Fathers of the Church, 1950), unless otherwise noted. On this topic in Tertullian, see also *On Baptism* 9. Latin text of [i]On the Soul[i] from J. H. Waszink, [i]Quinti Septimi Florentis Tertulliani De Anima[/i], Supplements to [i]Vigiliae Christianae[/i] (Leiden: Brill, 2010 [1947]).

32. Nasrallah, *Ecstasy of Folly,* 131.

33. Butler, *Bodies That Matter*, xiii.

34. Grosz, *Sexual Subversions,* 71. On this point, cf. Butler, *Bodies That Matter*, xiii.

35. See, for example, Tertullian's treatises *On the Apparel of Women, On the Veiling of Virgins, On the Crown, To His Wife, Exhortation to Chastity, On Monogamy, On Modesty, On Fasting, On Prayer, On Repentance,* and *Of Patience.*

36. Grosz, *Sexual Subversions,* 77. For those that have already become possessed, moreover, Tertullian claims that Christian exorcists are uniquely able to expel demons (*Apol.* 23.15).

37. Butler, *Bodies That Matter*, xxiii.

38. Tyler, "Against Abjection," 90.

39. According to Artemidorus, the appearance of a linen sheet in dreams could sometimes signal the dreamer's impending death (*Interpretation of Dreams* 2.3).

40. On this, see Ruth Padel, "Women: Model for Possession by Greek Daemons," in Averil Cameron and Amélie Kuhrt, eds., *Images of Women in Antiquity* (Detroit: Wayne State University Press, 1993), 3–19 [11].

41. Daniel-Hughes, *Salvation of the Flesh,* 70.

42. Translation from Ernest Evans, ed., *Tertullian's Treatise on the Resurrection* (London: SPCK, 1960).

43. Radler, "The Dirty Physician," 347, 365. For similar claims regarding this passage, see also Burrus, *Saving Shame,* 56; Perkins, *Roman Imperial Identities,* 161–169.

44. Petrey, *Resurrecting Parts*, 97.

45. Daniel-Hughes, *Salvation of the Flesh,* 69–70. On this point, see also Petrey, *Resurrecting Parts*, 97.

46. Daniel-Hughes, *Salvation of the Flesh,* 71. On the feminization of the flesh in Tertullian, see also Rivera, *Poetics of the Flesh,* 52.

47. Jennifer Glancy, "The Law of the Opened Body: Tertullian on the Nativity," *Henoch* 30.2 (2008) 267–288 [276–77], cited ap. Daniel-Hughes, *Salvation of the Flesh,* 71.

48. Petrey, *Resurrecting Parts*, 98–99.

49. On the various rites, see Véronique Dasen, "Childbirth and Infancy in Greek and Roman Antiquity," in Beryl Rawson, ed., *A Companion to Families in the Greek and Roman Worlds* (London: Blackwell, 2011), 291–314; Irene Mañas Romero and José Nicolás Saiz López, "Pueri nascentes: rituals, birth and social recognition in Ancient Rome," in Katharina Rebay-Salisbury and Doris Pany-Kucera, eds., *Ages*

and Abilities: The Stages of Childhood and Their Social Recognition in Prehistoric Europe and Beyond (Oxford: Archaeopress, 2020), 235–248.

50. Translation my own.
51. On this danger in the study of the abject, see Tyler, "Against Abjection," 84.
52. Tyler, "Against Abjection," 85.
53. Tyler, "Against Abjection," 85–7, emphasis mine.
54. Jasbir K. Puar, *The Right to Maim: Debility, Capacity, Disability* (Durham, NC: Duke University Press, 2017), xviii.
55. Christopher Frilingos, *Spectacles of Empire* (Philadelphia: University of Pennsylvania Press, 2004), 62–3.
56. Kotrosits, *The Lives of Objects*, 96.
57. I borrow this phrase from Rhiannon Graybill, "Fuzzy, Messy, Icky: The Edges of Consent in Hebrew Bible Rape Narratives and Rape Culture," *BCT* 15.2 (2019): 1–28 [13].
58. Simon Goldhill, "The Erotic Eye: Visual Stimulation and Cultural Conflict," in idem and Robin Osborne, eds., *Being Greek Under Rome: Cultural Identity, the Second Sophistic and the Development of Empire* (Cambridge: Cambridge University Press, 2001), 159–194 [183].
59. Goldhill, "The Erotic Eye," 182.
60. Tertullian's stereotype regarding the pantomime draws on that genre's gender-bending acting performances (i.e., one actor was expected to play all roles, regardless of gender). On the pantomime and other actors in this period, see H.A. Kelly, "Tragedy and the Performance of Tragedy in Late Roman Antiquity," *Traditio* 35 (1979): 21–44.

WORKS CITED

Arya, Rina. *Abjection and Representation? An Exploration of Abjection in the Visual Arts, Film and Literature*. Basingstoke, UK: Palgrave Macmillan, 2014.
Bataille, Georges. "Abjection and Miserable Forms," in Sylvere Lotringer, ed., *More & Less*. Brooklyn, NY: Semiotext(e)/Autonomedia, 1999, 8–13.
___. *Œuvres Complètes*. Paris: Gallimard, 1970.
Broeck, Sabine. *Gender and the Abjection of Blackness*. Albany, NY: State University of New York, 2018.
Burrus, Virginia. *Saving Shame: Martyrs, Saints, and Other Abject Subjects*. Philadelphia: University of Pennsylvania Press, 2008.
Butler, Judith. *Bodies That Matter: On the Discursive Limits of "Sex."* New York: Routledge, 1993.
___. *Gender Trouble: Feminism and the Subversion of Identity*. New York: Routledge, 1999 [1990].
Daniel-Hughes, Carly. *The Salvation of the Flesh in Tertullian of Carthage: Dressing for the Resurrection*. New York: Palgrave Macmillan, 2011.

___. "'Wear the Armor of Your Shame!': Debating Veiling and the Salvation of the Flesh in Tertullian of Carthage," *Studies in Religion/Sciences Religieuses* 39.2 (2010), 179–201.

Dasen, Véronique. "Childbirth and Infancy in Greek and Roman Antiquity," in Beryl Rawson, ed., *A Companion to Families in the Greek and Roman Worlds* (London: Blackwell, 2011), 291–314

Evans, Ernest, ed. *Tertullian's Treatise on the Resurrection*. London: SPCK, 1960.

Frilingos, Christopher. *Spectacles of Empire*. Philadelphia: University of Pennsylvania Press, 2004.

Glancy, Jennifer. "The Law of the Opened Body: Tertullian on the Nativity," *Henoch* 30.2 (2008), 267–288

Glover, T.R., tr., *Tertullian: Apology, De Spectaculis*, Loeb Classical Library 250. Cambridge, MA: Harvard University Press, 1931.

Goldhill, Simon. "The Erotic Eye: Visual Stimulation and Cultural Conflict," in Simon Goldhilll and Robin Osborne, eds., *Being Greek Under Rome: Cultural Identity, the Second Sophistic and the Development of Empire* (Cambridge: Cambridge University Press, 2001), 159–194

Graybill, Rhiannon. "Fuzzy, Messy, Icky: The Edges of Consent in Hebrew Bible Rape Narratives and Rape Culture," *The Bible & Critical Theory* 15.2 (2019), 1–28

Grosz, Elizabeth. *Sexual Subversions: Three French Feminists*. Sydney: Allen & Unwin, 1989.

___. *Volatile Bodies: Toward a Corporeal Feminism*. Bloomington, IN: University of Indiana Press, 1994.

Hennefeld, Maggie, and Nicholas Sammond. "Introduction: Not It, or, the Abject Objection," in *Abjection Incorporated: Mediating the Politics of Pleasure & Violence*, eds. Hennefeld and Sammond (Durham: Duke University Press, 2020), 1–31.

Kelly, H.A. "Tragedy and the Performance of Tragedy in Late Roman Antiquity," *Traditio* 35 (1979), 21–44

Kotrosits, Maia, and Carly Daniel-Hughes, "Tertullian of Carthage and the Materiality of Power," in Kotrosits, *The Lives of Objects: Material Culture, Experience, and the Real in the History of Early Christianity* (Chicago: University of Chicago Press, 2020), 85–106, 193–201.

Kristeva, Julia. *Powers of Horror: An Essay on Abjection*, translated by Leon S. Roudiez. New York: Columbia University Press, 1982.

Mañas Romero, Irene, and José Nicolás Saiz López, "Pueri nascentes: rituals, birth and social recognition in Ancient Rome," in Katharina Rebay-Salisbury and Doris Pany-Kucera, eds., *Ages and Abilities: The Stages of Childhood and Their Social Recognition in Prehistoric Europe and Beyond* (Oxford: Archaeopress, 2020), 235–248.

Padel, Ruth. "Women: Model for Possession by Greek Daemons," in Averil Cameron and Amélie Kuhrt, eds., *Images of Women in Antiquity* (Detroit: Wayne State University Press, 1993), 3–19.

Perkins, Judith. *Roman Imperial Identities in the Early Christian Era*. New York: Routledge, 2009.

Petrey, Taylor G. *Resurrecting Parts: Early Christians on Desire, Reproduction, and Sexual Difference*. New York: Routledge, 2016.
Proctor, Travis. Demonic Bodies and the Dark Ecologies of Early Christian Culture. Oxford: Oxford University Press, 2022.
Puar, Jasbir K. *The Right to Maim: Debility, Capacity, Disability.* Durham, NC: Duke University Press, 2017.
Quain, Edwin A., tr, "Tertullian On the Soul," in Rudolph Arbesmann, Sister Emily Joseph Daly, and Edwin A. Quain, trans., *Tertullian Apologetical Works and Minucius Felix Octavius*. New York: Fathers of the Church, 1950.
Radler, Charlotte. "The Dirty Physician: Necessary Dishonor and Fleshly Solidarity in Tertullian's Writings," *Vigiliae Christianae* 63 (2009), 345–368.
Spivak, Giyatri. "Extreme Eurocentrism," *Lusitania: A Journal of Reflection and Oceanography* (1992), 55–60.
Turcan, Marie, ed. *Tertullien: Les Spectacles*, Sources Chrétiennes 332. Paris: Éditions du Cerf, 2012 (1986).
Tyler, Imogen. "Against Abjection," *Feminist Theory* 10.1 (2003), 77–98.
Villalobos Mendoza, Manuel. *Abject Bodies in the Gospel of Mark*. Sheffield: Sheffield Phoenix Press, 2012.

Chapter 9

Paul Trading Barbs
Sexual Invective as Gendered Violence

Joshua M. Reno

Paul traffics in sexual slander with the intention of creating social boundaries within the communities to which he wrote. Prominent among his obloquies are sexual "subordination," "excess," and especially insinuations of sex work. His accusations and stereotypes exhibit xenophobia and misogyny conventional to the moralists of his time. And like his contemporaries, Paul deployed sexual slander seemingly to settle scores in other arenas of power.[1] As ever with Paul, control over these fledging communities seems to be his primary goal. While Paul was by no means the only ancient to peddle sexual invective, few other authors can claim to have the same impact. Paul's words, internalized and sacralized through centuries of protective and apologetic readings, represent one of the most well-read corpora of sexual abuse in history. The aim of this chapter is to unearth and elucidate two examples of Pauline sexual invective: first, Paul's brazen wish for genital mutilation in Galatians 5:12, and second, Paul's insidious exploitation of virginity discourse in 2 Corinthians 11:2–4. To do that I will sketch the milieu of ancient sexual slander—its tropes and functions—in Greek and Roman sources. Finally, I will conclude by discussing the impact Paul has on the present when his words are thoughtlessly reproduced at the pulpit or the lectern.[2]

SEXUAL INVECTIVE IN ANTIQUITY

Sex functioned as character witness in ancient discourse. Every aspect of sexual intercourse was open to scrutiny, and any deviation—perceived or fabricated—was a weakness to be exploited in public opinion. The who, what, where, when, why, and how of sexual activity were crucial details that rivals could cherry pick to paint the picture of saint or slut.[3] Invective was built on the standard logic of antiquity: *probabile ex vita* (i.e., character witness or assassination).[4] This logic hinges on two further assumptions: (1) Character Fixity and (2) Compounding Vices. The former assumption reasons that the character of an individual, established through invective, is elucidative of past, present, and future actions.[5] The second assumption indicates that any one deviation was persuasive evidence of multiple infractions if not a proclivity for any and every violation.[6] The adaptability of invective made it an efficacious and ubiquitous phenomenon of antiquity's agonistic society, utilized by authors and orators of diverse periods, locations, and cultures, and deployed in various media throughout the ancient Mediterranean. Despite this diversity, certain standard *topoi* persist,[7] including prominently gender and sexual deviances.[8] The same basic categories of insult exhibit a lengthy and diverse history well into late antiquity.[9] Below we will discuss two such tropes: the *os impurum* and slut-shaming.

OS IMPURUM

Aversion to *os impurum* ("defiled mouth") runs throughout Greek and Roman societies.[10] Impurity was contagious, much like disease, and could be communicated via close contact. In these societies, where a kiss was a medium of greeting, the dread of a foul mouth was acute.[11] Physical defilement was not the only concern. Common sense permitted guilt by association. Whatever activity besmirched the mouth of one man was likely one shared by those who willingly greeted him with a kiss. An opaque line separated approval from association, and thus critical importance was placed on cautious discernment of whose mouth passed purity muster. In the socio-sexual system of Greek and Roman societies, performing oral sex was considered degrading and defiling, especially for men. Unsurprisingly, therefore, insinuations that a rival (or their close associates) was a cunnilinctor or fellator were stock sexual abuse.

Athenian comics, like Aristophanes, exploited this taboo to great effect lambasting poets and politicians alike for performing oral sex.[12] Much like English, euphemistic or dysphemistic metaphors conflating food and drink with oral sex were regular. So, Aristophanes's crass Sausage Monger berates Paphlagon (*Eq.* 706–707): "So crabby! Come on, what shall I give you to eat [*kataphagein*]? On what will you munch [*phagois*] most happily? On a little weenie?"[13] Elsewhere, the language is much more direct: "This guy should gobble my cock [*to peos houtosi dakoi*]" (*Eq.* 1010)! Fellators were not the only targets of derision. Cunnilinctors also suffered disrepute: (*Pax* 885): "Oh no, my friend, once he's knelt down he'll lap her soup right up!" Cunnilingus conceived as ingestion is still clearer elsewhere (*Pax* 386–388): "If you recall having devoured [*katedēdokōs*] that welcome piglet [*choiridion*[14]] of mine, don't look on that as foul at this point."

Aristophanes is by no means alone. His iambic predecessors, Archilochus and Hipponax, were infamous for their sexual abuse, and whose poetry influenced Aristophanic slander.[15] Greek iambic traditions and comic ridicule profoundly influenced later Roman and Greek writers. This is nowhere clearer than during the late Republic and early Principate periods. The Latin poet Catullus (first century BCE) often invokes oral sex at others' expense, so in *Carmina* 80 he berates a certain Gellius for "gobbling [*vovare*] a man's full-grown mainmast" and in another, he lampoons Rufa for sucking off [*fellat*] Rufu(lu)s (*Carm.* 59). Amelius and another, Vettius, both suffer similar abuse for performing anilingus (*Carm.* 97, 98). Martial imitates Catullus in producing scornful poetry that inveighs against oral play. Apicius is accused of having a "repulsive tongue [*linguae malae*]" despite not speaking ill of any one (*Epigr.* 3.80). Martial also lampoons a certain Chione indicting her oral proclivity by insinuating her panties would be more effective on her face (*Epigr.* 3.87). In Greek, Lucian lampoons the willingness of a rival to have his mouth penetrated when drunk like that of Polyphemus's eye in *The Odyssey* (*Pseudol.* 27).

Comics and satirists are not the only public figures to deploy sexual slander. The public forum was full of aggressive and antagonistic attacks on sexual decorum. Athenian political rivals, Demosthenes and Aeschines, lampooned each other with stinging barbs. Aeschines (*Tim.* 130–131; cf. *Tim.* 167; *Fals. Leg.* 99, 127) warns the Athenians not to trust the words of his rival because that man's mouth has been defiled as a *kinaidos*. Elsewhere Aeschines *(Fals. Leg.* 23, 88) alleges that Demosthenes's whole body—even his mouth—was up for public sale. Demosthenes (*Cor.* 162, 242) in turn euphemistically labels Aeschines a *kinados* ("fox") and likewise indicates that, as far as Aeschines is concerned, everything is up for sale (*Fals. Leg.* 121, *peprakota pant'*).[16] Cicero (*Dom.* 10.25, 83) similarly attacks Clodius by insinuating that his associate Cloelius estranged Clodius and Clodia with his tongue.[17] The correlation of cunnilingus and hematophagy, especially menstrual blood, is also levied against the consul Mamercus Scaurus by Seneca the Younger (*Ben.* 4.31.2–5; cf. *Ep.* 87.16), and Lucian (*Pseudol.* 27) too accuses one of his critics, whom he facetiously names Rhododaphne, of similar offences.

Such insinuations were not neutral. Performing oral sex was closely associated with ancient disruptive deviants like the *cinaedi, pathici,* and eunuchs.[18] One graffito highlights the hunger of a *cinaedus* (*CIL* IV.1825): "Cosmus, you jockey, you massive *cinaedus* and cock-sucker: you hunger after naked males." Similarly, Catullus (*Carm.* 16) threatens anal and oral rape on his rivals Aurelius and Furius, whom he labels *pathicus* and *cinaedus* respectively. Eunuchs especially were considered to be identifiable by their effeminate behavior. They took a woman's role in sex and so were often associated with terms like *malakos* and *kinaidos*.[19] Eunuchs were thought to utterly lack sexual self-control, but worse still was their alleged proclivity for all manner of subordinate sexual behavior. In essence, these mutilated men did not *take pleasure* from sexual partners; rather, eunuchs were notorious for *giving pleasure*. With men, eunuchs were thought to enjoy being penetrated, either anally or orally. With women, eunuchs were frequently indicted for digital or oral stimulation of their mistresses.[20] So Martial roasts Baeticus for not "licking male middles" as he should, but instead, Baeticus is said to favor *cunnus* (*Epigr.* 3.81). Jerome naturalizes the connection between cunnilingus and castration exhorting women not to associate with eunuchs lest they give way to evil tongues (*lingua iniquorum*).[21] Of course, eunuchs were (in)famous for all manner of subordinate sexual stations, yet nothing is more debased, effeminate, subordinate than pleasuring a woman with one's mouth.[22] Eunuchs were considered, therefore, the basest humans—neither male nor female, but some transgressive *monstrum*—and as such eunuchs could be used as a curse against effeminate, non-castrated men.[23] To be labeled a eunuch was registered beyond the physical-anatomical sphere. Castration had sociological results: the death of manhood as a socio-ideological state.

GALATIAN CUNNILINCTORS

Paul's attack in Galatians 5:12 is made against advocates of Gentile circumcision, real or rhetorical. So, he states, "Would that those disturbing you actually emasculate themselves [*apokopsontai*]!" Paul's use of *apokoptō* is marked. Not only does this verb denote castration, but eunuchs were also labeled *apokopos* in Greek (cf. Latin *apocopus*).[24] Paul insinuates that these men should emasculate themselves and thus become eunuchs.[25] Such a caustic gibe has heavy significance in the gender economy of Classical antiquity. Eunuchs were considered deviant, abominable figures, most notably due to their characteristic (caricatured) effeminacy. Paul's opening salvo then indicates that these rivals ought to emasculate themselves, transforming themselves from men to transgressive, effeminate eunuchs. Branding rivals as eunuchs, Paul is quickly able to intimate something yet more nefarious about these rivals and their gospel. These men are impure, lustful for the flesh, and given to oral deviance.

There is good cause to consider *os impurum* as a potential allusion in Paul's bitter wish. Paul orients his distinction between his gospel and his opponents' gospel on slavery. Paul's is a gospel of freedom; theirs is a gospel of slavery. Eunuchs were normally slaves and as such could be expected to endure every manner of sexual use among ancient Greeks, Romans, and Jews.[26] So, like the enslaved generally, we have every reason to think that slavery would have included oral sexual service of master and mistress.[27] Paul's words evoke this milieu.[28] Chapter 5 opens with Paul's labored statement: "In his freedom, Christ has emancipated us. So stand firm and do not put on again a yoke of slavery." Paul situates his rivals' gospel as subjugation, one that places the Galatians in bondage and emasculates them for the purpose of carnal license. By contrast, Paul's is a gospel of freedom, mutual deference, and sexual propriety.

More tantalizing still is Paul's use of *katesthiō* ("to devour") in 5:15. As pointed out above, "to eat" is a regular euphemism for oral sex.[29] Both Greek and Latin exhibit a predilection for this metaphor, which was not limited to a technical set of vocabulary. Unsurprisingly, both languages offer a variety of consumptive verbs in these metaphors, the most common of which were *katesthiō* in Greek and *devoro* in Latin. So one Pompeiian graffito reads, "Calistus, eat (*devora*) it [dick]" (*CIL* IV.1854). Or, Aristophanes (*Pax* 716–717) writes with standard dysphemism, "You'll gulp down so much soup in three days, and so many boiled sausages and tender meats you'll devour [*katedei*]." Further, Paul also uses *daknō*, a verb used by Aristophanes's Sausage Monger in a nasty bit of fellatio humor (*Eq.* 1010). Inveighing against Paphlagon (Cleon), the Sausage Monger exclaims: "This guy should gobble my cock [*to peos houtosi dakoi*]!"[30] Paul's charge that the Galatians' freedom must not become a license for the flesh (*aphormēn tē sarki*, 5:13) resonates with sexual overtones. Euphemistic use of *sarx* persists in 5:16, with the *epithumia sarkos*, and 5:17, where the flesh lusts (*epithumei*). Shortly thereafter Paul lists the produce of the flesh, prominent among them *porneia, akatharsia,* and *aselgeia* (5:19).[31] In the midst of this flesh-fest, Paul intones three sexually charged terms opening the possibility of hearing a sly insinuation of sexual deviance. Such men are eunuchs in mind, even if they have not yet made themselves eunuchs in body. Paul alleges their actions already identify them as such, and he tacitly serves as the masterful physiognomist able to protect others not so adept at reading the physical manifestations of effeminacy.[32] Thus, one can well read Paul as indicating that his Galatian opponents are as good as castrates, who were stereotyped for their oral pleasure, a statement followed up with an argument that subtly positions his opponents' view as servile, orally deviant, sexually intemperate, given to serving each other's "flesh." There is good cause, therefore, to read Paul's caustic insult as insinuating that his opponents were deficiently masculine, as evidenced by "fleshly" beliefs given to (oral) sexual impropriety.

Paul savages these rivals, collapsing circumcision and castration, slavery and salacity, and insinuates that these men actually become what they are in all but flesh. Put another way, Paul's wish is rhetorically achieved by demonstrating they are sexually subordinate, servile eunuchs, even if their manhood hasn't yet been mutilated. Philodemus (*Anth. Graec.* 5.126) produces a similar effect by deriding a man who paid far more than he for a far less beautiful sex worker. Philodemus concludes: "Either I've absolutely lost my mind, or after this that guy's twins ought to be removed with an axe." Sexual deviance, especially publicly-witnessed sexual excess, in both instances is reduced to effeminacy. For Philodemus, a man driven to abject sexual slavishness ought to have his manhood removed for his physical body to reflect the emasculated state of his mind. Paul likewise reduces his rivals to the physical state that their devotion to circumcision has caused. Paul purports to protect the Galatian communities from a similar fate. In a rhetorical sl(e)ight of hand, Paul deploys a certain physiognomic prowess exposing these rivals as they really are. However much they may appear to be masculine rivals to Paul's authority, these men are *truly* lecherous castrates, a fact made clear by Paul whose physiognomic discernment cuts through their false deportment.[33]

The construction of a castrated caricature, of (rhetorical) rivals neither man nor woman, has major soteriological implications within the argument of this letter.[34] One of Paul's central claims in this epistle hangs on his use of the pre-Pauline baptismal formula: "There is no Jew or Greek. There is no slave or free. There is no male and female" (3:28). Thus, interpreters have understood baptismal initiation to have relegated such distinctions to the past, though these identities were not likely abolished in Galatian reality (cf. 1 Cor 7:17–24).[35] Why the tripartite formula changes in its final iteration has been a conundrum for interpreters. Many have insisted on coherence with the previous two items and thus have glossed Paul's Greek as "neither male nor female," indicating a "metaphysical removal of the *biological* sex," not merely "social emancipation but androgyny."[36] Some feminist interpreters have pointed out, Paul was not equalizing or unifying male and female but rather subsuming the female in the male. Kahl rightly labels Galatians as remarkably phallocentric, with Paul obsessively focused on the state of the foreskin.[37] This colors Paul's (supposedly) liberative statement "there is no male *and* female."[38] Paul's language suggests something similar to the *Gospel of Thomas* 114, where every woman who becomes male will enter the kingdom of heaven.[39] There is a transformation of female into male, from imperfection to perfection in ancient conception. This coheres well with the standard one-sex model of fe/male promoted by ancient philosophical and medicinal intellectuals.[40] Eunuchs, however, threaten this ancient model in that "their potential to transgress the boundaries of masculinity . . . challenge[s] the prevailing ethos of penetration that (they thought) was meant to correspond exclusively to elite imperial free males."[41] Since Christ's body is only male, then to be one with it, all believers must be male too.[42] As eunuchs, however, Paul's opponents are neither male nor female, but rather mark some monstrous, transgressive third gender.[43] Not only are they outside of the binary Paul invokes, but they also run against the grain, moving from male toward female, imperfecting and degenerating. Paul's invective performs a wholesale castration, cutting off his opponents' masculinity and so any claim to share in Christ.

SLUT-SHAMING

Ancient women endured a great amount of slut-shaming. Interrogation of the who, what, where, when, why, and how of women's sexual choices were ubiquitous and the answers, whether found or fabricated, were used to classify and valuate women. In this context, virginity was an ancient discourse of power wielded by men to control the sexual activity and productivity of ancient free-women. Virginity fabricated the illusion of a natural, innate dichotomy between chaste and unchaste women—between the *parthenos* and the *pornē* (or *matrona* and the *meretrix*). This discourse proved invaluable in controlling women's bodies, sexuality, and fecundity through the implementation of social and legal systems aimed to conform beliefs, attitudes, and practices to male-assigned norms.[44] Deviations from or contraventions of these norms were felt by men to be grievous assaults on the integrity of the household and male guardian to which a woman belonged. Though virginity was confined to women, it belonged to men. A father delivered his daughter's *parthenia* to his son-in-law at the wedding. In this respect, father and husband exhibit parallel functions. Fathers protected a woman's sexuality until marital consummation, and husbands secured a woman's sexuality (ideally) until death. Contravention of either father or husband was categorized in the same conceptual nexus: infidelity.[45]

Examples of infidelity abound from chaste women in adverse circumstances (e.g., Penelope, Lucretia) to allegations of tawdry wives (e.g., Clytemnestra, Phaedra, Sempronia, Messalina, Lesbia, or Clodia).[46] Indeed, accusations of promiscuity were ubiquitous in Roman satire.[47] The anxiety over sexual infidelity in Greek and Roman cultures was not merely sociological. Adultery entailed not just a breach of promises between partners. Rather, adultery intimated penetration of wife *and* household. Corner illuminates the socio-sexual concerns spatially, "Adultery overturned the exclusivity of the house and of domestic sexuality and brought the loose, open sexuality of the outside into the home and so could be spoken of as turning the *oikos* into a brothel."[48] Adultery and sex work were coextensive both morally and spatially. Through adultery the realm of sex work penetrated the household, despoiling the exclusive authority of the *kyrios* including his sexual authority over those who inhabit it.

Accusations of adultery thus easily elided into sex work.[49] At Athens, the enslaved, sex workers, and adulteresses were barred from the Thesmophoria (Isaeus 6.48–50). At Rome, Augustan legislation penalized husbands who did not prosecute their wives for adultery with the threat of prosecution for pimping.[50] In fact, the *Lex Iulia* on adultery legislated that the sex worker's infamous toga also be donned by convicted adulteresses.[51] Olson rightly suggests that this conceptual ambiguity is purposeful, "they [*moecha* and *meretrix*] are the same type of woman in our author's minds . . . [authors] felt they did not need to be distinguished absolutely. An adulteress *was* a whore."[52] In oratory, the line between the two had been blurred by prominent figures like Apollodorus, Isaeus, and Cicero, who employed "symbolic prostitutehood" against politically prominent women, whose actions threatened social hierarchies through "threateningly independent" sexual activity that undermined ideological paradigms like the *univira*.[53] Strong argues that "the common thread in all of these insults is not merely that the woman acted as a prostitute, but that she was publicly available and slept with men of low status, even slaves. She is disloyal not just to her family but to the social order itself."[54] In short, the central issue at question is disloyalty and *meretrix* was libel through which authors levied *infamia* against women felt to have circumvented patriarchal sexual mores. Glazebrook notes that guilt by association with sex work was an effective tactic of *pathos*, arousing suspicion, anger, hatred, and fear against both the woman and those men associated with her.[55] *Pornē*, then, was not simply the discursive counterpart to *parthenos* but was also an effective slur which male authors deployed to discredit and disparage women. Of course, sex work came with a conceptual framework that swelled with its own vernacular, images, and nexus of ideas. Authors did not necessarily need to come out and say "whore!" in order to accuse a woman. Indeed, conceptual matrices extended as far as labels like "work, public, and common" or "filth, degradation, and impurity" or "shame, lechery, and infidelity."[56]

CHRIST'S *PORNĒ*

Second Corinthians 11 begins by capitalizing on a metaphor in which Paul has betrothed the Corinthians to one man, presenting a pure virgin to Christ. There can be no confusion that Paul delivered to *one* man a *chaste* virgin—no surreptitious affairs, no miraculous conceptions. This scene fabricates a triad wherein the Corinthians function as a nearly agentless product of the socio-sexual exchange between Paul and Christ. Paul then claims that he and his Christ are not the Corinthians' only suitors and expresses concern that his chaste virgin may be seduced. He appeals to Eve who was beguiled by the serpent. Like his contemporaries, Paul likely understood Eve's deception to include sex.[57] By ancient standards, mental corruption was an adulterer's great crime.[58] Paul's metaphor, then, has already soured as he deploys standard prejudices built on misogynistic tropes about Eve to insinuate that the Corinthians are incapable of maintaining chastity in the face of cunning rivals. The next verse contains the brunt of Paul's slanderous assertions. While Pauline scholars have focused on Paul's reference to another *Jesus*, *Spirit*, and *Gospel*, my contention is that the weight of Paul's rhetoric comes not in these words but instead emphasis is placed on a stark repetition of *otherness*.

Paul's statement in 2 Cor 11:4 is littered with euphemistic undertone that continues to excoriate the Corinthians as sexually promiscuous. Three times Paul reiterates (an)other: Jesus, Spirit, and Gospel. Ancient ideal was that of the *univira*, or a "woman of one husband." Thus, *allos anēr* intimates a corruption of this ideal, a failure of fidelity. The language is standard in allegations of adultery[59] and in decrees of divorce or remarriage.[60] Aeschylus (*Ag.* 611–612) has Clytemnestra falsely claim not to know "the delight . . . of *another man*." Conversely, Lucretia reasons that "it is shameful . . . to live unlawfully with *another man*" (Diod. Sic. *Bibl. hist.* 1021.4). This trope comes off prominently in the Greek Novel where idealized virginity is pronounced. Thus, Chariton (*Chaer.* 2.11.1) has Callirhoe declare, "I want to die as the wife of Chaereas alone. This is sweeter to me than parents, homeland, and child: not to receive experience from *another man*."[61] The phrase *allos anēr* contributes to ancient virginity discourse that contrasted the untouched virgin with the used, unfaithful woman.

Paul too wields this stigma as a cudgel. So he asserts the Corinthians have been seduced by some *other* Jesus (*allos Iēsous*), other than Paul's chosen bridegroom. Already Paul conjures the image of a randy young woman more interested in sexual fulfillment than a proper marriage. Further, the Corinthians received some *other* spirit (*pneuma heteron lambanete*). Otherness doubles down on infidelity buttressed by the sexual undertones of (1) *pneuma* which could denote semen[62] and (2) *lambanō* that regularly was used of sexual reception, whether of experience with a man or reception of his semen.[63] Finally, Paul alleges the Corinthians welcomed some *other* gospel (*euaggelion heteron . . . edexasthe*). Once again Paul reiterates infidelity and here fills out the image insinuating the Corinthians have welcomed (*dechomai*[64]) another proposal (*euaggelion*[65]) with accompanying wedding bed.

The apodosis of this sentence has received startlingly little comment. The climax of all Paul's salacious slander is the seemingly innocuous phrase *kalōs anechesthe*. However, a standard denotation of the *echō* root was "to have sex with." This is seen widely in Greek literature, including the Septuagint and Paul.[66] When used in its compound forms these roots may denote toleration of sexual advances, as Aristophanes's heroine Lysistrata demonstrates:

> And if he overcomes me unwillingly by force . . . I will put up with him disagreeably (*kakōs parechō*) and will not fuck for him. (*Lys.* 225–228)[67]

Conversely, compounds of *echō* may intimate a promiscuous willingness to "put out." So, Strato (*Anth. Graec.* 12.11) recounts: "yesterday, while having [*echōn*] Philostratus for the night, I was impotent, despite him—how should I put it?—accommodating everything [*panta paraschomenon*]." In this sense, the terms indicate not so much "putting up" as "putting out." In a bitter Catch-22, subordinate partners who are complaisant were decried as overeager, disgraceful, and undesirable. It is this contrast between those who "put up" and those who "put out" that separates the violated *parthenos* from the vile *pornē*.

Paul's term *anechomai* also denotes tolerating something undesirable, and could be used to indicate toleration of sexual advances or activity. Lucian's (*Pseudol.* 27) diatribe against the *pseudologistēs* offers a telling example.

> And while you were yourself already drunk there, holding a wooden *kylix*, ready-to-fuck Polyphemus, a young man you hired, came to you as Odysseus, wielding his unbent stake, exceedingly well shaped, as if to put out your eye. . . . And you as the Cyclops opened up your mouth, and letting it gape as wide as possible, you endured (*ēneichou*) your mouth "being blinded" by him, or rather like Charybdis seeking to gulp down that "No One" whole along with his seamen, his rudder, and his furled sails.

Lucian reveals that even willing fellatio could be described using *anechomai*. Ideal women, like boys, were expected to resist as in Achilles Tatius where degrees of resistance, feigned or not, are felt (e.g., *Leuc. Clit.* 2.7).[68] So, Clitophon tolerates unhappily sex with Melite (5.27), though here every effort is made to excuse him by showing that he has sought to save himself for Leucippe. Conversely, when Melite's desire is depicted, resistance is not part of the narrative, only her lustful passion, temporarily attenuated by Clitophon's promise of intercourse (5.21).

Philological analysis demonstrates that *anechomai* denotes tolerance, with intimations of perverse willingness or upright reluctance added by context. Paul provides just such context: *kalōs*, which mirrors in reverse Lysistrata's oath to put up with sexual advances "disagreeably" (*kakōs*). The Corinthians "put up with this agreeably" or perhaps "put out well enough." The sexual metaphor built over 2 Cor 11:1–3 insinuates that the Corinthians eagerly "fuck around" with other suitors. Paul berates the Corinthians depicting them as a woman who puts out easily, a point he powerfully reiterates in vv. 19–20. They are not just a bride seduced, then, but a lascivious fiancée open to and willingly putting out for any newcomer.

IMPACTS OF SEXUAL INVECTIVE

Traditional interpretations of the Pauline epistles have conscripted passages such as these to posit rival missionaries to Paul. Scholars have thus beat these barbs into rivets in an effort to construct ideological opponents against which Paul rails. Pauline sexual invective is converted to Pauline theological juxtaposition, and entire epistles are interpreted through reconstructive mirror-readings. The nature of sexual invective, however, makes the results of these readings extremely dubious. Moreover, by converting sexual invective into theological juxtaposition, scholars have inadvertently internalized and sacralized Pauline sexual invective, with all its attendant violence, as part of Christian theological and sexual discourses.[69] Scholars, then, have contributed to the authorization of sexual slander as an expedient tactic for discrediting and dismissing theological rivals, and have sanctioned Paul's sexual prejudice(s) becoming complicit in the violence perpetrated by Paul and his interpreters against sexual and gender minorities.

In Galatians, Paul's intention is plainly not to offer a description but to discredit and deride. If only these men would emasculate themselves so their (public) bodies would reflect their (surreptitious) proclivities! Their mouths are sullied like those of eunuchs and should not be welcomed with a holy kiss, much less respected as authorities within the community. Such rivals are unmanned by Paul's rhetoric which conflates circumcision with castration, effeminacy, and salacity. Castration, then, is not the only violence lurking in Paul's words. Paul's invective presumes a set of ancient binaries that prioritizes and valorizes a form of masculinity which depreciates femininity saddling it with a host of sociomoral deficiencies.[70] Men such as these—who *receive penetration from* and *give pleasure to* dominant partners—suffer, according to Philo (*Spec.* 3.37), great disgrace at the hands of "the feminine disease" (*noson thēleian*) that "exchanges the manly nature for the feminine" (*tēn arrena phusin eis thēleian metaballein*).[71] "Eunuch" is an accusation alleging these men are dominated sexually and simultaneously the verbal weapon with which Paul (attempts to) dominate them (and the Galatians) socially. Thus, Paul's sexual invective, assigning sociosexual roles based on ancient prejudices of the ideal prepuce, relies foundationally on ancient misogyny. In short, eunuchs are considered imperfect, and therefore deficient, men, *precisely because* eunuchs "suffer like women" in a sexual context. Representing opponents as effeminate eunuchs, Paul can then build on further misogynistic prejudices. Lack of self-control, reified in sexual contexts by "the passion of desire" or *porneia*,[72] is a predilection of eunuchs insofar as self-control (*enkrateia*) is fundamentally a *masculine* virtue.[73] Furthermore, the fact that self-control is the virtue of a slaveholding society cannot be understood to be coincidence. The body and its impulses are meant to be mastered by the mind and reason. This tenant of ancient philosophy correlates precisely with ancient kyriarchy. That is the mind ought to control the body just as man ought to control woman, father control children, master control the enslaved. Self-control is as much a masculine virtue as are those household codes which uphold the statutory superiority of the freeborn, adult, male citizen.

In the case of 2 Corinthians 11, the weight of Paul's rhetoric comes from the repetition of *another*, a dog-whistle term for chastity, virginity, and infidelity. The Corinthians are, as Paul depicts them, his statutory inferiors. Paul's status supersedes their own in both gender and generation. The Corinthians are his daughter to whose sexuality and fecundity his analogy grants him rights. Paul complicates this image insinuating his daughter has been adulterated (*phtharē*) and his language participates in a culture of slut-shaming and victim blaming. Converting ideological uniformity to sexual purity maximizes the *pathos* of his claim, fomenting disgust at any alternative perspective, and *minimizes* the *logos* for Corinthian autonomy. Paul's metaphor, therefore, robs the Corinthians of ideological agency in the same way that daughters were robbed of sexual agency. Conversion is, therefore, a manipulative tactic in the power struggle waged between Paul and the Corinthians. This tactic weaponizes the male, misogynistic management of women's sexuality in an effort to undermine analogously the ideological liberty of the Corinthian community. The ideological sphere, untethered and uncurtailed, is converted to the sexual so that Paul can delimit it as unquestionably as he does women's sexuality.

Reception of Pauline sexual invective has had far reaching impacts beyond scholarship. Paul's words continue to wield influence on sociomoral discourses of gender, sexuality, and bodily autonomy. For instance, in Galatians Paul elides circumcision and mutilation (cf. Phil 3:2) insinuating his opponents are mutilated, effeminate eunuchs and are excluded from the baptismal promise of Gal 3:28. There Paul insists that male and female will be collapsed into just male (cf. *Gos. Thom.* 114).[74] Melissa Harl Sellew offers a trenchant and personal critique in her trans-centered reading of Thomas: "Someone like me, who in a sense is female long mistaken for a male, who in some people's eyes, though not my own, is perhaps a *male who made himself female*, now has to give up her womanhood and attempt to gain some semblance of maleness? That is not going to happen."[75] Paul's perspective represents a real and present danger for trans women, especially as modern interpreters convert Paul's misogyny into transmisogyny. Further, the rigid binary of Paul's language continues to harm intersex persons through Christian theological reflections on the normative body that encourage medicalized "management" of intersex individuals.[76] What was an expedient rhetorical tactic through which Paul hoped to curry favor for himself among the Galatians and delegitimate any potential rival perspective, continues to contribute to a culture that values masculinity above femininity. Further, insofar as Paul demands conformity under the guise of uniformity and unity even to the extent of threatening violence on those who do not conform (Gal 5:12; 1 Cor 4:21), penal power continues to be wielded against the gender margins to demand ideological and corporeal conformity to androcentric, cisnormative patriarchy.[77]

Paul's depiction of the Corinthians as the *pornē* of Christ in 2 Corinthians 11 continues to have ramifications for women and sex workers. Paul deploys patriarchal virginity/infidelity tropes to both shame the Corinthians and assert his control over them. Simultaneously, Paul can claim that the Corinthians should rightly be his chaste *parthenos*, and also that the Corinthians have become a notorious sex worker through infidelity to Christ their betrothed. Already in antiquity, Paul participates in a prejudicial discourse that is astonishingly tone deaf given that many/most sex workers were enslaved and the enslaved were expected to put out at their master's whim. The reception of Paul's prejudice continues to play powerfully in notoriously misogynistic slut-shaming and the stigmatization of those who have acquired capital through the sexual employment of their own bodies. Perhaps less obviously, Paul's language participates in and contributes to male management of women's bodies and sexualities. Research continues to show that Christian Purity Culture(s) applies more stringently to women (e.g., modest dress).[78] Assumptions like "boys will be boys" excuse boys from the purity standards that constrain women and perpetuate rape culture through the assumption that women's bodies and sexualities are the purview of men.

These exempla share in common conversion of the ideological to the sexual. In both instances, Paul leverages ancient sexual discourse(s) through a metaphorical matrix in the first instance to empower his *ideological* perspective with Greco-Roman masculinity and in the second to delegitimize his opponents' *ideological* perspective through aspersions of sexual deviancy and gender deficiency. Paul's use demonstrates clearly how this tactic can be exploited to gaslight insiders and malign outsiders. The communities to which he wrote are assured that they are unqualified to self-determine (e.g., Gal 3:1; 2 Cor 11:3) and told in no uncertain terms they are not permitted to associate with outsiders whose murky identities Paul exposes as deviant.

Paul's words were already dangerous and manipulative in antiquity; however, their reception by scholars has reinforced their power and contributes to the gaslighting of communities against whom Paul's words continue to be weaponized. "It's just a joke," is a standard refrain of gaslighters in defense of reprehensible comments, especially when confronted by individuals belonging to the (typically) racial, sexual, or gender identity used as the butt of the "joke." This tactic invalidates the abused by trivializing their perspective and shifting blame to them for not understanding the abuser's "humor" and thus "antagonizing" their abuser. Paul's apostolic authority seems to have unduly protected his invective from censure. Thus, Betz claims Gal 5:12 is "an after-thought," a "joke," one which Paul's peers were doing and merely "salts his argument."[79] Similar terms abound (e.g., sarcasm, irony[80]), all of which tacitly whitewash Paul and demand readers see Paul's best intentions. It is insisted, especially to sexual and gender minorities, that the neutral, impartial reading of Paul (i.e., the historical-critical) recognizes the gravity of the apostle's argument. Thus, Paul's comments, whose power hinges on scorn toward (enslaved, forcibly castrated) eunuchs and (socio-physically constrained) women, are presented in scholarship as the condonable solecisms of an impassioned, but ultimately just, apostle. The ends justify the means—according to traditional thinking—since Paul's intentions were to protect orthodoxy. Those hurt, offended, or harmed by Paul's misogynistic invective are declared "too sensitive." Paul was "just joking." Justification, it seems, simply declares Paul right.

NOTES

1. Marilyn B. Skinner, *Sexuality in Greek and Roman Culture*, 2nd ed. (Malden, MA: Wiley-Blackwell, 2014), 284–86.

2. This chapter is based on the research of my dissertation: Joshua M. Reno, "Holy Obscenity: Sexual Invective in the Pauline Corpus," (PhD diss., The University of Minnesota, 2021).

3. Questions ranged considerably: Who had sex with whom? Who penetrated whom? How did they have sex (e.g., anal, intercrural, manual, oral, vaginal)? What were the respective statuses of the partners (e.g., virgin, betrothed, married; child, parent; free, freed, slave; citizen, foreigner; man, woman, eunuch; etc.)? How often did they have sex (e.g., once, regularly, excessively)? When did they have sex (e.g., day, night; festival, holy day)? Where did they have sex (e.g., private, public, marriage bed, brothel, temple)? Why did they have sex (e.g., procreation, work, lust)?

4. Valentina Arena, "Roman Oratorical Invective," in *A Companion to Roman Rhetoric*, ed. William Dominik and Jon Hall (Malden, MA: Blackwell, 2007), 155.

5. Jess Miner, "Crowning Thersites: The Relevance of Invective in Athenian Forensic Oratory," (PhD diss., The University of Texas at Austin, 2006), 11.

6. W. Jeffrey Tatum, "Social Commentary and Political Invective," in *A Companion to Catullus*, Blackwell Companions to the Ancient World. Edited by Marilyn B.

Skinner (Malden, MA: Blackwell, 2007), 335. See e.g., Cicero, *Inv.* 2.33; [Cicero,] *Rhet. Her.* 2.3. [2.5]; Seneca, *Ep.* 18.14–15; 47.19; Diogenes Laertius, *Vit.* 7.127.

7. Arena, "Roman Oratorical Invective," 149. See the useful table provided by Alexandra Robinson, *Jude on the Attack: A Comparative Analysis of the Epistles of Jude, Jewish Judgement Oracles, and Greco-Roman Invective*, LNTS 581 (New York: Bloomsbury, 2018), 120–121.

8. Christopher Craig, "Audience Expectations, Invective, and Proof," in *Cicero the Advocate*, ed. Jonathan Powell and Jeremy Paterson (New York: Oxford University Press, 2004), 191. Similarly, J. Roger Dunkle, "The Greek Tyrant and Roman Political Invective of the Late Republic," *TAPA* 98 (1967): 166–167. See also Amy Richlin, *The Garden of Priapus: Sexuality and Aggression in Roman Humor*, Rev. ed. (New York: Oxford University Press, 1992), 96–104; Anthony Corbeill, *Controlling Laughter: Political Humor in the Late Roman Republic*, (Princeton Legacy Library: Princeton University Press, 1996), 99–173; Rebecca Langlands, *Sexual Morality in Ancient Rome* (New York: Cambridge University Press, 2006), 281–318; Wilhelm Süss, *Ethos: Studien zur älteren griechischen Rhetorik* (Leipzig: Teubner, 1910), 249–250. Miner, "Crowning Thersites," 71–107; Nancy Worman, *Abusive Mouths in Classical Athens* (New York: Cambridge University Press, 2008), 213–274; Jess Miner, "Risk and Reward: Obscenity in the Law Courts of Athens," in *Ancient Obscenities: Their Nature and Use in the Ancient Greek and Roman Worlds*, ed. Dorota Dutsch and Ann Suter (Ann Arbor: University of Michigan Press, 2015), 125–150; Deborah Kamen, *Insults in Classical Athens* (Madison: The University of Wisconsin Press, 2020), 79–81; Severin Koster, *Die Invektive in der griechischen und römischen Literatur*, BKPh 99 (Meisenheim am Glan: Anton Hain, 1980), 363.

9. Kamen, *Insults*, 8–9, 21–22, 49–52, 79–81; Miner, "Crowning Thersistes," 5–8, 16–26. See also Werner Krenkel, "Sex und politische Biographie," in *Naturalia non turpia: Sex and Gender in Ancient Greece and Rome*, Schriften zur antiken Kultur- und Sexualwissenschaft, eds. Wolfgang Bernard and Christiane Reitz (New York: Georg Olms, 2006), 233–263; Jason von Ehrenkrook, "Effeminacy in the Shadow of Empire: The Politics of Transgressive Gender in Josephus's 'Bellum Judaicum,'" *Jewish Quarterly Review* 101 (2011): 145–163; Richard Flower, *Emperors and Bishops in Late Roman Invective* (New York: Cambridge University Press, 2013), 103.

10. Jeffrey Henderson, *The Maculate Muse: Obscene Language in Attic Comedy*, 2nd ed. (New York: Oxford University Press, 1991), 183–186; Werner Krenkel, "Fellatio and Irrumatio," in Bernard and Reitz, Naturalia non turpia, 210–215, 219–223, 224–231; Werner Krenkel, "Tonguing," in Bernard and Reitz, Naturalia non turpia, 265–268, 271–275, 277–284, 285–287, 297–301; Richlin, *Garden of Priapus*, 26–30, 69, 82–83, 99, 128, 132, 149–151, 246 n. 36; Corbeill, *Controlling Laughter*, 99–127; Craig A. Williams, *Roman Homosexuality*, 2nd ed. (New York: Oxford University Press, 2010), 218–224.

11. Catullus, *Carm.* 37.20; 39.17–21; 97; 98; Martial, *Epigr.* 1.94; 2.10, 12, 20; 11.61; 12.55, 59.

12. Worman (*Abusive Mouths*, 62–120) identifies the Aristophanic correlation of professional speech and lascivious mouths.

13. All translations are mine unless otherwise noted.

14. Porcine terminology was among the most common metaphors for *kusthos* ("cunt"), e.g., Aristophanes, *Ach.* 764–808. See LSJ, A.I.2; BrillDAG, A; Henderson, *The Maculate Muse*, 131–132; J. N. Adams, *The Latin Sexual Vocabulary* (Baltimore: Johns Hopkins University Press, 1982), 82.

15. See Worman, *Abusive Mouths*, 8–14; Kirk Ormand, "Toward Iambic Obscenity," in Dutsch and Suter, *Ancient Obscenities*, 44–70.

16. Worman, *Abusive Mouths*, 247–260; Kamen, *Insults*, 79–81.

17. Corbeill, *Controlling Laughter*, 112–124. See also Krenkel, "Tonguing," 286.

18. Ps.-Archilochus, *Fr.* 328.9; Martial, *Epigr.* 3.77, 81. See also graffiti: *CIL* 1825a, 1826, 1827.

19. Peter Guyot, *Eunuchen als Sklaven und Freigelassene in der griechisch-römischen Antike*, Stuttgarter Beiträge zur Geschichte und Politik 14 (Stuttgart: Klett-Cotta, 1980), 38–41. See, e.g., Terence, *Eun.* 357, 375, 473, 606; Juvenal, *Sat.* 6.366–367. For stereotypical depictions of eunuchs as corruptively effeminate see Plato, *Leg.* 695A-B; Curtius Rufus, *Alex.* 10.1.22–38. N.B. the definitions provided by late antique lexicographers: Zenobius 2.62; Hesychius, *Lex.* β 106; Suda, *Lex.* β 46

20. J. David Hester, "Eunuchs and the Postgender Jesus: Matthew 19.12 and Transgressive Sexualities," *JSNT* 28 (2005): 22–23. See Terence, *Eun.* 479; Epictetus, *Diatr.* 2.19.20.

21. Jerome, *Epist.* 108.20; see also Gregory of Nazianzus, *Or.* 43.47; Theophylact Simocatta, *Epist.* 43 H; Aristaenetus, *Ep.* 1.21. For the connection between eunuchs and cunnilingus see Krenkel, "Tonguing," 282; Mathew Kuefler, *The Manly Eunuch: Masculinity, Gender Ambiguity, and Christian Ideology in Late Antiquity* (Chicago: The University of Chicago Press, 2001), 97–98.

22. Galen, 12.249 (Kühn); cf. Martial, *Epigr.* 7.67.14; Aristophanes, *Equit.* 1280–1289.

23. Guyot, *Eunuchen*, 41–42. See Terence, *Eun.* 696, 860.

24. All the various terms for eunuchs in Greek and Latin directly reference the fact of castration. See Guyot, *Eunuchen*, 21–22.

25. Similarly, Joseph A. Marchal, *Appalling Bodies: Queer Figures Before and After Paul's Letters* (New York: Oxford University Press, 2019), 79–102. The precise object of excision seems to matter little to Paul. Whether the castration removes the testes or the glans penis, the resulting figure was considered a cut, mutilated non-man, whose deviance from physical manhood was expected to be mirrored by sexual deviance (from manhood).

26. Jennifer A. Glancy, "The Sexual Use of Slaves: A Response to Kyle Harper on Jewish and Christian *Porneia*," *JBL* 134 (2015): 215–229; Glancy, "Early Christianity, Slavery, and Women's Bodies," in *Beyond Slavery: Overcoming Its Religious and Sexual Legacies*, ed. Bernadette J. Brooten (New York: Palgrave, 2010), 147–149; Krenkel, "Tonguing," 282.

27. Krenkel, "Tonguing," 282. See Terence, *Eun.* 486; Seneca the Elder, *Contr.* 4.Praef.10; 10.4.17; Petronius, *Satyr.* 75.11; Seneca the Younger, *Ep.* 47.7; 95.24; *Brev.* 12.5; Martial, *Epigr.* 9.6; Chariton, *Chaer.* 2.6.2; *CIL* 4.8380.

28. Joseph A. Marchal ("The Usefulness of an Onesimus: The Sexual Use of Slaves and Paul's Letter to Philemon," *JBL* 130 [2011]: 749–770) has made the case that

Paul's emphasis on the usefulness (*achrēston* and *euchrēston*) of Onesimus carries the socio-sexual undertones of the sexual use of enslaved persons (Phlm 11–20).

29. Krenkel, "*Fellatio* and *Irrumatio*," 220–221; Krenkel, "Tonguing," 271–275, 277–281. See also Adams, *The Latin Sexual Vocabulary*, 138–141; Henderson, *The Maculate Muse*, 47–48, 52.

30. See also Aristophanes, *Ach.* 1208–1221; *Nub.* 709–715; *Av.* 441. Hipponax (*Fr.* 84.11) and Lucian (*Asin.* 32; *Meret.* 5.3.4) use *daknō* in erotic contexts. See also Catullus, *Carm.* 8.18; Martial, *Epigr.* 9.73 (?). Note the extended cock-fight metaphor, ripe with sexual innuendos, at *Eq.* 496–497 (cf. Demosthenes, *Or.* 54.8–9).

31. On *porneia* see Joshua M. Reno, "Pornographic Desire in the Pauline Corpus," *JBL* 140 (2021): 163–185. *Akatharsia* and *aselgeia* can be fruitfully read in the context of *os impurum*, on which see Richlin, *The Garden of Priapus*, 29; Krenkel, "Tonguing," 265–266.

32. Marchal's (*Appalling Bodies*, 109) observation is apt: "Paul's rhetorical efforts seem to be less defenses of *the* gospel or *the* community, endangered from the outside than a response, angry and volatile, to a (perceived [or I would suggest, fabricated]) encroachment on *his* gospel and *his* (perceived) community, from another potential option about the embodiment of communal life, likely even from within these assembly communities."

33. Maud Gleason, *Making Men: Sophists and Self-Presentation in Ancient Rome* (Princeton: Princeton University Press, 1995), 76–81.

34. Marchal, *Appalling Bodies*, 105–108.

35. Daniel Boyarin, *A Radical Jew: Paul and the Politics of Identity* (Berkeley: University of California Press, 1994), 186–187. However, Melissa Harl Sellew ("Reading the *Gospel of Thomas* from Here: A Trans-Centred Hermeneutic," *JIBS* 1 [2020]: 78–79) correctly describes Paul's tactic as "erasure" and "masking" of difference.

36. Hans Dieter Betz (*Galatians: A Commentary on Paul's Letter to the Churches in Galatia*, Hermeneia [Minneapolis: Fortress, 1979], 196) follows the immensely influential reading of Wayne A. Meeks, "The Image of the Androgyne: Some Uses of a Symbol in Earliest Christianity," *HR* 13 (1974): 165–208.

37. Brigette Kahl, "Gender Trouble in Galatia? Paul and the Rethinking of Difference," in *Is There a Future for Feminist Theology*, eds. Deborah F. Sawyer and Diane M. Collier (Sheffield: Sheffield Academic Press, 1999), 57–73.

38. Marchal, *Appalling Bodies*, 78.

39. See Harl Sellew, "Reading the *Gospel of Thomas* from Here," 82–86.

40. Thomas Laqueur, *Making Sex: Body and Gender from the Greeks to Freud* (Cambridge: Harvard University Press, 1990), 5–6, 25–31; Brooke Holmes, *Gender: Antiquity and Its Legacy* (New York: Oxford University Press, 2012), 46–56.

41. Marchal, *Appalling Bodies*, 106.

42. See Kari Vogt, "'Becoming Male': A Gnostic and Early Christian Metaphor," in *The Image of God: Gender Models in Judaeo-Christian Tradition*, ed. Kari Elisabeth Børresen (Minneapolis: Fortress, 1995), 170–186; Lone Fatum, "Image of God and Glory of Man: Women in the Pauline Congregations," in Børresen, *Image of God*, 63–64. Contrast Kahl, "Gender Trouble in Galatia?" 71–72; Kahl, "No Longer Male:

Masculinity Struggles Behind Galatians 3:28?" *JSNT* 79 (2000): 43–46. For criticisms of these approaches see Elisabeth Schüssler Fiorenza, "Ideology, Power, and Interpretation: Galatians 3:28," in *Rhetoric and Ethic: The Politics of Biblical Studies* (Minneapolis: Fortress, 1999), 159–173.

43. Guyot, *Eunuchen*, 38–41.

44. Virginity was considered a feminine quality during the time of Paul, see Achilles Tatius, *Leuc. Clit.* 5.20. Virginity was sociolinguistically tied to young women in Greek and Roman cultures: *parthenia, koreia, virginitas*. See Susan Treggiari, *Roman Marriage: Iusti Coniuges from the Time of Cicero to the Time of Ulpian* (New York: Oxford University Press, 1991), 105–106; Amy Richlin, *Arguments with Silence: Writing the History of Roman Women* (Ann Arbor: University of Michigan Press, 2014), 68–70. On ancient virginity generally, see the definition of Giulia Sissa, *Greek Virginity*, trans. Arthur Goldhammer (Cambridge: Harvard University Press, 1990), 88–91; see also the extensive examination of Mary F. Foskett, *A Virgin Conceived: Mary and Classical Representation of Virginity* (Indianapolis: Indiana University Press, 2002), 25–73.

45. Corruption of an upstanding daughter carried the same terminology and legal ramifications as corruption of an upstanding wife: *moicheia*.

46. See e.g., Hesiod, *Op.* 695–705; Semonides, 7.50–56; Aeschylus, *Cho.* 595–601; Euripides, *Ion* 1090–1097; *Hipp.* 407–418; Aristophanes, *Eccl.* 225; *Pax* 980–986; *Thesm.* 789–800; Juvenal, *Sat.* 6.200–241.

47. Richlin, *Arguments with Silence*, 70.

48. Sean Corner, "Bringing the Outside In: The *Andrōn* as Brothel and the Symposium's Civic Sexuality," in *Greek Prostitutes in the Ancient Mediterranean 800 BCE–200 CE*, ed. Allison Glazebrook and Madeleine M. Henry (Madison: University of Wisconsin Press, 2011), 65.

49. This elision is prominent in the Jewish Scriptures (e.g., Jer 3:6–9; Hosea 1–3; Isaiah 62; Ezekiel 16), as well as Greek and Roman literature: *ILS* 9455; Demosthenes, [*Neaer*.] 59.67; Tacitus, *Ann.* 2.85.2; Suetonius, *Tib.* 35.2. Conversely, brothels were feared to function as rendezvous for trysts: see Tacitus, *Ann.* 15.37; Juvenal, *Sat.* 6.114–141; Suetonius, *Calig.* 41.1.

50. Kelly Olson, "*Matrona* and Whore: Clothing and Definition in Roman Antiquity," in *Prostitutes and Courtesans in the Ancient World*, ed. Christopher A. Faraone and Laura K. McClure (Madison: University of Wisconsin Press, 2006), 193–194.

51. Thomas A. J. McGinn, *The Economy of Prostitution in the Roman World* (Ann Arbor: University of Michigan Press, 2004), 251–252. On the treatment of adulteresses as sex workers see Hans Herter, "The Sociology of Prostitution in Antiquity in the Context of Pagan and Christian Writings," in *Sex and Difference in Ancient Greece and Rome*, ed. Mark Golden and Peter Toohey (New York: Edinburgh University Press, 2003), 70.

52. Olson, "*Matrona* and Whore," 192–193.

53. Anise K. Strong, *Prostitutes and Matrons in the Roman World* (New York: Cambridge University Press, 2016), 98. See also Allison Glazebrook, "The Bad Girls of Athens: The Image and Function of *Hetairai* in Judicial Oratory," in Faraone and McClure, *Prostitutes and Courtesans*, 130–135.

54. Strong, *Prostitutes and Matrons*, 117.
55. Glazebrook, "The Bad Girls of Athens," 132, 134–135.
56. Konstantinos K. Kapparis, "The Terminology of Prostitution in the Ancient Greek World," in Glazebrook and Henry, *Greek Prostitutes*, 226–231. See also J. N. Adams, "Words for 'Prostitute' in Latin," *RhM* 1265 (1983): 350–353.
57. 4 Macc 18:7–9; Irenaeus, *Haer.* 1.30.7; Clement, *Strom.* 3.14; Apoc. Abr. 23.1; Apoc. Mos. 19.6; 2 En. 31.6. See also Philo *Agr.* 108; *Leg.* 2.79–81. Paul's choice of *phtheirō* ("to corrupt") suggests he also understood Eve's seduction to be sexual.
58. Lysias, *Or.* 1.33; Xenophon, *Symp.* 8.20; Dionysius of Halicarnassus, *Ant. rom.* 13.10.15; Isocrates, *Demon.* 32; Polybius, *Hist.* 28.21.3; Diodorus Siculus, *Bibl. hist.* 29.2.1; 30.17.1; Philo, *Leg.* 3.148; *Ios.* 50; *Migr.* 66, 224; *Mos.* 1.305; Musonius, *Fr.* 20.49; Plutarch, *Ag. Cleom.* 54.2.
59. Hosea 3:3; Job 31:9–10; Mark 10:11–12 // Matt 19:9 // Luke 16:18 (cf. Deut 24:1–4; Jer 3:1). See also Diodorus Siculus, *Bibl. hist.* 1.59.3 (= Hecataeus, *Fr.* 25.728 [3a,264,F]); 10.21.4; *Vita. Aesopi* 109; Plutarch, *Dion* 51.1; Dio Chrysostom, *Or.* 15.5; Lucian, *Hermot.* 34; Herodian, *Pros. cath.* 3,2 p. 164 (§ 220); *Historia Alexandri* 84 (rec. φ). Some authors playfully adapt this trope: Euripides, *Hipp.* 1100; *Hel.* 1626; Gen 29:19; Tob 6:13; 7:10; T.Ab. 10.
60. Mark 10:11–12 // Matt 19:9 // Luke 16:18 (cf. Deut 24:1–4). See also Euripides, *Fr.* 953.27–32; Isaeus, *Cir.* 36; *Euph.* 5; Menander, *Asp.* 132–135; Dionysius of Halicarnasus, *Ant. rom.* 8.41.4; *Isaeo* 17; Physiologus, *Phys.* 27.
61. See also Chariton, *Chaer.* 3.7.5; 5.6.5; Achilles Tatius, *Leuc. Clit.* 5.18.4; Xenophon, *Eph.* 1.11.4.
62. On ancient physiology of semen see Giulia Sissa, "*Phusis* and Sensuality: Knowing the Body in Greek Erotic Culture," in *A Companion to Greek and Roman Sexualities*, ed. Thomas K. Hubbard (Malden: Wiley-Blackwell, 2014), 270. See e.g., Aristotle, *Gen. an.* 736b [2.3]; Galen, *Sem.* 2.5; Hierocles, *Elem. eth.* 1. On Paul's awareness of this conceptual framework see Troy W. Martin, "Paul's Argument from Nature for the Veil in 1 Corinthians 11:13–15: A Testicle Instead of a Head Covering," *JBL* 123 (2004): 75–84.
63. Chariton, *Chaer.* 2.11.1; 4.4.9; Ptolemaeus, *Diff. voc.* 61; Diodorus Siculus, *Bibl. hist.* 1.59.3 (= Hecataeus, *Fr.* 25.728 [3a,264,F]); Philo, *Spec.* 1.106; *Vitae Aesopi* 109. Several authors playfully adapt this language: Diodorus Siculus, *Bibl. hist.* 34/35.37 (= Posidonius, *Fr.* 189); Apollonius, *Ep.* 46; Plutarch, *Pyr.* 29.11.
64. *Dechomai* was used to indicate receipt of dowries or proposals, as well as sexual intercourse. Euripides, *El.* 1198–1200; *Ion* 60; *Med.* 978–979; Herodotus, *Hist.* 9.111.5; Aristophanes, *Av.* 1725–1730; Menander, *Dysk.* 730–749; Diodorus Siculus, *Bibl. hist.* 4.54.6 (= Dionysius Scytobrachion, *Fr.*14.394 [1a,32,F]); Plutarch, *Cat. mai.* 24.6–7; *Cat. min.* 30.9; Dio Cassius, *Hist. rom.* 48.39.2; Heliodorus, *Aeth.* 6.8.2. See also Hom. *Hym. Aphr.* 137–142; Pindar, *Pyth.* 3.94–95; Euripides, *Med.* 956–958, 1003–1004; Aristophanes, *Pax* 1204–1206; Plato, *Leg.* 742c; Diodorus Siculus, *Bibl. hist.* 4.54.6; Dio Cassius, *Hist. rom.* 48.39.2.
65. *Euaggelion* often referred to more colloquial good news, such as weddings: P.Oxy. 46.3313.1–8; Longus, *Daphn.* 3.33.1; Achilles Tatius, *Leuc. Clit.* 5.12.3; Chariton, *Chaer.* 6.5.1–10; Menander, *Georg.* 42–84, esp. 83–84.

66. Exod 2:1; Deut 28:30; Isa 13:16; 1 Cor 5:1. See also Josephus, *A.J.* 7.151; Philo, *Leg.* 2.236.

67. See also Aristophanes, *Lys.* 160–163. *Parechō* also carries this sexual connotation in Lucian, *Dial. meretr.* 5.4; *Dial. mar.* 13.1

68. Kenneth J. Dover, *Greek Homosexuality: Updated and with a New Postscript* (Cambridge: Harvard University Press, 1989).

69. This history is perhaps no more egregious than in Christian anti-Judaic invective, on which see Susanna Drake, *Slandering the Jew: Sexuality and Difference in Early Christian Texts* (Philadelphia: University of Pennsylvania Press, 2013); Drake, "Sexual Slander," in *The Oxford Handbook of New Testament, Gender, and Sexuality*, ed. Benjamin H. Dunning (New York: Oxford University Press, 2019), 593–606. However, the LGBTQIA community has borne the brunt of much Christian anti-queer/trans invective, on which see Heather R. White, "How Paul Became the Straight Word: Protestant Biblicism and the Twentieth-Century Invention of Biblical Heteronormativity," in *Bodies on the Verge: Queering Pauline Epistles*, ed. Joseph A. Marchal (Atlanta: Society of Biblical Literature, 2019), 289–307. Dale B. Martin, *Sex and the Single Savior: Gender and Sexuality in Biblical Interpretation* (Louisville: Westminster John Knox, 2006), 17–35, 51–64.

70. David M. Halperin, *One Hundred Years of Homosexuality: And Other Essays on Greek Love* (New York: Routledge, 1990), 133; John J. Winkler, *The Constraints of Desire: The Anthropology of Sex and Gender in Ancient Greece* (New York: Routledge, 1990), 54; Catharine Edwards, *The Politics of Immorality in Ancient Rome* (New York: Cambridge University Press, 1993), 81; Williams, *Roman Homosexuality*, 137–176.

71. Here Philo condemns pederasty (*paiderastein*). He begins by lambasting the *erōmenos* for being treated like a woman—and, indeed, treating himself like a woman through attention to hair, makeup, perfume, and beauty. He continues (*Spec.* 3.39) to condemn the *erastēs* for pursuing non-procreative sex (i.e., wasting his seed) and for being "a guide and teacher of unmanliness and effeminacy (*anandrias kai malakias*). The culture of pederasty results in rewards for "lack of self-control and effeminacy" (*akrasias kai malakias*) granted to "effeminate men" (*androgynous*, *Spec.* 3.40). Valorization of effeminacy, Philo concludes (*Spec.* 3.41), has resulted in some men desire "the transition into women" (*metabolēs tēs eis gynaikas*) and they "castrate their genitals" (*ta gennētika prosapekopsan*).

72. Reno, "Pornographic Desire," 177–184.

73. Stephen D. Moore, *God's Beauty Parlor: And Other Queer Spaces in and around the Bible* (Stanford: Stanford University Press, 2001), 160–163.

74. See Vogt, "'Becoming Male,'" 170–186.

75. Harl Sellew, "Reading the *Gospel of Thomas* from Here," 83.

76. Joseph A. Marchal, "Bodies Bound for Circumcision and Baptism: An Intersex Critique and the Interpretation of Galatians," *TSE* 16 (2010): 163–182.

77. Perhaps the most egregious and visible example of this is so-called conversion therapy. However, the weaponization of sexuality against non-conformers permeates Christian discourse and is often exploited to defend sexually abusive religious leaders through slut-shaming and victim-blaming. Robert Downen, Lise Olsen, and John

Tedesco, "Abuse of Faith: 20 Years, 700 Victims: Southern Baptist Sexual Abuse Spreads as Leaders Resist Reforms," *The Houston Chronicle*, 10 Feb. 2019, https://www.houstonchronicle.com/news/investigations/article/Southern-Baptist-sexual-abuse-spreads-as-leaders-13588038.php.

78. Katie Gaddini, "Practising Purity: How Single Evangelical Women Negotiate Sexuality," in *Intersecting Religion and Sexuality: Sociological Perspectives*, RSO 27 (Leiden: Brill, 2020), 109.

79. Betz, *Galatians*, 270. Compare J. Louis Martyn, *Galatians: A New Translation with Introduction and Commentary*, AB 33A (New York: Doubleday, 1997), 478. Martyn may identify Paul's "wish" (469) as a "rude, obscene, and literally bloody picture at their expense." However, Martyn converts castration into "trust in the redemptive power of religion" and thus a palatable "wish" for Paul to make.

80. D. F. Tolmie, "The Interpretation and Translation of Galatians 5:12," *AcT* 2 (2009): 90–93.

WORKS CITED

Adams, J. N. *The Latin Sexual Vocabulary*. Baltimore: The Johns Hopkins University Press, 1982.

———. "Words for 'Prostitute' in Latin." *Rheinisches Museum für Philologie* 126 (1983): 321–358.

Arena, Valentina. "Roman Oratorical Invective." Pages 149–160 in *A Companion to Roman Rhetoric*. Edited by William Dominik and Jon Hall. Malden, MA: Blackwell, 2007.

Betz, Hans Dieter. *Galatians: A Commentary on Paul's Letter to the Churches in Galatia*. Hermeneia. Minneapolis: Fortress, 1979.

Boyarin, Daniel. *A Radical Jew: Paul and the Politics of Identity*. Berkeley: University of California Press, 1994.

Corbeill, Anthony. *Controlling Laughter: Political Humor in the Late Roman Republic*. Princeton Legacy Library. Princeton: Princeton University Press, 1996.

Corner, Sean. "Bringing the Outside In: The *Andrōn* as Brothel and the Symposium's Civic Sexuality." Pages 60–85 in *Greek Prostitutes in the Ancient Mediterranean, 800 BCE—200 CE*. Edited by Allison Glazebrook and Madeleine M. Henry. Madison: The University of Wisconsin Press, 2011.

Craig, Christopher. "Audience Expectations, Invective, and Proof." Pages 187–213 in *Cicero the Advocate*. Edited by Jonathan Powell and Jeremy Paterson. New York: Oxford University Press, 2004.

Dover, K. J. *Greek Homosexuality: Updated and with a New Postscript*. Cambridge: Harvard University Press, 1989.

Downen, Robert, Lise Olsen, and John Tedesco. "Abuse of Faith: 20 Years, 700 Victims: Southern Baptist Sexual Abuse Spreads as Leaders Resist Reforms." *The Houston Chronicle*, 10 February, 2019, https://www.houstonchronicle.com/news/investigations/article/Southern-Baptist-sexual-abuse-spreads-as-leaders-13588038.php

Drake, Susanna. *Slandering the Jew: Sexuality and Difference in Early Christian Texts*. Divinations: Rereading Late Ancient Religion. Philadelphia: University of Pennsylvania Press, 2013.

———. "Sexual Slander." Pages 593–606 in *The Oxford Handbook of New Testament, Gender, and Sexuality*. Edited by Benjamin H. Dunning. New York: Oxford University Press, 2019.

Dunkle, J. Roger. "The Greek Tyrant and Roman Political Invective of the Late Republic." *Transactions and Proceedings of the American Philological Association* 98 (1967): 151–171.

Edwards, Catharine. *The Politics of Immorality in Ancient Rome*. New York: Cambridge University Press, 1993.

Fatum, Lone. "Image of God and Glory of Man: Women in the Pauline Congregations." Pages 56–137 in *The Image of God: Gender Models in Judaeo-Christian Tradition*. Edited by Kari Elisabeth Børresen. Minneapolis: Fortress, 1995.

Flower, Richard. *Emperors and Bishops in Late Roman Invective*. New York: Cambridge University Press, 2013.

Foskett, Mary F. *A Virgin Conceived: Mary and Classical Representation of Virginity*. Indianapolis: Indiana University Press, 2002.

Gaddini, Katie. "Practising Purity: How Single Evangelical Women Negotiate Sexuality." Pages 103–121 in *Intersecting Religion and Sexuality: Sociological Perspectives*, Religion and the Social Order 27. Leiden: Brill, 2020.

Glancy, Jennifer A. "Early Christianity, Slavery, and Women's Bodies." Pages 143–158 in *Beyond Slavery: Overcoming Its Religious and Sexual Legacies*. Edited by Bernadette J. Brooten. New York: Palgrave Macmillan, 2010.

———. "The Sexual Use of Slaves: A Response to Kyle Harper on Jewish and Christian *Porneia*." *Journal of Biblical Literature* 131 (2015): 215–229.

Glazebrook, Allison. "The Bad Girls of Athens: The Image and Function of *Hetairai* in Judicial Oratory." Pages 125–138 in *Prostitutes and Courtesans in the Ancient World*. Edited by Christopher A. Faraone and Laura K. McClure. Madison: The University of Wisconsin Press, 2006.

Gleason, Maud W. *Making Men: Sophists and Self-Presentation in Ancient Rome*. Princeton: Princeton University Press, 1995.

Guyot, Peter. *Eunuchen als Sklaven und Freigelassene in der griechisch-römischen Antike*. Stuttgarter Beiträge zur Geschichte und Politik 14. Stuttgart: Klett-Cotta, 1980.

Halperin, David M. *One Hundred Years of Homosexuality: and Other Essays on Greek Love*. New York: Routledge, 1990.

Harl Sellew, Melissa. "Reading the *Gospel of Thomas* from Here: A Trans-Centred Hermeneutic." *Journal for Interdisciplinary Biblical Studies* 1 (2020): 61–96.

Henderson, Jeffrey. *The Maculate Muse: Obscene Language in Attic Comedy*. 2nd ed. New York: Oxford University Press, 1991.

Herter, Hans. "The Sociology of Prostitution in Antiquity in the Context of Pagan and Christian Writings." Pages 57–113 in *Sex and Difference in Ancient Greece and Rome*. Edited by Mark Golden and Peter Toohey. New York: Edinburgh University Press, 2003.

Hester, J. David. "Eunuchs and the Postgender Jesus: Matthew 19.12 and Transgressive Sexualities." *Journal for the Study of the New Testament* 28 (2005): 13–40.
Holmes, Brooke. *Gender: Antiquity and its Legacy*. New York: Oxford University Press, 2012.
Kahl, Brigette. "Gender Trouble in Galatia? Paul and the Rethinking of Difference." Pages 57–73 in *Is There a Future for Feminist Theology?* Edited by Deborah F. Sawyer and Diane M. Collier. London: Bloomsbury, 1999.
———. "No Longer Male: Masculinity Struggles Behind Galatians 3:28?" *Journal for the Study of the New Testament* 79 (2000): 37–49.
Kamen, Deborah. *Insults in Classical Athens*. Madison: The University of Wisconsin Press, 2020.
Kapparis, Konstantinos K. "The Terminology of Prostitution in the Ancient Greek World." Pages 222–255 in *Greek Prostitutes in the Ancient Mediterranean, 800 BCE—200 CE*. Edited by Allison Glazebrook and Madeleine M. Henry. Madison The University of Wisconsin Press, 2011.
Koster, Severin. *Die Invektive in der griechischen und römischen Literatur*. Beiträge zur klassischen Philologie 99. Meisenheim am Glan: Anton Hain, 1980.
Krenkel, Werner. "*Fellatio* and *Irrumatio*." Pages 205–231 in *Naturalia non turpia: Sex and Gender in Ancient Greece and Rome*, Schriften zur antiken Kultur-und Sexualwissenschaft. Edited by Wolfgang Bernard and Christiane Reitz. New York: Georg Olms, 2006.
———. "Sex und politische Biographie." Pages 233–263 in *Naturalia non turpia: Sex and Gender in Ancient Greece and Rome*, Schriften zur antiken Kultur-und Sexualwissenschaft. Edited by Wolfgang Bernard and Christiane Reitz. New York: Georg Olms, 2006.
———. "Tonguing." Pages 265–302 in *Naturalia non turpia: Sex and Gender in Ancient Greece and Rome*, Schriften zur antiken Kultur-und Sexualwissenschaft. Edited by Wolfgang Bernard and Christiane Reitz. New York: Georg Olms, 2006.
Kuefler, Mathew. *The Manly Eunuch: Masculinity, Gender, Ambiguity, and Christian Ideology in Late Antiquity*. Chicago: The University of Chicago Press, 2001.
Langlands, Rebecca. *Sexual Morality in Ancient Rome*. New York: Cambridge University Press, 2006.
Laqueur, Thomas. *Making Sex: Body and Gender from the Greeks to Freud*. Cambridge: Harvard University Press, 1990.
Marchal, Joseph A. "Bodies Bound for Circumcision and Baptism: An Intersex Critique and the Interpretation of Galatians. *Theology & Sexuality* 16 (2010): 163–182.
———. "The Usefulness of an Onesimus: The Sexual Use of Slaves and Paul's Letter to Philemon." *Journal of Biblical Literature* 130 (2011): 749–770.
———. *Appalling Bodies: Queer Figures Before and After Paul's Letters*. New York: Oxford University Press, 2019.
Martin, Troy W. "Paul's Argument from Nature for the Veil in 1 Corinthians 11:13–15: A Testicle Instead of a Head Covering." *Journal of Biblical Literature* 123 (2004): 75–84.

Martyn, J. Louis. *Galatians: A New Translation with Introduction and Commentary*. Anchor Bible 33A. New York: Doubleday, 1997.

McGinn, Thomas A. J. *The Economy of Prostitution in the Roman World*. Ann Arbor: University of Michigan Press, 2004.

Meeks, Wayne A. "The Image of the Androgyne: Some Uses of a Symbol in Earliest Christianity." *History of Religions* 13 (1974): 165–208.

Miner, Jess. "Crowning Thersites: The Relevance of Invective in Athenian Forensic Oratory." PhD diss., The University of Texas at Austin, 2006.

———. "Risk and Reward: Obscenity in the Law Courts at Athens." Pages 125–150 in *Ancient Obscenities: Their Nature and Use in the Ancient Greek and Roman Worlds*. Edited by Dorota Dutsch and Ann Suter. Ann Arbor: University of Michigan Press, 2015.

Moore, Stephen D. *God's Beauty Parlor: And Other Queer Spaces in and around the Bible*. Stanford: Stanford University Press, 2001.

Olson, Kelly. "*Matrona* and Whore: Clothing and Definition in Roman Antiquity." Pages 186–204 in *Prostitutes and Courtesans in the Ancient World*. Edited by Christopher A. Faraone and Laura K. McClure. Madison: The University of Wisconsin Press, 2006.

Ormand, Kirk. "Toward Iambic Obscenity," Pages 44–70 in *Ancient Obscenities: Their Nature and Use in the Ancient Greek and Roman Worlds*. Edited by Dorota Dutsch and Ann Suter. Ann Arbor: University of Michigan Press, 2015.

Reno, Joshua M. "Holy Obscenity: Sexual Invective in the Pauline Corpus." PhD diss., The University of Minnesota, 2021.

———. "Pornographic Desire in the Pauline Corpus." *Journal of Biblical Literature* 140 (2021): 163–185.

Richlin, Amy. *The Garden of Priapus: Sexuality and Aggression in Roman Humor*. Rev. ed. New York: Oxford University Press, 1992.

———. *Arguments with Silence: Writing the History of Roman Women*. Ann Arbor: University of Michigan Press, 2014.

Robinson, Alexandra. *Jude on the Attack: A Comparative Analysis of the Epistles of Jude, Jewish Judgement Oracles, and Greco-Roman Invective*. LNTS 581. New York: Bloomsbury, 2018.

Schüssler Fiorenza, Elisabeth. *Rhetoric and Ethic: The Politics of Biblical Studies*. Minneapolis: Fortress, 1999.

Sissa, Giulia. *Greek Virginity*. Translated Arthur Goldhammer. Cambridge: Harvard University Press, 1990.

———. "*Phusis* and Sensuality," Pages 265–281 in *A Companion to Greek and Roman Sexualities*. Edited by Thomas K. Hubbard. Malden, MA: Wiley-Blackwell, 2014.

Skinner, Marilyn B. *Sexuality in Greek and Roman Culture*. 2nd ed. Malden, MA: Blackwell, 2014.

Strong, Anise K. *Prostitutes and Matrons in the Roman World*. New York: Cambridge University Press, 2016.

Süss, Wilhelm. *Ethos: Studien zur älteren griechischen Rhetorik*. Leipzig: Teubner, 1910.

Tatum, W. Jeffrey. "Social Commentary and Political Invective." Pages 333–353 in *A Companion to Catullus*. Edited by Marilyn B. Skinner. Malden, MA: Blackwell, 2011.

Thrall, Margaret E. *A Critical and Exegetical Commentary on the Second Epistle to the Corinthians*. 2 vols. ICC. Edinburgh: T&T Clark, 2000.

Tolmie, D. F. "The Interpretation and Translation of Galatians 5:12." *Acta Theologica* 2: 86–102, 2009.

Treggiari, Susan. *Roman Marriage:* Iusti Coniuges *from the Time of Cicero to the Time of Ulpian*. New York: Oxford University Press, 1991.

Vogt, Kari. "'Becoming Male': A Gnostic and Early Christian Metaphor." Pages 170–186 in *The Image of God: Gender Models in Judaeo-Christian Tradition*. Edited by Kari Elisabeth Børresen. Minneapolis: Fortress, 1995.

von Ehrenkrook, Jason. "Effeminacy in the Shadow of the Empire: The Politics of Transgressive Gender in Josephus's 'Bellum Judaicum.'" *Jewish Quarterly Review* 101 (2011): 145–163.

White, Heather R. "How Paul Became the Straight Word: Protestant Biblicism and the Twentieth-Century Invention of Biblical Heteronormativity." Pages 289–307 in *Bodies on the Verge: Queering Pauline Epistles*. Edited by Joseph A. Marchal. Atlanta: Society of Biblical Literature, 2019.

Williams, Craig A. *Roman Homosexuality*. 2nd ed. New York: Oxford University Press, 2010.

Winkler, John J. *The Constraints of Desire: The Anthropology of Sex and Gender in Ancient Greece*. New York: Routledge, 1990.

Worman, Nancy. *Abusive Mouths in Classical Athens*. New York: Cambridge University Press, 2008.

Chapter 10

Ambivalent Wedding Imagery in Matthew's Jerusalem Narrative

Laura Robinson

The language of Jesus as the "bridegroom" and the eschaton as a "wedding supper" is familiar to readers of the New Testament. Jesus is described as a bridegroom in all four canonical Gospels (Matt 9:15; Mark 2:19; Luke 5:35–6; John 3:29), Paul uses the language of betrothal to describe the relationship of the Corinthian church to Jesus (2 Cor 11:2), and the deutero-Pauline epistles use the imagery of marriage to describe Christ and the church (Eph 5:23–33). All of this culminates in the imagery of a new Jerusalem and Jesus being joined at a wedding feast of the Lamb in Revelation (21:2), where eschatological salvation is depicted as a final wedding between Jesus and his community.

To the modern, western reader, the language of weddings often carries romantic, even sentimental connotations. Weddings are occasions where love matches are affirmed between autonomous individuals entering a contract of their own choosing. But this is of course not an accurate measure of an ancient marriage, or an ancient wedding. Ancient weddings were complex economic affairs requiring extensive prenuptial negotiations concerning property, money, and family. In literature and mythology these negotiations often break down into violence, in which the bride is at once party to the proceedings and also a commodity over which other parties debate. The wedding in ancient literature is a site where the groom and his family battle against the bride's family for goods and loyalty. The bride and her agency are not entirely erased, but she is often sidelined.

In light of this, the role of the wedding as an image of eschatological salvation—as the union between a church community and its messiah—deserves a serious reevaluation. Does the tone of these eschatological passages change if we set aside our own understandings of weddings? What if instead we focused on what the image of the wedding in antiquity involves, namely, the exchange of power, commodities, including the bodies of human beings? How might this shape how we understand the theology of these passages?

A serious reckoning with the image of the wedding as a place where power and resources are contested and won helps to explain why the wedding imagery in Matthew's Gospel in particular is so violent. Tense weddings appear twice in Matthew's Jerusalem narrative: once in Matt 22:1–14 (the Parable of the Banquet) and again in Matt 25:1–13 (the Parable of the Ten Virgins). The wedding as symbol of eschatological judgment is a unique emphasis in the latter chapters of Matthew. Luke also includes the parable of the banquet, but only Matthew states the occasion for which the banquet is held. Furthermore, while Luke places the banquet parable *en route* to Jerusalem (Luke 14:1, 15–24), Matthew places it in the eschatologically-loaded setting of the Temple during Jesus's Passion. The parable of the virgins who are divided in their ability to successfully respond to a wedding feast occurs in Matthew alone.

Since Matthew uses wedding images so distinctively, surely this invites the question: Why weddings? What is it about weddings that leaves Matthew reaching for marriage imagery in his most apocalyptic chapters? Why do the weddings end badly for several attendees? And who is getting married? In her 2005 monograph *While the Bridegroom Is with Them*, Marianne Blickenstaff argues that depictions of force, destruction, and division in the context of a wedding is not peculiar to Matthew. Weddings in antiquity are often portrayed as tense occasions in which hostile parties are forced into close quarters, with the threat of violence and loss looming over the proceedings. In her eagerness to subvert traditional readings of these parables, though, Blickenstaff misses the most striking part of what her research reveals: weddings, understood through a first-century Judaean lens—as opposed to a sentimental twenty-first-century Western one—function as a perfect diorama for Matthew's understanding of the imminent end and his own community's place in light of it. In Matthew's literary and cognitive world, weddings are models for the eschaton precisely because they are places in which dramatic and sometimes violent transfers of loyalty occur.

Drawing from Blickenstaff's research on the violent wedding, in this chapter I take a two-pronged approach to the subject of wedding imagery in Matthew. First, I ask what the literary and historical background literature concerning weddings shows us about how Matthew's audience would have pictured a wedding. What cognitive associations did a wedding carry in antiquity? And secondly, I examine what this model of eschaton-as-wedding can show us about how Matthew and his readers see themselves, their opponents, and Israel in light of the imminent end. In the first part of the chapter,

I examine Jewish and Greco-Roman sources to show that in these literary traditions, weddings are stages of changing alliances that carry associations of joy and anticipation, union and fear, and separation and loss. In the second part of the chapter I will show how the double-edged wedding is for Matthew the ultimate illustration of the eschaton: a radical rearranging of orders and allegiances in which certain individuals are included or excluded, sometimes violently, from the new social structure created in the marriage. In the third and final section, I discuss why this imagery matters, and how the modern reader might make sense of it.

FORCE AND FESTIVITY IN ANCIENT LITERARY WEDDINGS

We would commit a massive oversight if, in our pursuit of more ambivalent portrayals of weddings, we ignored the fact that weddings in the ancient world were causes for celebration. While we receive few details about weddings in the OT, the references we have indicate that marriages were special occasions featuring music, feasting, and, for the upper classes at least, decadence. Jacob's (Gen 29:22) and Samson's (Judg 14:10) weddings are both seven-day festivals. Royal weddings feature music and elaborate garments for both bride and groom (Ps 45: 8, 13), and ordinary citizens are also said to have "marriage songs" (Ps 78:63). In 1 Maccabees, a full band and guests accompany a bridal party (1 Macc 9:39), and in John, Jesus attends a wedding at which guests are said to have drunk excessively (John 2:10). In the Talmud, rabbis dance at weddings, exuberantly praise the bride, and encourage other attendees to do the same (*b. Ketub.* 16b-17a). While marriage customs in practice probably varied dramatically between eras and classes, we have plenty of examples that demonstrate that in the Jewish world, weddings were environments of extended and even excessive festivities.

In Greco-Roman literature, upper-class weddings are also times of celebration. Wedding hymns and poems express a sentimental ideal of married life, which suggests that singers expect weddings to be happy affairs. Brides and grooms are portrayed as joyful and eager, and the expectation of lasting affection and romantic love for the couple fills the hymnic language (Catul. 61; Statius, *Sil.* 1.2). Historians describe the bride's wedding clothes as richly ornamented and loaded with symbolic significance; grooms are expected to look their best but less emphasis is placed on their appearance. Accompanying celebratory dinners feature music, meals and crowds (Cicero, *Clu.* 166, Plautus, *Aul.* 325ff).

The overwhelming majority of both Jewish and Greco-Roman wedding references indicate that wedding imagery does not anticipate violence, and to suggest otherwise would be to overstate the double-edged nature of wedding imagery. Though, as we will see, tense or violent weddings were common tropes in first century literature, and Matthew's audience could fully expect the wedding of the king's son in Matt 22 to be convivial. The union of the bride with the groom is a positive outcome and calls for appropriate acclaim. We can be sure that both Jewish and Gentile audiences would have read about a royal wedding and known to expect a spectacular party.

However, even when weddings proceeded peacefully, both Jewish and Greco-Roman literature acknowledges that the wedding will necessarily require the loss of one's previous family connections, especially for the bride. A wedding in the ancient world was, after all, a transaction. Before the wedding both families would have undergone extensive financial negotiations—and, if the family was royal, political negotiations—in order to determine whether or not a wedding would take place. Once an agreement about the bride and her price had been reached, the wedding ritual itself publicly confirmed that the bride had been disassociated from her parents' home and was now a member of her husband's family. As it was practiced in Greece, Rome, and Judea, the ritual act of the wedding procession was a physical enactment of a bride's separation from her family. In a typical procession the bride would be led (or borne on a litter) from her father's house to the home of her future husband, accompanied with companions, music, and sometimes the groom. Such an event served as a conspicuous announcement that the bride was officially separated from her father's household and transferred to that of her husband.

Hebrew Bible literature affirms this separation. The poet of Psalm 45 urges the bride to "forget (śkḥ; LXX *epilanthanomai*) (her) people and (her) father's house" (Ps 45:10–11) because of the surpassing greatness of her new people and house; for the most part, brides in the OT take his advice. The paradigmatic brides of Jewish literature—indeed, the ones who appear in Matthew's genealogy of Jesus (in Matt 1:1–17), particularly Rahab and Ruth—marry into Jesus's family at the expense of their own families, if not their entire countries.

Loss as inherent to weddings is even more explicit in Greco-Roman literature. The wedding ceremony as recounted in Roman histories acknowledges through symbolic ritual that the bride through marriage has now been separated both from her childhood family. Wedding songs urge the bride on the morning of her wedding to leave her mother and come meet the groom, and in some records the bride is ritually pulled from her mother's arms in a show of mock force. The "mourning bride," terrified of sex, adulthood, and the loss of her parents, appears in several Roman wedding songs (Catul. 61.81, 62.21), though other hymns wonder if brides coyly affect such tears in order to appear modest before the groom's family (Catul. 66:15–18). Records of other rites suggest that weddings constituted a girl's complete break with her childhood identity. Ancient historians do not describe the ritual in detail, but we have some records of brides dedicating their girlhood clothing and dolls as sacrifices to the gods before their weddings. The symbolism is hard to miss. To be a bride is to be severed from one's family and identity as it existed before the wedding in order to be fully integrated into a new family's life.

The line between ritualized separation and real separating violence grows blurrier as we look further back into Rome's founding mythology, and to what Romans saw as their civilization's paradigmatic "first wedding": the rape of the Sabine women. For ancient historians, the tale of their ancestors building families through abducted brides was not a shameful episode of military brutality, but a story that successfully captured the essence of Roman marriage. According to Livy, after the Sabine women were abducted from their homes, they were so successfully assimilated into Roman culture that they helped negotiate a peace between Rome and the Sabines that established Roman hegemony over both groups (Liv. 1.13). Though the harmony was never quite frictionless, this incident that began with mass abduction and rape managed to solidify peace alongside Roman (and patriarchal) dominance. Ancient and modern historians have noted that this process of separation, tension, and male triumph is actually a fair encapsulation of how some ancient writers understood the marriage process. Brides were taken with varying degrees of trauma from their parents, thus creating an environment of rivalry and tension between the families of the bride and groom. The tension was only resolved when the groom was established as the fitting victor, the bride was incorporated into the groom's family through childbearing, and the two divisive factions were united.

It is not accurate to say that in many settings, the consent of the bride in a marriage was utterly irrelevant in a contest between a husband, father, and rivals. Roman marriage contracts and ketubahs allowed for the bride's right of refusal, and keep scrupulous track of her own marital property in the event of divorce. Nonetheless, it remains true that marriage was not an initiative taken by the bride, and the imagery of non-consent permeated wedding mythology. Romans were apparently comfortable enough with the story of the Sabine women that Roman historians suggest that imagery inspired by the abduction permeated contemporary weddings. Plutarch describes the spear point worn in a bride's hair on her wedding day as reminiscent of the Romans taking Sabine brides by force (*Quaest. rom.* 87), the groom's carrying the bride over the threshold as symbolic of a Sabine bride's abduction (*Quaest. rom.* 29), and the good-luck wedding cheer of "Talasio!" as inspired by slaves dragging a beautiful woman to a soldier named Talasius, warning that other men should not try to steal her (*Quaest. rom.* 31).

The ritualized pulling of the bride from her parents was also thought to be inspired by the Sabine abduction. Whether these cheers, rituals, and bridal garments were actually inspired by the Sabine women's abduction or not, we cannot ignore the fact that multiple early historians proposed a plausible and even tasteful connection between a historical/mythical mass rape and contemporary wedding imagery. The fact that they understood Romans to have incorporated these images into wedding rituals suggests that these authors were comfortable with the idea that their ancestors had built their families by force and were willing to pass these images down as folklore.

Jewish literary tradition also portrays Israelites as using force to acquire brides. The raid of Jabesh-Gilead (Judg 21:10–12) and festival at Shiloh (Judg 21:23–24) end in mass kidnapping, an episode strikingly similar to the rape of the Sabine women. Even when a wedding is not itself a violent exchange of the bride as property, bridegrooms often have to violently exchange other property (or commit violence more generally) to make a wedding in the first place. David acquires one hundred Philistine foreskins to marry Michal (1 Sam 18:26–27), and Othniel must capture Keriath-Sepher to marry Achsah (Judg 1:12–13); these stories are in keeping with the Hebrew tradition of attaining a bride by a deed of valor, usually in war. Samson's wedding creates a debacle in which the characters struggle to prevent the transfer of property (Judg 14:12–15:6). This results in the violent exchange of clothes and the bride, and finally the deaths of most of the characters.

Finally, since the festival atmosphere of ancient weddings amassed large crowds of kin, weddings in first-century literature often serve as environments in which enemies are conveniently brought together for a climactic showdown. Violence breaks out at weddings for reasons entirely unrelated to the proceedings. Would-be brides and bridegrooms are killed or maimed before, during, and immediately after their weddings in several genres of literature (authors take special interest in the tragic blending of wedding and funeral imagery in such cases). Josephus says that Jonathan and Simon Maccabeus kill four hundred people in one wedding party to avenge Judas's death (*Ant.* 13.18–21). Even God seems to think that weddings are good settings for confrontation. For example, God prompts Samson to marry a Philistine girl, because "he (God) was seeking an opportunity against the Philistines" (Judg 14:3).

There are no obvious allusions to any of these particular literary or historical weddings in Matthew's Gospel. Whether Matthew had any of these specific references consciously in mind while redacting his Jerusalem narrative is unclear. However, we cannot ignore the fact that the sheer volume of literature shows that treat weddings high-stakes exchange of family allegiance and personal property. When one adds large crowds of potentially hostile intermingling families, weddings served as the perfect setting for tension and violence in both Hellenistic and Jewish literature. And given how frequently this is mentioned in the ancient world, surely Matthew and his audience would have known this. Thus, in the cognitive environment of Matthew's original audience, a wedding scene in literature would have certainly evoked images of joy and festivity, but could also portend danger.

MATTHEW'S APOCALYPSE IN LIGHT OF AMBIVALENT WEDDING IMAGERY

We now turn our attention to what Matthew reveals about the eschaton in his wedding parable, namely, the Parable of the Wedding Banquet (22:1–3), and the Parable of the Ten Virgins (25:1–5).

First, a note about casting decisions: who exactly does Matthew think is getting married? Given the Hebrew Bible trope of Israel as bride and God as her jilted, jealous, but ultimately faithful husband (Isa 54:4–6; Ezek 16:7–34; Hos 2:19), it might seem most natural to assume that God is the most likely candidate to serve as groom and Israel is the bride. In post-exilic prophetic texts, Israel's ultimate hope is often portrayed as divine marriage. Occasionally, Israel is a new bride, joining God for the first time, but more often the happy couple is reconciling after a long and tumultuous separation. If we follow this pattern, we would read these parables as Matthew's take on the prophetic divine marriage trope: Israel's eschatological salvation has come, and she has been reunited to God.

However, the bridegroom in both Matthean parables is more clearly Jesus. In the parable of the tenants, which precedes the parable of the wedding banquet, the father-son duo is obviously God and Jesus (21:33–41), so it seems most natural to assume that the father-son pair in the wedding banquet is God and Jesus as well. Jesus also implicitly identifies himself as the bridegroom when he quotes himself in the bridegroom's conversation with the foolish virgins. The virgins call for the bridegroom by shouting "Lord! Lord!" (25:11) like the unfortunate "workers of lawlessness" in Matt. 7:22–23, and the groom responds that he "does not know them" (25:12) just as Jesus "never knew" the workers of lawlessness in 7:23. More explicitly, Jesus calls himself the bridegroom (*nymphios*) earlier in the gospel (9:15). Though this last pericope is apparently adapted from an earlier passage in Mark 2:19, Matthew follows the thread of Jesus-as-bridegroom imagery far more extensively than his predecessor does.

Israel's long-awaited wedding has finally arrived in both parables, but the groom we would expect from reading the prophets is not waiting for her. Jesus is. What are we to make of this? It is insufficient to simply say that Matthew sees Jesus as the eschatological groom of his people and leave it at that. Matthew obviously knows the Hebrew Bible divine marriage tradition. He alludes to it twice when Jesus calls his audience an "adulterous" (*moichalis*) generation (Matt 12:39; 16:4), reminiscent of God's oft-repeated charge against Israel in the Prophets. Matthew also echoes other tropes that bolster the divine marriage, such as employing feminized imagery to describe Jerusalem ("Daughter Zion" in Matt 21:5) and using Isaiah 62 in a fulfillment quotation, which leans heavily on divine marriage imagery (Matt 21:5). But Matthew comfortably ascribes God's role as groom, and the subsequent matrimonial honors, to Jesus himself.

It seems most likely that Matthew is deliberately quoting a standard prophetic motif to describe Israel's salvation (that is, the final marital union between God and Israel) and reformatting it to refer to Jesus, the savior-husband to whom Israel really needs to be united. It also seems as though Matthew has retrojected future elements of salvation recounted in prophetic literature back into past history, and blurs the line between Israel's future salvation and the emergence of her king in the historical past. This is particularly apparent in the Triumphal Entry, where Matthew employs a line about future divine marriage in a fulfillment text (Matt 21:5 quoting LXX Isa 62:11) and also depicts Jesus processing with an entourage into Jerusalem in a suspiciously first-century groom-like manner. The final union between Christ and his people is still in the future, but the process has already started by the time Jesus arrives in Jerusalem. This union is not the union between God and Israel that the prophets long for, but it is the one that will truly bring about eschatological salvation.

So Israel is getting married to Jesus. What does this portend for her? As we have seen, for Israel to marry Jesus she must first be severed from her previous life and family. Jesus makes his displeasure at Israel's previous stewards plain in the extended woe oracles in Matthew 23, but his intention to wrestle Israel from its previous caretakers is made explicit earlier in the parable of the tenants. Here, Matthew draws yet again on a prophetic trope, depicting Israel as a vineyard (Isa 5, Jer 12:10, Ezek 19:10–14) and its religious leaders as tenants who maim and murder anyone who comes to collect the landowner's due (21:34–36). After the tenants kill many of the landowner's slaves (a clear allusion to the accusation of prophet-slaying, also cited in 23:34 and 37), they finally trigger their own destruction when they kill the landlord's son (21:38–9). The tenants seem to be under the mistaken impression that with enough resistance they would be able to take the vineyard for themselves, but this is not the case. The "chief priests and Pharisees" (21:45) will lose the kingdom of God, which will subsequently go to a people (*ethnos*) (21:43) that produces the results God is looking for. The period of Israel's history in which it was cared for and managed by Pharisees, Sadducees, and their post-temple heirs is over. God's rule over the people will now be mediated through a different community than the one that came before.

Furthermore, just as marriage in the ancient world severed brides from their childhood identity and habits, the eschaton signals Israel's coming-of-age and a change in her identity. Jesus manifests this when he parades into Jerusalem and immediately changes everything about Israel's cultural and spiritual center that he does not like. On his first day in Jerusalem, he drives out the money-changers from the temple (Matt 21:12–13), comes dangerously close to defiling the sanctuary by illegally bringing in the blind and lame (21:14), disposes of an inadequate fig tree (21:18–22), and ultimately declares that Israel's temple will be cleared away completely (24:1–2). Jesus assumes the right to reorganize space and ritual in Israel to a standard that he prefers, and the resistance of Israel's previous custodians (recorded in 21:16, 23) is summarily dismissed. Israel's old customs are no longer relevant now that Jesus has emerged. What he says, goes.

We see in the above examples that Matthew thinks that Israel's salvific marriage has already started, and his vision of what must happen to Israel in order to accomplish this—a severing from old structures and reincorporation into new ones—are consistent with other ancient literary and historical expectations of marriage in the ancient world. These expectations are present throughout Matthew's entire Jerusalem sequence, not simply the wedding pericopes. With this appraisal of Matthew's expectations behind us, we are now prepared to take on the question of the specific parables that include wedding imagery: the Parable of the Wedding Feast, and the Parable of the Ten Virgins.

One element that stands out in both parables is that the necessity of completely submitting oneself to the program of the groom and his family extends also to the wedding guests. Both parables feature divisions between guests, between those who greet the wedding in the way that the bridegroom and his father expect, and those who do not. In the Parable of the Ten Virgins, the women who are allowed access to the party are those who functionally take on bridal traits, rejecting their companions and choosing to receive the groom instead of sharing (25:9). The choice of groom-over-friends is clearly the correct one: Jesus praises guests who prefer to meet the groom in the way that befits his wedding day, and he treats the delay of the "foolish virgins" as a total failure. Not only do they not gain admittance to the feast. The host declares he does not even know them (Matt 25:11–12).

The necessity of submitting oneself to the demands of the bridegroom also appears in the Parable of the Wedding Banquet. This parable includes two sequences of the host winnowing the guests. In the first round he culls guests who neglect the invitation and kill the slaves (22:4–5), and in the second round he culls a guest who attends the wedding without a wedding garment

(22:12–13). Matthew distinguishes between those who prioritize their own livelihoods (22:5) and come on their own terms, and those to acquiesce to the wishes of the host. The weddings in Matthew's parables are so all-consuming that even the guests begin to act like brides. They leave behind their old clothes and old life, and adapt to the standards of the new family who has summoned them. When the groom draws hard lines between those who side with him and those who do not, the separation already inherent to first-century weddings is taken to new extremes.

The second element that stands out in the Parable of the Wedding Banquet is conflict. Unsurprisingly, the large-scale demands of the groom are met with resistance, and some characters use the occasion of the wedding to settle scores. A more subtle example of this is the guest with no wedding garment (22:11–14). Despite the fact that this second-string guest accepted the invitation, he still is not dressed appropriately, and is subsequently ejected from the party. At first glance this detail seems exceptionally odd. The man has been brought by surprise to a wedding, so of course he is not dressed for the occasion. But when we compare Matthew's text with Luke's, it seems more likely that Matthew is coding deliberate resistance on the part of the guest. For one thing, Matthew's wedding is less rushed than Luke's banquet. There is considerably more urgency in the Lukan parable, whose slaves are told to go out immediately and gather in the city's outcasts right off the street (Luke 14:21). Matthew's guests come neither immediately nor off the street. It is not clear but still more conceivable that in Matthew the guest had time to prepare. Secondly, Davies and Allison argue that evidence from the LXX and patristic writers suggests that "wedding clothes" in Matthew's context likely referred only to "clean clothes" or clothes provided by the host, and not to expensive formal wear. From all of this, it seems as if Matthew is trying to build the case for a deliberate slight on the guest's part. Given what we have seen about ancient propensities for starting fights at weddings, this is not a surprise. The guest contradicts the host, and is subsequently banished for his resistance.

Far more dramatic is the blatant resistance of the first guests. While some are simply indifferent and ignore the invitation in favor of their own farms and businesses (22:5), others actually kill the slaves who invite them (another accusation of prophet-killing, in 22:6). Once again, we have an occasion in which would-be guests take advantage of a wedding to start trouble. In a clear nod to the destruction of Jerusalem in 70 CE—which Matthew envisions as God's own doing—the violence of this refusal escalates and eventually devolves into civil war and destruction (22:7). The wedding incites conflict against the king and even open revolt, which is settled squarely in favor of the groom and his father. This wedding can be fought, as all weddings can, but those who resist it do so at their own peril.

Finally, what truly sets these weddings apart from their violent counterparts in ancient literature is their inevitability. In the weddings we examined in the first section of the chapter, wedding-resisters stood a real chance of preventing a wedding from happening, either by killing the groom, the bride, or enough of the guests. But there is no real possibility of stopping the eschatological wedding in either parable where it appears. The absence of half the guests in the Parable of the Ten Virgins hardly delays the proceedings. Likewise, not even a bloody failed coup and the absence of every original invited guest can prevent the wedding in the parable of the wedding banquet. However vigorously it may be fought, Israel's eschatological fulfillment will occur when it is united to Christ, and no amount of resistance can prevent it.

WHY DOES THIS MATTER? THE WEDDING AS IMAGE OF THE ESCHATON AND THE MODERN READER

Because weddings involve such complete changes of allegiance, breaks with old lifestyles, and exchanges of property, Matthew views them as mini-apocalypses and incorporates them into his eschatology. Jesus and his father claim a bride for themselves. Relevant parties resist the union, and the tension springing from such an occasion spills over into violence, both in the recent past (i.e., the Jewish War) and in the imminent future (i.e., the final judgment). So in light of the fact that Matthew pictures the eschaton as a wedding, and that weddings are portrayed as unusually fraught events that pit two competing parties against each other, what are we to make of this?

It might be jarring for the modern reader to imagine a wedding as a scene of gendered violence, with a bridegroom as a victorious aggressor over a bride. Crucially, Matthew does not use explicit imagery of sexual violence to describe eschatological salvation in his wedding parables. Nonetheless, it is inescapable that bridal consent is not of critical interest to him. Nor is it of interest to many of the voices beyond mythological depictions of ancient marriage. What the people of Israel think or want is not foregrounded, and images of exclusion and violence are prevalent in both wedding parables.

This should change how we understand conversion, ecclesiology, and community participation in Matthew's Gospel. Eschatological victory for Matthew is violent and occurs in the context of marital domination. This is a text that is not terribly interested in the consent of the converted. Matthew's Gospel does not narrate seduction. It narrates conquest, particularly on the missiological field. Likewise, the language of weddings makes it clear how much Matthew's Gospel is interested in ecclesiology as a victory between Jesus and his rivals. Matthew is interested in the dispute between Jesus and opponents (Pharisees, Sadducees, et. al.), and this arena of dispute is inseparable from how Matthew understands the union of Jesus and Jesus's people. Matthew frames the future of Jesus's people as a contest between Jesus and his opponents, while leaving the relationship between Jesus and his people somewhat ambiguous. No parable includes the voice of the bride, Jesus's people, in the narration. The consent of the bride figure in these parables is not of interest to our author. The contest for her loyalty happens around her.

A fuller examination of wedding imagery in Matthew's Gospel brings the stakes of Matthew's theology to the fore. This is a text that understands conversion in highly gendered, competition-centered ways. Matthew's Jesus has a bride in view who is won in the arena of force and domination, and his eschatology must be understood in this framework.

NOTES

1. Luke recounts a similar story of servants "keeping their lamps burning" while waiting for their master to return late from a wedding feast (Luke 12:35–40), but the servants are not identified as virgins, and the parable also ends on a far more positive note.

2. Suzanne Dixon, "The Sentimental Ideal of the Roman Family," in *Marriage, Divorce, and Children in Ancient Rome,"* ed. by Beryl Rawson (New York: Oxford University Press, 2000), 103.

3. Karen K. Hersch, *The Roman Wedding: Ritual and Meaning in Antiquity* (New York: Cambridge University Press, 2010): 112–114,

4. Hersch, *Wedding*, 137.

5. Jo Ann Hackett, "1 and 2 Samuel," in *Women's Bible Commentary, 20th Anniversary Edition*, ed. Carol A. Newsom, Sharon H. Ringe, and Jacqueline E. Lapsey (Louisville, KY: Westminster John Knox Press, 2012), 156.

6. Michael L. Satlow, *Jewish Marriage in Antiquity* (Princeton: Princeton University Press, 2001), 171.

7. "Since royal brides were often from other people, the implication would be that she needs to turn her back on her own culture, her loyalties, and her religion, like Ruth. Foreign brides such as Solomon's and Ahab's notoriously did not do so." John Goldingay, *Psalms Vol. 2: Psalms 42–89*, BCOTWP (Grand Rapids, MI: Baker Academic, 2007), 60. Thus in Goldingay's estimation, brides who do not adequately forget their homelands are dangerous liabilities to society.

8. Rebekah (not listed, but no doubt known to Matthew) leaves her family abruptly, cutting short the ten-day preparation period that her mother and brother propose (Gen 24:54–61). Rahab's family joins with Israel alongside her when she marries Salmon, but against the backdrop of the destruction of their entire city (Josh 6:25) and the loss of her national identity, and presumably her occupation, too, if she was in fact a prostitute. Amy H. C. Robertson, "Rahab and her Interpreters" in *Women's Bible Commentary, 20th Anniversary Edition*, ed. Carol A. Newsom, Sharon H. Ringe, and Jacqueline E. Lapsey (Louisville, KY: Westminster John Knox Press, 2012), 109–112.

Ruth, like Rahab, cuts herself off from her people, gods, and homeland for the sake of her Israelite mother-in-law (Ruth 1:16–17), and Bathsheba is only available for marriage into the line of David after David himself arranges her husband's murder (2 Sam 11:26–27).

9. Susan Treggiari, *Roman Marriage: Iusti Coniuges from the Time of Cicero to the Time of Ulpian* (New York: Oxford University Press, 1993): 166.

10. Hersch, *Wedding*, 66–67.

11. See Gary B. Miles's overview in his chapter "Roman Marriage," pages 179–219 in *Livy: Reconstructing Early Rome* (Ithaca, NY: Cornell University Press, 1995).

12. See Stevenson's examples in "Women of Early Rome as *Exempla* in Livy, *AB Urbe Condita*, Book 1," *CW* 104.2 (2011), 179.

13. Blickenstaff, *While the Bridegroom Is with Them: Marriage, Family, Gender, and Violence in the Gospel of Matthew* (London: T&T Clark, 2005), 34–35. See also Miles, *Livy*, 190–91.

14. Grubbs 78–9, Levine 10.

15. Treggiari, *Roman Marriage*, 166.

16. "The perpetuation of such explanations for a Roman wedding custom suggests that abduction continued to express one aspect of the marriage relationship as Romans perceived it." Miles, *Livy*, 188.

17. The Shiloh pericope, though, is less forgiving than Roman historians generally are about the Sabine women; the author concludes that the Benjaminites' raiding at Shiloh proved that the age of the Judges was a period of anarchy (Judg. 21:25).

18. Victor P. Hamilton, "Marriage," in *The Anchor Bible Dictionary*, ed. David Noel Freedman (New York: Doubleday, 1992), 4:563.

19. Blickenstaff finds examples in Xenophon, Achilles Tatius, and Lucian, among others (*Bridegroom*, 33).

20. The link between weddings and the outbreak of hostilities is even more pronounced in the Apocrypha. In the 1 Maccabees account of this same incident the bridegroom and his wedding party are "heavily armed" and even in the midst of celebration are aware that the festivities could turn violent (1 Macc 9:39).

21. The pericope occurs in the same setting and with much of the same wording in Luke 5:34.

22. Mark is the only other Gospel to use this term, at the end of Jesus's exhortation to "take up his cross and follow him" (Mark 8.38). Luke tells the story of Jesus criticizing the generation for seeking a sign and receiving the "sign of Jonah" that Matthew describes, but Luke describes the generation only as *ponēros*. Matthew seems to be uniquely seizing on the imagery of adultery in a manner that neither Mark nor Luke do.

23. Most commentators see Jesus's procession into Jerusalem as a triumphal entry for a victorious king, such as 2 Kgs 9:13 and 1 Macc 13:51. Hare includes a list of possible parallels in Hare, *Matthew*, 238. However, in the ancient world there was considerable overlap between nuptial imagery and royal imagery. Brides and grooms alike wore crowns, sat on special chairs, and were served by attendants. The groom in Songs of Solomon is carried on a litter on his wedding day, as were many later brides and grooms (Songs 3:9–10). Other possible common images include the festive

crowds and use of "tree branches" as opposed to Mark's "straw." In the Talmud, rabbis dance before the bride holding myrtle branches (*b. Ketub.* 16b-17a).

24. Apparently not the people of Israel at large, per Matt 21:45.

25. Davies and Allison explore a few reasons why they might think this, none of which are terribly convincing claims on the vineyard. Davies and Allison, *Matthew 21–28*, 183.

26. Davies and Allison 140, citing LXX 2 Bar 5:6–8 and *m. Hag.* 1.1. Hare refutes, arguing that the blind and lame are in the temple already when Jesus meets with them, and notes that rabbinic literature treated the blind and lame as permitted to attend festivals but not required (Hare, *Matthew*, 242). Rabbinic literature is difficult to use as a source for immediate post-temple belief and practice, though, and it seems entirely possible that Matthew would have assumed the blind and lame were not in the temple per 2 Sam 5:8.

27. Jesus's determination to rearrange temple space to better suit him becomes even more obvious when one compares this fig tree incident to the one in Mark's gospel. (11:12–14, 20–25). Matthew has altered Mark's account to show that Jesus's plans for the temple are effective immediately. Mark also portrays Jesus as spending a night in Bethany before returning to clear the temple (11:11, 15–19), whereas in Matthew Jesus proceeds directly to the temple to clear it.

28. Davies and Allison, *Matthew 21–28*, 204.

29. Mistreatment of a king's slaves is seen as an instigation of violence in 1 Chron 19. Nolland uses the term "rebellion" and "uprising" to describe the murder of the king's slaves. Nolland, *Matthew*, 887.

30. Kenton L. Sparks, "Gospel as Conquest: Mosaic Typology in Matthew 28:16–20," *CBQ* 68, no. 4 (2006): 651–63.

WORKS CITED

Blickenstaff, Marianne. *While the Bridegroom Is with Them: Marriage, Family, Gender, and Violence in the Gospel of Matthew*. London: T&T Clark, 2005.

Davies, W. D. and D. C. Allison. *Matthew 19–28*. International Critical Commentary. London: Bloomsbury T&T Clark, 2004.

Dixon, Suzanne. "The Sentimental Ideal of the Roman Family." Pages 99–113 in *Marriage, Divorce, and Children in Ancient Rome*. Edited by Beryl Rawson. New York: Oxford University Press, 2000.

Goldingay, John. *Psalms Vol. 2: Psalms 42–89*. Baker Commentary on the Old Testament Wisdom and Psalms. Grand Rapids, MI: Baker Academic, 2007.

Hackett, Jo Ann. "1 and 2 Samuel." Pages 150–163 in *Women's Bible Commentary, 20th Anniversary Edition*. Edited by Carol A. Newsom, Sharon H. Ringe, and Jacqueline E. Lapsey. Louisville, KY: Westminster John Knox Press, 2012.

Hersch, Karen K. *The Roman Wedding: Ritual and Meaning in Antiquity*. New York: Cambridge University Press, 2010.

Levine, Amy-Jill. "The Gospel of Matthew." Pages 465–477 in *Women's Bible Commentary, 20th Anniversary Edition*, edited by Carol A. Newsom, Sharon H.

Ringe, and Jacqueline E. Lapsey. Louisville, KY: Westminster John Knox Press, 2012.
Luz, Ulrich. *Matthew 21–28*. Hermeneia. Translated by James E. Crouch. Minneapolis: Fortress Press, 2005.
Miles, Gary B. *Livy: Reconstructing Early Rome*. Ithaca, NY: Cornell University Press, 1995.
Nelson, Andrew E., "Who Is This? Narrative of Divine Identity of Jesus in Matthew 21:10–17," *Journal of Theological Interpretation* 7.2 (2013):199–211
Nolland, John. *The Gospel of Matthew*. New International Greek Testament Commentary. Grand Rapids: Eerdmans, 2005.
Robertson, Amy H. C. "Rahab and Her Interpreters." Pages 109–112 in *Women's Bible Commentary, 20th Anniversary Edition,* edited by Carol A. Newsom, Sharon H. Ringe, and Jacqueline E. Lapsey. Louisville, KY: Westminster John Knox Press, 2012.
Saldarini, Anthony J. *Matthew's Christian-Jewish Community*. Chicago/London: University of Chicago Press, 1994.
Sanders, E. P., and Margaret Davies. *Studying the Synoptic Gospels*. London/Philadelphia: SCM Press/Trinity Press International, 1989.
Satlow, Michael L. *Jewish Marriage in Antiquity*. Princeton: Princeton University Press, 2001.
Stanton, Graham N. *A Gospel for a New People: Studies in Matthew*. Edinburgh: T&T Clark, 1992.
Stevenson, Tom. "Women of Early Rome as *Exempla* in Livy, *AB Urbe Condita*, Book 1." *Classical World* 104.2 (2011): 175–189.
Treggiari, Susan. *Roman Marriage:* Iusti Coniuges *from the Time of Cicero to the Time of Ulpian*. New York: Oxford University Press, 1993.

Chapter 11

Virgin Acts

Blinding, Castration, and the Violence of Male Chastity

Jeannie Sellick

According to the *Acts of John*, as the apostle John prepares for death, he readies both himself and his disciples for his departure. He hosts a "last supper," leaves his disciples with a departing prayer, and asks a select (but unsuspecting) few to dig him a grave outside the city gates. As he lies in the newly made grave, John has one final task—to issue a deathbed plea for his salvation. John does not argue that his salvation has been earned through converting many followers, resurrecting numerous people in Christ's name, nor from spreading the good news. Rather, in a unique twist, John appeals to Christ on account of his bodily purity. John cries out that despite the fact that he tried to get married three times, he is ultimately coming to his death a virgin with his "love for [Christ] kept stainless" (*Acts John* 113:16–17). As a closing argument, John offers up his undefiled, pure body. His salvation lies in his identity as a perpetual virgin for Christ.

John's deathbed plea is from a section of the *Acts of John* known as the *Metastasis*. While it is typically presented at the end of any publication of the *Acts of John*, I find it a useful framework through which to better understand the inner workings of the tradition as a whole. I offer up John's virginity as a lens through which to better understand this tradition's relationship with sexuality. Each of the loosely associated apocryphal acts of the apostles generally treats bodily purity as a high form of Christian practice, but the *Acts of John* has a particularly fraught relationship with *male* sexuality—complete with necrophilia, penis severing, and a divinely given illness to prevent marriage. Sexual violence perpetrated by men in the apocryphal acts, and more broadly early Christian literature, is nothing special. What is significant, however, is that in these stories from the extant early *Acts of John*, the violence is inflicted both by and *toward* men.

In this essay, I will visit three instances of sexual violence from the *Acts of John* in which men are dually the perpetrators and victims of sexual violence. Each of these, as I will show, centers on the male sexual appetite and body. Both the perpetrators and the victims are, at least in part, men. The moments of violence inflicted on the male body also serve as an important crux in the text. Following each instance of sexual violence, the male perpetrator/victim is converted to an ascetic form of Christianity. Sexual violence in this tradition is therefore a catalyst for celibacy. I argue that the violence in the *Acts of John* serves the function of making male sexuality strange and dangerous while allowing celibacy to stand in as the safer, more normative option.

The first act comes from John's time in Ephesus, where he meets a young man whose affair with a married woman has caused him to murder his disapproving his father and hatch a plan to kill his mistress, her husband, and himself. Following the apostle's intervention, however, the young man instead slices off his genitals as a show of his devotion to his newly ascetic life. Our next scene revolves around a case of attempted necrophilia. When a wealthy young man named Callimachus cannot convince the Christian Drusiana to sleep with him, he attempts to rape her corpse but instead is temporarily killed by a serpent sent by God. And for our third act, we will turn to John himself and his relationship with Jesus. John's deathbed plea for salvation gives insight to his own "conversion" to lifelong celibacy, a commitment made only after his attempts to get married resulted in Christ blinding the apostle for two years. These pieces come together to sketch an image of male sexual desire as violent and subversive, not merely to women, but destructive to the men themselves. Standing next to these violent acts, Christian ascetic practice is rendered normative. As a final illustration, I turn to a discussion of John's virginity found in the late fourth century polemical treatise by Jerome, *Against Jovinian*. Jerome's use of John in this text not only lays bare his familiarity with traditions from the *Acts of John* but also shows how the sexual ethics of the Johannine universe could be leveraged in support of a male virginal ideal in later antiquity.

ACT I: CASTRATION

Let us kick off with a wholesome tale of adultery, patricide, and penis severing. While in Ephesus, John is inspired by a dream to spend his morning walking outside the city gates. John and his cohort walk until suddenly they encounter a distressed young man running along the road with a sickle in his hand. John stops the nameless youth and questions him. Apparently, the young man had been engaged in an affair with a co-worker's wife. When his father found out, a fight ensued, and the youth kicked his disapproving father seemingly to death. By the time he encounters John, the young man has hatched an even more sinister plan. When confronted, he reveals to John:

> I have accomplished a wretched and inhuman act, and knowing that I would be arrested, I decided to do something even more violent and cruel to myself: to die at once. For my father was always advising me to live a dignified life, free from adultery, yet I could not bear his refutations of me, and so I kicked him to death. And when I saw what had happened, I hastened to the woman on whose account I had become the murderer of my father. And I resolved to kill her, her husband, and last of all, myself. (*Acts John* 49:7–14)

Left unchecked, the youth's sexual desire has already led to patricide and is now leading him to commit a double homicide and his own suicide—four deaths born of desire. John being John, however, he refuses to let this plan come to fruition. He makes a deal with the young man. He bargains, "if I raise [your father] for you, will you withdraw from that woman who has already led you astray?" (*Acts John* 50:4–5). The man agrees and, upon seeing his father alive and whole again, he is instantly converted.

Yet after John raises his father, the young man decides to see his mistress one last time. He races over to her house, takes the sickle, and cuts off his penis and testicles. He throws them down before the woman, proclaiming, "It is on account of you that I became the murderer of my father and of you two and even of myself! You have the likeness and cause of this thing. But as for me, God has shown me mercy so that I might witness his power!" (*Acts John* 53:5–7). Here the young man has blamed his behavior on two external sources. The first, of course, is his mistress (*moikalis*) who, like many women in Christian texts, carries the burden of being a "stumbling block" for young men. But the young man *also* blames his own body—specifically his genitals. By severing his genitals, he attempts to separate himself from his sin while preventing such behavior from ever happening to him again.

Thinking he has gone above and beyond in his dedication to his new lifestyle, the young man gleefully runs to tell John about what he's done. At first blush, it would seem to attentive readers of the canonical gospels that the actions of this young man are not merely admirable but moreover fall in line with Jesus's *own words*. In chapter 9 of the Gospel of Mark, Jesus states that if any part of the body causes a person to stumble, they should cut it off, for it is better to entire the Kingdom of God "maimed" than go to hell with their hands, feet or eyes intact (Mark 9:42–50). Despite modern interpreters' reticence to read this passage literally, Candida Moss has persuasively argued that Christ's injunction here fits within ancient understandings of therapeutic amputation and that it could be (and occasionally was) read literally by some Christians. By severing his genitals, the "likeness and cause" of his sin, is the young man not doing precisely what Christ had dictated? For John, no.

In a somewhat shocking twist, John does not greet the castration with praise, but with his disapproval. He chastises the young man and claims it was on account of Satan that he removed his "troublesome things [*ta akaira*] as if it were a virtuous deed" (*Acts John* 54:4–5). John goes on to explain that rather than destroy his penis and testicles, the man should have destroyed the sinful thought that revealed itself through his body. For the organs, he continues, are not themselves harmful; but rather it is the "invisible springs" [*ai aphaneis pēgai*] that bring shameful emotions to the surface that destroy men (*Acts John* 54:7–9). While John's negative reaction to the auto-castration may seem understandable or even logical to modern readers, self-amputation, and even castration, was not necessarily taboo in the ancient world. Though tempting to read John's reaction as a natural or logical one for this situation, it is possible that the text here is doing the work of *making* bodily amputation in general—and castration in particular—taboo. In John's eyes, the young man's bodily castration is as misdirected as the affair was in the first place. The affair, the murder, the castration—these are all the fruits of sexual desire. Though the story has a happy ending full of resurrection and conversion, it comes at the cost of the youth's body, now forever mutilated by the consequences of his own sexual desire.

ACT II: NECROPHILIA

Let us turn to another episode from John's time in Ephesus, this one featuring a love triangle. Our second act concerns the formerly married couple, Drusiana and Andronicus. While the couple initially had a rocky transition from the married to the celibate life, by the time we meet them in Ephesus the two who are now living "as brother and sister," and considered vital members of John's posse. One day Drusiana catches the eye of a distinguished young man, "an emissary of Satan," named Callimachus. While his friends informed him of Drusiana's marriage to Andronicus and of her dedication to celibacy, Callimachus could not be persuaded to give up the chase. Although she adamantly rejects his advances, Drusiana, so full of distress that she has become a "stumbling block" (*skandalon*) to a non-Christian man, falls ill and dies (*Acts John* 64).

This may seem like the natural ending to a tragic story. The toxicity of Callimachus's desire is so great that it causes Drusiana's death. But the universe of John's stories is not one to display such tragedy without conversion, and the reader expects a twist of fate on the horizon. Unperturbed by her death, Callimachus, "inflamed by the most dangerous lust and force of the manifold Satan," hatches an even more nefarious plan (*Acts John* 70:3–4). While John and his disciples grieve her death, Callimachus bribes a steward named Fortunatus, and then sneaks into Drusiana's tomb with the intention of raping her corpse. Since she had refused him in life, he intends to "insult" her corpse now that she is dead. As he begins to strip the clothes from Drusiana's lifeless body, he laments, "What have you benefited, miserable Drusiana? Were you not strong enough to do while living this thing, which, perhaps, would not have harmed you had you done it willingly yourself?" (*Acts John* 70:14–16). Luckily, as Callimachus is about to remove her undergarment a giant serpent thwarts his design. The snake immediately bites and kills the steward Fortunatus and then sits upon the would-be necrophile, appearing to kill him as well.

The next morning, John and Andronicus return to the sepulcher and are surprised to see a beautiful young man smiling next to the grave. Instantly recognizing the man as a servant of God, John inquires as to why he is present at such a scene. The "beautiful one" replies that he is there both for Drusiana, whom he promises to resurrect momentarily, but also, he is there "for the sake of the man who has died near her tomb" (*Acts John* 73:6–7). Following this revelation the young man immediately returns to heaven but when John, still a bit confused, turns to the other side of the sepulcher he is met with a monstrous sight—Drusiana's stripped corpse, a dead servant, and Callimachus dead under the weight of a giant snake. Seeing Drusiana, Andronicus immediately figures out what has happened but requests that John resurrect Callimachus to elicit a confession. John commands the snake to move and "awakens" Callimachus.

This night, unsurprisingly, has been quite transformative for the would-be necrophile. Callimachus recounts how his wicked plan was thwarted not only by the appearance of the serpent but also by the "beautiful young man" who covered Drusiana's body with a cloak and according to Callimachus instructed him, "Die so that you may live!" The newly repentant Callimachus now sees the error of his ways and asks for John's forgiveness:

> I beseech you, do not neglect to free me from this calamity and terrible crime, and offer to your God a man who was deceived by shameful and abominable treachery. If only you could break open my chest and show my thoughts! Since now this thing presses upon my soul, a great pain, that not long ago I had thoughts which I ought not to and, having been tempted by a cruel disposition, I brought the greatest sorrow upon myself. (*Acts John* 76:24–30)

John, of course, forgives him and raises Drusiana. Despite the protests of Callimachus, Drusiana then raises Fortunatus, and they all leave as one happy spiritual family. Well, everyone aside from Fortunatus who after being resurrected, subsequently dies again from the snake bite. In the end, it seems, the servant takes the brunt of responsibility for the rich man's wickedness.

Like in our first story, readers can see here that it is Callimachus's sexual desire that drives him to do the otherwise unthinkable. His sexual desire is stronger than Drusiana's marriage, her vows of celibacy, and even her death. His sexually driven actions cause the deaths of Drusiana, Fortunatus, and even his own (temporary) violent end. In both the story of the castrated young man and the failed necrophile, the sexual appetites and desires of these two men are the very root of their wickedness—not only because they are sexually active but because sexuality is the *cause* of their subversive violence. Patricide and necrophilia would have been unsavory and taboo acts even to the most sex-positive audiences. And as I argued above, the text works hard to depict self-mutilation as something to be considered misdirected at best, and more likely taboo. Yet it is also only through these acts of violence that these men can emerge as Christians. In these two instances, sexual violence is important in that it gives way to transformation. Suddenly celibacy feels comfortable, safe, and normative in comparison with the violent acts associated with male sexuality.

While my focus up until this moment has been on the effects of sexually driven violence on the male perpetrators, I would be remiss if I failed to address the role the women play in these stories. Both episodes contain the idea of women as "stumbling blocks" who carry the responsibility of male infatuation. As the young man's *moikalis*, the married woman from the first episode is very nearly murdered on account of the youth's guilt and lust. And although she is saved, the woman is in the end the victim of a sexually driven assault against her person when the young man throws his severed genitals at her. And it is notable here that while the sexual violence of the youth becomes a catalyst for his Christian transformation, no such opportunity is extended to the woman. This dynamic is even more insidious in the story of Drusiana and Callimachus. As discussed above, the stress of having become a *skandalon* to Callimachus is so intense that Drusiana dies. And while the Lord instructs Callimachus to "die so that [he] may live," perhaps a more accurate way of understanding this is that *Drusiana* must die so that Callimachus may live. It is Drusiana's death that sets into motion her rapist's salvation. And when all is said and done, she is expected to welcome Callimachus into the spiritual family as if nothing happened.

This dynamic is hardly surprising in the realm of early Christian literature. The idea that men often use women to "think with" is hardly new; but this feels like something even more nefarious. In her work on early Christian hagiography, Virginia Burrus has noted that the genesis male authored *vitae* of holy women revolves around the woman's death—that the Life (death) of women inevitably gives way to the story of her male hagiographer. Though the men of our episodes in the *Acts of John* are hardly hagiographers, they violently write the stories of their salvation on the bodies of women. Though the men in these episodes find themselves as the dual perpetrators/victims of violent acts, the violence serves as a catalyst for their eventual salvation. The same, however, cannot be said of the women they leave in their wake.

ACT III: BLINDING

For our final act, the "grand finale" if you will, let us return to John's deathbed. As John's followers dig him a shallow grave, he makes a final plea for this salvation on the basis of his sexual purity. John cries out to Christ:

> You, who up until the present hour, have preserved my purity for yourself and [kept me] untouched from sex with a woman. Who, when I wished to marry in my youth, appeared to me and said: "*I need you, John!!*" Who, when again I wished to give myself in marriage, arranged a bodily sickness for me. Who, when for the third time I wished to get married, thwarted me and then on the third hour of the day while in the sea said to me: "*John, if you were not mine, then I would have allowed you to marry.*" Who blinded me for two years, causing me to grieve and pray to you. Who in the third year, opened the eyes of my mind and graciously restored my perceiving eyes. Who, once I was able to see clearly, described for me the grievousness of looking closely at a woman . . . Who cut me off from the foul passion of the flesh . . . Who has rendered my love for you stainless . . . And now, since I have accomplished the task with which you entrusted me, Lord Jesus, deem me worthy of your rest and grant me my end in you, which is indescribable and unutterable salvation. (*Acts John* 113)

As with the previous two episodes, John's deathbed speech has a strong emphasis on desire as a disease and bodily punishment as a means for curtailing sexuality. Like the other young men of this text, John's desires can only truly be "cured" by Christ. And while John chastised the young man from our first episode for castrating himself, it seems that Christ's cure for John was to remove *his* "troublesome members," albeit only temporarily. Yet the most intriguing aspect of this final act is that John's virginity was not actively preserved by him, but *by Christ*. In fact, in this scene the violence is not committed by John—the sexually desirous mortal man—but by Christ. Each time John sought to get married, Jesus intervened on the grounds that John belonged to him—so much so that he blinds his beloved. There is no evidence here or elsewhere that John's sexuality causes him to commit any kind of violence. Instead, for John, his desire serves as a catalyst for him to be the victim of sexual violence.

Gerard Loughlin has noted that this scene between John and Jesus, as well as the traditions it inspired, is dripping with queerness. On even the most straightforward reading, the relationship between John and Christ in the *Metastasis* is queer. John and Jesus are in a relationship that precludes one from having sex with anyone else, and Jesus appears possessive of John's exclusivity. Although the text stops short of calling the apostle a "bride of Christ," John's depiction comes as close as it can to granting him the title without crossing that line. As Loughlin has highlighted, this scene is far from the only example of John being depicted as Christ's bride in the ancient and medieval world. Some medieval interpretations of the Wedding at Cana from the Gospel of John imagined the titular apostle as the bridegroom. This story is expanded upon in a homily from the Venerable Bede in which, upon meeting Jesus, John leaves his bride-to-be at the alter and instead spends the night sleeping upon Christ's breast. But the queerness of both this scene and of the *Acts of John* as a whole is rich and multifaceted. Borrowing the definition of queerness set forth by Amy Hollywood and Virginia Burrus yet succinctly articulated by Rebecca Krawiec as "a challenge to the normative discourses of sexuality," a queer reading of the *Metastasis* can help us better understand both John and the other men in this text.

When we adopt this broader definition, John's virginity queers him in several ways. The first and most obvious way is that John sublimates his sexuality to Jesus and figures them in a kind of relationship. This places two male presenting figures in, if not a marriage, an exclusive relationship. Another layer is that lifelong virginity was certainly considered non-normative in a second century Greco-Roman context. Furthermore, John also sublimates his sexuality not simply to a man, but a deity, a situation that, at least in my view, is not generally considered normative. With this broader understanding of queerness, however, we can expand the definition to include not just John, but also the other men of the text. The young man, Callimachus, and John each shed their heteronormative desires in favor of lifelong celibacy. Of particular note, however, is that the queerness both in the *Metastasis* and in the *Acts of John* tradition as a whole operates positively. It is John's virginity that grants him salvation. It is the relinquishing of sexual appetite that saves Callimachus and the young man. The removal of one's "troublesome members"—whether literally or metaphorically—affords each of these three men salvation.

When we examine these occasions of sexual violence in the *Acts of John*, we find a tradition that affirmed the salvific potential of queerness. While this potential provides an enticing interpretation to many modern readers, it is not merely an invention of their heuristic methods. Indeed, there is at least one church father who also interprets John's virginity through a queer lens, albeit unwittingly. Let us now turn to everyone's favorite translator, saint, and curmudgeon, Jerome.

"VIRGINITY NEVER DIES": JEROME AND JOHN

At the height of the late fourth century so-called Jovinian controversy, Jerome pens a two-part polemical treatise, *Adversus Jovinianum*. Since the controversy revolved primarily around Jovinian's assertion that virgin women were no better than their married counterparts, Jerome spends the entirety of his first book defending virginity, presumably female virginity. Yet *Adversus Jovinianum* does not only defend the primacy of virgin women, it also advocates for the superiority of virgin *men*. As the chief exemplar of male chastity, Jerome employs the beloved virgin disciple, John.

Jerome uses John to prove that virgin men are far superior to their married and even formerly married counterparts. He accomplishes this by directly comparing John to his formerly married apostolic peer, Peter. Jerome makes it clear who the better apostle is:

> And yet John, one of the disciples, who tradition dictates was the youngest of the Apostles, and who was a virgin when he found faith in Christ, remained a virgin, and *on that account, he was loved more by the Lord*, and reclined upon the breast of Jesus. And what Peter, who used to have a wife, did not dare to ask, he requested [John] to ask. And after the resurrection, when Mary Magdalene announced that the Lord had risen, both men ran to the sepulcher, but [*John*] *arrived first*. And while they were fishing in a boat on the lake of Gennesaret, Jesus was standing upon the shore, and the Apostles could not perceive who they saw; the *virgin alone recognized a virgin* (*solus virgo virginem agnoscit*), and said to Peter, "It is the Lord." (*Jov.* 1.26)

Jerome goes on to explain that while Peter is "an apostle only," John was an apostle, evangelist, and a prophet. He writes, "Virginity expounded [upon things] which marriage could not understand, and to briefly sum it up and show how great was the privilege of John, or rather, *the virginity in John*, the Virgin Mother was entrusted by the Virgin Lord to the Virgin disciple" (*Jov.* 1.26). For Jerome, John is the prototype of the perfect apostle, evangelist, and man. According to Jerome, John's virginity is not merely a sign of a superior status, rather he is superior *because* of his virginity. John's strength is derived from his virginity, and it is that chastely derived strength that would have made him the most ideal cleric, even above Peter. John's virginity provides him with a premier access to Christ's body and to a knowledge that is unavailable to the other disciples. If given the choice to be like Peter, a respected apostle but still second best, or like John an apostle who ran fast, had superior knowledge, and even got to lay on Jesus's chest, why would you not choose the latter?

While it should come as no surprise to us that Jerome would have been familiar with the traditions of the wider Apocryphal Acts of the Apostles, is it possible that Jerome's depiction of John may be colored by the apostle's characteristics in the wider *Acts of John*? Jerome shows familiarity with some of the broad traditions from the early extant *Acts of John*. He clearly references both the tradition identifying John as the beloved disciple and discusses other apocryphal narratives about the apostle. While John has long been identified with the "beloved disciple," there is no explicit reference within the New Testament canon to John—or the beloved disciple for that matter—being a virgin. Where might Jerome's understanding of John as the virgin disciple have come from? Tertullian may be the first extant author to describe John's chastity. In *On Monogamy*, he describes John as a "noted voluntary celibate of Christ's." A more explicit depiction of John as a virgin comes from Epiphanius of Salamis. The *Panarion* cites John's virginity several times. Epiphanius claims that Jesus was referencing John and James in Matthew 19:12 since they "remained virgins and neither cut off their members with their own hands nor married . . . " He again cites John and James as virgins when explaining why Mary was pledged to John. Finally, and most importantly for our purposes here, Epiphanius shows familiarity with John's deathbed prayer from the *Acts of John*. While we cannot say with certainty whether Jerome read the *Acts of John*, particularly not the version we now have, he occupied a similar social and theological space as other patristic authors clearly familiar with its traditions. It stands to reason that Jerome's understanding of John as a perpetual virgin can be traced either directly or indirectly to stories from the *Acts of John*. And it is Jerome's understanding of John's perpetual virginity that makes the figure of John so ripe for Jerome's creation of a virgin/chaste masculinity in his own writings.

If we pull these threads together, an intriguing image appears. For Jerome, John's virginity queers him. As depicted in both the Acts and *Adversus Jovinianum*, John's virginity is central to his relationship with Christ. Jesus does not merely love John; he *needs* him. He needs him to spread the good news, to run fast, to recline upon his chest. Jerome portrays John's decision to remain pure for Christ as one elevates him above not only the other apostles, but also other men. By being Christ's special virgin, Christ's "bride" if you will, John is given premier access to knowledge and spaces that his formerly married apostolic peers are not. In his willingness to submit fully to Christ, the queer John-like man can surpass other "holy men." Armed with his virginity, he is able to go further and deeper into his relationship with Jesus.

Yet there is one significant difference in how John's virginity is presented Jerome's writings. In the *Acts of John*, Jesus thrusts John's virginity upon him; while in Jerome's view of the relationship, John's perpetual chastity is entirely voluntary. He does not mention John attempting to get married, having his engagements thwarted by illness or even John being blinded. Jerome is clear that John *made himself* a "eunuch out of love" for Christ (*Jov.* 1.36). John's decision to voluntarily submit his sexuality to Christ may make him both theologically and socially more palatable. Theologically, for Jerome, virginity must be a *choice*, this is why, according to Jerome, Paul makes it clear that there is "no command from the Lord" on virginity (*Jov.* 1.12). If someone is not making the active choice to abstain from sex, then that abstention is not a sacrifice. This change is socially significant because John, even in a relationship with a deity, cannot dare to have both his sexual agency lost *and* his masculinity intact. In book one of *Adversus Jovinianum*, Jerome makes an argument in favor of virgin or celibate priests by laying out a framework for a virginal masculinity. Speaking once of his own chastened sperm, Jerome boasts that his "seed is one hundred times more fertile" than any married man's (*Epist.* 22, 19:2). John is not merely a virginal ideal but moreover, he is a Christian masculine ideal. In Jerome's view of celibate prowess, the virgin male is still queered—his restrained sexuality still a challenge to the normative discourse—but ultimately his superiority is maintained.

CONCLUSIONS

While the early Christian apocryphal acts generally show a preference for chastity over sex and marriage, the *Acts of John* emphasizes the uniquely illicit, dangerous, and violent nature of male sexuality. The madness of desire can cause a man to kill his father, castrate himself, and rape a corpse. Although the titular apostle's desire for marriage is the most "vanilla" of the group, perhaps it is Jesus's own mad desire that leads him to blind John. In these episodes, we see that sex and violence are intimately intertwined. The attempt to fulfill sexual desire leads to violence in such a way that the very act of sex itself comes to hold a violent potential. A reversal of order is created. The preconceived norm of sex—here, heterosexual sex—is suddenly made strange, made problematic, even made queer. Whereas the queer position—the refusal of sex, the adoption of lifelong celibacy, the sublimation to a deity—is presented as an option full of companionship, salvation, and normativity. In essence, the *Acts of John* queers normativity and normalizes queerness; making the "normative" illicit and the queer laudable. It is this transformation that makes the traditions of John, his converts, and his relationship with Christ ripe to be picked up by later Church fathers like Jerome and used for the creation of a uniquely powerful, queer virility.

NOTES

1. A huge thank you to everyone who listened to, read, and provided feedback on this paper. I am particularly indebted to Candida Moss, Rebecca Draughon, Jennifer Barry, Janet Spitter, Karl Shuve, and, of course, Eric Vanden Eykel and Christy Cobb for their insightful notes, lines of inquiry, and feedback.

2. All translations unless otherwise stated are mine. For this paper I am using the "early" Acts of John as reconstructed by Eric Junod and Jean-Daniel Kaestli. *Acta Iohannis*. CCSA 1–2. Turnhout: Brepols, 1983.

3. The Metastasis traditionally encompasses sections 106–115.

4. Our modern emphasis on seeing the encratism of these texts has been called into question by Yves Tissot in their piece, "Encratism and the Apocryphal Acts" (in *The Oxford Handbook of Early Christian Apocrypha*, ed. Andrew F. Gregory [Oxford: Oxford University Press, 2015]). While there are clear instances of an encratic teaching in the stories of the Acts of John, Andrew, & Thomas, Tissot sees less evidence in the Acts of Peter and Acts of Paul.

5. The full episode encompasses sections 48–54.

6. As Janet Spittler has noted, the Greek here is a little ambiguous as to whether or not the father is actually dead. In the Greek, the young man says that he kicked his father and "made him mute" (*aphōnon ethēken*). See Spittler's forthcoming, "Resurrection in the Acts of John," section 3 for a discussion of the ambiguity in this scene.

7. As David Konstan has noted, the figure of John in the Acts of John is more focused on the reconciliation and conversion of families to Christianity rather than splintering the familial unit, as is the case in many of the other Apocryphal Acts. See "Acts of Love: A Narrative Pattern in the Apocryphal Acts." *JECS* 6.1 (1998): 15–36.

8. Candida Moss, *Divine Bodies: Resurrecting Perfection in the New Testament & Early Christianity* (New Haven: Yale University Press, 2019), chapter 2, especially pp. 45–64.

9. Daniel F. Caner, "The Practice and Prohibition of Self-Castration in Early Christianity," *VC* 51 (1997): 396–415. Also see Moss, *Divine Bodies*, chapter 3 for a breakdown of the early Christian debate about the necessity of reproductive parts in a sexless heaven.

10. From what we can reconstruct, Drusiana seems to have been converted first which follows a pattern of female/wife conversion we see throughout the Apocryphal Acts of the Apostles. As expected, a vital part of her conversion included abstaining from sex with her husband, Andronicus. When he threatens her with either sex or death, she opts for death. Eventually, Andronicus sees the light and becomes a follower of John as well. See *Acts John* 63: 4–14 for a detailed reference to this situation being explained to Callimachus.

11. Spittler has noted the ambiguity surrounding death in this scene as well. Initially the text merely describes Callimachus as "fallen" when he sees the serpent kill

Fortunatus. When describing the events, Callimachus says that the sight of God's messenger is what "made [him] a corpse." And both John and the narrator later refer to Callimachus as a "corpse" before being resurrected. See Spittler, "Resurrection in the Acts of John," section 4.

12. This echoes the scene from Mark 16:5 in which the women are greeted at Christ's tomb by a young man dressed in a white robe.

13. For more on this dynamic, see Christy Cobb's piece in this volume, "Euclia's Story: Coordinated Sexual Assault, Violence, and Willfulness in the *Acts of Andrew*."

14. A special thank you to Jennifer Barry for alerting me to the importance of this issue and for directing me to the work of Virginia Burrus.

15. For a discussion of this dynamic in the Apocryphal Acts of the Apostles, see Kate Cooper, *The Virgin and the Bride: Idealized Womanhood in Late Antiquity* (Cambridge: Harvard University Press, 1996). See also Shelly Matthews, "Thinking of Thecla: Issues in Feminist Historiography." *JFSR* 17:2 (2001), 39–55.

16. Virginia Burrus, *The Sex Lives of Saints: An Erotics of Ancient Hagiography* (Philadelphia: University of Pennsylvania Press, 2004), esp. Chapter 2.

17. Gerard Loughlin, *Queer Theology: Rethinking the Western Body* (Oxford: Blackwell Publishing, 2007), 1–4.

18. Eleanor S. Greenhill, "The Group of Christ and St. John as Author Portrait: Literary Sources, Pictorial Parallels." 406–16 In *Festschrift Bernard Bischoff zu Seinem 65. Geburtstag*, eds. Johanne Autenrieth and Franz Brunhölzl (Stuttgart: Anton Hiersemann, 1971), 408–412.

19. Virginia Burrus, "Queer Father: Gregory of Nyssa and the Subversion of Identity," in *Queer Theology: Rethinking the Western Body*, ed. Gerard Loughlin (Oxford: Blackwell, 2007), 147–62. Amy Hollywood, "Queering the Beguines: Mechthild of Magdeburg, Hadewijch of Anvers, Marguerite Porete," in *Queer Theology*, 163–74. I was initially alerted to this framework, along with the chapters of Burrus and Hollywood, by Rebecca Krawiec's "The Memory of Melania," in *Melania: Early Christianity through the Life of One Family*, ed. C.M. Chin and Caroline T. Schroeder (Oakland: California University Press, 2017), 130–141. Krawiec uses this understanding of queerness to provide a queer reading of Melania the Elder in Palladius's *Lausiac History*. Krawiec argues that in both Melania ascetic and Palladius's depiction of her, Melania's gender is queered and thus she is granted access to spaces and tasks that women are not typically allowed.

20. For a full discussion of the Jovinian controversy, see David Hunter, *Marriage, Celibacy, and Heresy in Ancient Christianity: The Jovinianist Controversy* (Oxford: Oxford University Press, 2007).

21. Emphasis mine. Unless otherwise indicated, all translations of *Adversus Jovinianum* are mine. The Latin edition of *Adversus Jovinianum* comes from Jacques-Paul Minge, *Patralogia Latina*, volume 23, Col 0211A—Col 0338A.

22. Emphasis mine.

23. John 20:4.

24. John 13:25; John 21:20.

25. Tamás Adamik, "The Influence of the Apocryphal Acts on Jerome's Lives" in *The Apocryphal Acts of John*, ed. Jan Bremmer (Kampen: Kok Pharos Publishing

House, 1995), 175. Though the specific evidence Adamik uses to make connect the Acts with Jerome's hagiography is rather tenuous, he persuasively argues that Jerome was familiar with apocryphal literature. He does this primarily by quoting Jerome's *On Illustrious Men*, 7: "We rank among the apocryphal writings the journey of Paul and Thecla and the whole tale of the baptized lion."

26. Jerome, *On Illustrious Men*, 9.

27. Most significantly, in his *Commentary on Matthew*, Jerome references both the legend of John being placed in burning oil and the legend of his voluntary death, both from the broad Johannine apocryphal tradition.

28. Alan Culpepper, *John, the Son of Zebedee: The Life of a Legend* (Columbia, SC: University of South Carolina Press, 1994). According to Culpepper the first evidence of an author connecting John with the "disciple of the Lord, who also leaned on his breast" comes from Irenaeus in book 3 of *Against the Heresies*, 3.1.1. Culpepper, page 124.

29. Tertullian, *On Monogamy,* 17. Yet, as Culpepper has suggested, it is unclear whether Tertullian is referring to John the Apostle or John the Baptist. For his discussion see *John, Son of Zebedee*, pg. 140 and 179 fn. 10.

30. Epiphanius, *Panarion*, 58.4.5–6. Translation by Philip R. Amidon, S.J. in *The Panarion of St. Epiphanius, Bishop of Salamis: Selected* Passages. Pg. 203.

31. Epiphanius, *Panarion*, 78.13.4.

32. Epiphanius, *Panarion*, 79.5.3.

33. Jerome here quotes 1 Corinthians 7:25. He is adamant that virginity was not made a requirement because it is more noble to do something voluntarily than by compulsion. Compare with his treatment of this issue in *Letter 22*, 20.2.

34. Jeannie Sellick, "Female Bodies, Male Asceticism: Why the Jovinian Controversy Rests on Female Virginity." *Studia Patristica*, 2022 (forthcoming).

35. I address Jerome's vision of masculine virginity in my dissertation, "The Strongest Seed: Jerome's Fashioning of Ascetic Masculinity in Late Antiquity" (University of Virginia, forthcoming).

WORKS CITED

Adamik, Tamás. "The Influence of the Apocryphal Acts on Jerome's Lives." Pages 171–182 in *The Apocryphal Acts of John*. Edited by Jan Bremmer. Kampen: Kok Pharos Publishing, 1995.

Burrus, Virginia. *The Sex Lives of Saints: An Erotics of Ancient Hagiography*. Philadelphia: University of Pennsylvania Press, 2004.

———. "Queer Father: Gregory of Nyssa and the Subversion of Identity." Pages 147–162 in *Queer Theology: Rethinking the Western Body*, ed. Gerard Loughlin (Oxford: Blackwell Publishing, 2007).

Caner, Daniel F. "The Practice and Prohibition of Self-Castration in Early Christianity." *Vigiliae Christianae* 51 (1997): 396–415.

Cooper, Kate. *The Virgin and the Bride: Idealized Womanhood in Late Antiquity.* Cambridge: Harvard University Press, 1996.

Culpepper, Alan. *John, the Son of Zebedee: The Life of a Legend.* Columbia, SC: University of South Carolina Press, 1994.

Greenhill, Eleanor S. "The Group of Christ and St. John as Author Portrait: Literary Sources, Pictorial Parallels." Pages 406–16 in *Festschrift Bernard Bischoff zu Seinem 65. Geburtstag.* Edited by Johanne Autenrieth and Franz Brunhölzl (Stuttgart: Anton Hiersemann, 1971).

Hollywood, Amy. "Queering the Beguines: Mechthild of Magdeburg, Hadewijch of Anvers, Marguerite Porete." Pages 163–174 in *Queer Theology: Rethinking the Western Body*, ed. Gerard Loughlin (Oxford: Blackwell Publishing, 2007).

Hunter, David. *Marriage, Celibacy, and Heresy in Ancient Christianity: The Jovinianist Controversy.* Oxford: Oxford University Press, 2007.

Junod, Eric and Jean-Daniel Kaestli, eds. *Acta Iohannis.* Corpus Christianorum Series Apocryphorum 1–2. Turnhout: Brepols, 1983.

Konstan, David. "Acts of Love: A Narrative Pattern in the Apocryphal Acts." *Journal of Early Christian Studies* 6.1 (1998): 15–36.

Krawiec, Rebecca. "The Memory of Melania." Pages 130–141 in *Melania: Early Christianity through the Life of One Family*. Edited by C.M. Chin and Caroline T. Schroeder. Oakland: California University Press, 2017.

Loughlin, Gerard, ed. *Queer Theology: Rethinking the Western Body*. Oxford: Blackwell Publishing, 2007.

Matthews, Shelly. "Thinking of Thecla: Issues in Feminist Historiography. *Journal of Feminist Studies in Religion* 17.2 (2001): 39–55.

Moss, Candida., *Divine Bodies*: *Resurrecting Perfection in the New Testament & Early Christianity.* New Haven: Yale University Press, 2019.

Sellick, Jeannie. "The Strongest Seed: Jerome's Fashioning of Ascetic Masculinity in Late Antiquity." PhD Diss, University of Virginia, forthcoming.

———. "Female Bodies, Male Asceticism: Why the Jovinian Controversy Rests on Female Virginity." *Studia Patristica* (forthcoming 2022).

Tissot, Yves. "Encratism and the Apocryphal Acts." Page 407–423 in *The Oxford Handbook of Early Christian Apocrypha*, edited by Andrew F. Gregory. Oxford: Oxford University Press, 2015.

Chapter 12

Assaulting the Virgin

How the Protevangelium of James Hides Sexual Violence

Eric Vanden Eykel

In the mid to late-second century CE, an anonymous author penned what would become a highly influential account of the birth and early life of Mary, the mother of Jesus. Today that text is known to scholars as the *Protevangelium of James* (henceforth PJ).[1] In this text, readers encounter Mary as a uniquely pure and remarkable creature. Like Jesus's own conception in Matthew and Luke (Matt 1:20; Luke 1:34–45), Mary's conception in PJ is a supernatural one that seems to occur in the absence of a human father (PJ 4:4). Her childhood, as well, is extraordinary. She walks at six months, for example, and when her mother Anna she sees this, she builds a miniature sanctuary in her bedroom to shield her from anything in the world that could possibly compromise her purity (PJ 6:4). When Mary turns three, her parents transfer her to the care of the priests in the Jerusalem Temple. She lives there, in the Holy of Holies, until she is twelve (PJ 7–8; 15:11). Suggestions abound regarding the purpose of this text. Some argue that it was written in praise of Mary, while others have suggested it was meant to defend her from slander. Others suggest that it is the product of curiosity, an attempt to answer the question "What sort of person was the mother of Jesus?" Few have addressed the fact that in this text Mary is also the victim of sexual assault.

My focus in this chapter is one of the more dramatic and violent episodes in the text; it occurs directly after the birth of Jesus, when a woman named Salome "examines" Mary's postpartum condition and experiences disastrous consequences as a result. My argument is that Salome's actions in this episode constitute sexual assault, and that while the author of PJ ultimately condemns this violation, they also use this instance of sexual violence to emphasize what they see as the enduring theological significance and sanctity of Mary's body.

I begin by contextualizing the Salome episode within PJ, and by highlighting some of the reasons why scholarship on this text has neglected to analyze this problematic episode in these terms. I then discuss the episode in more detail, and compare it with the story on which it is patterned, namely, that of Thomas and his doubt in the Gospel of John. I conclude by comparing the Salome episode with the scene immediately preceding the birth of Jesus, when Joseph witnesses the stilling of the created world. I suggest that the juxtaposition of these scenes evokes certain traditions about the giving of the law at Sinai, and that this encourages readers to understand Mary not only as the means through which Jesus enters the world, but also the continued dwelling place of the deity even after she has given birth.

Before beginning, I want to note that the argument in this chapter began as a conversation with one of my undergraduate students. She approached me after a class session on PJ and remarked that this text and any discussion of it should come with a content warning. As she explained what she had seen in Salome's actions, she also shared—through many tears—that an episode in her own past is what made this violent reading so vivid and transparent to her. Because of my own positionality, I did not recognize this episode as sexual assault in my previous research on PJ. I am thankful for this student, for her willingness to share her story with me, and for the sharp and necessary reminder that our perceptions of the world are not uniform, objective things.[2]

THE BIRTH OF JESUS

The story of Jesus's birth in PJ spans several chapters near the end of the text. The author is clearly familiar with both Matthew and Luke, and we can see this in the way that they attempt to harmonize these disparate accounts. Mary and Joseph live in Bethlehem (as they do in Matthew), yet in PJ they still travel in order to register in a census (as they do in Luke). PJ's account of Jesus's birth is more detailed than anything we find in Matthew or Luke. Mary gives birth to Jesus in a cave just outside Bethlehem, while she and Joseph are on the road. When she begins to labor, Joseph leaves her in a cave while he heads to the hill country to search for a Hebrew midwife. When he departs the cave, he has a strange vision in which he sees all of creation standing still. Up until this point everything has been narrated in third person. But as soon as Joseph sets foot outside the cave, the perspective shifts, and he begins to share the details of his vision directly with the reader using first-person pronouns (PJ 18:2–11). We will return to this episode later in this chapter.

When Joseph succeeds in finding a midwife, they return to the cave, at which point a dark cloud descends and a bright light obscures their vision (PJ 19:12–15). When these recede, the midwife and Joseph behold a no-longer-pregnant Mary nursing her newborn infant Jesus (PJ 19:16). The midwife is awed by everything that she sees, and she looks for somebody with whom to share this miraculous news. Immediately she encounters Salome, a previously-unmentioned character who is apparently loitering about the entrance of the cave.[3] The midwife remarks to her: "Salome, Salome, I have an incredible thing to tell you! A virgin has given birth, but her vagina (*phusis*) doesn't convey this" (PJ 19:19).[4] What the midwife considers to be incredible is not that Mary has *conceived* a baby virginally, but that her body has returned in a seemingly miraculous way to its pre-pregnant state after giving birth.[5]

Scholars who have analyzed this scene in the past have generally not commented on the problematic nature of the midwife's declaration, namely, that it is an exceptionally personal and revealing one—she has just made a public declaration about the appearance and physical status of Mary's genitals. Mary has here been exposed, and that exposure sets in motion a process that will culminate in disaster. For when the claim is delivered to Salome, she responds to it with disbelief and skepticism. She says: "As the Lord my God lives, unless I insert my finger and examine her vagina [*phusis*], I will not believe that a virgin has given birth" (PJ 19:19). The midwife leads her into the cave and orders Mary: "Situate yourself, for there is no small disagreement concerning you" (PJ 20:1). Mary complies, and Salome approaches her and "inserted her finger into [Mary's] vagina [*phusis*]" (PJ 20:2). Yet as soon as she does this, her hand bursts into flames and begins to wither. She cries out: "Damn my wickedness [*anomia*] and my faithlessness [*apistia*], for I have tested the living God! And see, now my hand is falling away from me in fire" (PJ 20:3–4). The deity, it would seem, is not pleased.

ASSAULTING THE VIRGIN

This scene is uncomfortable in almost every way. From the moment that the midwife announces the physical status of Mary's vagina, to Salome's assault, it tends to make readers squirm. It is entirely possible to interpret the spontaneous combustion of Salome's hand as somehow intended to provide some dramatic or, dare I even suggest, "comic" relief. Scholars who have written on this episode generally do not frame what happens here in positive or jovial terms, but neither have they gone so far as to label it properly. Most if not all have opted for the sterile, medical language of "postpartum examination" or something similar.[6] But in order to fully understand this episode, we need to be willing to call it what it is: Salome's assault of the Virgin.

Reasons for why scholars of PJ have shied away from this more accurate designation are complicated and, I would surmise, not necessarily nefarious. One possible explanation for the lack of clarity could be the utter strangeness of this episode within the context of PJ. As the other contributions to this volume make clear, authors of early Christian literature are more than comfortable using sexually explicit and violent imagery of rape, assault, and murder to serve a variety of rhetorical and theological aims. On the one hand, it should not surprise us when sexual violence appears in an ancient or early Christian text. Yet this episode *is* strange, especially when one considers its broader context. The author of PJ upholds Mary as an utterly pure and innocent creature, and one of the central and recurring themes throughout the text is the consistent and effective protection of Mary and her purity. Whether it is the sanctuary that her mother builds for her (PJ 6:2), the Holy of Holies in the Jerusalem Temple (PJ 8:2; 15:11), or the house of the elderly Joseph (PJ 9:11), the message of PJ is both clear and consistent: Mary is safe. For this author to now formulate a story in which Mary of all people is the victim of sexual assault is an odd move, to say the least. It is at least possible that readers don't see the assault because they have been conditioned to assume Mary's safety as a known variable. We don't see what we aren't looking for.

There are also categorical reasons for why this episode hasn't been properly labeled. Salome's actions in the cave simply don't fit the definition of assault as it is generally framed, specifically in the context of ancient literature. One could argue, for example, that this scene doesn't compute as an instance of sexual violence because this particular act of violence is committed by a woman, against another woman. While such things undoubtedly happened in the ancient world, literary examples are exceedingly rare. It is far more common for sexual assault to be committed by men, against women.[7] Because of the lack of *comparanda*, it is easy to interpret the episode as a sort of medical exploration by Salome. There's also the issue of whether Salome's actions toward Mary were actually unwelcome on Mary's part. When the midwife enters the cave and instructs Mary to prepare herself for this test, Mary doesn't resist. She complies with the midwife's instruction to position herself, and she seems to do so without any hesitation or protest (PJ 20:1–2). So, isn't it the case that Mary has "consented" to this? Or should that make any difference?

In her pointed discussion of rape stories in the Hebrew Bible, Rhiannon Graybill notes that the presence of "consent" has for some time been the litmus test for determining whether a something "counts" as rape or not. "It has become common to describe consent as an idea simple as a stoplight," she argues. "Green ('yes!') means go, red ('no!') means stop, yellow means proceed with caution." But as she also points out: "Sex is not a traffic pattern, and neither is rape."[8] Graybill suggests that in order to come to a better understanding of rape stories in the Hebrew Bible, we need to move the discussion away from this standard criterion of whether "consent" is present. When "consent" is the definitive standard by which we determine whether a story is one of sexual assault or rape, we are able to dismiss some stories—like the Salome episode—as categorically something different. Graybill suggests, instead, that many stories of sexual violence occupy the more amorphous categories of "fuzzy, messy, and icky." The usefulness of these categories is precisely in the reality that they are difficult to define with precision. "Everyday language," Graybill writes, "with its imprecisions and casual; disregard for fixed definitions, helps to capture something slippery about experience."[9]

Graybill's categories can help readers of PJ better see Salome's actions for what they are. It is arguably inaccurate to label what Salome does to Mary as "rape," but at the same time it is disingenuous to call it a "postpartum examination." This interaction exists more accurately, truthfully, and uncomfortably between these two poles. It remains difficult to define with any real precision, and yet there is the keen sense that it is a clear violation of Mary's body. The action is altogether "fuzzy, messy, and icky," but at the end of the day it is also intrinsically and unequivocally wrong. This is evidenced by the fact that Salome's hand begins to burn and wither as a result of her crime. If it is the case that the author of PJ condemns this graphic and violent assault, then why include it in the first place? What's the point?

A TALE OF TWO DOUBTERS

It has long been noted that Salome's assault of Mary is patterned off the story of so-called "Doubting Thomas" found in John 20. The similarities between the two stories are far from subtle. Both Thomas and Salome express disbelief in the face of a seemingly impossible claim. For Thomas, the claim that the crucified Jesus is no longer dead, but alive (John 20:25). For Salome, it is that Mary's body has remained "virginal" even after she has given birth to Jesus (PJ 19:18). Both Thomas and Salome indicate that they will believe only if they can investigate matters for themselves. And they express this in nearly identical terms. When the disciples deliver the news to Thomas, he responds: "Unless [*ean mē*] . . . I insert my finger [*balō ton daktulon mou*] in the mark of the nails and my hand in his side, I will not believe [*ou mē pisteusō*]" (John 20:25). Similarly, when the midwife announces her news to Salome, she responds: "Unless [*ean mē*] I insert my finger [*balō ton daktulon mou*] and investigate her vagina [*phusis*], I will not believe [*ou mē pisteusō*]" (PJ 19:19).

One of the more glaring differences between these parallel stories of Salome and Thomas is that while Salome goes through with her test, Thomas stops short. When Jesus appears to Thomas and offers his body for examination, Thomas sees Jesus and then exclaims "My lord and my god" (John 20:28). While artistic representations of this scene often depict Thomas a knuckle or two deep into Jesus's side, in the Gospel of John there is no physical examination of Jesus's body. Thomas sees Jesus, and this is enough for him to believe the claim that Jesus is no longer dead. But the same is not true for Salome. Once the midwife instructs Mary to prepare herself, Salome wastes no time, and instead thrusts her finger into Mary. And as noted, the consequences of this are severe and disastrous. Both Thomas and Salome cry out to their god, although their respective motivations for doing so could not be more different. Thomas makes a confession of faith (John 20:28). Salome, expresses agony and a plea for forgiveness (PJ 20:3–7).

Thomas's story in John 20 is about one disciple of Jesus seeking to confirm an impossible claim. Likewise, the Salome episode exists for this purpose. Like Thomas, Salome indicates that she needs some kind of tactile proof in order to accept what has been presented to her. But unlike Thomas, whose disbelief dissolves when he sees the body of Jesus, Salome is not satisfied with just seeing the body of Mary, for the object of her curiosity is hidden from plain sight.[10] Yet even after she is punished for her assault, Salome's story realigns with Thomas's. Because like Thomas, Salome ultimately makes a sort of faith confession. As her hand is melting away in the flames, and angel appears and instructs her to pick up the infant Jesus. She does as she is told, and adds: "I will honor [*proskuneō*] him, because he has been born King of Israel" (PJ 20:10). She is healed instantly and then departs the narrative just as suddenly as she arrived (PJ 20:11).

Through its alignment with the Thomas pericope, the Salome episode serves to confirm the claim of the midwife, namely, that the birth of Jesus has not affected the physical integrity of Mary's body (PJ 19:18). In keeping with the theme of purity and virginity present throughout the text, Mary remains "the Virgin of the Lord" even after giving birth. But the story accomplishes this goal only because of its dependence on the Thomas pericope. After Jesus has appeared to Thomas, he says: "Have you believed because you have seen me? Blessed are those who have not seen and yet have come to believe" (John 20:29). Throughout John's Gospel, signs performed by Jesus engender belief in those who witness them. But here the author acknowledges that readers of his Gospel do not have the benefit of seeing with their own eyes. Instead, they have to take his word for it. And in doing so, they are doing the harder thing. I suggest that the same dynamic is present in the Salome episode. And while Salome's quest to validate the midwife's claim takes a different path than that of Thomas, the reader's task is ultimately the same in both cases. Because they cannot be present to hazard their own investigation, they must believe the impossible in the absence of tangible proof.

At this point we have yet to address the question of why the author of PJ chooses to tell this story in this way. Could the same goal not have been accomplished by following the Thomas pericope more closely? Could Salome not have just looked at the body of Mary and then confirmed the truth of the midwife's announcement? Why does the author choose to turn his protagonist into the victim of sexual assault? What is accomplished by subjecting Mary to violence like this? In this final section, I argue that the juxtaposition of the Salome episode with the vision of Joseph that immediately precedes Jesus's birth evokes traditions about the giving of the law at Sinai. I suggest that this connection establishes Mary both as a sort of divine conduit as well as the unique dwelling place of the deity.

THE WORLD STOOD STILL

Just before Jesus is born, the author of PJ uses the character of Joseph to further underscore the unusual and unique nature of the birth. When he departs the cave to find a midwife, he has a vision of the cessation of time and the utter stillness of all created things. Joseph's vision is narrated in the first person, and it has the effect of slowing the fast-paced narrative of PJ to an almost-complete stop, beckoning the reader to pause in wonder at what is taking place back in the cave, in his (and the reader's) absence:

> Now I Joseph was walking and yet not walking. And I looked up to the pole of heaven and I saw it fixed. I saw the air utterly astonished, and the birds of heaven resting. Then I gazed upon the earth and I saw a bowl sitting there, and workers reclining, their hands in the bowl. The ones chewing were not chewing, and the ones taking did not take, and the ones raising to their mouths did not raise, but their faces were all looking up. I saw sheep being driven, but the sheep were still. And the shepherd was raising his hand in order to strike them, but his hand was stuck, raised. I observed the torrent of the river and saw little goats, their mouths hovering over the water, but not drinking. And then, in an instant, everything resumed its course. (PJ 18:2–11)

The shift in narrative aspect from third to first person persists halfway into next chapter, as Joseph finds a midwife and speaks with her. It will return to the third person (in PJ 19:11) as abruptly as it switched in the first place.[11]

The first-person narration serves an important function within the narrative world of PJ. Like the so-called "we passages" in the New Testament Acts of the Apostles (16:10–17; 20:5–15; 21:1–8; 27:1–28:16), the shift in perspective has a way of "validating" the contents of the vision for the reader. This is not secondhand, but "straight from the source."

The shift also has a way of slowing the reader down and thus encouraging them to marvel along with the rest of creation at the importance of the events transpiring in the cave. But perhaps most significantly, Joseph's "I" draws the reader away from the cave and away from Mary, forcing them to follow Joseph as he leaves. The author of PJ perhaps senses that this temporary abandonment will unsettle his readers, and he plays with this dynamic in the way that he crafts Joseph's vision. The reader perhaps judges Joseph for leaving Mary alone, but then suddenly they are traveling away from the cave with him. And as they begin to witness the stilling of creation alongside Joseph, they find themselves drawn into that eager expectation.

In the early 1990s, François Bovon published a short chapter on this scene in which he explores exactly how the vision of Joseph (the stillness of time specifically) functions within the author's worldview.[12] Bovon's argument in that chapter is twofold. First, he suggests that the vision of Joseph is supposed to correspond in some way to the Lukan shepherds who are at rest in the field when the angels come to announce the birth of Jesus (in Luke 2:8). Second, and more significantly for our purposes in the present chapter, he argues that the suspension of time in Joseph's vision signifies the dawning of a new eschatological era. "The created world is immobilized," he maintains, "because God is about to act."[13] Noting that the pause in time is only temporary, Bovon suggests that Jesus's birth here is understood only as the first stage in God's eschatological action. The birth of Jesus for this author is but a glimpse of the end, and not the end itself.[14]

Bovon lists a number of ancient sources in this chapter that also describe the cessation of time, but he only explores a small handful of these in any depth. One that he names but then doesn't comment on is *Shemot Rabbah*, an aggadic midrash on Exodus. This text is an outlier for studying PJ because it was probably written several hundred years after PJ. By addressing that text here I am not claiming any sort of literary dependence, and Bovon's citation of it likewise is not a claim of this sort. Yet while the author of PJ is certainly not citing a text that does not exist yet, it is entirely possible that they are familiar with some form of the traditions present in this text.[15] Here we are concerned with Chapter 29, which is a commentary on the giving of the law at Sinai (in Exod 20).

The focus of *Shemot Rabbah* 29 is on the first words of the Decalogue: "I the LORD am your God." What follows is a series of reflections on the theophany in Exodus 19:18, in which the mountain trembles and is covered with smoke, with the voice of God speaking in the distance to Moses as the sound of thunder. The earth and the people quake not because they fear punishment, but because through the giving of the Law, God is giving new life to creation. There is also a sense here that what happens at the giving of this new life will happen again at some point in the future. The commentary continues: "If the earth trembled when He gave life to the world, how much the more so when he comes to punish the wicked for transgressing the words of the Torah?" (*Shem. Rab.* 29:9).[16]

For the purposes of this analysis, the most significant portion of the *Shemot Rabbah* is what happens near the end of chapter 29, when the ground stops quaking and God begins to speak: "When God gave the Torah no bird twittered [or flew], no ox lowed, none of the Ophanim stirred a wing, the Seraphim did not say 'Holy, Holy,' the sea did not roar, the creatures spoke not, the whole world was hushed into breathless silence and the voice went forth: I am the LORD your God" (*Shem. Rab.* 29:9). The stillness of the natural world is interpreted not only as an expression of fear or awe, but of the oneness and uniqueness of the God of Israel. The story of Elijah and the prophets of Ba'al in 1 Kings 18 is cited as an illustration. In the *Shemot Rabbah*, it is not just Ba'al who doesn't respond to the wailing of his prophets; the natural world quiets as well: "God silenced the whole world, both those in heaven and those on earth, and the whole world became waste and void, as if no creature was in the world" (*Shem. Rab.* 29:9). Connecting this back to Exodus, the point is made: "How much more natural was it then that when God spoke on Mount Sinai, the whole world became silent, so that all creatures might know that there is none beside Him" (*Shem. Rab.* 29:9).

I have two suggestions for how we might understand Joseph's vision in light of this midrash. First, that the stillness of creation is a commentary on the identity of the one being born in the cave. The reader of PJ is already aware that Jesus will not be a regular human child. At the annunciation scene, Mary is told that he will be "son of the Most High" (PJ 11:7). The stillness that precedes his birth in PJ 18:2–11 could be read as the author's attempt to restate and reaffirm this divine identity. Alternately, the author of PJ may be framing the birth of Jesus as an event similar to what happens at the giving of the Law in Exodus. Perhaps Jesus is, for this author, a sort of "new law," or perhaps the author is echoing the Pauline sentiment that Jesus is the *telos nomou*, the law's completion (Rom 10:4). If we understand Jesus as a sort of "new law," or as the completion of the law, then this casts Mary as Sinai. And if we reread the story of Jesus's birth and Salome's assault in this light, correspondences between these stories become remarkably clear.

The Israelites arrive at the base of Sinai in the nineteenth chapter of Exodus. The mountain is veiled in a thick smoke, indicating that God has indeed arrived among the people and that the giving of the law is imminent

(Exod 19:18). We find a similar setting of the scene in PJ, when Joseph and the midwife arrive at the cave and find it overshadowed by a dark cloud (PJ 19:13), indicating similarly that God is somehow present in the cave. Upon seeing the cloud, the midwife in PJ echoes Mary and Simeon in the Gospel of Luke (2:29–32) and exclaims: "My soul has been magnified today, because today my eyes have seen a miracle, because salvation has been born to Israel" (PJ 19:14). It is tempting to suggest that the midwife (like Simeon) is referring to the newborn infant Jesus, but notably, she has not yet seen Jesus. Her awe is directed not at him, but at the cloud that prevents anyone from seeing whatever miraculous thing is happening behind it. And just as the cloud in Exodus 19 obscures the peoples' view of the mountain, and thus the giving of the law, so too does the cloud in PJ obscure the peoples' view of Mary, and thus the birth of Jesus.

Fire is also present in Exodus as well as PJ. In Exodus, it is the source of the cloud that covers the mountain, but also indicates the divine presence (Exod 19:18; 24:17). The fire on the mountain is known to the reader of Exodus because the narrator describes it, but this is not the case with the fire in PJ. Unlike the dark cloud that keeps the midwife and Joseph from approaching the cave and witnessing the birth of Jesus, the fire that issues forth from Mary's body is as much a surprise to the reader as it is to Salome whose hand is suddenly and violently consumed by it. The fire in PJ is understood as the author's condemnation of Salome's assault, but when reading this account through the lens of Exodus, it is also possible to interpret it as indicative of the divine presence. This would suggest that the deity is somehow uniquely and powerfully present within Mary, an observation that becomes ever more striking when we recall that Salome's assault occurs *after* Jesus has been born. Mary's body in this text persists as a sacred and inaccessible terrain.

A final component of the Exodus account that has an implicit parallel in PJ is the instruction given to the people to not touch the mountain. Before the cloud and the fire arrive, God commands Moses: "Set limits for the people all around, saying, 'Be careful not to go up the mountain or to touch the edge of it.'" (Exod 19:12). Those who fail to observe this rule are to be killed with arrows or stones (Exod 19:12–13). There is no explicit prohibition in PJ against people touching Mary, but one of the primary emphases of the text is that Mary is guarded carefully from impurity for her entire life. There are a few examples of people in PJ who do touch her, albeit not in the same way as Salome does. Her mother holds her and feeds her when she is an infant (PJ 5:10), and when she is brought to the temple the priest welcomes her with a kiss and places her on the steps of the altar, where she dances for those gathered (PJ 7:7). The fact that Salome is punished for her touch suggests that something about it is fundamentally different from these other examples.

If I am correct that Salome's touch is an instance of sexual assault, then it certainly is different from anything that Mary has encountered in the course of the narrative. It is also possible to understand Salome's punishment as another echo of the giving of the law in Exodus, although notably, the punishment for touching the mountain in Exodus is not burning by fire, but being killed by arrows and stones. It is of course not necessary for every detail to match exactly in order for the argument to be made for literary allusion.

There is a final connection worth highlighting that bolsters this reading, which is from the New Testament Epistle to the Hebrews.[17] The author of Hebrews writes: "You have not come to a thing that can be touched, a blazing fire, and darkness, and gloom, and a tempest" (Heb 12:18). There's an interesting and well-attested textual variant in the first part of this passage that suggests an alternate reading: "You have not come to a *mountain* that can be touched."[18] Given the reference to fire, darkness, as well as its context within Hebrews, it seems fairly obvious that even without this variant reading, the author of Hebrews is speaking about the mountain in Exodus as something that is strictly off limits. In characteristically supersessionist language, the author then contrasts the untouchable mountain with a number of things that at least implicitly *can* be touched, including "Jesus, the mediator of the new covenant" (see Heb 12:22–24). The suggestion that the author makes here is that while the mountain of the "old covenant" is off limits, and cannot be touched, the mediator of the new covenant (Jesus) is not off limits, and in fact *can* be touched.

This comparison in Hebrews is particularly striking considering how the Salome episode in PJ ends. Salome does not die or burn up completely. Rather, as she screams about the flames that engulf her hand, an angel appears and tells her the antidote: she will be healed if she touches Jesus. She does this, and she is cured immediately and leaves the cave justified. The body of Mary remains strictly off limits, and those who test its boundaries are punished. The body of Jesus, on the other hand, is approachable and has the capacity to heal those who would touch it. It is possible to argue that the dynamics present in this scene echo and perpetuate the supersessionism of Hebrews. As some might phrase it: "the old covenant is bad and violent while the new one is peaceful and loving." I would suggest that such an interpretation is less than helpful in the broader context of PJ. Mary is not here replaced by Jesus. Rather, she continues to exist alongside him, and what Salome's assault makes clear is that Mary's body remains not only virginal, but sacred as well.

CONCLUSION

We now return to the question that has been following us throughout this chapter: Why did the author of PJ introduce a story in which his protagonist is the victim of a sexual assault? This question becomes ever more sharp in light of the text's central aim of demonstrating that Mary's purity has never been at risk. One way of addressing this question is to say that the assault reinforces for the reader that they can believe the claim of the midwife, namely, that Mary's body remains unaffected by the birth of Jesus. On this same note, the assault and its punishment also serve as a fairly graphic warning to those readers who would question the truth of such a claim. Essentially, those who dare to doubt whether Mary's virginity remains intact are following in Salome's footsteps. And we know how that turned out. But I would also like to suggest another reading, which is that the language of sexual assault here is meant to evoke a visceral and even violent reaction in readers. The episode is uncomfortable, possibly by design, and what Salome does to Mary should be met by readers with disapproval, disdain, and disgust. The connection of this episode with the giving of the law in Exodus gives the scene a more theological tenor. Mary is not simply "the Virgin of the Lord." She is the location where the deity is both uniquely and powerfully present. And just like the mountain in Exodus, failing to respect her boundaries could cost you.

NOTES

1. This title was created in the sixteenth century by Guillaume Postel, who is often credited with the "rediscovery" of the text and its reintroduction into the West. In antiquity it circulates under various other headings. Discussion of dating and provenance in Lily Vuong, *Gender and Purity in the Protevangelium of James*, WUNT 2.358 (Tübingen: Mohr Siebeck, 2013), 32–39; Eric Vanden Eykel, *"But Their Faces Were All Looking Up": Author and Reader in the Protevangelium of James*, RJFTC 1 (London: T&T Clark, 2016), 23–24. Translations of the *Protevangelium* in this chapter are my own, and for these I use the standard Greek text in Ronald Hock, *The Infancy Gospels of James and Thomas*, SB 2 (Santa Rosa: Polebridge, 1995), 32–77. Readers interested in a recent English translation, commentary, and bibliography should consult Lily Vuong, *The Protevangelium of James*, ECA 7 (Eugene, OR: Cascade, 2019).

2. She gave me permission to share this, but she also requested to remain anonymous.

3. Modern readers have formulated a number of hypotheses regarding who the author and ancient readers of the *Protevangelium* would have understood Salome to be. For our purposes, the question of her identity is peripheral to the function that she serves in this episode.

4. The Greek noun I have translated here as "vagina" is *phusis*, which is often translated here and in other texts as "nature." Yet context suggests that this is a rather unsubtle reference to Mary's vaginal opening. On this point, see John J. Winkler, *The Constraints of Desire* (New York: Routledge, 1990), esp. 217–20; see also Mary F. Foskett, *A Virgin Conceived: Mary and Classical Representations of Virginity* (Indianapolis: Indiana University Press, 2002), 159. Similar uses in Hippocrates, *Mul.* 2.143; Antonius Liberales, *Metam.* 4; Artemidorus Daldianus, *Onir.* 5.63.

5. For the ancient reader, conception of a child outside of normal, natural means would have been more understandable than the idea that a woman's physical integrity could be maintained through the process of giving birth. As Walter Bauer so famously remarked: "One does not argue the question whether a virgin can conceive, but whether she can give birth without losing her characteristic condition" (Bauer, *Das Leben Jesu im Zeitalter der neutestamentlichen Apokryphen* [Tübingen: Mohr, 1909; repr., Darmstadt: Wissenschaftliche Buchgesellschaft, 1967], 69).

6. This comment is directed at my own scholarship on PJ as well as others who have published on this text. See for example Vanden Eykel, *"But Their Faces,"* 146–49; idem., "Protevangelium Iacobi," pages 93–105 in *The Reception of Jesus in the First Three Centuries. Volume 2: From Thomas to Tertullian: Christian Literary Receptions of Jesus in the Second and Third Centuries*, ed. Chris Keith et al. (London: T&T Clark, 2019), 103–4.

7. Most of the examples in this volume are a case in point. Jeannie Sellick's chapter on the Acts of John involves men committing violence against men, and in Christy Cobb's chapter on the Acts of Andrew, it is Maximilla who plans and facilitates her husband's rape of Euclia. Maximilla does not rape Euclia, but she is the reason why Euclia is raped. All other chapters deal with sexual violence as involving a male and a female. Rhiannon Graybill ("Fuzzy, Messy, Icky: The Edges of Consent in Hebrew Bible Rape Narratives and Rape Culture," *The Bible and Critical Theory* 15 [2019]: 4, n. 15) notes a few instances in the Hebrew Bible of sexual violence committed against men, including Jeremiah (Jer 20:7), Noah (Gen 9), and Lot (Gen 19:30–38). She also notes that such an interpretation for these stories is not necessarily standard. In terms of Roman literature, it is possible to understand Martial's character Philaenis (e.g., in *Epi.* 7.67) as a female who preys sexually on other females, but this is far from certain.

8. Graybill, "Fuzzy, Messy, Icky," 3.

9. Graybill, *Texts After Terror: Rape, Sexual Violence, and the Hebrew Bible* (New York: Oxford University Press, 2021), 12.

10. Salome is clearly in search of some type of physical evidence, but the precise nature of that evidence remains unclear. Some have suggested that she is searching for an intact hymen, but Julia Kelto Lillis points out (in "Paradox in Partu: Verifying Virginity in the *Protevangelium of James*," *JECS* 24 [2016]: 9–10) that the hymen as an indicator of physical virginity is almost entirely absent from our ancient gynecological manuals. Soranus alone references it (*Gyn.* 1.3.17) and then only to refute the idea.

11. This seemingly clumsy adjustment in perspective has been cited as evidence that the vision of Joseph was originally part of PJ. This argument is possibly bolstered by the absence of the vision from some MSS, including the Bodmer V codex (our

oldest extant copy of PJ), as well as Vat.gr. 455 and 654. Yet others have argued that the presence of the vision in all other MSS of PJ suggests that it was part of the narrative from the beginning, and as such, those MSS that do not have the vision have simply chosen to exclude it for whatever reason. There are a number of MSS that include the vision but adjust the narrative perspective to the third person throughout, which certainly makes the vision itself less jarring.

12. Bovon, "The Suspension of Time in Chapter 18 of *Protevangelium Jacobi*," in *The Future of Early Christianity*, ed. B. A. Pearson (Minneapolis: Fortress Press), 393–405.

13. Bovon, "Suspension," 403.

14. Bovon, "Suspension," 403.

15. Tim Horner, for example (in "Jewish Aspects of the Protoevangelium of James," *JECS* 12 [2004]: 313–335), argues that the author of PJ is familiar with certain Mishnaic traditions.

16. Translations of *Shemot Rabbah* are from the Soncino Edition (London: Soncino Press, 1983).

17. Hebrews is a text with which the author of PJ is likely familiar. See, for example, the argument in Vanden Eykel, *"But Their Faces,"* 131–34.

18. This reading is found in the Majority Text, Codex Bezae, among others.

WORKS CITED

Bauer, Walter. *Das Leben Jesu im Zeitalter der neutestamentlichen Apokryphen*. Tübingen: Mohr, 1909. Repr., Darmstadt: Wissenschaftliche Buchgesellschaft, 1967.

Foskett, Mary F. *A Virgin Conceived: Mary and Classical Representations of Virginity*. Bloomington: Indiana University Press, 2002.

Graybill, Rhiannon. "Fuzzy, Messy, Icky: The Edges of Consent in Hebrew Bible Rape Narratives and Rape Culture." *The Bible and Critical Theory* 15 (2019): 1–28.

———. *Texts After Terror: Rape, Sexual Violence, and the Hebrew Bible*. New York: Oxford University Press, 2021.

Hock, Ronald F. *The Infancy Gospels of James and Thomas*. Scholars Bible 2. Santa Rosa: Polebridge, 1995.

Horner, Tim. "Jewish Aspects of the *Protoevangelium of James*." *Journal of Early Christian Studies* 14 (2004): 313–335.

Lillis, Julia Kelto. "Paradox in Partu: Verifying Virginity in the *Protevangelium of James*." *Journal of Early Christian Studies* 24 (2016): 1–28.

Vanden Eykel, Eric. *"But Their Faces Were All Looking Up": Author and Reader in the Protevangelium of James*. Reception of Jesus in the First Three Centuries 1. London: T&T Clark, 2016.

———. "Protevangelium Jacobi." Pages 93–105 in *From Thomas to Tatian: Christian Literary Receptions of Jesus in the Second and Third Centuries CE*. Vol. 2 of *Reception of Jesus in the First Three Centuries*. Edited by Chris L. Keith, Helen K. Bond, Christine Jacboi, and Jens Schröter. London: Bloomsbury T&T Clark, 2019.

Vuong, Lily. *Gender and Purity in the Protevangelium of James*. Wissenschaftliche Untersuchungen zum Neuen Testament 2.358. Tubingen: Mohr Siebeck, 2013.

———. *The Protevangelium of James*. Early Christian Apocrypha 7. Eugene, OR: Cascade, 2019.

Chapter 13

Five Husbands

Slut-Shaming the Samaritan Woman

Meredith J. C. Warren

This essay[1] pushes back against the many readings, both scholarly and popular, of the Samaritan woman at the well (John 4) as an example of Jesus's "radical inclusivity."[2] It argues that receptions of the passage as inclusive often perpetuate the tendency known as "slut-shaming," a tactic frequently employed to denigrate women and police their sexualities. Slut-shaming techniques are common both in biblical commentaries and in popular readings of John 4, and, I argue, are also employed by the author of John. Slut-shaming is the attempted denigration of a person, usually a woman or girl, because of her perceived sexual deviancy or promiscuity. Viewed through this lens, it becomes evident that the passage is hardly a call for inclusion of women or Samaritans. In the end, the character of the Samaritan at the well becomes just another woman for men to "think with."[3] While finding inclusive readings of scripture is an important part of an ethical interpretive framework for religious communities, readings of this passage as an inclusive text run the risk of participating in the same slut-shaming that occurs in the biblical text. What is more, the pattern of slut-shaming in scholarship on John 4 reinforces damaging norms within the academy, norms which enable a culture of sexism and rape culture to flourish within our guild.

In John 4, Jesus famously encounters a Samaritan woman with whom he carries on a lengthy repartee while his disciples have gone food-shopping. Because he dialogues at length with a woman in general, and a Samaritan in particular, who challenges him on several points and is knowledgeable about inner-Jewish boundary debates and theological questions, the account is often held up as an example of Jesus's magnanimous inclusivity, especially (and problematically) over and against other Jews.[4] It is only when he miraculously reveals that he knows her entire sexual history that he gets the upper hand in the discussion and she in turn becomes an "apostle to the Samaritans." Like the popular notion that Jesus "even" deigned to dine with so-called sinners like tax collectors and sex workers, here the Samaritan woman's Otherness—in terms of her gender, her Samaritan identity, and, most importantly of her sexual history—is exploited in order to portray Jesus as generous and benevolent.

This essay investigates the many levels at which the Samaritan woman has been slut-shamed, contributing to the prevalence of rape culture in biblical interpretation. I will demonstrate how past readings of Jesus and the Samaritan woman tend to gloss over how slut-shaming occurs in the text, and how they even reinforce the slut-shaming performed by Jesus in their own comments on John 4, or try to apologize for the woman's sexual history by providing alternate, socially-acceptable justification for the number of her partners. After contextualizing the Samaritan woman's sexuality through the lenses of slut-shaming and the *femme fatale*, I conclude by connecting scholarly approaches to the Samaritan woman's promiscuity to issues of rape culture and sexism in the field of biblical studies as a discipline.

READINGS OF THE TEXT AS INCLUSIVE

There exists the prevalent view that Jesus's benevolence is proven through just how magnanimously he consorts with sinners.[5] Jesus's forgiving nature is often evidenced by claiming that he "hung out" or dined with sex workers, especially but not exclusively in the popular imagination.[6] For example, the Twitter bio of @JesusOfNaz316, a popular account impersonating Jesus, reads: "Carpenter who hangs out with fishermen, alcoholics, and prostitutes."[7] However, the biblical texts do not include such a gathering. Instead, Jesus does not look favorably on women's sexual activity,[8] paid or otherwise. By way of context for examining the account involving the Samaritan woman, it is important to interrogate this particular perception of Jesus as friend of women. Notably, there is no description of Jesus ever dining or socializing with sex workers. Instead, in Matthew 21:28-32, the Parable of the Two Sons, Jesus uses tax collectors (*telōnai*) and what the NRSV translates as prostitutes (*pornai*) to insult the elders and chief priests. Nowhere do any of the Gospels describe Jesus encountering a *pornē*, although he does encounter tax collectors and more generic sinners (*hamartōloi*) elsewhere (Matt 9:10, 10:3, 11:19; Mark 2:15–16; Luke 3:12, 5:27, 29–30, 7:34, 15:1). It's likely that the original idiom was indeed *telōnai kai pornai* because of the phrase's origins in the Q source, which tends to favor gendered pairs, in this case tax collectors (male profession with negative social connotations) and sex worker (female profession with negative social connotations).[9] In Luke 7:37, a text often assumed to reference Jesus dining with a sex worker, the woman is described only as being a sinner and from the city; her sin is just as generic as (or perhaps even more generic than) those sinners associated with tax collectors in Matthew's text.[10] Jesus's reputation is much rosier than his narrated behavior warrants. Regardless, in every case, the phrase is used as a hyperbolic insult designed to denigrate Jesus's opponents; it is not a rallying cry to inclusivity. As with other examples of this kind of comparison, the tax collectors and sinners are being used *to think with*. They exemplify how poorly "this generation" is abiding by Torah; they stand as hyperbolic examples of just how low the bar is. Jesus in these examples is not arguing for inclusion but rather using women, sinners, and tax collectors to shame his real interlocutors.

But likewise, there is the problem of using this popular assumption to elevate Jesus's reputation irrespective of whether it reflects the gospel accounts or historical record; this claim, that Jesus dined with sex workers, is intended to juxtapose two contrasting individuals. On the one hand, Jesus, son of God, forgiver of sins, all around swell dude. On the other hand, this line of thinking goes, a woman whose profession is a sin so damning that she should be used emphatically to indicate the true boundlessness of Jesus's forgiveness. For example, Monique Alexandre's treatment of early Christian women includes the claims that the Gospels represent a "marked change" from the position of women in early Judaism[11]; the "traditional hierarchy was overturned" by Jesus's involvement with women, she writes, linking this claim to Matthew 21:31 and John 4 in almost the same breath.[12] Luise Schottroff argues that Jesus's compassion in John 4 actually liberates a woman who is "suffering to be freed from her prison."[13] In other words, the prevailing, seemingly progressive or even feminist, eagerness to wave a giant foam finger at Jesus's feminism—often linked to the perception that he hung out with imaginary sex workers—actually does nothing to recognize the autonomy, humanity, or acceptability of sex work itself, and instead only further emphasizes the gulf between perceived sexual sin and righteous forgiveness. I wholeheartedly agree with the rallying cries raised by scholars such as Elisabeth Schüssler Fiorenza and others that we need an ethics of biblical interpretation that preferences inclusivity and justice.[14] Previous Christian-liberationist and Christian-feminist readings aimed to create space for women within the church, but an ethics that privileges Christian women is hardly inclusive.[15] Likewise, inclusivity fails if it is at the expense of sex workers, Jews, and others used by the text to propagate a rhetorically powerful argument for following Jesus. In effect, presenting Jesus as inclusive could be understood to participate in the phenomenon called slut-shaming.

This approach also occurs in scholarship on the Samaritan woman; she is used as an example of Jesus's radical inclusivity precisely because of her perceived sexual indiscretions. For example, Paul Anderson in his *Christology of the Fourth Gospel* writes that "In general, the treatment of women in John is more elevated than in Matthew. This is illustrated by the fact that the Samaritan woman becomes a follower of Jesus and even an 'apostle to the Samaritans'" (Jn. 4:7–42).[16] Jerome H. Neyrey describes the encounter in this way: "she represents the quintessential deviant (non-Jew, unclean, shameless, even sinner); but in her transformation, she exemplifies the radical inclusivity of Jesus' circle."[17] As in the example of the tax collectors, sinners, and prostitutes in the synoptic gospels, the Samaritan woman is used to shame Jesus's true interlocutors, and not as a symbol of inclusion for all. She is juxtaposed to the clueless disciples—*even* an adulterous Samaritan woman, the lowest of the low, understands more than they.

SLUT-SHAMING

Slut-shaming is a cultural phenomenon that is as contemporary as it is long-lived; it is a pervasive feature of both recent and ancient times. Slut-shaming is a means of restricting women's sexual activity by using a woman's sexual history, reputation, or activity to discredit her.[18] It is a form of sexual slander[19] especially aimed at promiscuity, hence the colloquial use of the term "slut" to denote (in particular) a woman who has multiple sexual partners. Slut-shaming as a social tool is used to mark its subject as "deserving disrespect."[20] It is "a societal process that is predominantly directed at women, where individuals are publicly exposed and shamed for their 'perceived sexual availability, behavior or history.'"[21] As a phenomenon, slut-shaming connects the perceived promiscuity or sexual deviance with shame. Shame is intimate, deeply connected with the self (the person experiencing shame) but it is also relational, in that shame is a public emotion. Shame serves to alienate—it isolates the victim from community: "Shame is the intensely painful feeling or experience of believing we are flawed and therefore unworthy of acceptance and belonging."[22] Shame is a powerful emotion, and in slut-shaming it is weaponized.

Slut-shaming can happen to flesh-and-blood individuals and literary figures alike; if literary, it can happen within the text itself or crop up in later receptions. It almost always happens to women rather than men or male characters due to patriarchal expectations that men should be fully actualized human beings whereas women (and their sexuality) should be presided over by men. Women outside these norms are considered dangerous. Recognizing slut-shaming in biblical accounts and in scholarly assessments of biblical texts is important because it reveals the scaffolding supporting systemic sexism in biblical texts as well as in the guild. Slut-shaming in antiquity might be tempting to wave away with a claim of "it was different back then" but in reading John 4 more closely there are suggestions that we need not understand Jesus's reaction to the woman's history as automatic or necessary. However, I will suggest in this article that it is not just the author of John's gospel who passes judgment on the Samaritan woman's sexual past; scholars do as well. It is more difficult to wave away a history of scholarship that amplifies Jesus's disdain for her and which attempts to interpret that disdain as acceptance instead. What is more, that scholarship reflects a profound issue at the heart of our discipline: slut-shaming is but one part of systemic rape culture in the guild.

FIVE HUSBANDS?! SLUT-SHAMING THE SAMARITAN WOMAN

This is the context in which to examine the interaction between Jesus and the unnamed Samaritan woman. The tendency outlined above to read Jesus as inclusive as seen in academic and popular treatments of the Samaritan woman is one of the ways that she is slut-shamed. The significance of Jesus's rudeness to her, and his sexualizing of her in the midst of a conversation, has been problematically overlooked, so that scholars often (inadvertently) replicate his slut-shaming of her. Thus, there are two parallel incidents of slut-shaming connected to the Samaritan woman. One occurs at the level of narrative, where Jesus reveals the woman's history as a tactic to convince her of his identity through his knowledge of her life. This event is constructed by the author, who intends the interaction to have an effect on the implied audience.

The second example of the phenomenon operates within scholarly discussion of the biblical scene and has two ways of manifesting: either by expanding on Jesus's slut-shaming (the commentator takes on the role of Jesus) or by reimagining the woman's sexual history as virtuous, or acceptable within the normative sexual roles for women (the commentator takes on the role of rescuer). In other words, in conjunction with the tendency to use the Samaritan woman to showcase Jesus's radical inclusivity, there are two ways to slut-shame: one emphasizes the frowned-upon sexual activity as a negative, while the other attempts to downplay non-normative sexual activity in an attempt to defend the character from accusations of sluttiness. Both of these approaches understand sluttiness to be bad. At each level, the slut-shaming takes place in public, as is implied in the phenomenon of slut-shaming: the conversation between the woman and Jesus is at the well, a public space; it is reported in a gospel, to be read in community; it is commented on by scholars with the expectation (however naïve) that their work might be widely read.

In the first category, some scholars read in further details about the woman's sexuality.[23] Brown's commentary describes the woman as "mincing and coy,"[24] but acknowledges her role in bringing about what he calls the "conversion" of the Samaritan peasants.[25] Generally she is acknowledged as being an important witness to the spread of the news of Jesus, often mentioned in the same breath as Nicodemus.[26] But unlike Nicodemus, she remains unnamed. Instead she is marked by her foreignness, that she is Samaritan.[27] The Samaritan woman's foreignness—that she is known only by her ethnic identity and not given a name, as Nicodemus is—aligns with her perceived adultery.[28] Indeed, sexual shaming is connected with the sexual depravity associated with "foreigners" in antiquity,[29] as evidenced by the pervasiveness of the association between idolatry and adultery in the Bible, from the prophets to Revelation's Babylon. The fact that as a Samaritan, the woman shares a God and a portion of her scripture with Jesus does not exempt her from judgment, either of adultery or idolatry,[30] and indeed her foreignness makes her sexual deviancy all the more likely in the minds of ancient authors and readers.

It is widely accepted that the encounter with the Samaritan woman is modelled after so-called betrothal scenes that are prevalent in the Hebrew Bible.[31] The expectation of a betrothal at the end of the scene is subverted, however, when Jesus enquires about her marital status, and we discover that she is not the virginal daughter of Jesus's relation but rather a woman who has already been married several times. This information is revealed not through the woman's own admission but because of Jesus's telepathic ability to "tell her everything she had ever done" (John 4:17–19, 39). This feat is part of how John reveals Jesus's true identity.[32]

Raymond Brown's Anchor Bible commentary on the passage indicates that Jews could marry three times; in that context, the Samaritan woman's five marriages and (at least) six relationships might seem excessive, or as Brown phrases it, "markedly immoral."[33] Brown is far from the only commenter to remark unfavorably on the woman's relationship status; she has also been called a "five-time loser"[34] and a woman who has led an "immoral life, which has exhibited profligacy and unbridled passions for a long time."[35] More neutrally, couching his discussion in the gendered social norms that worked as cultural currency in antiquity, Neyrey observes that, even if she were a widow (offering Mark 12:20–23 for comparison), "her current non-marital relationship . . . suggests either adultery or concubinage," which he states would be a mark of shame in a world in which women's sexual exclusivity was a sign of her honor.[36]

Neyrey's comment highlights the important dynamic of the economy of honor and shame in antiquity. This so-called honor/shame dichotomy lends itself to analyzing how slut-shaming functions in the conversation as well as how it is perpetuated in scholarship. Neyrey is correct that sexual promiscuity and participation in non-normative sexual encounters was honor-removing for women and for the men to whom those women belonged. As such, slut-shaming was a common tactic in antiquity.[37] In a Jewish context, we need look no further than Josephus when he reports on the women of the Herodian court, or in a later Christian context, the slut-shaming of Theodora by Procopius in *The Secret History*. In both cases, slut-shaming is used by authors to denigrate the women in question for political gain.[38] A narrative of repentance, where a woman comes to her senses and gives up her lascivious past, only reinforces that the previous slutty behavior is shameful.

There are also scholars who see the woman's promiscuity as extending to her interactions with Jesus himself. Eslinger, for example, sees the conversation between Jesus and the Samaritan woman as rife with sexual *double entendres*.[39] For example, Eslinger notes that "drinking water from a well" could connect to the warning against promiscuity in Proverbs 5:15–18, and that the phrase living water, aside from its use for flowing water elsewhere in the Hebrew Bible, is used with sexual undertones in Jeremiah 2:13, since the text uses the phrase to point to Israel's infidelity to her husband Yahweh.[40] The woman herself initiates this flirtation, according to Eslinger, since she is the one who first uses a double-entendre when she, pointing out that Jesus is a man and she a woman, reminds him that Samaritans and Jews do not *sygchrōntai* (v 9)—which, with the dative, can mean to have sexual intercourse.[41] The desire depicted by the evangelist does not only belong to the Samaritan woman. While interpreters focus on the woman's seemingly insatiable desire for husbands, Jesus's desire is crucial for understanding the scene: Jesus desires that the woman desire the water he is offering.[42] Scholars who focus on the woman's desire, either in her current or past relationships or her current interactions with Jesus, desexualize Jesus in order to remove any hint of sexual shame lingering about him, shame that might rub off the woman and contaminate Jesus.

In this context, and with the betrothal type-scene lurking in the background, Eslinger argues that the conversation between Jesus and the Samaritan woman is flirtatious, and the woman's response to Jesus's offer of the living water reflects her understanding that he is making advances; Eslinger calls her come-back "provocative" and her use of double-entendre here lascivious, since she alludes to the "well" of Jacob, who "watered so many."[43] For the reader, who knows what Jesus means because of the previous three chapters of John's Gospel, Jesus's response is not as innuendo-laden as it might be to the Samaritan woman, who, Eslinger suggests, might have been encouraged by Jesus's claim that she will thirst no more after being satisfied with the flowing fountain of his living waters. Enough to satisfy even a woman with five previous husbands. Wink, wink. When Jesus directs her to go and get her husband, then, he does so with the intention of putting a stop to this flirtation; "Had she not been making sexual advances, had Jesus not understood them, and had the reader not understood both the woman and Jesus, his command to go call her husband would make no sense here. Jesus tells her to go get her husband exactly when she expected to commit adultery against the man."[44] Eslinger describes the woman as embarrassed by what she might consider Jesus's change in tone and reads her subsequent responses as attempts to "maintain her respectability."[45] In this reading, Jesus plays along with the woman's advances long enough to cause her embarrassment, and then showcases her promiscuity by revealing her marital status and adulterous behavior, twice over. Jesus does not appear compassionate or even forgiving, but Eslinger's argument puts Jesus in the playful position of violating gendered social customs as a participant in this sexualized repartee. Jo-Ann Brant observes that the conversation with the Samaritan woman rounds out Jesus's character, but its result, if we are expecting one thing based on the trope of the betrothal at the well, is comedy because of her previous husbands. Brant acknowledges that Jesus's response is not sympathetic or necessarily accepting of the woman's status, from a narrative perspective, because the comedy resides in the rejection of the woman because of her sexual history.[46] The key points here are the sexual nature of the banter and that Jesus's aim is to cause embarrassment: the slut-shaming is present in the text itself. This is not an inclusive Jesus when it comes to sexuality.

The second category of slut-shaming is subtler. Feminist commentators have hastened to point out the woman's role as dialogue partner. This move is an attempt to rehabilitate the Samaritan woman by showing how she and Jesus are equal partners (or even that she is his superior) in this debate about the Living Water. Mary Rose D'Angelo avers that "the text imputes neither sin nor shame to the woman" since Jesus does not require the woman's repentance (cf. John 5:14).[47] Regarding her previous marriages, scholars such as Gail O'Day remind us that the text nowhere says that she was divorced; the woman may simply be an unfortunate widow or trapped within regulations around Levirate marriage.[48] This, however, does not do away with the issue of the Samaritan woman's current relationship, and the widow reading removes some of the rhetorical effect of the dialogue between Jesus and the Samaritan woman. Jesus's request that the woman go and bring her husband to him reads pretty heartless in this scenario; her husbands are dead, and perhaps, as a widow four times over, she was reluctant to go through the formalities this time around. But what this explanation also attempts to do is wipe away any hint of stain on the woman for these previous marriages and her current illicit relationship. Schottroff details the socio-historical context in which chain marriages such as the Samaritan woman's might have occurred, and notes that in her report to her community, she does not view herself as a victim of that situation, having been liberated by her conversation with Jesus, in which, Schottroff claims, Jesus does not appear judgmental about her sexual past.[49] Attempting to rehabilitate the Samaritan woman reinforces normative feminine sexuality; rehabilitating her implies that her sexuality is only acceptable within legitimate heterosexual marriage(s). In doing so, attempts to "rescue" the Samaritan woman's reputation participate in the shaming of alternative relationships implied by the Samaritan woman's history. In other words, providing "safe" or virtuous explanations for the number of husbands in the Samaritan woman's past reinforces the binary of "slut" and "virtuous woman."[50] As Sweeney observes, this tendency may be an unconscious defensive mechanism (especially given the systemic rape culture in the discipline of biblical studies) "in which some women distance themselves from other women in efforts to protect their own social standing and to secure preferential treatment from those in power."[51] In both attempting to rescue the Samaritan woman from accusations of sexual impropriety and in attempting to uphold her as a model of Jesus's radical inclusivity, scholars align themselves with Jesus in his scorn for the woman's current marital status. They likewise include themselves in what they identify as Jesus's model inclusivity when they praise her eventual acceptance of Jesus as a messiah.

A SHAMELESS WOMAN

One way of understanding the precise mechanism of slut-shaming in John 4 and its interpretation is through the lens of the *femme fatale*. If scholarship which participates in slut-shaming is as ineffective at enforcing sexual norms on the Samaritan woman as that which seeks to rehabilitate her, the Samaritan woman becomes dangerous. As Caroline Blyth describes her, the *femme fatale* is "the terrifying woman whose malignant eroticism has the power to intoxicate her victims and drag them mercilessly toward destruction or even death."[52] Her characteristics are her heightened sexuality and her dangerous allure to those (men) she encounters. The threat of the *femme fatale* works alongside the rubric of slut-shaming because it implies that there is something wrong with women who seek their own sexual pleasure rather than existing only to please men; namely, they are dangerous. Though the construct of a *femme fatale* is not equivalent to slut-shaming, I believe the trope engages with a form of slut-shaming by attaching women's sexual independence to death and danger for male sexual integrity. A woman who refuses to be shamed is potentially fatal.

The Samaritan woman's response to Jesus's question about her marital status illustrates her refusal to be shamed—her shamelessness. "Shamelessness [. . .] engages self-humiliation, transforming it into a poignant, even defiant, acceptance of human finitude and vulnerability."[53] She "leans in" to Jesus's attempt to humiliate her, responding plainly about her current and past relationships. I can almost imagine her exhaustion at having to field such questions (*again?*); I can almost hear the disappointment in her voice when what she thought was an intellectual conversation among equal sparring partners dissolves into yet another evaluation of her personal life. Perhaps these disappointments are familiar to some of my readers, as well. But her shamelessness, her unapologetic response to Jesus's invasive question, gives her a certain power. Perhaps reminiscent of Sarah in Tobit, the Samaritan woman's marriages can be read as dangerous—and potentially even fatal—for her partners. We are given no clues about how the marriages ended. Most scholars assume divorce, the insatiable Samaritan woman flitting from one relationship to another. As mentioned just above, feminist interpretations, attempting to excuse just how many husbands the Samaritan woman has had, posit that she is a widow many times over.[54] Although less slutty in this reading, her potential liaison with Jesus is more deadly by a factor of five. As well, the Samaritan woman's foreignness contributes to her danger as *femme fatale*.[55] Her sexual allure as she encounters Jesus, and the way he pulls back from the banter at just that moment, indicate that the thrill of speaking with her is not just about her gender or her foreignness as Samaritan. Especially when the choice is between ordinary mortal "water" and the water of life offered by Jesus, the concept of death lingers near the couple as they debate.

The Samaritan woman's characterization as *femme fatale* is not limited to the biblical text's depiction of her but lurks under the surface of many commentaries on the text. While the concept of a *femme fatale* was not a named idea at the time John was writing his gospel, the idea that women were dangerous, sexual beings whose uncontrolled activity could lead to men's downfall was certainly prevalent; one only need look at the reception history of Eve for an example.[56] It has certainly impacted biblical scholarship's engagement with John 4. Though scholars do not mention the phrase, the titillation and gleeful horror with which commentators have described her sexual history clearly mark her as one. Blyth notes that the *femme fatale* is a figment of our imagination, not a historical person, but this makes her no less real. Rather, she reflects her creator's ideas about gender and society: "the fatal woman often functions as an 'anxiety pointer'—a scapegoat upon which the insecurities and preoccupations currently threatening dominant social discourses are projected."[57] In attempting to heighten the sexual elements of the Samaritan woman's erotic past on the one hand, and to dampen them by rehabilitating her sexuality into widowhood, scholarship shares this anxiety about how the woman disrupts these "dominant social discourses" with her shamelessness. Fears of women's liberation and independence from men and the heteronormative family unit contributed to the artistic proliferation of the fatal woman. Whether in the context of the Augustan moral reforms or the most recent reaction against feminism in the form of the alt-right movements and their trickle-down effects, women's sexuality is often at the heart of social angst, in scholarship as well as in culture more broadly.

CONCLUDING THOUGHTS

Scholarship's preoccupation with pointing out (or trying to sweep under the rug) the Samaritan woman's sexual past is a reaction against her shamelessness. She threatens to undo our popular assumptions about Jesus, the "self-denying and solitary knight": his single-ness, his celibacy, his open-armed acceptance of all types of people, his divinity.[58] Jesus fits the shameless slut's target victim profile in his ascetic rejection of the pleasures of the world, and yet is able to emerge victorious from this battle; in pointing out the woman's status, he resists her power. The slut-shaming she endures in scholarship is indicative of biblical scholars' overarching discomfort, not necessarily at what her sexuality might mean for Jesus, who skillfully resists her seeming advances; rather, slut-shaming serves to justify Jesus's rudeness to her, and thus to maintain his reputation as a Good Guy faced with such a deadly seductress.

What seems to be missing in the discussion of John 4 is any consideration of the woman's experience in her own community. Commentators are so focused on Jesus's mingling with a scandalous woman, pointing out how tolerant, norm-bending, or flirtatious he might be, without noticing that the woman herself might have a very different experience among her neighbors. Neyrey's discussion in *The Feminist Companion to the Gospel of John* focuses on the general gender norms for ancient Greek and Roman society, including ancient Judea.[59] He points out the numerous places in texts by Roman and Greek authors, including Philo, that articulate how and where a woman should participate in society, and the honor-shame currency to which women's sexuality is tied. There are two key verses in John 4 which are under-appreciated in my view: John 4:28–29. In those two verses, the woman goes back to the city and speaks to her community.[60] Later, in John 4:39–40 we learn that "many Samaritans from that city believed in him because of the woman's testimony," specifically that Jesus had known about her previous husbands and her current partner; but the fact that the woman's testimony is believed *in her own community*, where presumably her domestic life would be widely known, suggests that scholars assume too much about Jesus's own response to the woman. In other words, the Samaritans in the story seem largely unbothered by the woman's life, at least unbothered enough for the woman to feel empowered to speak freely to her community about her encounter, and unbothered enough to take her seriously. Jesus's interaction with the woman is rendered less remarkable when we decenter him and recenter the Samaritan woman; indeed, his behavior is comparably much less radical and much more unkind than that of the Samaritan community in which the woman lives.

Recognizing Jesus as contributing to the slut-shaming of this woman through his rudeness has an illuminating effect on several aspects of scholarship and the guild. First, it highlights one ramification of attempts to uplift Jesus as wholly inclusive or wholly tolerant, despite ambiguous and conflicting evidence. That consideration involves the false claim, rarely made by scholars but frequently repeated in popular discourse and by our students, that Jesus and the New Testament God are loving and kind, in opposition to the Old Testament God (somehow a distinct entity), who is (according to this view) intolerant, hateful, and violent.[61] It would be easy to juxtapose the idea of a tolerant, sex-worker friendly Jesus with the horrific account of the concubine in Judges 19, for example. I hope that by unpacking scholarly discomfort with the Samaritan woman's sexual history and her present activity, and identifying slut-shaming rhetoric in many commentaries, this will provide support for those of us who wish to push back against the false dichotomy of a loving New Testament and vengeful Old Testament idea of God, which is both a result and a cause of anti-Judaism. In fact, gender-based violence is prevalent throughout ancient Jewish, early Christian, and Hellenistic/Roman texts, including those that came to be Scripture. This is not something to elide by coming up with excuses for the woman's multiple marriages (maybe she was simply a very unlucky widow!).

I am reminded as I conclude this essay of a quotation from the film *Clue*:

Colonel Mustard: How many husbands have you had?

Mrs. White: Mine, or other women's?

Colonel Mustard: Yours.

Mrs. White: Five.

Colonel Mustard: FIVE?

Mrs. White: Yes, just the five. Husbands should be like Kleenex: soft, strong, and disposable.[62]

The quotation is from Mrs White, a seductive character with red lipstick played by Madeline Kahn. Mrs White's previous husbands have all died under mysterious circumstances. When a female character (or a real-life woman) is depicted as being both attractive and dangerous (particularly from the perspective of heterosexual men), she, like the Samaritan woman, is a *femme fatale*, unashamed (and even proud!) of her sexual past. The scholarly reproduction of the slut-shaming narrative around the Samaritan woman and the discomfort with her husbands has ramifications for women in the field as well. As Blyth notes, the depiction of women as *femme fatale* "reinforces and sustains dominant cultural ideologies about women's marginal placement in the world and the inherent dangers of their agency and empowerment."[63] This view illuminates how many academic readings of her are slut-shaming. As illustrated by the diagram in figure 13.1 from the University of Alberta's Sexual Assault Centre,[64] slut-shaming is on the spectrum of sexual violence in that it supports a system of rape culture. When women in control of their own sexual and marital choices and pleasures are seen as shameful, then gendered violence that befalls them is depicted as a consequence of their own moral failure, or even as "deserved." Rape culture is not merely hypothetical; it culminates in more physical forms of violence including rape and murder; what begins as "attitudes and beliefs" at the bottom of the pyramid, quickly escalates to the "normalization of violence," "removal of autonomy," and "physical expressions of violence." The Samaritan woman's story fits so smoothly within the existing rape culture of the discipline that it has not even been noticed that she is so shamed.

The Samaritan woman's treatment in a good portion of academic work written about her cannot but have an effect on the construction and reinforcing of cultural norms within the academy, and in particular, for women scholars within biblical studies. Rape culture is inescapable, and biblical studies is no exception.[65] Sexual harassment is rampant in our field.[66] The example of Helmut Koester's harassment and assault of Elaine Pagels,[67] among his other women graduate students at the time, is but one recognizable name among a sea of much more ordinary incidents of rape culture. A survey on harassment conducted by the LGBTQ+ Task Force of the Society of Biblical Literature in early 2020 found that 5 percent of members have experienced or witnessed inappropriate behavior at SBL meetings.[68] There was no data collected about the gender of those responding, but if the demographics of the respondents reflects the membership, then it's possible that that 5 percent is mostly women and trans members; this means that up to 15–20 percent of women (likely higher among trans respondents) experienced and/or witnessed such behavior. Speaking about Jan Joosten's conviction in 2020 for child pornography, Esther Hamori wrote on Twitter that this is "what it looks like when systems prioritize the perspective and reputation of men."[69] Hamori's comment leads me to consider what systems of analysis we use that "prioritize the perspective and reputation" of Jesus, and how insidious

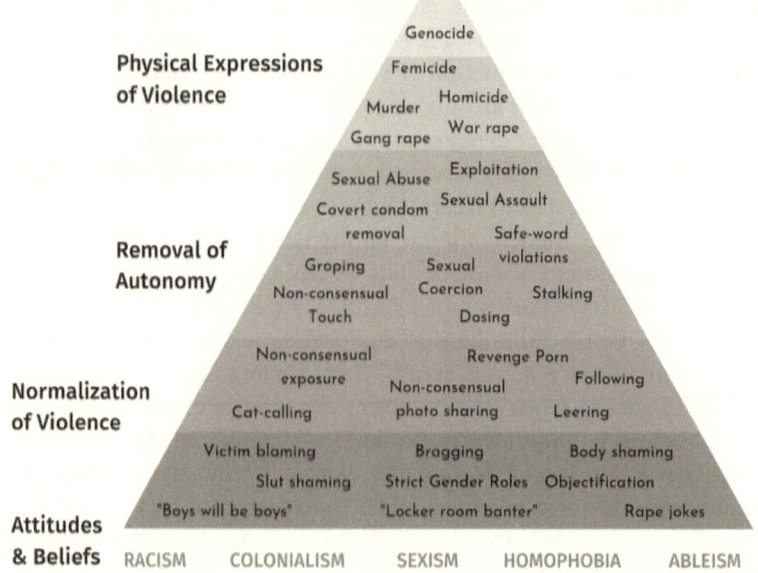

Figure 13.1. Pyramid of Sexual Violence. *Source*: Used with permission from the Sexual Assault Centre of the University of Alberta.

rape culture is in our lives and scholarship. As uncomfortable as it might be to some, it is important to challenge the prioritization of Jesus's reputation, and the power structures behind that drive, that has for centuries been the lens through which Jesus's interaction with the Samaritan has been viewed. There are real ramifications for upholding this view of Jesus, and one of them is the perpetuation of rape culture.

NOTES

1. A special thank you to Elizabeth Castelli who provided me with access to articles and chapters that were not available to me due to the COVID-19 pandemic, during which this essay was written. I would also like to express my gratitude to Michelle Fletcher who helped me think through the relationship between *femmes fatales* and

slut-shaming. This chapter was published previously, in open access format, as "Five Husbands: Slut-Shaming the Samaritan Woman," *BCT* 17.2 (2022): 51–70.

    2. For a critique of the concept of the inclusive Jesus, see Markus Bockmuehl, "The Trouble with the Inclusive Jesus," *HBT* 33 (2011): 9–23; Bockmuehl does not address Jesus's inclusivity vis a vis women, however, he does point out the danger of the so-called inclusive Jesus for Christian Judeophobia.

    3. Claude Levi-Strauss coined the phrase "good to think with" in 1962 (*Totémisme Aujourd'hui* [Paris: Presses Universitaires de France, 1962]). With regard to women as tools for men to think with, Peter Brown appears to have originated that usage. (*The Body and Society: Men, Women, and Sexual Renunciation in Early Christianity* [New York: Columbia University Press, 1988]).

    4. See Monique Alexandre ("Early Christian Women" in *A History of Women in the West. Volume 1: From Ancient Goddesses to Christian Saints*, ed. Pauline Schmitt Pantel [Cambridge, MA: The Belknap Press of Harvard University Press, 1992], 418–420) for a particularly clear example of this dynamic in scholarship.

    5. Portions of this section were originally drafted and appear in a slightly different form in Sara Parks, Shayna Sheinfeld, and Meredith J. C. Warren, *Jewish and Christian Women in the Ancient Mediterranean* (London: Routledge, 2022), 171–172.

    6. Jennifer Wright Knust makes a related observation about feminist biblical interpretations of the woman caught in adultery (John 7:53–8:11) ("Can an Adulteress Save Jesus? The Pericope Adulterae, Feminist Interpretation and the Limits of Narrative Agency" in *The Bible and Feminism: Remapping the Field*, ed. Katherine Southwood, with Anna Fisk; [Oxford: Oxford University Press, 2017], 402–431).

    7. Archived at https://bit.ly/JesusOfNazBio

    8. Or men's, for that matter.

    9. Sara Parks, *Gender in the Rhetoric of Jesus: Women in Q* (Lexington, 2019), 94–96.

    10. *kai idou gynē hētis ēn en tē polei hamartōlos*. The *Women's Bible Commentary* identifies her as a prostitute due to Luke's description of her being from the city (Schaberg and Ringe 2014). Kathleen Corley argues that the woman's identification as "from the city" would be enough to mark her as a "streetwalker" (*Private Women, Public Meals* [Peabody MA: Hendrickson, 1993], 124), but I do not find this argument convincing. Corley cites Osborne (1987), who looked at this combination of woman/sinner/city in Jewish literature in partial support of this conclusion.

    11. Alexandre, "Early Christian Women," 419. This position, as in this example, is often (inadvertently?) connected with a pernicious anti-Judaism, in which Jesus's engagement with women is also dangerously presented *in contrast* to his Jewish contemporaries. See discussion in Parks, *Gender*, 4.

    12. Alexandre, "Early Christian Women," 420.

    13. Luise Schottroff, "Die Samaritanerin am Brunnen (Joh 4)," in *Auf Israel hören. Sozialgeschichtliche Bibelauslegung*, eds. Renate Jost, Rainer Kessler, and Christoph M. Raisig (Lucerne: Edition Exodus, 1992), 121. Translation mine, from: "Er hat sich nicht dadurch also Prophet oder Messias erwiesen, dass er wunderbares Wissen über verborgene Untaten hat, wie fast durchweg in der Auslegung dieses Texts behauptet

wird, sondern dass er einer Unterdrückten und Leidenden zur Befreiung aus ihrem Gefängnis hilft."

14. Elisabeth Schüssler Fiorenza, *Rhetoric and Ethic: The Politics of Biblical Study* (Minneapolis: Fortress, 1999), esp. 195–197.

15. Parks, *Gender*, 58–59.

16. Anderson, *The Christology of the Fourth Gospel: Its Unity and Disunity in the Light of John 6*, WUNT 2 (Tübingen: Mohr Siebeck, 1996).

17. Neyrey, Jerome H. "What's Wrong with This Picture? John 4, Cultural Stereotypes of Women, and Public and Private Space." Republished in *The Feminist Companion to John* (Sheffield: Sheffield Academic, 2003), 118; he goes on to say that "the Samaritan woman could be the Johannine 'representative' of Jesus's inclusion of *Gentile* disciples, even those culturally labeled *unclean*, including '*sinners*' and even '*courtesans*.' She would, then, typify the most radical inclusivity of membership in the circle of Jesus' disciples."

18. Brian N. Sweeney, "Slut Shaming," in *The SAGE Encyclopedia of Psychology and Gender*, ed. Kevin L. Nadal (Sage Publications, 2017), 1578.

19. Susanna Drake, "Sexual Slander," in *The Oxford Handbook of New Testament, Gender, and Sexuality*, ed. Benjamin H. Dunning (Oxford: Oxford University Press, 2019), 593; Jennifer Wright Knust, *Abandoned to Lust: Sexual Slander and Ancient Christianity* (New York: Columbia University Press, 2006), 3, 116.

20. Sweeney, "Slut Shaming," 1579.

21. Lewis Webb, "Shame Transfigured: Slut-shaming from Rome to Cyberspace," *FM* 20.4 (2015) np, who here quotes L. Gong and A. Hoffman, "Sexting and slut-shaming: Why prosecution of teen self-sexters harms women," *GJGL* 13 (2012), 577–589, here 580. See also L. Tanenbaum, *I Am Not a Slut: Slut-shaming in the Age of the Internet* (New York: HarperCollins, 2015).

22. Brené C. Brown, *I Thought It Was Just Me: Women Reclaiming Power and Courage in a Culture of Shame* (ebook; New York: Gotham, 2007), 5.

23. Luise Schottroff reports some appalling commentary by German scholars of the mid-Twentieth century, including Bultmann, remarking that "Die Warnung vor dem Verhalten der 'schlechten Frau' dient der Disziplinierung der Frauen und ihrer Anpassung an das herrschende Frauenbild ("Die Samaritanerin," 116).

24. Raymond Brown, *John*, ABC (2 vols; New York: Doubleday, 1966), 175.

25. Raymond Brown, *John*, 184.

26. The Samaritan woman and Nicodemus may be a Johannine "gender pair" according to Margaret M. Beirne, *Women and Men in the Fourth Gospel: A Genuine Discipleship of Equals* (London: Sheffield Academic, 2003), esp. 67–104; Parks, *Gender in the Rhetoric of Jesus*. See also Colleen Conway, "Gender Matters in John" in *A Feminist Companion to John: Volume II*, edited by Amy-Jill Levine, 79–103. Cleveland: Pilgrim, 2003.

27. Gail R. O'Day, "John," *The Women's Bible Commentary*, eds. Carol A. Newsom and Sharon H. Ringe (Louisville, KY: Westminster/John Knox Press, 1992), 294–302 (295). Cited in Stephen D. Moore, "Are There Impurities in the Living Water That the Johannine Jesus Dispenses? Deconstruction, Feminism, and the Samaritan Woman"

in *A Feminist Companion to the Gospel of John*, Vol 1., ed. Amy-Jill Levine, with Marianne Blickenstaff (Sheffield: Sheffield Academic Press, 2003), 78–97, here 81.

28. It is worth noting the close association between terms for adultery and sex work in antiquity. See J. Adams, 1983. "Words for 'Prostitute' in Latin," *Rheinisches Museum für Philologie*, volume 126, numbers 3–4, pp. 321–358; M. McCoy, "The Politics of Prostitution: Clodia, Cicero, and Social Order in the Late Roman Republic," in *Prostitutes and Courtesans of the Ancient World*, eds. C. Faraone and L. McClure (Madison: University of Wisconsin Press, 2006), 177–185.

29. Drake, "Sexual Slander," 593.

30. Some commenters on the scene suggest an allegorical reading of the five husbands as the five books of the Samaritan Torah (Origen, *In Jo.* 13.8; GCS 10:232), or instead as the gods worshipped by the people of Samaria according to 2 Kings 17:29–34, e.g., Brown, *John*, 17 and Jennifer Wright Knust, "Marriage, Adultery, and Divorce," in *The Oxford Handbook of New Testament, Gender, and Sexuality*, ed. Benjamin H. Dunning (Oxford: Oxford University Press, 2019), 531.

31. Robert C. Culley pointed out the recurring motif of the Betrothal Scene at the Well in *Studies in the Structure of Hebrew Narrative* (Philadelphia: Fortress, 1976). On its re-use in John, see Jo-Ann A. Brant, "Husband Hunting: Characterisation and Narrative Art in the Gospel of John," *BibInt* 4.2 (1996), 205–223; Kasper Bro Larsen, *Recognising the Stranger*, 124–5. Ellen B. Aitken suggests that John 4 best compares with the Rachel narrative in Genesis 29 ("At the Well of Living Water: Jacob Traditions in John 4," in *The Interpretation of Scripture in Early Judaism and Christianity: Studies in Language and Tradition*, ed. C. A. Evans (London: T & T Clark, 2000), 342–52.

32. Larsen, *Recognising the Stranger*, 134.

33. Raymond Brown, *John*, 171. Brown notes that the five marriages have, since antiquity, also been interpreted as symbolic, for example of the five books of the Samaritan Pentateuch (171, citing Origen, *In Jo.* 13.8; GCS 10:232) or to idolatrous worship of five previous 'pagan' gods and the current Samaritan god/ba'al who is not a husband because he, unlike Yahweh, is not the true Jewish *ba'al* (*ba'al* meaning both god and husband/lord).

34. Paul D. Duke, *Irony in the Fourth Gospel* (Atlanta: John Knox Press, 1985), 102.

35. Theodor Zahn, *Das Evangeliumdes Johannesausgelegt* (Leipzig: Deichert, 6th edn, 1921), 244. Moore ("Impurities," 211n18) lists a number of other shockingly negative sexualizing statements made by scholars about the Samaritan woman's life. See also discussion of similar statements in German scholarship in Schottroff, "Die Samaritanerin."

36. Neyrey, "What's Wrong with This Picture," 110.

37. Webb, "Shame Transfigured."

38. Roland Betancourt, *Byzantine Intersectionality: Sexuality, Gender, and Race in the Middle Ages* (Princeton: Princeton University Press, 2020), esp. 59–88.

39. Lyle Eslinger, "The Wooing of the Woman at the Well: Jesus, the Reader, and Reader-Response Criticism," *Lit. Theol.* 1.2 (1987), 167–183.

40. Eslinger, "Wooing," 170. Likewise, in Song of Songs 4:12, the metaphor of a cistern of water is employed in a sexual context. See also Brant, "Husband Hunting," 214.

41. Eslinger, "Wooing," 176, & n. 25.

42. Moore, "Impurities."

43. Eslinger, "Wooing," 177.

44. Eslinger, "Wooing," 178.

45. Eslinger, "Wooing," 179.

46. Jo-Ann Brant, "Husband Hunting."

47. Mary Rose D'Angelo "(Re)presentations of Women in the Gospels: John and Mark" in *Women and Christian Origins*, eds. Ross Shepard Kraemer and Mary Rose D'Angelo (Oxford: Oxford University Press, 1999), 134.

48. Gail O'Day, "John" in Newsom, Carol A., and Sharon H. Ringe eds. *The Women's Bible Commentary* (London: SPCK, 3rd ed), 521–22.

49. Schottroff, "Die Samaritanerin," 121.

50. Moreover, even if the Samaritan woman is an equal conversation partner with Jesus in this scene, the fact remains that Jesus uses her "shameful" unmarried situation as a rhetorical weapon to disarm her and persuade her of his identity.

51. Sweeney, "Slut Shaming," 1580.

52. Caroline Blyth, *Reimagining Delilah's Afterlives As Femme Fatale: The Lost Seduction* (London: Bloomsbury, 2017), 9.

53. Burrus, *Saving Shame: Martyrs, Saints, and Other Abject Subjects* (Philadelphia: University of Pennsylvania Press, 2008), 3.

54. O'Day, "John," 521; Schottroff, "Die Samaritanerin."

55. Rebecca Stott, *The Fabrication of the Late-Victorian Femme Fatale: The Kiss of Death* (Basingstoke: Macmillan, 1992), 37–8; as quoted in Blyth, *Reimagining*, 16.

56. See Sara Parks, "The Reception of Eve in Early Judaism and Late Antiquity," in *The Routledge Handbook to Eve*, ed. Caroline Blyth (London: Routledge, 2022).

57. Blyth, *Reimagining*, 21.

58. Blyth, *Reimagining*, 15.

59. Neyrey, Jerome H. "What's Wrong with This Picture? John 4, Cultural Stereotypes of Women, and Public and Private Space." *BTB* 24. 2 (May 1994): 77–91.

60. Neyrey (111) says that the woman goes back to the public space, the marketplace, to speak only with "males" (sic) rather than the private spaces of the city to speak with "females" (sic) but the text nowhere infers the gender of the Samaritans the woman speaks with or the gender of those who respond. John 4:28-29 reads: "*aphēken oun tēn hydrian autēs hē gynēynē apēlthen eis tēn polin kai legei tois **anthrōpois**; deute idete anthrōpon hos eipen moi panta hosa epoiēsa, mēti houtos estin ho christos* "; *Anthropos* is an unmarked word for person, though grammatically masculine, and can refer to, in the plural, mixed-gender groups. The LSJ also notes that the term can be used to refer to a woman or single-gender groups of women.

61. Eva Mroczek has developed a teaching resources on this topic, available here: https://docs.google.com/document/d/1BG5PvCO5pTTATcgBF-Da5j9p0myFg-g9wj1ECkrRhFbI/.

62. Jonathan Lynn, *Clue*, 1985.

63. Blyth, *Reimagining*, 180.

64. University of Alberta Sexual Assault Centre, "Create Change around Sexual Violence." Archived at https://bit.ly/UAlbertaSAC.

65. Blossom Stefaniw, "Feminist Historiography and Uses of the Past," *SLA* 4.3 (2020), 260–283. See also, for example, two recent examples of biblical scholars Jan Joosten and Richard Pervo, both convicted of possession of child pornography, as outlined in these essays by Jonathan Poletti (who also discusses several other biblical scholars and theologians with the same convictions; https://medium.com/belover/when-bible-scholars-are-child-pornographers-ea6f62fe0b3f) and Johanna Stiebert (https://www.shilohproject.blog/privilege-beyond-bounds/?fbclid=IwAR2WHfTUrwHqNOs2jf7xJKa_iTSWaWeP1NqAC5gB2epUixwNGT61YIrBUkk). Beth Alpert Nakhai has written about sexual harassment and assault in the context of archaeological excavations: https://www.chronicle.com/article/how-to-avoid-gender-based-hostility-during-fieldwork/.

66. And as the 2019 Membership Report for the Society of Biblical Literature states, "Members identifying as women continue to represent about 25% of the membership." https://www.sbl-site.org/assets/pdfs/sblMemberProfile2019.pdf 2019 is the most recent year for which data is published at the time of publication. For a discussion about gender representation in one field of biblical studies, see Rollens 2020.

67. Jana Reiss, "Elaine Pagels on Grief, Her #MeToo story, and Why We Find Meaning in Religion." *ReligionNews* (26 October 2018). https://religionnews.com/2018/10/26/elaine-pagels-on-grief-her-metoo-story-and-why-we-find-meaning-in-religion/; Elaine Pagels, *Why Religion? A Personal Story* (Harper Collins 2018).

68. "LGBTQ+TaskForceSurvey_HarrassmentQuestions.xlsx," attached file from correspondence with Christopher Hooker, Director of Membership and Programs for Society of Biblical Literature, 23–28 July 2021.

69. https://twitter.com/ProfEstherJ/status/1275147273446608896 Stephen Young also points out that men's reputations are treated as more valuable than "the bodies of women and children" https://religiondispatches.org/love-the-scholarship-but-hate-the-scholars-sin-himpathy-for-an-academic-pedophile-enables-a-culture-of-abuse/?fbclid=IwAR3mNjY_diVxOr5pe21lXVMMRQz6Z88X45gkT8JnYKLfXlJfe8to7rEWPLQ.

WORKS CITED

Adams, J. "Words for 'Prostitute' in Latin." *Rheinisches Museum für Philologie* 126.3–4 (1983): 321–358.

Aitken, Ellen B. "At the Well of Living Water: Jacob Traditions in John 4." Pages 342–352 in *The Interpretation of Scripture in Early Judaism and Christianity: Studies in Language and Tradition.* Edited by C. A. Evans. London: T & T Clark, 2000.

Alexandre, Monique. "Early Christian Women." Pages 409–444 in *A History of Women in the West. Volume 1: From Ancient Goddesses to Christian Saints.* Edited by Pauline Schmitt Pantel. Cambridge, Mass: The Belknap Press of Harvard University Press, 2002.

Anderson, Paul. *The Christology of the Fourth Gospel: Its Unity and Disunity in the Light of John 6*. WUNT 2; Tübingen: Mohr Siebeck, 1996.

Beirne, Margaret M. *Women and Men in the Fourth Gospel: A Genuine Discipleship of Equals*. London: Sheffield Academic, 2003.

Betancourt, Roland. *Byzantine Intersectionality: Sexuality, Gender, and Race in the Middle Ages*. Princeton: Princeton University Press, 2020.

Blyth, Caroline. *Reimagining Delilah's Afterlives as Femme Fatale: The Lost Seduction*. Library of Hebrew Bible/Old Testament Studies; 652. London, England: Bloomsbury T&T Clark, 2017.

Bockmuehl, Markus. "The Trouble with the Inclusive Jesus." *Horizons in Biblical Theology* 33 (2011): 9–23.

Brant, Jo-Ann A. "Husband Hunting: Characterization and Narrative Art in the Gospel of John." *Biblical Interpretation* 4.2 (2006): 205–223.

Brown, C. Brené. *I Thought It Was Just Me: Women Reclaiming Power and Courage in a Culture of Shame*. New York: Gotham, 2007.

Brown, Peter. *The Body and Society: Men, Women, and Sexual Renunciation in Early Christianity*. New York: Columbia University Press, 1988.

Brown, Raymond. *John*. Anchor Bible Commentary. 2 vols. New York: Doubleday, 1966.

Burrus, Virginia. *Saving Shame: Martyrs, Saints, and Other Abject Subjects*. Philadelphia: University of Pennsylvania Press, 2008.

Conway, Colleen. "Gender Matters in John." Pages 79–103 in *A Feminist Companion to John: Volume II*, edited by Amy-Jill Levine. Cleveland: Pilgrim, 2003.

Corley, Kathleen. *Private Women, Public Meals*. Peabody MA: Hendrickson, 1993.

Culley, Robert C. *Studies in the Structure of Hebrew Narrative* (Philadelphia: Fortress Press, 1976).

D'Angelo, Mary Rose. "(Re)presentations of Women in the Gospels: John and Mark." Pages 129–149 in *Women and Christian Origins*. Edited by Ross Shepard Kraemer and Mary Rose D'Angelo. Oxford: Oxford University Press, 1999.

Drake, Susanna. "Sexual Slander." Pages 593–606 in *The Oxford Handbook of New Testament, Gender, and Sexuality*. Edited by Benjamin H. Dunning. Oxford: Oxford University Press, 2019.

Duke, Paul D. *Irony in the Fourth Gospel*. Atlanta: John Knox Press, 1985.

Eslinger, Lyle. "The Wooing of the Woman at the Well: Jesus, the Reader, and Reader-Response Criticism." *Literature and Theology* 1.2 (1987): 167–83.

Gong, L. and A. Hoffman, "Sexting and Slut-shaming: Why Prosecution of Teen Self-sexters Harms Women." *Georgetown Journal of Gender and the Law* 13 (2012): 577–589.

Hamori, Esther. Twitter Post. 22 June 2020, 8:22pm. https://twitter.com/ProfEstherJ/status/1275147273446608896.

Knust, Jennifer Wright. *Abandoned to Lust: Sexual Slander and Ancient Christianity*. New York: Columbia University Press, 2006.

———. "Can an Adulteress Save Jesus? The *Pericope Adulterae,* Feminist Interpretation and the Limits of Narrative Agency." Pages 402–443 in *The Bible and Feminism: Remapping the Field.* Edited by Katherine Southwood with Anna Fisk. Oxford: Oxford University Press, 2017.

———. "Marriage, Adultery, and Divorce. Pages 521–538 in *The Oxford Handbook of New Testament, Gender, and Sexuality.* Edited by Benjamin H. Dunning. Oxford: Oxford University Press, 2019.

Larsen, Kasper Bro. *Recognizing the Stranger.* Leiden, The Netherlands: Brill, 2008.

Levi-Strauss, Claude. *Totémisme Aujourd'hui.* Paris: Presses Universitaires de France, 1962.

LGBTQ+ Task Force. "LGBTQ+TaskForceSurvey_HarrassmentQuestions.xlsx." In correspondence with Christopher Hooker (Director of Membership and Programs for Society of Biblical Literature) 23–28 July 2021.

McCoy, M. "The Politics of Prostitution: Clodia, Cicero, and Social Order in the Late Roman Republic." Pages pp. 177–185 in *Prostitutes and Courtesans of the Ancient World.* Edited by C. Faraone and L. McClure. Madison: University of Wisconsin Press, 2006.

Moore, Stephen D. "Are There Impurities in the Living Water That the Johannine Jesus Dispenses? Deconstruction, Feminism, and the Samaritan Woman." *Biblical Interpretation* 1.2 (1993): 207–227. Republished in *The Feminist Companion to John.* Volume 1. Pages 78–97. Edited by Amy-Jill Levine. Sheffield: Sheffield Academic, 2003.

Mroczek, Eva. "Mean, Angry Old Testament God vs. Nice, Loving New Testament God? Not So Fast." https://docs.google.com/document/d/1BG5PvCO5pTTATcgBF-Da5j9p0myFgg9wj1ECkrRhFbI/.

Nakhai, Beth Alpert. How to Avoid Gender-Based Hostility during Fieldwork." *The Chronicle for Higher Education.* 15 July 2018. https://www.chronicle.com/article/how-to-avoid-gender-based-hostility-during-fieldwork/.

Neyrey, Jerome H. "What's Wrong with This Picture? John 4, Cultural Stereotypes of Women, and Public and Private Space." *Biblical Theology Bulletin* 24, no. 2 (May 1994): 77–91. Republished in *The Feminist Companion to John.* Volume 1. Pages 98–125. Sheffield: Sheffield Academic, 2003.

Newsom, Carol A., Sharon H. Ringe, and Jacqueline E. Lapsley, eds. *The Women's Bible Commentary: Revised and Expanded Edition.* London: SPCK, 2014.

O'Day, Gail. "John." Pages 294–302 in *The Women's Bible Commentary.* Edited by Carol A. Newsom and Sharon H. Ringe. London: SPCK, 2012.

Osborne, Delores. "Women: Sinners and Prostitutes." Paper presented at the SBL Pacific Coast Region, Long Beach, California, April, 1987.

Pagels, Elaine. *Why Religion? A Personal Story.* Harper Collins 2018.

Parks, Sara. "The Reception of Eve from Early Judaism to Late Antiquity." In Caroline Blyth, ed. *The Routledge Handbook to Eve.* London: Routledge, 2022 (forthcoming).

Parks, Sara. *Gender in the Rhetoric of Jesus: Women in Q.* Lexington, 2019.

Parks, Sara, Shayna Sheinfeld, and Meredith J. C. Warren. *Jewish and Christian Women in the Ancient Mediterranean.* London: Routledge, 2022.

Poletti, Jonathan. "On Bible Scholars & Child Porn." *Medium.* 27 June 2020. https://medium.com/belover/when-bible-scholars-are-child-pornographers-ea6f62fe0b3f.

Reiss, Jana. "Elaine Pagels on Grief, Her #MeToo story, and Why We Find Meaning in Religion." *ReligionNews.* 26 October 2018. https://religionnews.com/2018/10/26/elaine-pagels-on-grief-her-metoo-story-and-why-we-find-meaning-in-religion/.

Rollens, Sarah. "Where Are All the Women in Q Studies? Gender Demographics in the Study of Q." Pages 223–253 in *The Q Hypothesis Unveiled: Theological, Sociological, and Hermeneutical Issues behind the Sayings Source*, edited by Markus Tiwald. Stuttgart: Kollhammer, 2020.

Schaberg, Jane D. and Sharon H. Ringe, "Luke" in Carol A. Newsom, Sharon H. Ringe, and Jacqueline E. Lapsley, eds. *The Women's Bible Commentary: Revised and Expanded Edition.* London: SPCK, 2014. NP eBook. Accessed July 8, 2021.

Schottroff, Luise. "Die Samaritanerin am Brunnen (Joh 4)." Pages 115–132 in *Auf Israel hören. Sozialgeschichtliche Bibelauslegung.* Edited by Renate Jost, Rainer Kessler, and Christoph M. Raisig. Lucerne: Edition Exodus, 1992.

Schüssler Fiorenza, Elisabeth. *Rhetoric and Ethic: The Politics of Biblical Study.* Minneapolis: Fortress, 1999.

Stefaniw, Blossom. "Feminist Historiography and Uses of the Past." *Studies in Late Antiquity* 4.3 (2020): 260–283.

Stiebert, Johanna. "Privilege Beyond Bounds: A Response to the Conviction of Jan Joosten." Shiloh Project. 26 June 2020. https://www.shilohproject.blog/privilege-beyond-bounds/?fbclid=IwAR2WHfTUrwHqNOs2jf7xJKa_iTSWaWeP1NqAC5gB2epUixwNGT61YIrBUkk.

Stott, Rebecca. *The Fabrication of the Late-Victorian Femme Fatale: The Kiss of Death.* Basingstoke: Macmillan, 1992.

Sweeney, Brian N. "Slut Shaming." *The SAGE Encyclopedia of Psychology and Gender.* Edited by Kevin L. Nadal. Sage Publications, 2017.

Tanenbaum, L. *I Am Not a Slut: Slut-Shaming in the Age of the Internet.* New York: HarperCollins, 2015.

University of Alberta Sexual Assault Centre. "Create Change around Sexual Violence." Accessed 21 July 2021. https://www.ualberta.ca/current-students/sexual-assault-centre/create-change.html. Archived at https://bit.ly/UAlbertaSAC.

Webb, Lewis M. "Shame Transfigured: Slut-shaming from Rome to Cyberspace." *First Monday* 20.4 (2015) NP. https://doi.org/10.5210/fm.v20i4.5464.

Young, Stephen. "Love the Scholarship but Hate the Scholar's Sin? 'Himpathy' for an Academic Pedophile Enables a Culture of Abuse." *Religion Dispatches.* 24 June 2020. https://religiondispatches.org/love-the-scholarship-but-hate-the-scholars-sin-himpathy-for-an-academic-pedophile-enables-a-culture-of-abuse.

Zahn, Theodor. *Das Evangeliumdes Johannesausgelegt.* Leipzig: Deichert, 1921.

Chapter 14

Revelation Naturalizes Sexual Violence and Readers Erase It

Unveiling the Son of God's Rape of Jezebel

Stephen Young

The book of Revelation is notoriously violent and sexist. These characteristics of the text amplify each other: gendered images in Revelation that carry classic misogynist stereotypes in Greek and Roman literary culture are often not so much about women as they are resources for depicting God's violent judgment and helping the text's hearers revel in it. For example, the writer of Revelation, "John," sees Rome as the ultimate end-times enemy whom Jesus will defeat for God.[1] His cipher for Rome is "Babylon," who is a "great whore" (17:1), and the depiction of Babylon in 16:19–19:3 has a variety of contours that were conspicuously gendered in ancient Mediterranean texts.[2] Within this literary context, she is a low-status prostitute who embodies many "quintessential" feminine characteristics: lack of self-mastery, excessive, luxuriating, dominated by passions, dangerous sexuality, and enticing men to immoderate behavior.

Babylon's transgressions of gendered norms are threats to society in the context of Greco-Roman narratives about the rising and falling of peoples, cities, and kingdoms: she feminizes kings by controlling them, is active instead of passive, and is an agent of spreading sexual immorality.[3] Ultimately God will incite her former clients to sexually brutalize, strip, eviscerate, devour, and burn her body (Rev 17:16–17; 18:8–9) while God's people—with whom the audience of Revelation is supposed to identify—celebrate exuberantly as they smell the aroma of her smoldering corpse for eternity (19:1–3). The writer thus imagines the climax of God's victory over defiling enemies in terms of sexual violence against and humiliation of a woman's body. As Meredith Warren forcefully emphasizes, "Make no mistake: stripping someone naked is a sexualized punishment."[4] The text wields misogynist ideals about masculinity and femininity to envision God's actions and make them feel appropriate. Though there are various intersecting registers of violence beyond gender in Revelation, violence reaches some of its peaks at viciously gendered points.

Revelation's violent misogyny is conspicuous, but perhaps more conspicuous is the overlooking or even suppression of it by many later interpreters. Biblical scholars often claim that the depiction of Jesus as "a Lamb standing as if it had been slaughtered" in Rev 5:6 controls other presentations of him and redefines the text's violence in terms of Jesus's self-sacrifice. Violent images elsewhere are therefore viewed as metaphorical or figurative, and Revelation becomes a text advocating radical non-violence.[5] Such claims tend to ignore its violently misogynist imagery and also, as Susan Hylen notes, "the rhetorical effect that the violent metaphors often have."[6] While the vast majority of Revelation's readers are not trained scholars, their engagements with the text are shaped by scholars' readings, especially as mediated via sermons, Bible study materials, and other Christian consumer media variously networked with scholarship. Especially over the last half century, as "non-violence" has become a more societally dominant moral ideal, non-scholarly readers have been increasingly *inattentive* to Revelation's violence. So regardless of the interpretive mechanics for how it happens, the text's violent misogyny becomes invisible or is erased in ways that mirror what Rhiannon Graybill calls reading strategies that "claim innocence."[7]

This chapter un-erases Revelation's gendered violence by developing powerful readings of Rev 2:19–28 that some feminist biblical scholars have proposed in which the Son of God not only assaults Jezebel, but rapes her. It is a minority reading of the text that does not register as an option for most interpreters. In the few cases where this uncomfortable reading is acknowledged as a possibility, the sexual assault is recategorized and justified. By lingering on the Son of God's rape of Jezebel, I argue that the current-day erasure of Revelation's gendered violence reflects how modern Christian consumers of the text inhabit its own interests and ways of imagining reality. Revelation does not simply *feature* sexual violence against women as something divinely authorized. Revelation goes a step further, and *normalizes* it.

John does not mark the hierarchical exploitation, subjugation, and brutality against women as something that is itself remarkable. Feminist scholars such as Tina Pippin, Lynn Huber, and Pamela Thimmes have noted that instead of featuring voices that represent those who would protest, the author of Revelation crafts his women with ideologies about masculinity and femininity that shape ancient literate male culture. So, while many modern Christian readers misread Revelation, they do tend to align with its patriarchal erasure of harm against women. In this chapter I urge readers to dwell in that unstable zone where the buffers between biblical text and later reception dissolve. Any discomfort that results can help us interrogate afresh the erasure of sexual violence in both Revelation and the settings of its later readers that have been shaped by long histories of patriarchy.

REVELATION 2:20–23 AS A SCENE OF MARTIAL RAPE

Revelation belongs to a genre of ancient Jewish and Christian writing known as an apocalypse. It was not uncommon for the writers of Jewish apocalypses to claim that parts of their text recorded letters that had been sent. *2 Baruch* 78–87 presents itself as a letter from Baruch to the nine and a half tribe, for example, and *1 Enoch* 92–105 is the *Epistle of Enoch*. Similarly, Revelation purports to contain seven letters dictated by Jesus himself to seven assemblies of Christ followers in Asia Minor (see Revelation 2–3).

The fourth letter in Rev 2:18–29 is "the words of the Son of God" dictated to "the angel of the assembly in Thyatira." After saying that the members of the assembly had started out well in their loyalty to him, he claims they have declined from their promising beginnings:

> But I have this against you: you tolerate that woman Jezebel, who calls herself a prophet and is teaching and beguiling my servants to practice fornication and to eat food sacrificed to idols. I gave her time to repent, but she refuses to repent of her fornication. Beware, I am throwing her on a bed, and those who commit adultery with her I am throwing into great distress, unless they repent of her doings; and I will strike her children dead. And all the churches will know that I am the one who searches minds and hearts, and I will give to each of you as your works deserve. (2:20–23)

The dominant reading of this passage in New Testament studies revolves around the phrase "I am throwing her on a bed." David Aune's commentary provides a good example:

> The expression . . . "I will throw her into a sickbed," is a Hebrew idiom that means "to cast upon a bed of illness," i.e., to punish someone with various forms of sickness (Charles, 1:71–72; see Exod 21:18; 1 Macc 1:5; Just 8:3) . . . it is surprising that "Jezebel" is not threatened with death, though her "children" are.[8]

The key point to note is that Aune, like many others, interprets *ballō autēn eis klinēn* (literally, "I am throwing her onto a bed") as a statement of punishing

Jezebel with the suffering of illness, arguing that *klīnē* does not simply mean bed, but sick bed or bed of illness.[9] The most common English Bible translations reflect this reading: "sickbed" or "bed of sickness" (CEB; ESV; HCSB; NASB; NKJV; RSV) and "bed of suffering" (NIV, NLT). The note of surprise in such interpretations is that while Jezebel doesn't face death, her children do. This suggests, as some commentators make explicit, that readers ought not dwell on anything shocking or uncomfortably terrible about how the Son of God punishes *her*. Together these commentaries and translations, plus the sermons and Bible Study materials shaped by them, circulate this reading and the invisible questions about what is notable in the passage that generate the reading.

Biblical scholar Tina Pippin quickly unmasks what this "traditional reading" makes invisible: "the female body is ignored."[10] Feminist New Testament scholars have thus sought to un-ignore the female body, just as the writer of Revelation does not ignore it either. Pippin, in her important and provocative book, *Death and Desire: The Rhetoric of Gender in the Apocalypse of John*, though reproducing the sickbed interpretation of *klīnē* in Rev 2:22, situates the depiction of what the Son of God does to Jezebel within the writing's overall "sexual oppression and stereotypes of woman as object of violence and desire."[11] Indeed, what happens to the figure of Jezebel is a signature example of "the role of the female [as] subordinate in the text . . . used or abused."[12] By attending to what Rev 2:20–23 itself emphasizes, Pippin un-erases the Son of God's violence against a woman's body.

Others have heeded Pippin's call to not ignore the female body. They have argued that John depicts not simply violence against Jezebel, but also the Son of God sexually assaulting her. Christopher Frilingos amplifies the gendered textures of Rev 2:22–23, noting that Jesus's actions "reinforce the femininity that Jezebel shares with Babylon." More to the point:

> The constellation of images produces an astonishing scene of submission and penetration: the sexual immorality of Jezebel is punished on a bed by the "fiery eyes" of the "one who searches minds and hearts." Domination is on display, even if the threat of sexual assault remains veiled behind a surface suggestion of illness.[13]

Dominant ideologies of masculinity and femininity in Greco-Roman literary culture hierarchically defined masculinity in terms of domination, self-mastery, penetration, activity, strength, and virtue versus penetrated, dominated, passive, weak, and vicious femininity.[14] The writer of Revelation amplifies the Son of God's hegemonic masculinity through an active masculine sexual mastery of Jezebel that "refeminizes" the woman as a passive recipient of male subjugation.

Some Feminist readers have dispensed with the sickbed reading of *klīnē* altogether, since the Greek word's basic meaning is "bed," not "sickbed." While "sickbed" is a possible meaning when context suggests it, nothing in Rev 2:18–29 introduces ideas of sickness or suffering from disease. The writer instead has the Son of God's voice load Jezebel with gendered sexual images: "she teaches and deceives [*plana*] my servants to practice fornication [*porneusai*] and to eat food sacrificed to idols" in 2:20 and "she refuses to repent of her fornication [*tēs porneias autēs*]" in 2:21. In 2:22, the Son of God mentions the men who commit adultery [*tous moicheuontas*] with Jezebel. I modified the NRSV's translation of 2:20 to emphasize the meaning of "deception" for *planaō*. This aligns with John's gendered polemic via the figure of Jezebel since one characteristic of femininity in ancient Jewish and Christian versions of wider gender ideologies is an irrational weak mind that's easily deceived and has the propensity to deceive.[15]

The Son of God repeatedly paints Jezebel with a transgressive sexual brush and then theorizes the nature of his punishments in Rev 2:23: "I will give to each of you as your works deserve." As Olivia Stewart Lester suggests, the Son of God's sexual assault of Jezebel is punitive and thus connected to John's repayment-according-to-works theory of punishment.[16] There is every reason to dispense with the sickbed reading of *klinē* and understand Jezebel's punishment on a bed as an expression of what, from the text's violently misogynist point of view, she deserves for her sexual misdeeds and deceptive leading of others into them. Thus, the Son of God throws her down on a bed (*ballō autēn eis klinēn*), which in context means he sexually assaults her.[17] Sarah Emanuel draws these threads together:

> The likelihood that Jezebel is being thrown on a sickbed seems very slim to me, given that the immediate context is full of references to fornication and adultery. *Kline* is only "sickbed" when it is situated within a context of sickness. The context of Revelation 2 ... is not of illness, but rather of sexual violence.[18]

The writer of Revelation thus sets a scene in which a feminine figure catalyzes decline from the Thyatiran assembly's promising beginnings (2:19) through her sexual misdeeds and deceiving of others into them. The Son of God re-masters the situation in 2:22–23 through a violent sexual humiliation of Jezebel, threat to cause "great distress" to those who were deceived "unless they repent *of her doings*" (emphasis mine), and the killing of her children. The gendered distinctions are crucial to note for the discussion below of this how passage's competitive rhetoric works: only "Jezebel" is punished severely with rape and the death of her offspring. Those men (implied given the imagery of adultery) she deceived may repent.

The writer of Revelation further positions the Son of God's throwing of Jezebel onto a bed within a frame of sexual violence by activating the imagery of warfare. One of the most common settings of rape in Greco-Roman literature is warfare, conquest, and the treatment of defeated enemies—in other words, martial rape. In one of Nestor's better-known speeches of the *Iliad*, he makes explicit that because Zeus favors the Greeks to defeat Troy, "let no man make haste to depart homewards until each has lain with (*katakoimēthēnai*) the wife of some Trojan, and has got requital for his strivings and groanings over Helen" (2.354–56; LCL). While this is not the same language as Rev 2:22's *ballō autēn eis klinēn*, the use of *katakoimaō* in this martial context refers to forceful bedding-down (i.e., rape) of the women of defeated Trojan men.[19] The next sentence (*Il.* 2.357–59) even has Nestor threaten to have any Greek who opts out of his command to rape Trojan women executed.

Marial rape is a norm within the *Iliad*'s mythmaking about Achilles's wrath and the Trojan war. In the lead-up to the fight between Paris and Menelaus, the Greeks' pact should the Trojans violate their oath includes both the utter defeat of Troy and their women being penetrated by [*migeien*] or made sexually subject to [*dameien*] victorious Greek men (*Il.* 3.301). Priam highlights the mass rape and ravaging of Trojan women should the city fall as though it is an obvious expectation (*Il.* 22.62–5). And Achilles's catastrophic wrath itself, the explicit subject of the *Iliad* (1.1), is kindled by Agamemnon taking Briseis from him in Book 1 when Achilles had slain her husband and three brothers and taken her as his sexual prize (19.291–300). Kathy Gaca synthesizes materials across the *Iliad* and *Odyssey* to show that both the rape and widespread ravaging of defeated women for sexual use or for selling to other men for sexual use were top-down goals of warfare in the literary world of these writings.[20]

Martial rape was not a phenomenon limited to Homeric sources. It pervaded depictions of war in Greek and Roman literature.[21] Discussions of war within Jewish literature of the Hellenistic and Roman eras also celebrate martial rape (Jdt 9:4). Josephus repeatedly emphasizes the outrage over the wives of Jewish men being taken for rape by Roman soldiers during the First Revolt (*J.W.* 7.377, 382, 385). And a revelatory writing similar to Revelation, *4 Ezra*, includes within its laments about the downfall of Jerusalem that "our virgins have been defiled, and our wives have been ravished" (10:22). Greek and Roman sources also specify that the decimation of the lineages of the conquered often accompanies martial rape (e.g., Diod. Sic. 13.57–58; Livy, *Ab Urbe Condita* 21.13.9; 4 Ezra 10:22–23). Caryn Reeder explains that these genocidal associations of wartime rape amount to a rhetoric of "destroying the future" of the conquered.[22]

The Son of God's violent punishment of Jezebel in Rev 2:22–23 would have resonated for ancient audiences within the cultural scripts of martial rape given how John positions Jesus among conquering divine warriors.[23] Scholars use the term divine warrior to indicate a deity who defeats divine opponents or their subordinates on earth. Sometimes the warrior is the high God, but often divine warriors are subordinates of the high God. As Adela Yarbro Collins shows in detail, mythology about divine warriors suffuses Revelation. The writing has three such figures: the high Jewish God and then his subordinates, Michael and especially the Lamb, who is identified as Jesus.[24] The first introduction of Jesus as a warrior comes very early in the text. Revelation 1:13–16 associates him with Dan 7:13–14's "one like a son of man" and furnishes him with an array of powerful characteristics (e.g., "from his mouth came a sharp, two-edged sword"). "The one like a son of man" was a passive figure whom the high God vindicates in Daniel 7, but by the first century CE some Jewish writers had turned him into an active warrior and judge. Revelation participates in this transformation when it coordinates Jesus's role as a warrior with the one like a son of man, who was known by then as an end-times agent of Israel's God.[25]

The letters to the seven assemblies of Revelation 2–3 immediately follow the introduction of Jesus as a martial figure. He is the speaker in each letter. Though they alternate their labels for him, almost all include some element of 1:13–19's warrior imagery. Thus the letter to the assembly at Thyatira commences with, "These are the words of the Son of God, who has eyes like a flame of fire, and whose feet are like burnished bronze" (2:18), which alludes back to 1:14–15 corresponding details about the one like a son of man's eyes and feet. The Son of God who speaks to the Christ followers at Thyatira and punishes Jezebel thus takes the stage as Revelation's signature divine warrior who defeats God's enemies.

John further activates the rhetoric of divine warfare and conquest by referring to a generic follower who obeys as "the one who conquers [*ho nikōn*]" in each of the seven letters of Revelation 2–3. In Rev 2:26–28, the Son of God coordinates their conquering with Jewish mythology about divine warriors: to the ones who conquer, "I will give authority over the nations; to rule them with an iron rod, as when clay pots are shattered—even as I also received authority from my Father." Mythology about divine warriors in texts of the Greco-Roman period often specifies that their victories result in receiving cosmic authority, which they use to confer benefits on their subordinates.[26] The Son of God's words in Rev 2:26–28 paraphrase Ps 2:8–9, which was a go-to passage among literate Jews who wrote about subordinate end-times warriors for Israel's God, the authority they would be given over the nations, and the rod of iron with which they would rule.[27] This martial imagery amplifies Rev 2:18–29's transgressive and feminizing sexual language about Jezebel to create a more suggestive setting for how "I am throwing her onto a bed" would have resonated. The Son of God is a masculine conqueror who humiliates his defeated feminized enemy by raping her and decimating her lineage.

Rhiannon Graybill argues that the interpretive and moral clarity that readers commonly seek runs up against the realities not only of how texts work, but sexual violence itself. Compared to the scripts often used to parse sexual violence in neat and clean ways (e.g., the "perfect victim" who fights back or perpetrators being overt evil strangers), these texts are "fuzzy, messy, icky."[28] Graybill's approach helps in thinking about the Son of God's aggression toward Jezebel. Drawing from the work of Sarah Emanuel, Meredith Warren, Olivia Stewart Lester, and others, I have argued that when the Son of God throws Jezebel on a bed in Rev 2:18–29, the imagery is not one of punishment with sickness, but of martial rape of a defeated enemy. Other feminist readers like Tina Pippin and Christopher Frilingos have left the nature of the sexual aggression ambiguous while firmly elucidating the passage's noxiously patriarchal volume. Our readings all emphasize the intersections of the Son of God's punishment of Jezebel with images of divinely sanctioned sexual violence elsewhere in Revelation plus John's affirmative wielding of wider literary culture's patriarchal schemes for thinking about reality. To borrow Graybill's words, these points "form a sticky corpus; they touch and contaminate each other. It is often difficult to speak of one . . . without the others creeping in."[29] While I argue that the Son of God's rape of Jezebel would resonate for many kinds of ancient bodies who encountered this text, perhaps the more important point is that Rev 2:18–29 is another piece of a sticky corpus of misogynist imagery in Revelation. Importantly, however, Revelation itself does not mark these matters as icky. They are, instead, the justified workings of God through his subordinate warrior, Christ. And as John repeatedly writes, hearers should exuberantly revel in them.

FEMINIZING "JEZEBEL" TO DUNK ON OTHER CHRIST TEACHERS

When the writer of Revelation throws the kitchen sink of sexually transgressive imagery at Jezebel, he's likely not claiming that a Christ teacher he opposes in Thyatira actually engages in such sexual practices or leads others into them. Neither is her name Jezebel. When we redescribe the gendered polemics of the Rev 2:18–29, the situation is more plausibly the following: there was a female Christ teacher whom the male writer of Revelation considered a rival.[30] Her version of piety toward the Jewish deity apparently could include the consumption of meat that had been slaughtered in cultic settings for Greek or Roman deities (i.e., *eidōlothytos*). John disagreed on this and other points, strongly. He responded with gendered sexual polemics, in particular by associating the woman with the notorious queen Jezebel of Hebrew lore. He feminizes his rival while aligning himself with masculine authority via the Jewish deity's eschatological agent, Christ. Just as John later feminizes Rome by sketching her judgment from God in visceral detail as a low-class whore who will be sexually violated, so he similarly casts Jezebel as a sexual deviant and scripts her punishment as masculine sexual domination by the Son of God.[31] As Robyn Whitaker insightfully puts it, "John fights a doctrinal dispute through sexual slander."[32]

John's gender slandering of a rival slots him alongside other writers and cultural leaders from Mediterranean antiquity like Cicero's *In Catalinam* or Irenaeus's claims about Marcus and other competing Christian leaders whom he depicts as sexually immoral in *Adversus Haereses*. As Catherine Edwards and Jennifer Knust have shown, delegitimizing an opponent by contesting their masculinity, depicting them as effeminate, and accusing them of excessive or illegitimate sexual action was one of the most recognizable rhetorical paths.[33] John is participating in a common practice of literate and elite culture. Indeed, his demonizing of powerful women (e.g., "Jezebel" and "Babylon the whore") who lure men into sexual vice, and even effeminize male rulers (see Rev 2:20, 22; 17:2, 18; 18:3, 9), is part of the same phenomenon as Augustan propagandists vilifying Cleopatra for being dominant over Marc Antony, feminizing him with her sexual allure.[34] John does not attack the female leader in Thyatira because she is a woman. But he does amplify ancient tropes about wild women who cause transgressions of the normative gender order (e.g., being vectors of sexual vice and feminizing free men) in ways that make his polemic against her more violently intense than against the male leader in Pergamum whom he rejects in 2:14 for the same sins of *porneia* and *eidōlothytos*.[35]

This understanding of Rev 2:18–29's language about the female Christ teacher in Thyatira also helps explain why the Son of God will murder her children (2:23) after raping her. Stories of martial rape in Greco-Roman literature tended to illustrate decimation of an enemy's lineage through the genocide of men and then the enslaving of children. But since in the scenario of 2:18–29, Jezebel's "children" would be the adult followers of the female Christ teacher in Thyatira, a martial rape narrative would involve their murder by the conquering victor.

A key takeaway is that attending to masculinity, femininity, and sexual violence when thinking about Revelation is not to read anachronistic concerns into the text. John makes these matters explicit, repeatedly: "But I have this against you: you tolerate that woman [*tēn gunaika*] Jezebel" (Rev 2:20). Sexual violence and gender are, furthermore, at the center of responsible historical study of how (a) the text works in its social contexts, (b) fits in Greco-Roman literary culture, and (c) could have been heard by ancient audiences. Feminist readers highlight gender and sexual violence in Revelation precisely as part of seeking a truthful historical reading, not to impose their ideologies on it. Sara Parks reminds us that to consider feminist questions "niche" as opposed to part of the fabric of scholarship is itself an activist decision. It is to opt for erasing the parts of our ancient data that do not fit male-centered fantasies about our sources and how to study them.[36] Unfortunately, such erasure is normative in the history of reading Revelation, and it contributes to the erasure not only of Revelation's promotion of sexual violence, but also of sexual violence in the worlds of Revelation's modern readers.

ERASING THE SON OF GOD'S RAPE OF JEZEBEL

Scholarly commentators are not the only people who often overlook the Son of God's rape of Jezebel. Christian readers have been overlooking this rape for centuries alongside their erasure of the Bible's promotion of sexual violence elsewhere. Joy Schroeder demonstrates how an impulse to protect the Bible from criticism melded with patriarchal ideals among ancient Christian writers such that their readings downplay biblical promotion of sexual violence—often by silencing and blaming women.[37] Contemporary Christians continue this tradition.

If we want to sample the reactions to Jesus's gendered violence in Revelation, the media materials that produce evangelical biblical reading-culture are a useful place to look. The section on Rev 2:18–29 in a popular guide for Bible study groups commences the discussion with, "What things in our world today make Jesus angry?" It then naturalizes Jesus's anger by reproducing Revelation's own polemic against Jezebel: "How do you think this woman was able to lead some of the Christians in Thyatira away from God's standard of holiness?" When this guide gets to the Son of God's violence against Jezebel in 2:22–23, it erases the assault on a woman's body while encouraging Christians to think of Jesus's actions as a positive model for how God works in their lives: "Has the Lord ever used harsh measures in your life, or in a friend's life, to bring you to repentance?" It even asks: "What instruments of chastening does Jesus threaten to use (vv. 22–23)?" No indication is given that participants should produce the answers of "rape and mass-murder of children," or even just "violence against women." The absurdity of spelling-that-out highlights how the guide's ideal readers will not notice Jesus's gendered violence. It can even conclude, "*Pray that God will shatter any moral complacency in your life*" (emphasis original).[38]

This Bible study does not help readers engage accurately and ethically with facets of Revelation 2 like rape, slut-shaming, mass murder, and violent patriarchy. It does not mark them as realities readers should notice, reject, and work to dismantle. Instead, it promotes uncritical identification with the violent man (because he's "the good guy"), what he voices about Jezebel, and John's own norms in Revelation 2. It may seem unremarkable that a conservative evangelical Bible Study naturalizes identification with Rev 2:18–29's presentation of Jesus. But a crucial part of critical thinking and truthful reading involves remarking on the unremarkable. That is the path to noticing how the Bible Study guide reproduces a culture of not-noticing violence against women and even feeling like such violence is acceptable.

The *Believer's Bible Commentary* ignores the violence to Jezebel's female body and reproduces the sick bed reading while the *NIV Life Application Study Bible*'s notes overlook the Son of God's actions against Jezebel in 2:22–23. The notes do focus on ways that the sexual activities discussed in the 2:18–29 "hurts us," "has tremendous power to destroy," "hurts others," and "undermines integrity and trust." But the harmful sex in view is Jezebel's "sexual immorality," which is interpreted as "sex outside of marriage" to align with evangelical family values, and not the rape narrated in the passage.[39] The *Apologetics Study Bible*'s notes ignore the actual treatment of Jezebel, choosing instead to assimilate the "great tribulation" of 2:22 (i.e., NRSV: "Those who commit adultery with her I am throwing into *great distress*") to the concept with the same name in Dispensationalist end-times schemes.[40]

The popular *New Bible Commentary* says nothing about the assault on Jezebel. It asserts "The language in vs 22–23 is clearly figurative, setting forth a punishment befitting the crime," perhaps anticipating that readers may squirm at the murder of children, to which the commentators next turn.[41] Craig Keener's *Bible Background Commentary* includes a paragraph on Rev 2:21–23 that neglects the ubiquity of martial rape in Greek, Roman, Jewish, and Christian sources. He instead explains that "disciples were sometimes called 'children,'" that God has allowed false prophets a chance to repent, and that the "biblical expectations" for judgment according to works have precedent.[42]

The dynamics at work in readings that render the Son of God's rape of Jezebel invisible mirror those seen across many Christian readers' responses to sexual violence elsewhere in biblical literature. Renita Weems's pioneering book from almost thirty years ago, *Battered Love: Marriage, Sex, and Violence*, demonstrates how Hebrew prophetic literature wields violently misogynist and rapist ideologies to imagine marriage, God's "love" for Israel, and divine punishment. It turns out that biblical writings naturalize and think-with sexual violence, and often not very subtly (e.g., see Deut 21:10–14; Ezekiel 16; 23).[43] Yet it is also a norm for readers not to notice these facets of biblical writings, especially when the Bible's moral exceptionalism or evangelical gender and sexual norms are at stake.

NOT "THE STANDARD OF THE TIMES" BUT THE REPRODUCTION OF RAPE CULTURE

When Christians erase the Son of God's rape of Jezebel in Revelation 2 or the sexual violence promoted elsewhere by biblical texts, they align with the patriarchal erasure of violence against women in biblical writings themselves. Ancient Mediterranean texts participate in the normalization of martial rape such that Gaca can succinctly refer to "a socially normative rape culture in antiquity."[44] Even the writings that seem to reject rape still reflect and participate in rape culture. As historians of sexuality and gender have shown, outrage about wartime rape tends to be male writers lamenting that *our* free women were raped by men from *other* people groups or from lower-statuses in the societal hierarchy (e.g., by slaves in a slave uprising).[45] Male leaders may also competitively depict martial rape by rival leaders, armies, or groups as an image of their irrational excess and failed masculinity: they could not master themselves and live virtuously.[46] These objections are not so much critiques of rape *per se* as reaffirmations of gendered and xenophobic assumptions in ways that strategically wield outrage about the wrong women being violated by the wrong men—all for rhetorical purposes other than overturning rape culture. The rape of enslaved women (or men, for that matter) by their enslavers or by authorized others did not register, and the humiliation of defeat also serves to sink the higher-status women among the conquered to make them legitimate targets of rape.[47]

The point is not that "rape was the standard of the times." Such a claim re-naturalizes rape culture by erasing its victims and the objections they certainly had. Rape of the "right women" was normalized within elite male ideologies that are reflected in most of our literary sources from Mediterranean antiquity. These texts were, by definition, the product of about one percent of the population, which is hardly enough to make claims about "the" standards of the times. Some ancient sources, furthermore, do reflect disgust, discomfort, and concern about forms of sexual violence against women. There were laws against rape, though their logics tend to follow the status distinctions discussed above and not modern versions of ideas about consent.[48] Even so, biblical and other ancient sources reflect a varied and violent patriarchal set of norms. And within these violent norms, the hierarchical exploitation, subjugation, and brutality against women is not something that is itself remarkable. When some readers erase the Son of God's sexual violence against Jezebel, they are inhabiting that contact zone where the violently patriarchal sensitivities of biblical sources overlap with white Christian versions of patriarchy that officially decry sexual violence while still reproducing rape culture.

As the #MeToo movement highlighted, the erasure of sexual violence and the silencing of victims have been crucial factors in keeping society hospitable to misogyny and rape. The erasure of the Son of God's gendered violence in Revelation then becomes more than an abstract issue. When it is normal to overlook sexual violence against women while reading the Bible, it will "come naturally" for folks shaped by such reading cultures to overlook sexual violence in the world of their daily lives. Conversely, it will feel uncomfortable when they encounter people trying to make sexual violence that looks bad for patriarchy visible. Such people may seem like inappropriate activists who are stirring up trouble instead of leaving well-enough alone when, in fact, it is also an "activist" decision on behalf of rape culture to ignore it.

We can get even more specific: institutions where upholding the Bible's "moral reputation" is a paramount value will do so by overlooking its sexual violence, downplaying it, or blaming its victims (e.g., Jerusalem in Ezekiel 16; Jezebel in Revelation 2). This will especially be the case in settings where claims about the Bible's perfection or inerrancy authorize its authority.[49] These institutions will then likely be places that similarly prioritize upholding the reputations of male leaders or doctrines by downplaying allegations of abuse and blaming victims. In other words, engagements with the Bible that identify with its moral reputation are communicating a message and creating a culture. It is a culture of identifying with exploitative misogyny, and, as Kristin Kobes Du Mez has recently discussed at length, this culture has a long history of predictable consequences that are devastating to women, children, and also men who do not conform to gender norms.[50]

The discomfort generated by feminist attention to rape scenes like Jesus's actions in Revelation 2 are not simply exercises in exposing a biblical writing. They are opportunities for what Graybill calls unhappy reading: "that is, reading strategies and tactics that do not insist that every act of reading comes to a 'happy ending.'"[51] If rape culture thrives on erasing, excusing, or downplaying sexual violence and silencing victims, then the unhappy reading can lead to the beginnings of disruption. To reverse the scenarios above: what if instead of overlooking the Son of God's rape of Jezebel, readers did something different. What if they instead label this as gendered sexual violence committed by Jesus, but then unequivocally reject it? What if they then commence grappling with the complexities of rape culture and how to go about un-making it? This solution is not simple, but it's a start.

NOTES

1. The writer of Revelation self-identifies as John (Rev 1:4, 9). Whether or not one considers "John" a "pseudonymous" attribution to a figure associated early with

Jesus (e.g., Gal 2:9), either way, as Greg Carey has argued, Revelation's characterizations of John naturalize the writer's authority for competitive use against other Christ teachers (*Elusive Apocalypse: Reading Authority in the Revelation of John* [Macon, GA: Mercer University Press, 1999]). In this chapter I refer to Revelation's writer as John without presuming the historical veracity of this attribution.

2. For Babylon as ultimate eschatological enemy in Revelation, see Rev 16:17–19:3. Understanding Babylon to be a cipher for Rome is a dominant—but not unanimous—position among scholars, and it is commonly noted that the writer is capitalizing on Babylon's mythic reputation as an evil and oppressive city in Hebrew prophetic literature. See Brian Blount, *Revelation: A Commentary* (Louisville, KY: Westminster John Knox, 2009), 309–14.

3. See Horace, *Odes* 3.6 for an example of imagining Rome's rise and then decline in terms of women transgressing such gender norms. For discussions of Revelation's Babylon and gendered stereotypes in Greco-Roman literary culture, see Paul Duff, *Who Rides the Beast?: Prophetic Rivalry and the Rhetoric of Crisis in the Churches of the Apocalypse* (New York: Oxford University Press, 2001), 109–11; Lynn Huber, *Thinking and Seeing with Women in Revelation*, LNTS 475 (New York: Bloomsbury, 2013), 63–73; Tina Pippin, "The Heroine and the Whore: Fantasy and the Female in the Apocalypse of John," *Semeia* 60 (1993): 67–82. On the resonances with images with lower-class, enslaved prostitutes in Roman culture, see Jennifer Glancy and Stephen Moore, "How Typical a Roman Prostitute Is Revelation's 'Great Whore'?," *JBL* 130 (2011): 551–69.

4. Meredith Warren, "Rape Jokes, Sexual Violence, and Empire in Revelation and This Is The End," in *The Bible and the Postsecular World: Essays in Honour of Philip Davies*, eds. Thomas Bolin and James Crossley (London: Routledge, Forthcoming). See also Olivia Stewart Lester's argument that Rev 17:16's forced-stripping of Babylon would have resonated as sexual violence (*Prophetic Rivalry, Gender, and Economics: A Study in Revelation and Sibylline Oracles 4–5*, WUNT2 466 [Tübingen: Mohr Siebeck, 2018], 60–62).

5. For example, David Barr, "The Lamb Who Looks Like a Dragon?: Characterizing Jesus in John's Apocalypse," in *The Reality of the Apocalypse: Rhetoric and Politics in the Book of Revelation*, ed. David Barr (Atlanta: SBL, 2006), 205–20. Or more broadly accessible: Greg Boyd, *The Crucifixion of the Warrior God: Interpreting the Old Testament's Violent Portraits of God in Light of the Cross* (Minneapolis: Fortress, 2017), 593–628. For a sustained critique of these approaches, see Paul Middleton, *The Violence of the Lamb: Martyrs as Agents of Divine Judgment in the Book of Revelation*, LNTS 586 (New York: Bloomsbury, 2018). For a brief critical rundown, see Candida Moss, *Divine Bodies: Resurrecting Perfection in the New Testament and Early Christianity* (New Haven: Yale University Press, 2019), 98–99, 173–75.

6. Susan Hylen notes the phenomenon of scholars making the slain-lamb the real (non-violent) message of Revelation and the common use of misleading dichotomies like figurative or metaphorical versus literal to downplay the text's violent language ("Metaphor Matters: Violence and Ethics in Revelation," *CBQ* 73 [2011]: 777–96).

7. Rhiannon Graybill, *Texts After Terror: Rape, Sexual Violence, and the Hebrew Bible* (New York: Oxford University Press, 2021), 26.

8. David Aune, *Revelation 1–5*, WBC 52A (Nashville: Thomas Nelson, 1997), 205.

9. See other commentaries, both academic (e.g., G.K. Beale, *The Book of Revelation: A Commentary on the Greek Text*, NIGTC [Grand Rapids: Eerdmans, 1999], 263) and aimed at pastors and Bible Study leaders (e.g., Blount, *Revelation*, 63; Robert Thomas, *Revelation 1–7: An Exegetical Commentary* [Chicago: Moody, 1992], 218; Ben Witherington III, *Revelation*, NCBC [New York: Cambridge University Press, 2003], 104).

10. Tina Pippin, "'And I Will Strike Her Children Dead': Death and the Deconstruction of Social Location," in *Reading from This Place*, vol. 1, eds. Fernando Segovia and Mary Ann Tolbert (Minneapolis: Fortress, 1995), 194.

11. Tina Pippin, *Death and Desire: The Rhetoric of Gender in the Apocalypse of John* (Louisville: Westminster John Knox, 1992), 71–72.

12. Pippin, *Rhetoric of Gender*, 69.

13. Christopher Frilingos, *Spectacles of Empire: Monsters, Martyrs, and the Book of Revelation* (Philadelphia: University of Pennsylvania Press, 2004), 109.

14. This understanding of gender in Greco-Roman sources is commonly called the penetration paradigm, Priapic model of masculinity, or the active vs. passive model. For a detailed explication focusing on Latin literature, see Craig Williams, *Roman Homosexuality*, 2nd ed. (New York: Oxford University Press, 2010), 13–14, 17–19, 94–99, 137–202, 258–67. For a brief rundown, see L. Stephanie Cobb, *Dying to Be Men: Gender and Language in Early Christian Martyr Texts* (New York: Columbia University Press, 2008), 24–32. There are important criticisms of these models that do not so much dispense with them as destabilize or note ways some ancient texts frame matters differently: see Maia Kotrosits, "Penetration and Its Discontents: Greco-Roman Sexuality, the *Acts of Paul and Thecla*, and Theorizing Eros without the Wound," *JHS* 27 (2018): 343–66.

15. For a clear example, "Why does the serpent speak to the woman and not to the man? . . . Woman is more accustomed to be deceived than man. For his judgments, like his body, is masculine and is capable of dissolving or destroying the designs of deception; but the judgment of woman is more effeminate, and because of softness she easily gives way and is taken in by plausible falsehoods which resemble the truth" (Philo, *QG* 1.33; LCL). See also Philo, *QG* 1.46; *Opif.* 151–52; *Let. Aris.* 250; 1 Tim 2:12–15. See below for discussion of gendered polemic.

16. Stewart Lester, *Prophetic Rivalry*, 60–62.

17. Stewart Lester, *Prophetic Rivalry*, 65–66.

18. Sarah Emanuel, *Roasting Rome: Humor, Resistance, and Jewish Cultural Persistence in the Book of Revelation* (New York: Cambridge University Press, 2019), 110 n. 52. Others also dispense with the sickbed reading to understand 2:22 as a scene of rape-as-punishment: Colleen Conway, *Behold the Man: Jesus and Greco-Roman Masculinity* (New York: Oxford University Press, 2008), 162; Stephen Moore, "Raping Rome," in *Untold Tales from the Book of Revelation: Sex and Gender, Empire and Ecology* (Atlanta: SBL, 2014), 148–49; Warren, "Sexual Violence"; Warren, "Sexual Violence and Rape Culture in the New Testament," *The Shiloh Project*, 31 May 2017, https://www.shilohproject.blog/sexual-violence-and-rape-culture-in-the-new-testament/.

19. I appreciate Kathy Gaca's insightful thoughts about the resonances of *katakoimaō* in *Il.* 2.355 in our email discussion of the passage.

20. Kathy Gaca has numerous publications on the topic. For a focus on Homeric literature, see "Ancient Warfare and the Ravaging Martial Rape of Girls and Women: Evidence from Homeric Epic and Greek Drama," in *Sex in Antiquity: Exploring Gender and Sexuality in the Ancient World*, eds. Mark Masterson, Nancy Sorkin Rabinowitz, James Robson (New York: Routledge, 2015), 278–97.

21. For a few examples: Herodotus, *Hist.* 1.146.2; Pausanias, *Descr.* 10.22.4; Caesar, *Bell. gall.* 7.14. This is a common point: e.g., Susan Guettel Cole, "Greek Sanctions against Sexual Assault," *CP* 79 (1984): 97–113; Gaca, "Martial Rape, Pulsating Fear"; Sara Elise Phang, "Intimate Conquests: Roman Soldiers' Slave Women and Freedwomen," *Ancient World* 35 (2004): 207–37.

22. Caryn Reeder, "Wartime Rape, the Romans, and the First Jewish Revolt," *JSJ* 48 (2017), 378–80.

23. For more detailed discussion of this paragraph's and the following's points about divine warriors, see Stephen Young, *Paul Among the Mythmakers: Gods, Sin, and Scriptures* (Under Review), Chapter 4, "Victorious Gods and the Benefits They Bestow: Christ the Warrior for Gentiles."

24. Adela Yarbro Collins, *The Combat Myth in the Book of Revelation* (Missoula: Scholars Press, 1976). On "the lamb" in Revelation being Jesus, see Aune, *Revelation*, 1:367–73. For Michael, see Rev 12:7–8.

25. Key examples of these first-century writings are 4 Ezra, the *Parables of Enoch*, Revelation, and Mark. On this development in the "one like a son of man," see John J. Collins, "The Son of Man in First-Century Judaism," *NTS* 38 (1992): 458, 464.

26. See Young, "Christ the Warrior for Gentiles."

27. Matthew Novenson, *Christ Among the Messiahs: Christ Language in Paul and Messiah Language in Ancient Judaism* (New York: Oxford University Press, 2012), 53–60.

28. Graybill, *Texts After Terror*, 1–29.

29. Graybill, *Texts After Terror*, 27.

30. Given the constraints of this chapter, I simply outline a reading that could be argued in detail elsewhere. For important examples of scholars offering redescriptions similar to the one in this paragraph, see Duff, *Who Rides the Beast*; Emanuel, *Roasting Rome*, 21–35, 95–125; Pamela Thimmes, "'Teaching and Beguiling My Servants': The Letter to Thyatira (Rev. 2.18–29)," in *Feminist Companion to the Apocalypse of John*, 69–87; Whitaker, "Sexual Slander in the Apocalypse of John."

31. On God's judgment of Babylon in Rev 16:19–19:3, see the discussion at the start of this chapter. See Duff's extensive analysis (in *Who Rides the Beast*) of Revelation that elucidates connections between Jezebel and Babylon.

32. Robyn Whitaker, "Invoking Jezebel, Invoking Terror: The Threat of Sexual Violence in the Apocalypse of John," in *Terror in the Bible: Rhetoric, Gender, and Violence*, eds. Monica Jyotsna Melanchthon and Robyn J. Whitaker (Atlanta: SBL, 2021), 114.

33. See Catherine Edwards, *The Politics of Immorality in Ancient Rome* (Cambridge: Cambridge University Press, 1993); Jennifer Knust, *Abandoned to Lust:*

Sexual Slander and Ancient Christianity (New York: Columbia University Press, 2006), 1–50. Knust even briefly uses John's polemics against Jezebel and Babylon in Revelation as examples of sexual slander in antiquity (*Abandoned to Lust*, 113–14).

34. Huber draws these connections (*Thinking and Seeing*, 67). On Cleopatra and Marc Antony, see Edwards, *Politics of Immorality*, 25–26, 63–68, 186–92; Knust, *Abandoned to Lust*, 15–16, 41–44.

35. This is a common point: Thimmes, "Teaching and Beguiling My Servants," 78–79; Whitaker, "Sexual Slander in the Apocalypse of John," 113–17.

36. Sara Parks, "'The Brooten Phenomenon': Moving Women from the Margins in Second-Temple and New Testament Scholarship," *BCT* 15 (2019): 46–64.

37. Joy Schroeder, *Dinah's Lament: The Biblical Legacy of Sexual Violence in Christian Interpretation* (Minneapolis: Fortress, 2007).

38. Quotations are from Douglas Connelly, *Seven Letters to Seven Churches*, Life Guide Bible Studies (Downers Grove: InterVarsity, 2017), 26–29.

39. William MacDonald, *Believer's Bible Commentary*, ed. Art Farstad (Nashville: Thomas Nelson, 2016), 2464; *NIV Life Application Study Bible*, Third Edition (Grand Rapids: Zondervan, 2019), 2217–18.

40. Ted Cabal, Chad Brand, E. Ray Clendenen, Paul Copan, and J.P. Moreland, eds, *The Apologetics Study Bible* (Nashville: Holman, 2017), 1581.

41. D.A. Carson, R.T. France, J.A. Motyer, G.J. Wenham, ed, *New Bible Commentary: 21st Century Edition* (Downers Grove: InterVarsity, 1994).

42. Craig Keener, *The IVP Bible Background Commentary: New Testament*, Second Edition (Downers Grove: InterVarsity, 2014), 734–35.

43. Renita Weems, *Battered Love; Marriage, Sex, and Violence in the Hebrew Bible* (Minneapolis: Fortress, 1995). For a few examples beyond Weems, Graybill, the scholarship on Revelation discussed in this chapter, and the other essays in this edited volume, see M.I. Rey, "Reexamination of the Foreign Female Captive: Deuteronomy 21:10–14 as a Case of Genocidal Rape," *JFSR* 32 (2016): 37–53; Johanna Stiebert, *Rape Myths, The Bible, and #MeToo* (New York: Routledge, 2020), 19–43.

44. Gaca, "Ancient Warfare and Ravaging Martial Rape," 280.

45. Again, among Jewish writings, see 4 Ezra 10:22. The book of Judith is another example: while Jdt 9:11 celebrates Israel's God as the protector of the weak and forlorn, 9:4 just a few sentences earlier seamlessly praises his handing over of the wives and daughters of defeated enemies for rape. For discussion of other sources in Greco-Roman literary cultures, see Guettell Cole, "Greek Sanctions against Sexual Assault"; Gaca, "Ancient Warfare and Ravaging Martial Rape," 280; Reeder, "Wartime Rape," 369, 380–82.

46. Reeder, "Wartime Rape," 280–81.

47. For discussions, see Gaca, "Ancient Warfare and Ravaging Martial Rape," 281–84, 288; Glancy, *Slavery in Early Christianity*; Reeder, "Wartime Rape," 366–68; Williams, *Roman Homosexuality*, 103–36. See also Cobb's essay in this volume for another example in early Christian literature of an enslaver who coordinates the rape of her enslaved worker (pages 37–52).

48. On such laws and ancient versions of ideas like consent, see Roland Betancourt, *Byzantine Intersectionality: Sexuality, Gender, and Race in the Middle Ages*

(Princeton: Princeton University Press, 2020), 19–57. See also Graybill's critical discussion of consent and her critique of the common scholarly claim that since women lacked certain types of autonomy "back then," consent was not a concept and therefore rape is an anachronistic idea for antiquity (*Texts After Terror*, 21, 30–39).

49. For discussion of how ideas about biblical inerrancy or perfection coordinate with white evangelical gender ideologies, see Stephen Young, "Biblical Inerrancy's Long History as an Evangelical Activist for White Patriarchy," *Religion Dispatches*, 8 Feb 2022, https://religiondispatches.org/biblical-inerrancys-long-history-as-an-evangelical-activist-for-white-patriarchy/.

50. Kristin Kobes Du Mez, *Jesus and John Wayne: How White Evangelicals Corrupted a Faith and Fractured a Nation* (New York: Liveright, 2020), 272–94. Her argument aligns with Megan Goodwin's important point that an overfocus on "religion" as opposed to white patriarchy as a factor in sexual abuse is a form of sensationalism that masks the ubiquity of "ordinary" sexual violence (*Abusing Religion: Literary Persecution, Sex Scandals, and American Minority Religions* [New Brunswick: Rutgers University Press, 2020]). The issue is not evangelicalism so much as white patriarchy, of which conservative evangelicalism is an intense historical and ideological manifestation.

51. Graybill, *Texts After Terror*, 4.

WORKS CITED

Aune, David. *Revelation 1–5*. Word Biblical Commentary 52A. Nashville: Thomas Nelson, 1997.

Barr, David. "The Lamb Who Looks Like a Dragon?: Characterizing Jesus in John's Apocalypse." Pages 593–628 in *The Reality of the Apocalypse: Rhetoric and Politics in the Book of Revelation*, ed. David Barr. Atlanta: SBL Press, 2006.

Beale, G. K. *The Book of Revelation: A Commentary on the Greek Text*. New International Greek Testament Commentary. Grand Rapids: Eerdmans, 1999.

Blount, Brian. *Revelation: A Commentary*. Louisville, KY: Westminster John Knox, 2009.

Boyd, Greg. *The Crucifixion of the Warrior God: Interpreting the Old Testament's Violent Portraits of God in Light of the Cross*. Minneapolis: Fortress Press, 2017.

Cabal, Ted, Chad Brand, E. Ray Clendenen, Paul Copan, and J.P. Moreland, eds, *The Apologetics Study Bible*. Nashville: Holman, 2017.

Carey, Greg. *Elusive Apocalypse: Reading Authority in the Revelation of John*. Macon, GA: Mercer University Press, 1999.

Carson, D. A., R. T. France, J. A. Motyer, G. J. Wenham, ed, *New Bible Commentary: 21st Century Edition*. Downers Grove: InterVarsity, 1994.

Cobb, L. Stephanie. *Dying to Be Men: Gender and Language in Early Christian Martyr Texts*. New York: Columbia University Press, 2008.

Cole, Susan Guettel. "Greek Sanctions against Sexual Assault," *Classical Philology* 79 (1984): 97–113.

Collins, Adela Yarbro. *The Combat Myth in the Book of Revelation*. Missoula, MT: Scholars Press, 1976.
Collins, John J. "The Son of Man in First-Century Judaism," *New Testament Studies* 38 (1992): 448–466.
Connelly, Douglas. *Seven Letters to Seven Churches*. Life Guide Bible Studies. Downers Grove: InterVarsity, 2017.
Conway, Coleen. *Behold the Man: Jesus and Greco-Roman Masculinity*. New York: Oxford University Press, 2008.
Du Mez, Kristin Kobes. *Jesus and John Wayne: How White Evangelicals Corrupted a Faith and Fractured a Nation.* New York: Liveright, 2020.
Duff, Paul. *Who Rides the Beast?: Prophetic Rivalry and the Rhetoric of Crisis in the Churches of the Apocalypse.* New York: Oxford University Press, 2001.
Edwards, Catherine. *The Politics of Immorality in Ancient Rome*. Cambridge: Cambridge University Press, 1993.
Emanuel, Sarah. *Roasting Rome: Humor, Resistance, and Jewish Cultural Persistence in the Book of Revelation*. New York: Cambridge University Press, 2019.
Frilingos, Christopher. *Spectacles of Empire: Monsters, Martyrs, and the Book of Revelation*. Philadelphia: University of Pennsylvania Press, 2004.
Gaca, Kathy. "Ancient Warfare and the Ravaging Martial Rape of Girls and Women: Evidence from Homeric Epic and Greek Drama." Pages 278–97 in *Sex in Antiquity: Exploring Gender and Sexuality in the Ancient World*, eds. Mark Masterson, Nancy Sorkin Rabinowitz, James Robson. New York: Routledge, 2015.
Glancy, Jennifer and Stephen Moore. "How Typical a Roman Prostitute Is Revelation's 'Great Whore'?" *Journal of Biblical Literature* 130 (2011): 551–69.
Goodwin, Megan. *Abusing Religion: Literary Persecution, Sex Scandals, and American Minority Religions*. New Brunswick: Rutgers University Press, 2020.
Graybill, Rhiannon. *Texts After Terror: Rape, Sexual Violence, and the Hebrew Bible*. New York: Oxford University Press, 2021.
Huber, Lynn. *Thinking and Seeing with Women in Revelation.* Library of New Testament Studies 475. New York: Bloomsbury, 2013.
Hylen, Susan. "Metaphor Matters: Violence and Ethics in Revelation." *Catholic Biblical Quarterly* 73 (2011): 777–96.
Keener, Craig. *The IVP Bible Background Commentary: New Testament*, Second Edition. Downers Grove: InterVarsity, 2014.
Knust, Jennifer. *Abandoned to Lust: Sexual Slander and Ancient Christianity*. New York: Columbia University Press, 2006.
Kotrosits, Maia. "Penetration and Its Discontents: Greco-Roman Sexuality, the *Acts of Paul and Thecla*, and Theorizing Eros without the Wound." *Journal of the History of Sexuality* 27 (2018): 343–66.
MacDonald, William. *Believer's Bible Commentary*, ed. Art Farstad. Nashville: Thomas Nelson, 2016.
Middleton, Paul. *The Violence of the Lamb: Martyrs as Agents of Divine Judgment in the Book of Revelation*. Library of New Testament Studies 586. New York: Bloomsbury, 2018.

Moore, Stephen. *Untold Tales From the Book of Revelation: Sex and Gender, Empire and* Ecology. Atlanta: SBL Press, 2014.

Moss, Candida. *Divine Bodies: Resurrecting Perfection in the New Testament and Early Christianity.* New Haven: Yale University Press, 2019.

Novenson, Matthew. *Christ Among the Messiahs: Christ Language in Paul and Messiah Language in Ancient Judaism.* New York: Oxford University Press, 2012.

Parks, Sara. "'The Brooten Phenomenon': Moving Women from the Margins in Second-Temple and New Testament Scholarship." *Bible and Critical Theory* 15 (2019): 46–64.

Phang, Sarah Elise. "Intimate Conquests: Roman Soldiers' Slave Women and Freedwomen." *Ancient World* 35 (2004): 207–37.

Pippin, Tina. *Death and Desire: The Rhetoric of Gender in the Apocalypse of John.* Louisville: Westminster John Knox, 1992.

———. "The Heroine and the Whore: Fantasy and the Female in the Apocalypse of John." *Semeia* 60 (1993): 67–82.

———. "'And I Will Strike Her Children Dead': Death and the Deconstruction of Social Location." Pages 191–98 in *Reading From This Place*, vol. 1, eds. Fernando Segovia and Mary Ann Tolbert. Minneapolis: Fortress, 1995.

Reeder, Caryn. "Wartime Rape, the Romans, and the First Jewish Revolt," *Journal for the Study of Judaism* 48 (2017): 363–85.

Rey, M. I. "Reexamination of the Foreign Female Captive: Deuteronomy 21:10–14 as a Case of Genocidal Rape." *Journal of Feminist Studies in Religion* 32 (2016): 37–53.

Schroeder, Joy. *Dinah's Lament: The Biblical Legacy of Sexual Violence in Christian Interpretation.* Minneapolis: Fortress, 2007.

Stewart Lester, Olivia. *Prophetic Rivalry, Gender, and Economics: A Study in Revelation and Sibylline Oracles 4–5.* WUNT 2.466. Tübingen: Mohr Siebeck, 2018.

Stiebert, Johanna. *Rape Myths, The Bible, and #MeToo*: Rape Culture, Religion, and the Bible. New York: Routledge, 2020.

Thimmes, Pamela. "'Teaching and Beguiling My Servants': The Letter to Thyatira (Rev. 2.18–29)." Pages 69–87 in *Feminist Companion to the Apocalypse of John*, ed. Amy-Jill Levine. London: T&T Clark, 2009.

Thomas, Robert. *Revelation 1–7: An Exegetical Commentary.* Chicago: Moody, 1992.

Warren, Meredith. "Sexual Violence and Rape Culture in the New Testament." *The Shiloh Project*, 31 May 2017, https://www.shilohproject.blog/sexual-violence-and-rape-culture-in-the-new-testament/.

Weems, Renita. *Battered Love; Marriage, Sex, and Violence in the Hebrew Bible.* Minneapolis: Fortress, 1995.

Whitaker, Robyn. "Invoking Jezebel, Invoking Terror: The Threat of Sexual Violence in the Apocalypse of John." Pages 107–120 in *Terror in the Bible: Rhetoric, Gender, and Violence*, eds. Monica Jyotsna Melanchthon and Robyn J. Whitaker. Atlanta: SBL Press, 2021.

Williams, Craig. *Roman Homosexuality*, 2nd ed. New York: Oxford University Press, 2010.

Witherington, Ben. *Revelation.* New Cambridge Bible Commentary. New York: Cambridge University Press, 2003.

Young, Stephen. "Biblical Inerrancy's Long History as an Evangelical Activist for White Patriarchy." *Religion Dispatches*, 8 Feb 2022, https://religiondispatches.org/biblical-inerrancys-long-history-as-an-evangelical-activist-for-white-patriarchy/.

Index of Ancient Sources

HEBREW BIBLE/OLD TESTAMENT

Genesis

9	213n7
19:30–38	213n7

Exodus

19	209, 210
19:12	210
19:12–13	210
19:18	208, 210
20	208
24:17	210

Deuteronomy

21:10–14	249

Joshua

6:25	180n8

Judges

1:12–13	174
14:3	174

14:10	171
14:12–15:6	174
19	68n27, 228
19:22	64
19–20	64
21:10–12	174
21:23–24	174
21:25	181n17

Ruth

1:16–17	181n8

1 Samuel

18:26–27	174

2 Samuel

5:8	182n26
11:26–27	181n8

1 Kings

18	209

2 Kings

9:30-37	46
17:29–34	233n30

Psalms

45	172

Proverbs

5:15-18	224

Isaiah

62	176

Jeremiah

2:13	223
12:10	176
20:7	213n7

Ezekiel

16	249, 251
16:7–34	175
19:10–24	176
23	249

Daniel

3	91
13	62

OTHER ANCIENT JEWISH TEXTS

1 Enoch

92–105	241

1 Maccabees

9:39	171, 181n20

2 Maccabees

7	91

4 Ezra

10:22	244, 255n45
10:22–23	244

Babylonian Ketubot

16b–17a	171

Josephus

Antiquities

13.18–21	174

The Jewish War

7.377	244
7.382	244
7.385	244

Shemot Rabbah

29	208
29:9	209

NEW TESTAMENT

Matthew

1:1–17	172		
1:20	201		
7:22–23	175		
9:10	218		
9:15	169, 175		
10:3	218		
11:19	218		
12:39	176		
15:1–5	175		
16:4	176		
19:12	194		
21:5	176		
21:12–13	177		
21:14	177		
21:16	177		
21:18–22	177		
21:28–32	218		
21:31	219		
21:33–41	175		
21:34–36	176		
21:38–39	176		
21:43	176		
21:45	176		
22:1–3	175		
22:1–14	x, 170, 178		
22:4–5	177, 178		
23	176, 177		
23:34	176		
23:37	176		
24:1–2	177		
25:1–13	x, 170		
25:9	177		
25:11	175, 177		
25:12	175, 177		

Mark

2:15–16	218
2:19	169, 175
5:27–31	72
8:38	181n22
9:42–50	187
11:12–14	182n27
11:20–25	182n27
12:20–23	222

Luke

1:34–45	201
2:8	201
2:29–32	210
3:12	218
5:27	218
5:29–30	218
5:35–36	169
7:34	218
7:37	219
12	100n12
12:35–40	88, 89, 180n1
12:41–48	88, 89
12:42	88
12:45	88
12:47	89
12:47–48	85, 99, 100n11
12:48	89
14:1	170
14:15–24	170
14:21	178
15:1	218
16:1–8	100n12

John

2:10	171
3:29	169
4	217, 221, 225, 226, 227
4:7–42	220
4:17–19	222
4:28–29	227, 234n60
4:39	222
4:39–40	227
5:14	224
20	205, 206
20:17	73
20:25	205
20:28	206
20:29	206

Acts

16:10–17	208
18	72
20:5-15	208
21:1-8	208
27:1–28:16	208

Romans

8:18	91

1 Corinthians

1:11	72
4:21	155
5–6	73
5–7	72
5:1–20	73
5:4–5	73
5:9	72
5:9–13	73
6:1–11	73
6:12–20	74
7	x, 47, 71, 74, 79
7:1	72, 75
7:2	76
7:3	75
7:4	75
7:5	76
7:7	75
7:9	76
7:10	75
7:10–11	76
7:12–14	76
7:15	77
7:15–17	76, 77
7:15–19	77
7:17–24	148
15	81n16
16:17	72

2 Corinthians

6:17	80n4
11	71, 78, 154, 155
11:1–3	152
11:2	169
11:2–4	143
11:3	78, 155
11:4	151
11:20–21	78
12:20–21	78

Galatians

3:1	155
3:28	72, 148, 154
5:12	143, 146, 155, 156
5:13	147
5:15	147
5:16	147
5:17	147
5:19	147

Ephesians

5:23–33	169

Philippians

3:2	154

Colossians

2:21	80n4

Hebrews

12:18	211
12:22–24	211

1 Timothy

2	71
2:12–15	253n15
2:15	78
5:11	78
5:14–16	78

Revelation

1:13–16	245
2	249, 250, 251
2-3	241, 245
2:18	245
2:18–29	241, 243, 245, 247, 248, 249
2:19	243
2:19–28	240
2:20	243, 247
2:20–23	241
2:21	243
2:22	243, 244, 247, 249
2:22–23	244, 248, 249
2:23	243, 247
2:26–28	245
5:6	240
16:17	252n2
16:19–19:3	239
17:1	239
17:2	247
17:16–17	239
18	247
18:3	247
18:8–9	239
18:9	247
19:1–3	239
21:2	169

OTHER EARLY CHRISTIAN TEXTS

Acts of Andrew

17–22	42
17.1, b	42, 43
17.2	42
17.4	43
18.1	42, 45
18.2	45
18.3	45
18.5	45
19.1	45
20.5	46
21.3	46
22.2	46
22.4	46

Acts of John

113	191
113:16–17	185

Acts of Paul and Thecla

9	30n24
26	57
27	57
28–39	57
31	57
41–43	57
165	30n24

Ambrose of Milan

De virginibus

1.1.2	53
1.2.5	54
1.2.7	56
1.2.8	56
1.2.9	56
1.10.57	55
2.1.2	53
2.3.19	57
2.3.20	57
2.4.26–27	58
2.6.39	55
3.1.1	54
3.7.32	60
3.7.33	60
3.7.34	60
3.7.35	60

Epistles

5.6	63
5.14	63
6.2	63
6.8	64
6.19	64

Athanasius of Alexandria

Apologia ad Constantium

33.49	114

Augustine of Hippo

City of God

1.14	96, 97
1.15	97
1.16	95, 97
1.17	96
1.19	96
1.20	96

Letters

111.2	90, 91
111.3	91
111.4	91
111.5	91
111.6	92
111.7	92, 93
111.8	94
111.9	94

2 Baruch

78–87	241

Chronicon Paschale

362	108

Clement of Rome

1 Clement

1–3	19
4–6	19

6.2	17, 18, 19, 20, 22, 23, 25, 26, 27, 30n24	
63.1	26	
65.1	18, 26	

Didache

2.2	3

Epiphanius of Salamis

Panarion

58.4.5–6	198n30
78.13.4	198n31
79.5.3	198n32

Epistle of Barnabas

19.5	3

Eusebius of Caesarea

De vita Constantini

3.55	110
3.55–58	109

Gregory of Nazianzus

Orations

4.86–87	109
4.87	115

Gospel of Thomas

114	148

Hippolytus of Rome

Elenchos (Refutation of All Heresies)

IX.2	6
IX.7.2–3	6
IX.8.1	6
IX.8–11	6
IX.11.1	7
IX11.3	7, 8
IX.12.1	6
IX.12.2	7
IX.12.9	7
IX.12.10–13	7
IX.12.15	6, 7
IX.12.16	8
IX.12.20	8
IX.12.21	8
IX.12.22	8
IX.12.23	9
IX.12.24	9
IX.12.25	2, 9, 10
IX.12.26	10

Jerome

Adversus Jovinianum

1.12	195
1.36	195
1.26	193

Epistulae

22.19:2	195

Martyrdom of Perpetua and Felicitas

18	22
20	22
21	57

Paulinus

Vita sancti Ambrosii

2.5	54
3.9	54

Protevangelium of James

4:4	201
5:10	210
6:2	204
6:4	201
7-8	201
7:7	210
8:2	204
9:11	204
11:7	209
15:11	201, 204
18:2–11	203, 207, 209
19:11	207
19:12–15	203
19:13	210
19:14	210
19:16	203
19:18	205, 206
19:19	203, 206
20:1	203, 204
20:2	203, 204
20:3–4	203
20:3–7	206
20:10	206
20:11	206

Sozomen

Ecclesiastical History

5.10.5–7	108, 110, 111
5.15.14–17	109

Tertullian

Apologeticus

15.4	22
15.5	22

On the Shows

1	127
4	129
6–12	127
8	129
9–13	128
17	134
23	134
24	127, 129
25	128, 134
26	129, 130, 131, 133
30	133, 134, 135

On the Soul

39	132
41	129
57	132

On the Flesh of Christ

4.1–3	131

On Monogamy

17	198n29

Theodoret

Ecclesiastical History

3.7.1	108

Index of Ancient Sources 269

GREEK AND ROMAN SOURCES

Achilles Tatius
Leucippe and Clitophon

2.7	152
5.21	152
5.27	152

Aelius Aristides
Isthmian Oration (Orat. 46)

46.27	25

Aeschines
Against Timarchus

130–131	145
167	145

On the False Embassy

23	145
88	145
99	145
121	145
127	145

Aristophanes
Equites

496–497	159n30
706–707	144
1010	144, 147

Lysistrata

160–163	162n67
228	152

Pax

885	144
386–388	145
716–717	147

Catullus
Carmina 80

16	145
59	145
97	145
98	145

Cicero
De domo sua

10.25	145
83	145

Pro Cluentio

166	171

Demosthenes
De corona

162	145
242	145

Diodorus of Sicily
Bibliotheca historica

13.57–58	244
1021.4	151

Herodotus

Histories

1.93	110
1.199	110

Homer

Iliad

1.1	244
2.354–56	244
2.357–59	244
3.301	244
22.62–5	244

Livy

Ab Urbe Condita

1.13	173
21.13.9	244

Lucian

Demonax

57	26

Pseudologista

27	145, 152

Martial

On the Spectacles

6	22
9	22
10	22
24	22

Epigrams

3.80	145
3.81	146
3.87	145

Petronius

Satyricon

28	89

Philodemus

Anthologica Graeca

5.126	148

Plautus

Aulularia

325ff	171

Plutarch

Quaestiones Romanae

29	173
31	173
87	173

Pseudo-Dio Chrysostom

Orations

37.26	24

Seneca the Younger

De beneficiis

4.31.2–5	145

Epistulae

87.16   145

Statius

Silvae

1.2   172

Strabo

Geographica

11.14.16	110
11.16	110
12.3.36	110
16.1.20	110

Strato

Anthologica Graeca

12.11   152

Index

Page references for figures are italicized.

abjectivity, 123–127
abortion, xi, 1–5, 10–12
apocryphal acts, 38, 51n50, 185–186, 194–195, 196n10, 197n15
Acts of Andrew x, 37–38, 40–44, 47–48, 49n6, 213n7
Acts of John xii, 185–186, 191–195, 213n7
Acts of Paul and Thecla 22, 30n24, 57
Adam and Eve, 82n27, 86
adultery, 3, 9–11, 58, 82n27, 116, 149–151, 181n22, 186–187, 222, 224, 231n6, 233n28, 242–243, 249
Affect Theory, vii, 71, 74
agency, x, 40, 73, 85, 102n36, 154, 169, 195, 229
Ahmed, Sara, x, 37–49
Ambrose of Milan:
    Agnes. *See* saints: Saint Agnes;
    and gender, 56, 60, 64–65;
    Antiochene virgin, 58–60, 67nn16–17;
    De virginibus. See Ancient Source Index;
    life, 54–55, 65n2, 67n23;
    Marcellina, 54–55, 59;
    Pelagia, 59–60;
    Thecla. *See Acts of Paul and Thecla*;
    violence, 53–54, 56–57, 61, 64–65
amphitheater:
    archaeology, *25*;
    history, 32n38, 26;
    function, 18–19, 23, 26;
    violence in, 17, 19, 23, 26.
    See also violence, blood: spectacles, martyr
androgyny, 148
animals:
    as metaphor, 22, 30n26;
    bears, 21–22, 24, 128;
    hunters of, 22, 24;
    in Roman arena, 22, 57;
    lions, 22, 57, 91;
    pigs, 107, 119n7;
    sacrificial, 117
Aphrodite (Venus):
    cult rituals, 109–110, 119.
    See also mythology, temple: Venus
apocalyptic, 88, 133, 170
Aristophanes, 144–145, 147, 152

ascetic (asceticism), 39, 44, 55,
    114, 186, 227
Augustine:
    enslavement, 7, 14n20, 85, 87–91,
        93–98, 99n2, 100n3;
    on sex, 86, 94;
    suffering servants, 89–91, 94;
    violence, 85–9, 94, 96, 98, 99n2;
    women, 91–94, 96–98

baptism, 72, 76, 101n20, 124,
    129, 148, 154
barbarian, 85, 91–93, 97, 101n20, 107–
    109, 111–112, 117
benefaction, 39, 42–43
Bishop Syagrius of Verona,
    53–54, 62–63.
    See also Bishop
        Ambrose of Milan
blood:
    menstrual, 145;
    ritual, 60;
    spectacles (of martyrdoms) in
        Roman arena, 22, 26.
    See also martyr
Briggs, Sheila, 7, 23
Butler, Judith, 123–125
Burrus, Virginia, 56, 96–97,
    125, 191–192

cannibalism, 111–112, 117
castration:
    and cunnilingus, 146. See also
        sex: cunnilingus;
    auto-, 188, 196n9;
    eunuchs, 145–148, 153–154, 156,
        158n19, 158n24, 195;
    in *Acts of John*, 188;
    in the Roman arena, 22;
    Paul's letters, 146–147, 149,
        154, 158n25
    See also ascetic, sex: celibacy

colonial:
    colonialism, 41;
    context, 17–18;
    Roman colonialism, 17–18,
        20, 25–28.
    See also enslavement
consent, x, 44, 87, 95, 173, 180, 204–
    205, 250, 255n48.
    See also Graybill, Rhiannon, rape,
        sex, violence
Constantine, 108–110, 117, 120n8
Corinth:
    church in, 18, 20, 23, 72–74,
        79, 61n16, 82n20, 142,
        150–155, 169;
    city of, 18, 23–24, 25,
        31n34, 32n36;
    enslavement in, 25, 26–28
corporeal, 43, 92, 123–130, 132–133,
    135, 137n26, 155

dehumanization, 38, 44, 115, 130
degradation, 9, 23, 27, 150
Deleuze, Gilles, 74–75
Diocletian, 55
disability:
    blindness, 152, 177, 181n26,
        186, 191, 195;
    illness, xi, 45, 92, 185,
        195, 241–243;
    physical, 177, 182n26
divorce, 151, 173, 224, 226
Donatists, 89, 101n20

enslavement:
    ancient institution of, 38,
        42–43, 92, 147;
    manumission, 42, 45;
    of peoples, xi-xii, 2–4, 6–11,
        20–21, 37–39, 41–44, 46–47,
        85, 87–88, 92, 99n2, 147, 150,
        154–155, 250;
    rhetoric of, 85–88, 98, 147.
    See also colonial: colonialism,
        dehumanization, rape
erotic:
    imagery, 59, 135;

lust, 58, 64, 94, 146–147,
   152, 189–190;
  sado-erotic(ism), 61, 113;
  suggestive of sexual acts, 226;
  the body as, 44, 60;
  voyeur, 53, 58–59, 65.
  See also sex
eschatology, 88, 179–180
Eusebius, 4,109–110, 114, 120n8
excretions, of the body:
  vomit, 125;
  feces, 125;
  semen, 151, 161n62

feminist (feminism):
  theory, x, 38–39, 41–42, 126, 148,
    219, 224, 240, 243, 246, 248;
  history, 40
feminine body, 50n13, 54, 61, 64–65,
  66n11, 153, 160n44, 225, 239, 243
fertility, 132, 195
Frankfurter, David, 56, 59, 61, 113

genitalia:
  castration. See castration;
  penis, 158n25, 185–188;
  vagina, 203, 206, 213n4
Glancy, Jennifer, 7, 9, 42, 44
Graybill, Rhiannon, x, 44, 204–205,
  213n7, 240, 246, 255n48
the Grimm Brothers, 39–42, 48–49

Hegel, Friedrich, 40–42, 50n20
Heliopolis, 107, 108–112, 114–118
Hellenism, 24–25, 32n36, 175, 228, 244
heresy, 4, 5–8, 88
Herodotus, 109–110, 112, 117, 120n6
Hippolytus, 1–11, 13n15
humiliation, 23, 44, 57, 125, 226, 240,
  243, 246, 250

idolatry, 86, 112, 127, 132, 222,
  233n33, 241, 243
imperialism:

hierarchy, 6, 18, 22, 28, 32n36,
  78, 118, 148;
 early Roman period, 18, 20, 22;
 legality, 10, 25, 27, 118, 120n8;
 violence in, 22–23,
  27–28, 85, 134

Jacob, 171, 223
jealousy, 17, 19, 23, 26–28, 175
Jerome, 4, 10, 113, 146, 186, 193–196
Jezebel, 240–251, 254n31, 255n33
John, Gospel of, 72, 169, 171, 192,
  202, 205–206, 217–218, 220–
  222, 224–227
John the Baptist, 115, 198n29
Jonah, 97, 181n72
Judaism:
 Jews, 3, 94, 107, 109, 147, 174,
  179, 217, 219, 222, 223, 244;
 practices, 107, 120n11, 171–172,
  174, 222, 223;
 scriptures, 19, 94, 222, 246;
 literature, 229, 241,
  243–245, 248;
 in the New Testament, 217,
  223, 245, 247
justice, 22, 25, 102n26, 219

Kotrosits, Maia, 27, 30n24, 75, 126
Kristeva, Julia, 123–125, 132

Lucretla, 95–97, 149, 151
Luke, Gospel of, 85, 87–88, 90, 99,
  169–170, 178, 201–202, 208, 210,
  219. See also Luke-Acts
Luke-Acts:body purity in,
  185, 196n10;conception in,
  201;enslavement, 87–88, 100nn10,
  100n12;narration in, 208;wedding
  metaphors, 169, 170

Mark, Gospel of, 72, 125, 129, 181n22,
  187, 218, 222
masculinity:

and virginity, 61, 65, 194–
  195, 198n35;
 enslavement and, 87, 154;
 martyrs and, 56, 57, 66n12;
 problems with, 12n3, 154, 240,
  242, 250, 253n14;
 sex, 147–149, 153, 155, 194–195,
  242, 247–248
Marcion, 131, 137n16
marginalization, x, 126, 132–133
marriage, 7, 10, 56, 72–73, 76–78, 108–
  110, 117, 151, 169–173, 176–177,
  179, 185, 188, 190, 191, 193, 195,
  222, 224–226, 228, 249–250
martyrs:
 culture of, 88, 91, 95, 101n18;
 enslavement, 20, 85–86, 92;
 gender, 19, 53, 55–60, 65,
  94–95, 97–98;
 texts, 22, 30n21, 31n28, 48,
  54–58, 59, 65, 67n15, 85,
  94, 95, 97;
 treatment of, *21*, 59;
 violence, 27, 48, 53–54, 57,
  60–61, 65, 85–86, 91, 95, 97.
 See also erotic: sado-erotic,
  execution, blood
Mary:
 and Jesus, 72, 202–203, 210, 212;
 birth, 131, 202, 210, 212;
 body, 202, 205–207, 210, 212;
 genitalia, 203, 205, 213n4;
 life, 201;
 sexual assault, 201, 203–206;
 virgin, 67n17, 205–206, 210, 212
Matthew, Gospel of, 170–180, 182n27,
 194, 201–202, 218–220
meals:
 cannibalism. *See* cannibalism;
 celebratory, 171, 169, 171, 177;
 feast days, 54, 118;
 ritual, 130.
 See also starvation
midrash, 208–209
miracle, 58–59, 91, 93, 97–98, 210

misogyny, 143, 153, 155, 240, 251
morality:
 of enslaved peoples, 8;
 sexual, 3, 71, 73–74, 77–78,
  82n24, 239, 242, 249
Moses, 19, 209–210
mutilation:
 general, 17, 47, 111;
 of genitalia, 46–47, 143, 154;
 self-, 190
mythology, 20, 169, 173, 174, 245.
 See also pagan (paganism)

naked:
 as spectacle, 57;
 forcibly, 22–23, 107, 240;
 relating to sexual desire, 113, 145
Nicodemus, 222, 232n26

original sin, 86–87, 90, 94–95, 114
orthodoxy, 18, 88, 156

pagan (paganism):
 general, 18, 20, 23, 107–109,
  111–114, 116, 118–119,
  120n8, 133;
 women, 19, 20, 114–115, 119n5
patriarchy, 72, 150, 155, 173, 220, 240,
 246, 248–251, 256n50
Paul:
 Corinthians, 26, 72–74, 76,
  78–79, 151–152, 154, 169
 death, 27;
 defining "Christian," 72;
 enslavement, 147–148;
 Galatians, 146–148, 153 *See also*
  Ancient Source Index;
 new law, 210;
 on sex, 47, 72–74, 76–79,
  80n4, 82n20, 143, 146–
  148, 150–154;
 suffering, 19;
 transmisogyny, 155–156
parables:
 enslavement, 88, 101n12;

eschatology, 179–180;
    of the Wedding Banquet, 170,
        175, 177–178;
    of the tenants, 176;
    of the Ten Virgins, 170, 175, 177,
        179, 180n1;
    of the Two Sons, 218
patricide, 186–187, 190
pedagogy, 47, 61
pederasty, 162n71
Pelagianism, 86
penetration. *See* sex: penetration
Peter, 19, 27, 88, 193
Perkins, Judith, 125–126
persecution, 20, 54, 58–60, 116
Plutarch, 173
pregnant (pregnancy):
    bodies, xi, 1–3, 5, 10–11, 203;
    birth, 10, 14n33, 41, 131–
        132, 201–204, 207–210,
        212, 213n5;
    nursing, 14n33, 203;
    rhetorical use of, 45, 63;
    reproductive will, 45, *See
        also* consent;
    womb, 41, 45, 126, 131–132
prostitution:
    brothels, 58, 62, 67n17,
        149, 160n49;
    and sex workers, 58, 74, 108–110,
        112–113, 116, 150, 180n8,
        218, 220, 231n10, 239, 252n3;
    ritual, 112–113, 116–118, 119n5,
        120n8, 120n11
purity, 37, 44, 47, 51n40, 60–61, 78,
    82n24, 96, 144, 150, 155, 185, 191,
    201, 204, 206, 210, 212

queer:
    theory, xii, 39–40, 75,
        192, 194–196;
    culture, 81n15;
    space, 135

rape:
    bestiality, 107, 111–112, 119n4;
    in the academy, 217–218, 221,
        225, 229, 230;
    language of, viii, 44, 92, 94,
        95–96, 205;
    martial, 243–244, 246, 249–250;
    necrophilia, xii, 185–
        186, 190, 195;
    of enslaved peoples, 87, 250, *See
        also* enslavement;
    of virgins, 111;
    slut-shaming, 217–218, 248;
    stories of, viii, 37, 41–42, 44,
        59–60, 96, 173–174, 205, 241;
    weaponization of, xi, 53–54,
        59–60, 62, 64–66, 92, 94,
        97–98, 145, 204, 213n7, 229,
        243,   248, 250;
    victim-blaming, 43, 95;
    #MeToo, 251.
    See also sex, violence
remarriage, 77, 151

Saints:
    Agnes, 54–61, 65, 66n13, 67n17;
    Clement's writing on, 19;
    martyrdom, 48, 97;
    Patropolis, 115;
    sexuality, 144;
    suffering, 48, 90
Salome:
    and Mary's body, 201–
        212, 213n10;
    and Thomas, 205–207
Samaritan woman:
    femme fatale, 217, 229;
    gender, 217–220, 224;
    in media, 218;
    Jesus, 220–221, 224,
        228, 232n17;
    outsider, 217, 222;
    rape culture, 218, 229;
    sexuality, 218–228, 233n35;
    slut-shaming, 218, 221,
        224, 227, 229

Samson, 171, 174
Satan, 73, 76, 80n9, 129, 188–189
Sebasteion, 71, 79
self-control, 65, 76, 146, 153–154, 162n71
sex:
    celibacy, 58–59, 67n16, 72–73, 186, 188, 190, 192, 195, 227;
    cunnilingus, 145–146, 158n21;
    homosexuality, 77, 78;
    necrophilia. *See* rape: necrophilia;
    penetration, 92, 103n37, 130, 148–149, 153, 242, 253n14;
    sexuality, xii, 23, 43, 77, 114, 149, 154, 185–186, 190, 192, 195, 218, 220, 222, 224–226, 228, 239, 250.
    voyeurism, *See* erotic: sado-erotic, erotic: voyeur.
    See also rape
shame:
    affect, 71, 74, 76–79, 81n16, 188, 220;
    crucifixion, 125;
    gender, 126–127, 131–132, 150, 155, 173, 218, 220, 222–227, 229;
    Genesis and, 86, 94;
    hierarchy of, 126, 223;
    sexual, 57, 62–63, 71, 76, 94, 96, 126, 151, 155, 188, 218, 220, 222–223, 227, 229;
    violence, 71, 75, 77–78, 94, 111.
    See also Affect Theory.
spirit:
    demonic, 128–130, 132;
    enslavement, 13;
    Holy, 13n15, 129;
    in Paul's letters, 73, 80n9, 151;
    marriage to Christ, 56
starvation, 39
Strabo, 109–110, 112, 117, 120n6
submission:
    colonial, 26;
    enslavement, 45, 98;
    sexual, 242.
    See also sex, rape
Susanna, 62
suicide, 7, 95–96, 98, 103n37, 117, 187

Talmud, 171 181–182n23
temple:
    Aphrodisian, 71;
    Jerusalem, 94, 201;
    of Apollo, 25;
    of the Word, 114;
    of Venus, 109–110;
    relating to religious space, 101n19, 118, 120n7, 170, 177, 204, 210
Tertullian:
    and gender, 124, 126, 130–131, 133–135;
    baptism, 129, 132;
    Marcion, 131, 137n16;
    Monarchianism, 13n15;
    myth, 22, 132;
    on resurrection, 125–128;
    Roman culture, 127–129, 133–135;
    writings, 123–124, 126–127, 129–132, 136, 194.
    See also Ancient Source Index
Thecla. *See Acts of Paul and Thecla*
Tobit, 226
torah, 80n6, 209, 219

victim-blaming. *See* rape: victim-blaming
violence:
    corporal punishment, 40, 43;
    disembowelment, 116–117
    murder, 3, 9–11, 37–38, 47, 91, 96, 108, 113, 120n8, 176, 181, 186–188, 190, 204, 229, 247–249;
    torture, 19–20, 22, 26–27, 31n28, 39, 41–42, 46, 48, 91, 134–135;
    execution, 18, 56

virgin:
   virginity, 53–55, 58–60, 62–65,
      111–114, 117, 143, 149,
      154–155, 160n44, 185–186,
      191–194, 206, 212;
   virginity test, xi, 54,
      62–64, 213n10.
   See also ascetic, sex

wedding:
   as metaphor, 56, 173, 177;
   celebration, 171, 173;
   economics of, 169–170, 172;
   feast. *See* meals: celebratory;
   power exchange, 170, 172, 179;
   rape, 171–174;
   sex, 151, 173;
   virginity, 149
willfulness, 37–42, 44–45, 47–49,
   85–86, 90, *See also* Ahmed, Sara,
   Affect Theory

xenophobia, 143

About the Contributors

Tara Baldrick-Morrone is a visiting assistant professor in the Study of Religions at Wake Forest University, where she teaches undergraduate and graduate courses on Christianities, gender, public history, and historiography. Her research considers how different conceptions of an ancient Christian past influence twentieth-century American politics and legislation of reproductive issues. She is currently working on her first manuscript, based on a revision of her dissertation, titled *Reproducing History: Abortion and Christian Moral Supremacy in America*.

Chance E. Bonar is a PhD candidate in the Committee on the Study of Religion at Harvard University, concentrating on the New Testament and early Christianity, and is also a William R. Tyler Fellow in Byzantine Studies at Dumbarton Oaks Research Library and Collection. His dissertation explores language of enslavement to God in the *Shepherd of Hermas*, and he works broadly on Christian literature, imperialism, anti-Judaism, and the function of authorship from the first to eighth centuries CE.

Christy Cobb is assistant professor of Christianity at University of Denver. She holds a PhD in Biblical Studies from Drew University, where she focused on New Testament and Early Christianity and received a certificate in Women and Gender studies. Cobb published her first book, *Slavery, Gender, Truth, and Power in Luke-Acts and Other Ancient Narratives* in 2019. Her research interests include Slavery, Gender/Sexuality, Ancient Narratives (Greek, Roman, Jewish, and Christian), and Acts of the Apostles.

Jennifer Collins-Elliott is a lecturer in the Department of Religious Studies at the University of Tennessee, Knoxville. Her research focuses on gender and violence in early Christian literature and on theories of sexual violence. She is currently completing her dissertation titled "'Bespattered with the Mud of Another's Lust': Rape and Physical Embodiment in Christian Literature of the 4th-6th Centuries CE" at Florida State University.

Arminta Fox is associate professor of religion at Bethany College in Lindsborg, Kansas, where she also founded and co-directs the Women and Gender Studies Program. In 2021, she received the Donna Meredith Humphreys Award for Excellence in Teaching. She is the author of *Paul Decentered: Reading 2 Corinthians with the Corinthian Women*, published in the *Paul in Critical Contexts* series with Lexington/Fortress Academic in December 2019, as well as several journal articles and chapter contributions on topics ranging from incarceration to vocation.

Midori E. Hartman is assistant professor of classical studies at Albright College. She holds a PhD in historical studies with an emphasis on Christianity in Late Antiquity from Drew University. Her primary research interests are Augustine of Hippo, ancient slavery, and rhetoric as it intersects with issues of gender, ethnicity, and animality.

LaToya M. Leary Francis is a PhD candidate in the Department of Religion at Florida State University. Her dissertation, "Rhetoric That Disables: Socially Disabling Conditions in the Ancient World," analyzes physical difference in Graeco-Roman, early Jewish, and early Christian texts, with a focus on their dis-abling rhetorical functions, and considers how the treatment of these "dis-abling" states or "defects" aid in the construction and advancement of certain identities.

Travis W. Proctor is assistant professor of religion and director of the Premodern Ancient World Studies (PAST) Program at Wittenberg University. He received his MA and PhD in ancient Mediterranean religions from the University at North Carolina at Chapel Hill. His research analyzes ancient Christian cultures (ca. 50–500 CE) from the perspectives of cultural studies, gender studies, and the environmental humanities, with special interests in embodiment, environmental history, space, and material cultures, and ritual studies. His book *Demonic Bodies and the Dark Ecologies of Early Christian Culture* was recently published with Oxford University Press.

Joshua M. Reno is lecturer in the Department of Classical & Near Eastern Religions and Cultures at the University of Minnesota. His research covers discourse(s) around sex work in Greek and Roman literature. He is the author of several essays on sex, gender, and the Pauline epistles, most recently "Pornographic Desire in the Pauline Corpus" (*Journal of Biblical Literature*, 2021). He is currently completing a book on Pauline sexual invective.

Laura Robinson is an instructor of religious studies and campus minister at Ferrum College in VA. She is also a doctoral candidate in religious studies (New Testament track) at Duke University. She holds an MA in Biblical exegesis (Wheaton College, 2013) and systematic theology (Wheaton College, 2014).

Jeannie Sellick is currently a PhD candidate in religious studies at the University of Virginia. Her forthcoming dissertation, *The Strongest Seed: Jerome's Fashioning of an Ascetic Masculinity in Late Antiquity,* revolves around the ascetic musings of the fiery, yet famous presbyter, Jerome. In her free time, Jeannie enjoys watching Marvel movies, eating Cheetos, and playing with her senior pup, Missy.

Eric Vanden Eykel is associate professor of religious studies at Ferrum College in Virginia. His research focuses on early Christian literature, with a particular focus on texts and traditions about the infancies and childhoods of Jesus and Mary. He is the author of *"But Their Faces Were All Looking Up": Author and Reader in the* Protevangelium of James (Bloomsbury) and *The Magi: Who They Were, How They've Been Remembered, and Why They Still Fascinate* (Fortress).

Meredith J. C. Warren is senior lecturer in biblical and religious studies at the University of Sheffield, and the director of the Sheffield Institute for Interdisciplinary Studies. She is also editor in chief of the *Journal for Interdisciplinary Biblical Studies*. The author of *My Flesh Is Meat Indeed: Nonsacramental Reading of John 6* (2015), *Food and Transformation in Ancient Mediterranean Literature* (2019), and co-author of *Jewish and Christian Women in the Ancient Mediterranean* (2022), Warren's current research includes gender, the senses, anti-Judaism, and apocalyptic literature.

Stephen Young researches myth, gender, divine hierarchies, and how history is imagined in the writings of ancient Jews and Christians. He is finishing his first book, *Paul Among the Mythmakers: Gods, Sins, and Scriptures* and preparing for the next project on gender and sexual violence in early Christianity. Stephen teaches in the Department of Languages, Literatures, and Cultures at Appalachian State University, rides his bicycle up as many mountains as he can, and holds a PhD in religious studies from Brown University.

www.ingramcontent.com/pod-product-compliance
Lightning Source LLC
Chambersburg PA
CBHW020111010526
44115CB00008B/784